Archipelagos of Sound

Archipelagos
of SOUND

Transnational Caribbeanities, Women and Music

EDITED BY

Ifeona Fulani

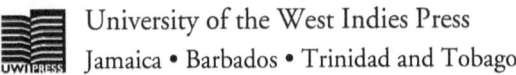
University of the West Indies Press
Jamaica • Barbados • Trinidad and Tobago

University of the West Indies Press
7A Gibraltar Hall Road, Mona
Kingston 7, Jamaica
www.uwipress.com

© 2012 by Ifeona Fulani

All rights reserved. Published 2012

A catalogue record of this book is available from the
National Library of Jamaica.

ISBN: 978-976-640-266-2

Cover illustration: Lennox Coke, *Island Rythm*.
Collection of Lennox Coke. Reproduced by courtesy of Lennox Coke.

Cover and book design by Robert Harris

Set in Adobe Garamond 11/14.5 x 27

Printed in the United States of America

Contents

Introduction / 1
Ifeona Fulani

PART 1 **FROM THE POSTCOLONIAL TO THE TRANSNATIONAL**

1 The Blackness of Sugar: Celia Cruz and the Performance of (Trans)nationalism / 19
Frances R. Aparicio

2 Louise Bennett in Performance: Pedagogies of Nation and Gender / 34
Donna Aza Weir-Soley

3 Between La Habana and Veracruz: Toña la Negra and the Transnational Circuits of *Música Tropical* / 69
B. Christine Arce

PART 2 **PERFORMING/CONTESTING IDENTITIES**

4 Guadaloupean Women Performing *Gwo Ka*: Island Presences and Transnational Connections / 93
Kathe Managan

5 Celia's Shoes / 119
Frances Negrón-Muntaner

6 Calypso Rose's Phallic "Palet" and the Sweet Treat of Erotic Aurality / 143
Lyndon K. Gill

| 7 | "Born in Chanel, Christen in Gucci": The Rhetoric of Brand Names and Haute Couture in Jamaican Dancehall / **171**
Andrea Elizabeth Shaw

| 8 | The Rhetoric of Hips: Shakira's Embodiment and the Quest for Caribbean Identity / **191**
Nadia Celis

PART 3   **AT THE DIASPORIC CROSSROADS**

| 9 | The Black Diaspora North of the Border: Women, Music and Caribbean Culture in Canada / **217**
Lisa Tomlinson

| 10 | Who Is Grace Jones? / **234**
Ifeona Fulani

| 11 | "LADIES A YOUR TIME NOW!": Erotic Politics, Lovers' Rock and Resistance in the UK / **258**
Lisa Amanda Palmer

| 12 | From Third Wave to Third World: Lauryn Hill, Educated and Unplugged / **279**
Cheryl Sterling

| 13 | Whose Rihanna?: Diasporic Citizenship and the Economies of Crossing Over / **299**
Heather D. Russell

| 14 | I and Ireland: Reggae and Rastafari in the Work of Sinéad O'Connor / **321**
Adam John Waterman

Contributors / **341**

Acknowledgements / **343**

Introduction

| IFEONA FULANI

The Caribbean is not a common archipelago but a meta-archipelago . . . it has the virtue of having neither a boundary nor a center. Thus the Caribbean flows outwards, past the limits of its own sea with a vengeance.

– Antonio Benítez-Rojo[1]

THE IMPORTANT ROLE THAT MUSICIANS, music and song play in the cultural and political life of Caribbean communities both nationally and transnationally, has increasingly become the subject of scholarly attention. Recent scholarship on the musical cultures of the Caribbean has expanded the terrain of cultural studies within the region and outside of it, but prior to this intensification of interest, ethnomusicologists documented the special role of music in the collective life of enslaved people in the Americas. Denied access to literacy by their colonial masters, the enslaved depended on aural and oral sources as resources for news and information from both nearby and from far afield. Singers were both artists in music and purveyors of information, comment and critique, a tradition still extant in communities at home in the Caribbean and abroad in its diasporas – calypsonians in Trinidad and *salseros* in New York are only two examples of this.

Paul Gilroy alludes to the *service* rendered to enslaved populations and their descendants by musicians who, he argues, extend their cultural role to serve as guardians of aural and oral traditions. In the practice of their art, musicians have functioned as protectors of the "embattled cultural sensibility" of their communities, a sensibility that survives and continues to serve as political and philosophical inspiration.[2] It is that "embattled cultural sensibility", examined through the lens of women, gender and sexuality, that this book addresses. The embattled terrain is defined by both the music and performance of gender and sexuality by the women who are the subjects of this volume's chapters, women who complicate normative racialized constructions of womanhood and foreground national and transnational identitarian politics, often within the commodified domain of the popular music industry.

The global reach and influence of Caribbean musics are remarkable, given the size of the island territories, populations and economies that comprise the region. A seemingly disproportionate number of artists from the Caribbean region have achieved fame that is not only transnational but, in some cases, translinguistic: the late Celia Cruz, Eddy Grant, Gloria Estefan, Marc Anthony, Sean Paul, Shakira and Rihanna, to name a few. Bob Marley, who was designated artist of the century by *Time* magazine in 2000, and whose album *Exodus* was named album of the century by *Rolling Stone* magazine is, perhaps, the most well known.

This global popularity is attributable to the creation, distribution and dispersal of Caribbean musics via commercial, social and cultural vectors that have created archipelagos of sound extending outward from the Caribbean region in all directions. Powered by the forces of globalization and the transnational movements of Caribbean people and culture, Caribbean musics travel in sonic flows that bear aesthetic imprints and lyrical discourses – as well as articulations of their "embattled cultural sensibility" – from their islands of origin to geographically far-flung diasporic and transnational Caribbean communities and other interested consumers. Metaphorically, the archipelagic form suggests the trajectory of the flow of Caribbean musics into the world even as it implies a sonic replication of the geography of Caribbean. My use of it extends Kamau Brathwaite's notion of "bridges of sound" by imaging a continuous virtual arc of sonic connections, extending beyond the African diasporic reach that Brathwaite invokes to stretch across the globe.[3] In this respect my use of the archipelagic metaphor comes closer to that suggested by Benítez-Rojo above, implying boundless, dynamic movement. Historically, in the Caribbean archipelago, the sea connected the islands as much as separated them. As the means by which people and cultural currents have crossed between islands, the sea has been the vector that linked the arcing islands and their clusters of population in a ceaseless flux.[4] Sonic archipelagos sustain connections within cultural communities through commercialization of culture, through the shared pleasure generated by the music, but also by enabling the sharing of concerns, sentiments and anxieties – cultural and political – articulated through the music.

The archipelagic shape – the defining curve of islands both separated and connected by water – vividly renders the cultural contradiction of the region: diversity within larger unity. Following Kamau Brathwaite, Edouard Glissant, Benítez-Rojo and others,[5] this volume assumes the persistence of unifying cultural patterns within the region, as well as the consequences of historical contiguities resulting from similar histories of slavery and colonialism that Tim Reiss describes as the "uniting circulation of cultural creation".[6] Sara Johnson illuminates the influence of musicians and music in sustaining a collective awareness of shared history and culture, arguing that two centuries before decolonization and independence, the inter- and circum-Caribbean movements of musicians generated a mutually sustaining awareness of interconnection as well as the importance of communication and collaboration between populations. The migrations of musicians were instrumental to forging this awareness, creating what Johnson terms an "inter-island aesthetic" that transcended linguistic difference and undermined colonial/political compartmentalization.[7] Grounded in the music traditions of Central Africa, this aesthetic evolved throughout the Caribbean in dynamic response to migrations of people and music between islands.

As Johnson explains, "this aesthetic was a critical element in the formation of national music traditions in the Caribbean . . . musical production was a cultural avant-garde . . . breaking colonial and linguistic barriers".[8] There is irony, then, in the tendency within the Caribbean and US academies to emphasize linguistic difference in ways that subtly subvert the survival of a shared historical consciousness and an "inter-island aesthetic". Recognizing the persistent awareness of inter-island connectivity among Caribbean peoples, the contributors to this volume resist the usual separation of Hispanic, francophone and anglophone Caribbean cultures. The chapters in the collection span the Caribbean and its diasporas, accenting both relation and diversity, to include writing on artists from Guadeloupe, Colombia, Cuba, Jamaica, Trinidad and Tobago, Barbados, and the United States.

Transnational Caribbeanities

That consumption of Caribbean musics extends beyond the Caribbean and its diaporas, and exerts cross-cultural influence, is readily confirmed by a survey of popular music over the last thirty years. The continuing globalization of the recording industry has increased the availability of Caribbean musics, while technology's infiltration of every aspect of modern life, via the Internet, cellular phones, MP3s and iPods has facilitated access, transmitting the musics, their messages and associated images across the globe. Caribbean cultures, already the products of creolization, inspire replication and syncresis as exemplified by the rapid spread of reggae outside of Jamaica where it emerged in the 1970s and its appropriation and localization by musicians elsewhere. Reggae has inspired black youth across the Caribbean,[9] white and Asian youth in Britain[10] and oppressed people across the continents of Africa, Asia and Australasia, seeding raggamuffin, rajamuffin, Japanese dancehall music as well as reggae Latino and *reggaetón*. Bands and artists performing "roots" reggae have proliferated globally, producing superstars such as the late Lucky Dube and Alpha Blondy in Africa, bands such as UB40 and the Specials in Britain, and lesser known reggae practitioners from Hopiland, in the United States, to New Zealand.

The spread and popularity of salsa music and dance within the Americas is an even stronger example of "circulatory mixing, the innovative cultural dynamic characteristic of Caribbean musics".[11] A hybrid evolved from Cuban genres such as *son* and *mambo*, salsa was brought to New York by Cuban musicians in the 1960s and 1970s. In New York, Cuban and Puerto Rican musicians developed new styles of salsa, fertilizing the many sub-genres of salsa that circulate globally. The dispersion of the music across national boundaries and the popularity of both the music and the dance in the Americas, exemplify the role of culture in sustaining community and transnational identities, while also contributing to the increasing commercial success and global popularity of salsa.[12]

Cultural transnationalism is, to an extent, facilitated by the global culture industry, fostering the globalization of Caribbean culture. Conversely, as Andrea Elizabeth Shaw's chapter in this volume demonstrates with reference to dancehall fashions, local Caribbean communities exploit the global market, consuming and transforming imported goods and cultural product. This process, termed "glocalization" by some scholars, asserts local and national identities and resists co-optation and cultural homogenization by the forces of economic globalization. Rather, creativity and innovation, at the level of the local, foster transnational cultures and identities, even while transformed themselves by the crossings of national boundaries. Following Carolyn Cooper's assertion of the cultural specificity of transnational discourses that may appear to be "gobal",[13] we conjecture that cultural manifestations in the transnation can often only be deeply understood with reference to the local: its history, cultural influences and condition. Frances Negrón-Muntaner demonstrates this in her chapter, "Celia's Shoes". She posits that the display of Celia Cruz's shoes at the Smithsonian enables us to "walk" through Celia's career, following her social and professional climb to success as a performer in Cuba, which was remarkable for an Afro-Cuban woman, and then as an exiled Cuban female singer in the nearly all Puerto Rican male club of salsa, eventually becoming a pan-Latino icon. Like the salsa of which she was queen, Celia Cruz's shoes are a representation of both *cubanía* and of the Cuban experience of exile in the United States.

Women and Music in the Caribbean

The chapters of this book examine the music, performance and cultural impact of culturally significant female Caribbean-born musical artists based either in the Caribbean or in the Caribbean's diasporas – women who are transnational or global superstars who have become potent symbols of their nations of origin. Second, the globalization of Caribbean musical forms is examined in terms of their influence on North American and European female recording artists, specifically Lauryn Hill and Sinéad O'Connor. The fields of contemporary Caribbean popular music are notoriously male dominated, which confers exceptional status onto the relatively few women who have reached national and transnational audiences. But while the women who are the focus of the chapters of this book are undeniably phenomenal as artists, they are also significant in the ways their artistic works embody the vitality, diversity and reach of Caribbean cultural influence and Caribbean cultural politics.

The contributors to this book take as a starting point the intersection of gender, race, culture and diasporization set against the region's history of conquest, colonialism and slavery, as well as the ongoing impact of globalization. We share the position of Keith Nurse, Christine Ho and other scholars of Caribbean culture, that globalization, far from being a recent phenomenon, has a six-hundred-year history grounded in the operations of European colonialism and Western imperialism. We understand the consequences of globalization's processes to extend beyond purely economic concerns and influence culture, cultural politics, society and the evolution of transnational identities.[14] Thus the collection also examines some of the many ways in which the globalization of Caribbean musics – specifically music made by women – has intervened in transnational and African diasporic feminist/womanist conversations on race, gender roles and identities, gender relations, sexuality, and national identities.

The collection reflects the responses of artists to the complex question of how the Caribbean-identified female subject negotiates the conundrums of living in the transnation. How does she respond to "the problematic of belonging", as Alexander Weheliye has termed the matrix of contradictory sentiments about conflicting national affiliations and yearnings for home?[15] Frances R. Aparicio, B. Christine Arce and Heather D. Russell, in their respective chapters about Celia Cruz, Toña la Negra and Rihanna, examine the representational status of these artists whose cultural significance spans the national and transnational, and who disrupt gendered, raced and nationalist borders. Ifeona Fulani, writing on Grace Jones's evolution as an artist in "Who Is Grace Jones", Cheryl Sterling, writing on Lauryn Hill in "From Third Word to Third Wave: Lauryn Hill Educated and Unplugged", and Adam Waterman, writing on Sinéad O'Connor's identification with Rastafari in "I and Ireland", examine their subjects' lyrical and performative interrogations of fixed notions of national identification, cultural belonging, political affiliation and artistic boundaries.

Commodified representations of the bodies of black and Latina Caribbean women circulated on album covers, in the popular press and on videos all shape globally prevalent stereotypes of Caribbean female physicality and sexuality. Such images perpetuate the long history of myth and racist attributions attached to bodies of women of colour that Magdalena Barrera acknowledges in her ironic naming of Jennifer Lopez "Hottentot 2000".[16] Given the extent that the arena of popular culture provides a stage for the enactment of social and cultural change – such as redefinitions of sexuality, contestations and play on gender identities, and gender conflicts – we give attention to the particular ways in which black women and Latina musicians engage the constellation of patriarchal, sexist and racist stereotypes that Myra Mendible, with specific reference to "the Latina body", aptly summarizes as "a historically contingent, mass-produced, combination of myth, desire, location, marketing and political expedience".[17] The chapters in this volume document the changing character and effects of that engagement, from Calypso Rose's lyrical articulation of the sweetness of same-sex desire in the 1970s, discussed in Lyndon K. Gill's chapter, to Nadia Celis's examination of Shakira's twenty-first-century lyrical and bodily discourse in "The Rhetoric of Hips".

Collectively, the chapters in this volume examine the multiplicity of ways in which female performers contest and/or subvert media representations of black women and Latina women, while also attending to seemingly contradictory instances of performances in which stereotypes are exploited for commercial purposes. In the Caribbean, mainstream cultural and gender-political attitudes to sexuality are articulated in popular culture with reference to media representations of raced and classed female bodies, and in public response to those representations. However, as Russell reveals in "Whose Rihanna?: Diasporic Citizenship and the Economies of Crossing Over", transnationally, the representational schema may be complicated by the demands of immigrant citizenship and the requirements of conformity to the expectations of new nation values – expectations that are particular to each raced and ethnic immigrant group.

The chapters in this volume explore innovations in music and performance styles by female recording artists in the Caribbean, and by artists in the far reaches of "outer-national" influence, that have generated new, hybrid and/or iconoclastic musical and performance styles out of older, previously male-dominated Caribbean forms. In her chapter, "The Black Diaspora North of the Border: Women, Music and Caribbean Culture in Canada", Lisa Tomlinson charts the growing presence of Caribbean women in Canadian hip-hop, reggae, dancehall and dub poetry, comparing areas where the three genres overlap in the creative musical forms of female artists. Kathe Managan's study, "Guadaloupean Women Performing *Gwo Ka*: Island Presences and Transnational Connections", explores the recent, increasing participation of women in the *gwo ka* musical tradition. Managan examines the influence of transnational connections on the relationship of Guadeloupean women with *gwo ka*, an icon of Guadeloupean identity and a largely male-dominated art form where, traditionally, women's participation was circumscribed.

The Structure of This Book

The chapters in this book are organized in a loose chronology from the early twentieth century to the early twenty-first century, following the shifts and trends in postcolonial studies, transnational studies and feminist cultural criticism as well as changes in patterns of influence and consumption brought about by the globalization of Caribbean musics. Additionally, and equally important, the ordering of the chapters acknowledges that artists emerging in the last twenty-five years are beneficiaries of the innovations and struggles of their predecessors, whose successes opened up the arena of popular music for succeeding generations of women.

The artists who are the focus of the chapters in part 1, "From the Postcolonial to the Transnational", each attained iconic status within their local, national and transnational communities and were artistic pioneers and ground-breaking innovators in music and lyrics. In chapter 1, "The Blackness of Sugar: Celia Cruz and the Performance of (Trans)nationalism", Frances R. Aparicio proposes that Cruz serves as a complex and intriguing icon of the relational nature of nationalism and transnationalism. Aparicio examines the figure of the Queen of Salsa and the tensions inherent in the constellation of transnational subjectivities that are constituted through her musical repertoire, her stage performances, her bodily aesthetics and her interviews. Cruz's diverse musical repertoire has functioned as a performative locus for the negotiations of her Cubanness and a pan-Latin American identity that also includes the United States. Aparicio examines Cruz's multiple crossings of racial and cultural boundaries and her easy assumption of diverse racial, national and historical identities, even while she simultaneously asserts her Cubanness through her stage performances.

In chapter 2, "Louise Bennett in Performance: Pedagogies of Nation and Gender", Donna Aza Weir-Soley considers the far-reaching influence of Louise Bennett, poet, folklorist and performance artist, who has influenced many other Jamaican artists and scholars to accept Jamaican Creole as the *de facto* official language of the Jamaican people. Bennett's critics point to the apparent contradiction between her middle-class origins and her endeavour to legitimize the language and worldview of the Jamaican working class. However, Weir-Soley argues that Bennett played a central role in the collective process of claiming self-worth for all Jamaicans whose sense of self had been severely compromised by the legacy of colonialism. Weir-Soley examines Bennett's subversive didacticism and her use of humour in her songs and recitations, deployed as a means of resisting co-optation by the discourses of colonialism and to highlight certain ironies inherent in their influence on the psyche of the colonized. Weir-Soley reminds us of the primacy of the singer's voice, as well as audience responsiveness to music's sonic character prior to the ascendancy of visual media from mid-twentieth century forward. The affective power of the vocal timbre and accentuation, heard in live performance or captured on records and on radio, evoked nationalist sentiment and identification as strongly as the character of the music.

In chapter 3, "Between La Habana and Veracruz: Toña la Negra and the Transnational Circuits of *Música Tropical*", B. Christine Arcé focuses on Toña la Negra, the Afro-Cuban musician who became famous in Mexico for her singing of boleros and Cuban *son*. In her analysis of Toña's success in Mexico, and in the city of Veracruz in particular, Arce reflects on the impact of African-inspired Caribbean music on Mexican musical culture and on the concurrent, yet paradoxical, deflection of the African presence in Veracruz. Arce's analysis underscores the persistence of transnational cultural flows within the Caribbean region and sheds light on the potential of music to permeate geopolitical and cultural barriers; for, despite her Cuban origins and evident blackness, Toña is a positive emblem of Mexicanity, playing a fundamental role in the creation of a national culture.

The chapters in part 2 of the book, "Performing/Contesting Identities", closely examine bodily aspects of performance and musical culture: dress, movement, the very fact of active participation – as in the case of Guadeloupean women participating in *gwo ka* – as well as lyrical discourse on the body. Based on ethnographic research in Guadeloupe, Kathe Managan's chapter, "Guadeloupean Women Performing *Gwo Ka*: Island Presences and Transnational Connections", examines the increasing participation of Guadeloupean women in the traditional form of music, song and dance known as *gwo ka*. *Gwo ka* performance is centred on a drum of the same name, made from a goatskin-covered barrel; *gwo ka* drumming, and the dance and singing that goes along with it, has existed in Guadeloupe from early in the colonial period.

The performance of *gwo ka* is a potent site of national identification traditionally dominated by men; however, Managan's reseach confirms that women seeking access to national sentiment increasingly lay claims to the form. Growing numbers of women participate in drumming, formerly an exclusively male activity, as well as singing and dancing. Managan also presents an illuminating selection of interviews with female *gwo ka* singers, dancers and drummers, whose lives exemplify and illustrate the complexities of transnational connections.

In chapter 5, "Celia's Shoes", Frances Negrón-Muntaner reflects on the career of Celia Cruz, Cuba's Queen of Salsa, motivated by a feeling of awe inspired by a beautifully crafted pair of Cruz's shoes on exhibition at the Smithsonian. The unique, hand-carved shoes, created by a Mexican master *zapatero*, weighed heavily in Negrón-Muntaner's hands as if they had carried not only the burden of Cruz's physical and psychic history but also the weight of Cubanness itself. Treating the shoes as a signifier of social status and gender, as well as ethnic and national identities, Negrón-Muntaner interprets the stories they convey about Celia's career: her rise from poverty to stardom, her migrations from Cuba to Mexico and subsequently to the United States. She argues that Celia's shoes bespeak the singer's shifting, multiple identities in ways that represent both the particularity of their owner's unique career and the Cuban exilic experience in the United States.

In chapter 6, Lyndon K. Gill proposes that we give a close critical *listen* to the grand dame of calypso music: McCartha Sandy-Lewis, better known as Calypso Rose. Lewis's 1968 song "Palet" provides the sonic focal point for Gill's analysis of Calypso Rose's sexual and gender politics, in particular her discourse in this song on female same-sex desire. In this chapter, Gill deploys Caribbean-American lesbian feminist poet Audre Lorde's re-conceptualization of the sensual as a bridge between the political and the spiritual in her classic essay "Uses of the Erotic: The Erotic as Power"[18] to read (and hear) Calypso Rose's song as a coded expression of erotic subjectivity. Gill deploys the concept of erotic subjectivity, recognizing that it brings together the political, sensual and spiritual as part of an interlinked way of experiencing and interpreting the world. Gill proposes that this perspectival trinity attends to various formal and informal power hierarchies (the political); sexual as well as non-sexual intimacy (the sensual); and sacred metaphysics (the spiritual). He deploys the concept as a lens to bring into view the mutually constitutive relationships among these seemingly separate, but actually linked epistemologies in the life and work of an exemplary artist.

In chapter 7, "'Born in Chanel, Christen in Gucci': The Rhetoric of Brand Names and Haute Couture in Jamaican Dancehall", Andrea Elizabeth Shaw explores the role of fashion in the Jamaican dancehall arena, and considers how fashion, specifically designer wear, is invoked and fetishized in song lyrics. The chapter title alludes to a lyric by Spice, a female Jamaican DJ, that Shaw contextualizes as part of the competition between women for primacy in the dancehall space. Shaw suggests that the intermingling of designer clothing and the Caribbean female body results in a potent signifier of femininity that renders the wearer of these designer items not only sexually superior to her counterpart clad in local fashion, but also deadly to her potential male conquests. Acknowledging that the most desired styles worn in the dancehall are North American or European in origin, Shaw extends her reading of the crucial importance of fashion in the reggae dancehall to explore some of the ways in which dancehall performers employ designer-wear discourse to negotiate the political and social tensions between the Caribbean and the First World.

Nadia Celis examines the place and status of bodies in the definition of Caribbean cultural identity in chapter 8, titled "The Rhetoric of Hips: Shakira's Embodiment and the Quest for Caribbean Identity". This chapter takes as its point of departure Shakira's most successful hit recording to date, the single "Hips Don't Lie", to illustrate a significant development in Shakira's portrayal of her personal and cultural identity. Celis deploys feminist theories of embodiment to support her argument that Shakira's corporeality and personality are paradigmatic of an "embodied subject". She examines Shakira's mobility across cultures, evident in the simultaneity of her identifications (as Colombian, Lebanese and Latina) to examine issues of "translation" faced by Caribbean bodies and subjects in their relations with transnational networks of meaning and globalized body politics. Shakira's polyvalent use of her body language breaks with local and global expectations regarding gender and ethnicity; Shakira's embodied self reveals the potential of bodies to foster alternative notions of subjectivity and of power relations. Shakira's "wise" body, her nomadism and her performative ability are considered as distinctive features of Caribbean identities, making of this artist an emblematic figure of the actual and potential contributions of the Caribbean to the search for alternative ways of being and coexisting in a postcolonial world.

The chapters in part 3 of the book take as their focus artists whose careers and cultural politics have been influenced by or illuminate diasporic cultural cross-currents. In chapter 9, "The Black Diaspora North of the Border: Women, Music and Caribbean Culture in Canada", Lisa Tomlinson reviews the rarely acknowledged contributions of Caribbean-Canadian women to the development of black music culture in Canada. While there have been to date a few successful Caribbean-Canadian female music artists in Canada and the diaspora, Caribbean-Canadian women's presence in the Canadian music industry remains marginal. In this chapter Tomlinson charts black women's presence in Canadian hip-hop, reggae, dancehall and dub poetry and examines the ways these forms overlap in the creative musical expressions of Caribbean-Canadian female artists.

In chapter 10, "Who Is Grace Jones?", Ifeona Fulani proposes that the visual and spectacular aspects of Jones's performance have for too long been the focus of scholarly attention, to the seeming neglect of the aural and musical, namely, Jones's songs and the accompanying music, the lyrics and her vocalization of them. In this chapter Fulani attempts to look beyond the fetishizing fixation with Jones's image and personae to reflect on the Jamaican and African diasporic cultural influences discernable in the subversive, transgressive elements in Jones's work. Fulani's reading is informed by the critical necessity of taking into account the particular histories that shape public response to, and perceptions of, black female performers on one hand and, on the other, the social and commercial pressures that forestall or negate overt expressions by black female performance of black female subjectivity. Fulani argues that fantasy, stereotype and fetish have influenced critical response to Grace Jones as an artist and have thus obscured important aspects of her artistic innovation. The result has been lack of recognition of the trajectory of Jones's artistic development and the increasing complexity in her music and performance over time.

In chapter 11, "'LADIES A YOUR TIME NOW!': Erotic Politics, Lovers' Rock and Resistance in the UK", Lisa Amanda Palmer traces the emergence of lovers' rock, a genre of Black British reggae music that first appeared in London during the 1970s in Caribbean nightclubs and on "pirate" radio stations. Palmer argues that within the political context of the dancehall scene, lovers' rock and roots reggae are seen as binary opposites of each other – lovers' rock being "soft", and therefore feminized, reggae concerned with romantic love, and roots as masculinized "serious" reggae concerned with black oppositional politics. Deploying black feminist theories on love and the erotic, Palmer challenges the gendering of lovers' rock by suggesting that the genre was part of a much broader and complex political expression of love and rebellion among Caribbean communities in Britain.

In chapter 12, titled "From Third Wave to Third World: Lauryn Hill, Educated and Unplugged", Cheryl Sterling argues that national parameters or boundaries do not apply to Lauryn Hill, as her music is a fusion of soul, pop, reggae and hip-hop. This fusion has generated a mythos such that everyone wants to claim her as their own. When she was a Fugee, people talked of a Haitian group with an amazing female singer. When she "married" a Marley, she became the Jamaican Lauryn Hill. The mythos of identity transcends actuality, for few speak of the New Jersey girl who was proclaimed as the "mother of hip-hop invention". In her chapter, Sterling explores the shifting morphology of Lauryn Hill as reflected in her music. Sterling argues that heard and read together, *The Miseducation of Lauryn Hill* and *MTV Unplugged No. 2* stand as a subjective chronicle of Lauryn Hill's own self-actualization, sought through an interrogation of the spiritual and political. Sterling traces distinct but intersecting theoretical paradigms in her reading of Hill's musical discourse. Third-wave feminism is evident in Hill's evolving political consciousness and the processes of re-diasporization are revealed in the ease by which she incorporates Caribbean aesthetics in her work and life.

When pop superstar (and Grace Jones impersonator) Rihanna burst on the scene in 2005 with her hybrid reggae, hip-hop and R&B style, particularly signalled by her highly successful hit "Pon de Replay", audiences hurriedly Googled to find information about her origins: "Barbados? Barbados!" In chapter 13, Heather D. Russell examines Rihanna's Caribbeanity in the context of what Alexander Weheliye describes as an attendant "diasporic citizenship", a matrix of factors that black popular cultural practice, translocationality, conflicting/contesting/reinforcing sites of national belonging and myriad realms of black expressivity often engender. Russell reviews the often heated and radically divergent public discourse in Barbados that, on the one hand, critiques Rihanna's "sexualized", "morally questionable" and "scantily clad" representations in media, but on the other demands formal national recognition of her for having drawn attention to Barbados as a nation. The dialectics of nation, race, identity and global economy inform Russell's analysis of the Barbados Tourist Board's decision to posit Rihanna as the "face of Barbados" in obvious denial that Rihanna is not phenotypically characteristic of the Afro-Barbadians who constitute the principal racial group in the country. Her acceptance as "sex symbol" who also embodies "crossover appeal" in the global popular cultural marketplace raises a complex of issues that Russell addresses in this chapter, in particular, the Barbadian public imagination of itself, which from a national perspective invariably feels both "proud" and "protective" of one of their daughters, and yet, from an economic perspective, concedes the expedience of invoking and marketing Rihanna as Bajan commodity.

Chapter 14 offers a reminder of the global proportions of the archipelagic sweep and influence of Caribbean musics and the politics that inform them. In "I and Ireland: Reggae and Rastafari in the Work of Sinéad O'Connor", Adam John Waterman examines O'Connor's deployment of reggae as mode of political critique and argues that Sinéad O'Connor's engagement with reggae music should be understood as evidence of a larger political commitment to the Rastafari movement. He proposes that, in O'Connor's rendering, Rastafari is not an exclusively Jamaican cultural formation, but a spiritual movement that speaks to the struggles of all colonized peoples. For O'Connor, Rastafari presents an alternative to the punitive Roman Catholicism that evolved in response to the Irish struggle against colonialism, one that transcends narrow national identifications and nurtures connections between anti-colonial struggles. Although Catholicism was an important element of the struggle against British occupation, in the postcolonial era, traditionalist Irish Catholicism nurtures a sense of Irish national distinctiveness based upon racial exclusivity and whiteness. By crossing "traditional" Irish musics with reggae beats, O'Connor's work opens a space through which to articulate an anti-colonial transnationality for the post–Cold War era.

If at the very least the chapters in this volume introduce readers to artists whose performance and artistic works contribute uniquely to the vitality, diversity and reach of Caribbean cultural influence and Caribbean cultural politics, then this book will have made its own contribution to the archipelagic flow.

Notes

1. Antonio Benítez-Rojo, *The Repeating Island: The Caribbean and the Postmodern Perspective*, trans. James Maraniss (Durham, NC: Duke University Press, 1996), 1–4.
2. Paul Gilroy, *The Black Atlantic: Modernity and Double Consciousness* (Cambridge, MA: Harvard University Press, 1993), 78–79.
3. Kamau Brathwaite, "Jah", in *The Arrivants: A New World Trilogy* (Oxford: Oxford University Press, 1978), 162.
4. See Benítez-Rojo's theorization of the Caribbean as ceaseless motion, in "a never-ending tale", *Repeating Island*, xi.
5. See Kamau Brathwaite, *Contradictory Omens: Cultural Diversity and Integration in the Caribbean* (Kingston: Savacou, 1985); Edouard Glissant, *Caribbean Discourse: Selected Essays*, trans. J. Michael Dash (Charlottesville: University Press of Virginia, 1992); Benítez-Rojo, *Repeating Island*.
6. Timothy Reiss, introduction, *Music, Writing and Cultural Unity in the Caribbean*, ed. Timothy Reiss (Trenton, NJ: Africa World Press, 2005), 28.
7. Sara E. Johnson, "Cinquillo Consciousness: The Formation of a Pan-Caribbean Musical Aesthetic", in *Music, Writing and Cultural Unity in the Caribbean*, ed. Timothy Reiss (Trenton, NJ: Africa World Press, 2005), 36.
8. Ibid., 37.
9. See Samuel Furé Davis, "Reggae in Cuba and the Hispanic Caribbean: Fluctuations and Representations of Identities", *Black Music Research Journal* 29, no. 1 (2009): 25–50.
10. See Carolyn Cooper, *Sound Clash: Jamaican Dancehall Culture at Large* (New York: Palgrave Macmillan, 2004), 20.
11. Reiss, 26.
12. See Elizabeth Chamberlin's documentary film *Salsa in Japan: A Japanese and Latino Mix* (Berkeley Media LLC, 2003), which explores the popularity of salsa dancing and salsa clubs in Japan.
13. Cooper, *Sound Clash*, 1.
14. See the introduction to *Globalization, Diaspora and Caribbean Popular Culture*, ed. Keith Nurse and Christine Ho (Kingston: Ian Randle, 2005).
15. Alexander G. Weheliye, *Phonographies: Grooves in Sonic Afro-Modernity* (Durham, NC: Duke University Press, 2005), 147.
16. M. Barrera, "Hottentot 2000: Jennifer Lopez and Her Butt", in *Sexualities in History: A Reader*, ed. K. Phillips and B. Reay (New York: Routledge, 2002).
17. Myra Mendible, "Embodying Latinidad", in *From Bananas to Buttocks: The Latina Body in Popular Film and Culture*, ed. Myra Mendible (Austin: University of Texas Press, 2007).
18. Audre Lorde, "Uses of the Erotic: The Erotic as Power", in *Sister Outsider: Essays and Speeches* (Freedom, CA: Crossing Press, 1984), 56.

Part 1.

FROM THE POSTCOLONIAL TO THE TRANSNATIONAL

1.

The Blackness of Sugar
Celia Cruz and the Performance of (Trans)nationalism

FRANCES R. APARICIO

ON OCTOBER 16, 1997 the Cuban singer Celia Cruz, known as the Queen of Latin Music, donated a bright orange Cuban rumba dress, a blonde wig, and a pair of her unique stage shoes to the permanent collection of the National Museum of American History. What could be seen merely as an entertainer's accessories, these objects point to the unique ways in which Celia Cruz uses her body, in addition to her voice and songs, as a site for performing transnationalism. Together, the three personal accessories serve as icons for the ways in which Celia Cruz has negotiated heterogeneous musical and cultural systems throughout sixty years of making music in Cuba, Latin America, the United States and internationally. The traditional rumbera dress, which suggests her years of singing with La Sonora Matancera, has served to visually construct Celia as a symbol of Cuban national identity and of *afrocubanismo*. For many years, the curious platform shoes without heels were custom-made for her by a Mexican shoemaker, thus indexing her affective and professional ties to Mexico and the larger sense of *latinoamericanismo* (Latin Americanism) that Celia has created through her music. Finally, her blonde wig metonymically reminds us of her incursions into Anglo music, her entry into the international entertainment scene and mainstream Hollywood.

These specific props, however, are only three out of an innumerable repertoire of dresses, shoes, wigs and songs that well illustrate the versatility with which Celia Cruz has entered diverse markets and created different audiences at particular historical moments. If her fame rests on her unique 'deep, metallic contralto' voice and her improvisational skills in the soneo, it is also the result of the diverse repertoires and styles that she has performed and literally embodied (Sabournin 1986: 553). In an interview with Raúl Fernández (1996), she commented that 'yo me meto en todo; lo que a mí me piden yo canto', adding that she even sang La Macarena at an event in New Orleans [I get into everything; I'll sing anything people want]. This versatility is, to be sure, due to the Cuban singer's genial musical talents that allow her to perform songs without having to rehearse. As Larry Harlow has commented, 'Esa señora es un genio' [That lady is a genius] (Rondón, 1980: 136).

Celia Cruz's repertoire is indeed vast. Her performances and recordings include, among many others, traditional Cuban santería music, pregones, guajiras, Afro-Cuban rumbas, guarachas, mambos and cha-cha-chá, boogaloo and salsa in the 1960s and 1970s, rock en español with Los Fabulosos Cadillacs, Brazilian music, Peruvian folkloric songs, Mexican rancheras, Puerto Rican bombas, and collaborations with Wyclef Jean and David Byrne in the United States. The stylistic and musical fluidity, coupled with her ever-changing bodily aesthetics, easily wins her audiences out of widely diverse communities. This versatility, facilitated by her musical talent, illustrates the multiple subjectivities that Celia Cruz has constructed for herself. Yet it does not diminish Celia Cruz's subject position which is strongly rooted in the Cuban exile experience. As George Lipsitz (1994: 5) notes, 'even under circumstances of global integration, local identities and affiliations do not disappear. On the contrary, the transnational economy often makes itself felt most powerfully through the reorganization of spaces and the transformation of local experience'. In this short article, I will trace the tensions between her public ideological position on Cuba and the multiple identities – including blackness – that she assumes and performs through her musical repertoire, professional history, public interviews, and the aesthetic construction of herself as a tropical diva.

As the singer of La Sonora Matancera during the 1950s, Celia Cruz was the female embodiment of Afro-Cuban music and música tropical in Cuba and throughout Latin America. Since her exile in 1961, she has served as the voice of Cuba in a different way. In her song, 'Yo soy la voz' (Cruz and Puente, 1969), the singing subject enumerates the evocative meanings that her voice carries. She is the voice of the Cuba of the past, 'el sabor tropical' [the taste of the tropics], the symbol of the Cuban son, of coffee and of sugar cane. In this song, the Queen of Salsa defines her voice as the vehicle for imagining pre-socialist Cuba and as a tool for articulating a metaphor between the singing subject and the national body of Cuba. If the voice is 'the locus of articulation of an individual's body to language and society' (Furman, 1991: 303), then Celia Cruz's performative Cuban grito, 'azúcar' [sugar] takes on added meaning. The performative use of this signifier emerged at a restaurant in Miami and it has become her universally recognized trademark.[1] Yet it carries within it the history of Cuba's plantation culture, the economics of slavery, and the racial and gender dynamics from which Cuban national identity and popular music emerge (Benítez-Rojo, 1996; Ortiz, 1947 [1995]; Rivero, 1989). Given these subtexts, the symbolic reiteration of the word 'azúcar' reaffirms the role of Celia Cruz's voice and body as an icon of Cuba's African-based heritage and mestizaje. Yet it also serves as a vestigial reminder of the US-dominated capitalist economy that was transformed by socialism, a nostalgic signifier given Celia Cruz's subject position as a Cuban exile.

Her 1998 recording, *Azúcar negra,* and its title song, render the single utterance of 'azúcar' much more complex. While sugar is white, the seemingly oxymoronic metaphor of 'black sugar' foregrounds the traces of slavery behind the national economy of the plantation, a blackness that is indeed reaffirmed in the title song 'Azúcar negra'. The initial, ritualistic African-style drumming in this cut composed by Mario Díaz indexes the genealogy of blackness in Afro-Cuban music. Again, this song establishes a metaphor between Celia as a singing subject and Afro-Cuban culture. When she states that her blood is black sugar and that her skin is marked by the rumba and the bongó, this discourse inscribes Africanness and black agency on her body, the traces of slavery that facilitated the economy of the island. Significantly, the lyrics also identify the singing subject as the daughter of a rich island, foregrounding the association between slavery and capitalism and simultaneously suggesting the nostalgic discourse of the Cuban exile subject.

Celia Cruz's musical repertoire is indeed an expression of afrocubanismo. Afro-Cuban vernacular poetics, including popular religious beliefs such as santería, popular oral traditions such as pregones and street slang, are the stylistic and discursive substance of many of Celia's songs. From the early hits with La Sonora Matancera, such as 'El yerberito moderno' and 'Burundanga', to the famous two-volume recording, *Homenaje a los santos,* which anthologizes some authentic African santería music with modern arrangements of songs dedicated to particular saints, Celia Cruz's music has consistently foregrounded the African legacy in Cuba's music, rhythms, and cultural heritage. Her singing in African languages, particularly in Lucumí, as in 'Lalle lalle' (Cruz, 1991) and 'Changó "ta veni"' (1989), her rhythmical dialogues with the drums, as in 'Quimbo Quimbumbia' (1969), and songs such as 'Azúcar negra' (1998), 'Bembelequá' (1994), and 'La cumbanchera de Belén' (1989), which foregrounds the figure of the black rumbera and her dancing movements, are all traditional expressions of afrocubanismo at multiple levels. Salsa hits such as 'Quimbara', according to Mayra Santos, 'are basically a call to the dance floor, where the purpose of rhyme, rhythm, and lyrics is to bring to consciousness the act of salsa itself, an act of bonding where audience, dancers, musicians, and singers come together as a community of "entendidos"' (1997: 184). As the Afroboricua writer Mayra Santos suggests here, this particular song by Celia Cruz enacts the ritualistic task of creating a translocal, mulatto and black working-class community through the Afrocuban vernacular poetics and rhythms that inform many of her songs.

If Mayra Santos proposes a 'translocal' definition of salsa anchored in a working-class, mulatto, pan-Caribbean cultural semiotics, Celia Cruz's own definitions of salsa music, on the contrary, have served to reaffirm a pre-socialist Cuban national identity racialized as white. In the continuing debate about the origins, authenticity and ownership of salsa music, Celia's definitions of salsa coincide with many who insist that it is only Cuban music recycled for an international market. In this vein, she has proposed that 'El yerberito moderno', which is a traditional Cuban pregón, is now called salsa. Salsa, for her, is a commercial label that has created a larger audience for Cuban music, for which she is very happy. And while Celia Cruz publicly recognizes the talents and collaborations of Puerto Rican and other Latino musicians in the development of salsa, she insists on conflating it with Cuban music. In an interview with Alberto Nacif (1997), Celia Cruz reveals the connection between this Cubanist definition of salsa and her own experience of exile:

> I have 37 or 38 years outside of my country, and the longing for it is precisely what allows me to conserve that feeling and never lose it. Today that thing that you call, or rather we call (because I'm also doing that) salsa, is nothing more than my Cuban music, variations of the son, but it needed another name so that it could be actualized and be successful. It was around that time that the great Cuban orchestras, which were the truly great exponents of Cuban music, were not allowed to travel to the

United States any longer. When that happened, Cuban music was starting to get pushed to the side. This was, of course, because the bands that were playing it were not around. So then the name salsa came along, and nothing really changed. It was still Cuban music. One of the few things that has changed is perhaps the addition of electronic instruments. In fact the Sonora Matancera didn't use electronic instruments until the very last minute, at which time they incorporated the electric bass. Also there is the fact that a lot of the musicians and the arrangers from today were born in other places like Puerto Rico, or New York, for example, Tito Puente, who have also been influenced by jazz, are playing salsa. However, that's not my style. I'll continue with my Cuban music until the last day. You can call it "salsa" or "sulso" or whatever you want to call it, it's still Cuban music. I will always have it present within me. I can be here in Mexico or in Venezuela or in Spain or Argentina, and my accent is still a Cuban accent. (Nacif, 1997: 2)

This lengthy reply is worth quoting since it suggests that Celia Cruz's definition of salsa has more to do with her own cultural deterritorialization than with wanting to deny the musical, stylistic and instrumental innovation of New York Puerto Rican salsa since the 1970s. When she distinguishes her style from that of Tito Puente, she is in fact contradictorily acknowledging that there are diverse styles of salsa under the rubric and that not all music labelled salsa is Cuban music. Yet this statement also reaffirms the fact that one of her most important contributions to the Latin popular music scene in the United States was to bring back, so to speak, the 'Cuban son aspect' (Rondón, 1980) during the salsa boom, what she refers to as her 'Cuban accent' in more metaphorical ways. Cesar Miguel Rondón (1980: 92), in fact, speaks of Celia Cruz as 'la propia guaracha personificada' and calls her influence on salsa 'matancerización salsosa'. Celia's musical style and performances have tropicalized (Aparicio and Chávez-Silverman, 1997) or, to be more specific, 'cubanized' songs and musical numbers from other national traditions, such as 'Cucurrucucú paloma' (1981). Yet Celia's reply, in itself, evinces the ambivalence between the discourse of Cubanness for and by the exiled subject, and the transnational audiences and musical styles that have emerged, ironically, out of her own political and geographical displacement.

Celia Cruz has been very vocal about her exile politics both in interviews and in her own musical repertoire and performances on stage. In interviews she has acknowledged her painful departure from the island and the personal repercussions that the exile status has imposed on her (Fernández, 1996; Nacif,

1997; Rath 1995). In her recordings, she has consistently included songs that either evoke a pre-socialist Cuba or imagine a post-socialist Cuba, a lyrical and desired reclaiming that has musically vocalized the hegemonic political agenda of the Cuban exile community in Miami.[2] Her stance has been overtly expressed in public performances and has informed, for example, the controversy over the visit of Silvio Rodríguez to Puerto Rico. As the opening act for the Concierto de las Américas in 1994, Celia Cruz sang José Martí's verses and publicly exhorted all presidents to bring Fidel Castro down. This appropriation of José Martí's discourse in the context of liberating Cuba from its socialist state is not unique to Celia Cruz, but a discursive strategy common to many Cuban singers in exile, such as Gloria Estefan and Willie Chirino (Guevara, 1997). With regard to class and race, it is interesting, although not necessarily contradictory, that despite Celia's urban, working-class black origins, she would become a central spokesperson for the politics of the early, white bourgeois, landholding Cuban exile community. The fact that in Cuba she sang to white audiences helps to explain this stance, since the revolution initially dismantled the economic infrastructure of the music clubs in which La Sonora Matancera performed (Fernández, 1996).

Her exile politics were clearly illustrated during her concert in Ann Arbor, Michigan, in November 1997. Celia responded to the presence of the Cuban community signalled by a large, Cuban flag in the audience. Following the dialogic modes of Afro-Caribbean music and exemplifying the power of her vocality, that is, the 'vital interrelationship between vocalization and audition' (Dunn and Jones, 1994: 2), Celia sang predominantly Cuban music: guajiras, sones, guarachas, mambos, many of them expressing a nostalgic and national sentiment towards Cuba. She picked up a little Cuban flag, which she held in her hand throughout the long performance, and enveloped herself in the large Cuban flag that the Cuban listeners offered her. Interspersed among songs and commentary, Celia would utter in Spanish comments against socialist Cuba and coded allusions about Fidel Castro. Speaking in Spanish during the whole concert in a region where Spanish is far from being a public language, these comments served as coded messages that privileged a particular Cuban exile ideology. Yet they were also received by a Hispanophone or bilingual public who may not have been politically in agreement with her, but who nevertheless enjoyed the politically imbued rhythms and the sonorous arrangements. Indeed, this particular concert established an unprecedented carnival-like environment, a dialogue between the singer and the audience, that fostered free and communal dancing in the aisles, listeners standing up and clapping, and some angry audience members who expected to see the show from their seats undisturbed by a participatory auditorium. Celia Cruz's unique musical style and collective performativity truly tropicalized Hill Auditorium in Ann Arbor, yet this transculturative event was mediated by the discourse of the Cuban exile. Perhaps the Queen of Latin Music felt safe and comfortable expressing her nostalgia for a pre-revolutionary Cuba to a highly responsive, warm and heterogeneous audience in a small, midwest college town far from the Latino politics of either coast. Yet, ironically, her political and politicized performance, like her traditional rumbera dresses and the new digitalized recordings of her performances with La Sonora Matancera, serve as visual and sonorous re-creations of that Cuba of the past. The image of 'azúcar negra' comes to mind, as Celia's black body, Afro-Cuban rhythms, and voice together indexed the cultural survival of slaves in Cuba while she simultaneously vocalized the discourse of a pro-capitalist, white Cuban bourgeoisie, also embodying colonial desire with her blonde wig.

As was recently observed in the *New York Times* (Ojito, 1998), '[I]n an era of crossover pop stars and the relentless Americanization of almost everything, Ms. Cruz . . . is an oddity. She has seen her popularity in this country grow even as she has clung resolutely to her roots, her language and her style.' This contradiction is significant for understanding the relational nature between national and transnational identities. Celia Cruz's insistence on retaining her Spanish after thirty years of residing in the United States, and despite her international fame, also illustrates a strategic nationalism that has not, interestingly, limited her access to a global market that advertises itself as English-only. When she comments publicly that her 'English is not good-looking' in a Caribbean, hispanicized English and insists on using Spanish on stage, she is indeed contributing to the increasing visibility of Spanish as a public language in the United States. Simultaneously, however, Spanish is also a dominant paradigm for *latinidad* that does not always include Latino younger generations nor Anglophone Latinos. In this regard, it can well function as a dominant marker of identity within the larger, Latino community.

Yet Spanish is also Celia's vehicle for vocalizing and constructing a Latin American identity. Her first song, which she performed for a radio amateur show in Havana and which won her a prize, was an Argentinean tango entitled

'Nostalgia'. As the singer for 'Las mulatas de fuego', a group of Cuban dancers who travelled to Mexico and other Latin American countries, Celia Cruz was a key figure in the initial dissemination of the mambo throughout Mexico and, eventually, of música tropical. She toured Mexico with Toña la Negra in 1961 and brought Cuban rhythms and musical genres to many parts of that country (Fernández, 1997). Likewise, her travels with La Sonora Matancera during the 1950s created audiences for Afro-Caribbean music in Colombia, Haiti, Venezuela, Costa Rica and Panama. Her recordings also circulated her vocal and improvisatory talents to all regions of Latin America. Significantly, these early tours cemented the intergenerational popularity that Celia Cruz is currently enjoying in the United States among Latino audiences. Not only US Latino adults who grew up listening to Celia Cruz in their respective countries constitute her Latino market but, as Mirta Ojito (1998) well observes, 'the more recent immigrants, who tend to be younger, attend her concerts buoyed by their own interest in her music but also by curiosity over a woman whose music their parents and grandparents danced to back in the 1950s' (Fernández, 1996; Walsh, 1998). Thus, Celia Cruz's vocality and song repertoire literally create a hemispheric community of Latino and Latin American listeners that crosses generations, national borders and cultural divides. It serves as a vehicle of cultural memory that unifies Latinos, at least temporarily, across age and national borders. In the United States, her performances in Spanish also serve, like Latin popular music, as public spaces where a colonized cultural identity is performed decolonizing itself, reaffirming its presence. That Celia Cruz's construction of *latinidad* within the United States has been facilitated by her past Latin American appearances reveals how the transnational circulation of music, in its production, performance and audition, is already always embedded in local experiences of national identities.

If within salsa music Celia Cruz's performances and recordings represent the traditional, Cuban sound, she has also embraced musical genres from diverse Latin American regions and folklores, such as Peruvian waltzes, Mexican boleros, Uruguayan songs, Dominican merengues and Puerto Rican bombas, thus hybridizing her own Cuban music with other Latin American folkloric rhythms and tunes. It was Celia who took Chabuca Granda's 'La flor de canela' into Mexico in 1957, where it was first recorded by los Hermanos Silva (Fernández, 1996). She has also interpreted Ismael Rivera's hits (Cruz, 1992), performed 'La cama de piedra' in her Mexican tours, and has two recordings dedicated to Mexico.³ She has recorded the Argentinean Palito Ortega's Nueva Ola hit, 'Corazón contento' from the 1970s (Cruz and Puente, 1969) and in 1988 she recorded 'Vasos vacíos' with *Los fabulosos Cadillacs*, entering the world of rock en español (Cruz *et al.*, 1997). In her stage appearances, she has played an important role as a cultural ambassador to Latin America throughout the world, having toured Europe, Japan, Greece, Finland, Africa, and most countries in Latin America, including Brazil. When Jean Franco (1994: 19) writes that Celia Cruz is the 'apostle of latinity' and that, as a singer, she has played the role of a Simón Bolívar in unifying Latin American countries, the Latin Americanist critic recognizes the alternative political power of popular culture. Celia's vocality in building a sense of community across national borders exemplifies what George Lipsitz (1994: 17) has described as 'the potential of popular culture as a mechanism of communication and education, as a site for experimentation with cultural and social roles not yet possible in politics'.

Much of this *latinidad* associated with Celia Cruz, however, has been imagined and constructed outside of Cuba and the geopolitical borders of Latin America. The years of Celia's growing fame were during the 1970s, when she performed with Willie Colón and Johnny Pacheco. Her record with the Dominican Johnny Pacheco, *Celia y Johnny* (1976), according to Raúl Fernández (1996), has been one of the most anthological Latin American repertoires ever recorded in the salsa industry. It includes the Brazilian hit, 'Usted abusó', 'Zambúllete', a Uruguayan song that Celia sings to Panama, and other hits such as 'Vieja Luna', the Peruvian 'Toromata', and 'Quimbara' (Rondón, 1980). The dialectics, then, between national and pan-American identities in the salsa industry resist fixed categorizations or boundaries. New York salsa during the 1970s responded both to local Puerto Rican experiences in the barrio as much as it created pan-Latino audiences in the United States and Latin America. New York itself, as Ruth Glasser (1995) has documented, has been, historically, a site of pan-Caribbean and Latin American musical borrowings and collaborations that produced what has been traditionally considered to be Puerto Rican national or even nationalist music. Yet, as the songs 'Pasaporte latinoamericano' (Cruz, 1998) and 'Latinos en Estados Unidos' (Cruz and Colón, 1981) suggest, Celia sings a Latina identity that emerges out of homogenizing the diverse experiences of migration and of cultural deterritorialization of Latin Americans, rendering them synonymous with the Cuban exile and its constructed otherness of the United States and of English. Through these songs, which she ultimately selects, she is resolving some of the ambivalences between her constructions of Cubanness and the transnational dimensions of her audiences and reconciling the fact that the US Latino market paved the way for her growing fame and mainstreaming.[4]

In the United States, Celia's traditional afrocubanismo is transformed in relation to the African-American community, thus extending this nationally based racial identity into hemispheric dimensions. Her hairstyles, for one, suggest these diasporic identities. During the 1970s she wore dreadlocks in a concert in Colombia and on the album cover of *Celia y Willie* (1981). Assuming blackness in the United States context, she also wore an Afro hairstyle in the album *Recordando el ayer* [Remembering the past] (Cruz, 1976) to signal the reaffirmation of the African heritage in her music. The politics of her hair also served as a visual marker of her solidarity with the claims of the black movement and of 'black is beautiful', a solidarity which Salsa music reaffirmed through its articulation with the political and social movements of the Young Lords and the Black Panthers (Pagán, 1997). In the 1960s, Celia performed boogaloos and in the 1990s she collaborated with The Fugees' Wyclef Jean in his hip-hop version of 'Guantanamera' (1997). Celia's prelude in Spanish of the traditional national song based on José Martí's verses assumes solidarity with African-American cultural expressions, yet these lyrics are also radically resemanticized by Wyclef Jean as they are overlaid with the hip-hop song that transforms the signifier Guantanamera into a Latina woman's name in Spanish Harlem and the song into a dialogue of desire between her and the singer. Like the African drumming in 'Azúcar negra', Celia's 'Guantanamera' has become one of the foundational lyrics for hip-hop music, a genealogy that is also evident in Wyclef Jean's own Afro-Cuban heritage.

Celia explained in an interview (Fernández, 1996) that in the Cuba of the 1950s she had heard, at a distance, 'of jazz in the United States, of Cab Calloway, the film Stormy Weather', yet she was 'never too interested'. By 1989 her concert at the Abyssinian Baptist Church in Harlem on 21 October 'underscored the connections between the various outposts of the African diaspora in the New World' (Watrous, 1989: 62). On stage with Mario Bauzá's orchestra, Tito Puente on the timbales and Chico O'Farill, Celia Cruz indeed embodied on stage the historical connections between Afro-Cuban rhythms and African-American jazz.

Perhaps the most illuminating example of the transnational circulation of Afro-Caribbean music is the fact that, from her exile in the United States, Celia Cruz herself has influenced musicians in Cuba. Her role as a musical 'transmigrant' (Basch *et al.*, 1994) is clearly evidenced in her interview with Alberto Nacif, who tells the Cuban singer the following anecdote:

> A couple of years ago when I was in Chicago for the last tour of the Muñequitos de Matanzas, I had six of them piled into my car, and as we were going to eat some dinner and then spend some time walking through the downtown Chicago area, I happened to put in a copy of your CD Azúcar Negra in the car, and they absolutely went crazy to hear your voice and to hear the quality of music that you were singing. They all asked me to make them copies for themselves, and refused to leave the car, even though we were all hungry, until the CD was done playing. That says a lot about the effect that you still have on the people of Cuba. (Nacif, 1997: 2)

Celia responded that she has never met Los Muñequitos de Matanzas but that she hears they're very good. Despite the rigid boundaries established by the US embargo on Cuba and Celia's own ideological boundaries, the members of socialist Cuba's most important folkloric Afro-Cuban group listen to Celia's homage to *afrocubanismo* in 'Azúcar negra' inside a car in Chicago, a city renowned for its jazz and blues. Mediated through CD technology, this musical encounter in Chicago between the music of the two Cubas attests to the diasporic and hemispheric nature of musical migrations.

A final instance of Celia's multiple musical hybridities is her incursion into Anglo music, particularly rock, and her mainstreamed presence in Hollywood and the US entertainment market, a hybridity signalled by her reiterated use of her blonde wigs. Before coming to the United States, her recording with La Sonora Matancera of 'Rock and roll' (1988), a guaracha hybridized with rock and roll rhythms, announces the emergence of rock and its entrance into Cuba, yet it locates it as the new rhythm that follows the mambo and the cha-cha-cha. This musical genealogy and the use of English in the song blur the binaries that have been imposed between Latin music and rock. If anything, it proposes that rock is part of the musical productions of the African diaspora in the Americas more than a sign of the cultural divides between the imperial Anglo and the colonized Latin American cultures. Celia's participation in the *Tropical Tribute to the Beatles* overtly articulates the connections between rock and Afro-Caribbean musics and the participation of Latino musicians in the development of rock, historically deemed as imperialist music from the perspective of Latin America. As Ralph Mercado (1996) writes in the liner notes, the unquestionable influence of the mambo and of Latin/Cuban jazz and rhythms during the 1950s and 1960s, the use of the clave beat in many of The Beatles' songs, and the cha-cha-cha beat in 'And I Love Her' and 'Obladi Oblada', are some of the traces of Latin influence in the compositions of 'the Fabulous Four'. Although this recording was received with lukewarm support by the Latino public, it is an important recognition of the underlying presence of Afro-Caribbean musical contributions to rock music, historically racialized as white from the Latin American perspective. Celia's interpretation of 'Obladi Oblada' shows the cyclical forces of musical migrations, for its Spanish lyrics about the love between Celia and her husband, Pedro Knight, in addition to the salsa rhythms and arrangements, tropicalizes the original text. The Spanish, salsified versions, of classics such as 'I Want to Hold your Hand' and 'Can't Buy me Love' and the interlingual soneos in the English songs speak to the local, Latino reality, thus repeating rock with a difference.

In terms of her 'spectacular body' (Parker *et al.*, 1992: 12), that is, the ways in which Celia Cruz's bodily aesthetics speak to the dialectics between national and transnational locations, the blonde wigs do not necessarily whiten Celia's repertoire but are, on the contrary, transculturated by her dark skin, her Spanish vocals, and the song repertoires that reaffirm afrocubanismo, a Cuban exile perspective and a hemispheric *latinidad*. Her changing fashions, her flashy style, glamorous, elegant, and, to some, extravagant stage costumes, serve as visual traces of social history since the 1950s. Her tropicalized, baroque and colourful attire serve as a visual reaffirmation of the Caribbean presence in the United States while it simultaneously makes Celia the embodiment of transnationalism. The fluidity with which the Reina Rumba imagines and reimagines herself as Afro-Cuban, Latin American, Latina and international may be easily dismissed as marketing strategies or as an instance of postmodernism. Rather, I propose that these multiple subjectivities and performative identities do not necessarily dilute or preclude national identities, but in fact are interpellated by them. Celia Cruz's singing and bodily aesthetics suggest more complex modes of understanding the cultural implications of the migrations of Latin popular music.

Acknowledgement

This essay was originally published by Frances R. Aparicio as "The Blackness of Sugar: Celia Cruz and the Performance of (Trans)nationalism", *Cultural Studies* 13, no. 2 (1999): 223–36. Reprinted unaltered by permission from Taylor and Francis.

Notes

1. According to Celia Cruz, once, when she was having lunch at a Cuban restaurant in Miami, the waiter asked her if she wanted Cuban coffee with or without sugar. She thought that was very strange given the fact that Cuban coffee is very strong and tastes bitter without sugar. So, she told him, 'With sugar! With sugar, my dear boy!' She told the story to her audience afterwards and she began screaming 'Azúcar, azúcar' during her performances. This information appeared in the website http://tyrone.Hob.corn/events/960315cruz/ (3-15-96).
2. Songs such as 'De la Habana hasta aquí' (1998), 'Yo regresaré' (1969), 'Yo soy la voz' (1969), and 'Cuando Cuba se acabe de liberar' (1994), are but some examples of both the nostalgic and utopic discourses around Cuba's liberation.
3. Among her innumerable recordings, see *México qué grande eres,* Secco SCLP 9227, and *A ti, México,* Tico, SLP 1164. No dates were available.
4. Based on his extensive interview with Celia Cruz, Raúl Fernández (1997) writes that Celia has not just been a singer, but that she has personally chosen each and every one of the hits that have become a success, at times against the wishes of composers, musicians and producers. In this light, her personal ideologies highly inform her musical selections.

References

Aparicio, Frances and Chávez-Silverman, Susana (eds) (1997) *Tropicalizations: Transcultural Representations of Latinidad,* Hanover and London: University Press of New England.
Basch, Linda, Glick Schiller, Nina and Christina Szanton Blanc, (1994) *Nations Unbound: Transnational Projects, Postcolonial Predicaments, and Deterritorialized Nation-States,* Langhorne, PA: Gordon and Breach.
Benítez-Rojo, Antonio (1996) *The Repeating Island: The Caribbean and the Postmodern Condition,* Durham and London: Duke University Press.
Cruz, Celia (1976) Celia, Johnny, Justo and Papo: *Recordando el ayer,* Vaya Records, LPS 88722.

—— (1988) *La reina del rítmo*, Peerless, SA de CV PCD-011-3.
—— (1989) *La incomparable Celia con la Sonora Matancera*, Palladium Latin Jazz and Dance Records, PCD-133.
—— (1991) *La dinámica Celia Cruz con la Sonora Matancera*, Seeco Tropical, 0019-2.
—— (1992) *Tributo a Ismael Rivera: Celia Cruz*, Vaya Records, JMVS 110.
—— (1994) *Irrepetible*, RMM Records, CDZ 81452.
—— (1998) *Azúcar Amarga*, RMM Records, RMD 80985.
Cruz, Celia and Colón, Willie (1981) *Celia y Willie*, Vaya Records, JMVS 93.
Cruz, Celia and Puente, Tito (1969) *Quimbo Quimbumbia*, Tico Records, TRSLP 1193.
Cruz, Celia *et al.* (1996) *Tropical Tribute to The Beatles*, RMM Records, RMD 82011.
Cruz, Celia *et al.* (1997) *Celia's Duets,* RRMM Records, RMD 82201.
Dunn, Leslie C. and Jones, Nancy A. (1994) 'Introduction', in *Embodied Voices: Representing Female Vocality in Western Culture,* Cambridge: Cambridge University Press.
Fernández, Raúl (1996) Interview with Celia Cruz, 15 September, Hollywood, CA: Jazz Oral History Project, The Smithsonian Institution.
—— (1997) 'Celia Cruz: artista de América Latina', *Deslinde,* 21, July/September 1997: 102–21.
Franco, Jean (1994) 'What's left of the intelligentsia? The uncertain future of the printed word', *NACLA Report on the Americas,* 28(2): 16–21.
Furman, Nelly (1991) 'Opera, or the staging of the voice', *Cambridge Opera Journal,* 3(3): 303.
Glasser, Ruth (1995) *My Music is my Flag: Puerto Rican Musicians and their New York Communities 1917–1940,* Berkeley: University of California Press.
Guevara, Gema (1997) 'La Cuba de ayer/La Cuba de hoy: the politics of music in the Cuban-American community', The Rhythms of Culture: Dancing to Las Américas. International Research Conference on Popular Music in Latin(o) America, 21–22 March, University of Michigan, Ann Arbor.
Jean, Wyclef (1997) *The Carnival,* Columbia Records, 487442-2.
Lipsitz, George (1994) *Dangerous Crossroads: Popular Music, Postmodernism, and the Poetics of Place,* New York and London: Verso.
Mercado, Ralph (1996) 'Introduction' to *Tropical Tribute to the Beatles,* RMM Records, RMD 82011.
Nacif, Alberto (1997) Interview with Celia Cruz (unpublished) 21 October, Ann Arbor, Michigan.
Ojito, Mirta (1998) 'Celia Cruz: longtime Salsa star with rising appeal', New York Times, 27 June.
Ortiz, Fernando (1947[1995]) *Cuban Counterpoint: Tobacco and Sugar,* trans. Harriet de Onís, Durham and London: Duke University Press.
Pagán, Adam (1997) 'Indestructible!: Diasporican identity, the Young Lords Party, and the cultural politics of music – a brief synthesis, 1960s–1970s', The Rhythms of Cul-

ture: Dancing to Las Américas. International Research Conference on Popular Music in Latin(o) America, 21–22 March, University of Michigan, Ann Arbor.

Parker, Andrew, Russo, Mary, Sommer, Doris, and Yaeger, Patricia (1992) 'Introduction' to *Nationalisms and Sexualities*, New York: Routledge.

Rath, Derek (1995) 'Celia Cruz: legendary lady of Latin music', *The Beat*, 14(6): 42–5.

Rivero, Eliana (1989) 'From immigrants to ethnics: Cuban women writers in the U.S.', in A. Horno-Delgado *et al.* (eds) *Breaking Boundaries: Latina Writings and Critical Readings*, Amherst: The University of Massachusetts Press.

Rondón, César Miguel (1980) *El libro de la Salsa: Crónica de la música del Caribe urbano*, Caracas, Venezuela: Editorial Arte.

Sabournin, Tony (1986) 'Celia Cruz', in H. Wiley Hitchcock and S. Sadie (eds) *The New Grove Dictionary of American Music*, London: Macmillan.

Santos, Mayra (1997) 'Salsa as translocation', in C. Fraser Delgado and J.E. Muñoz (eds) *Everynight Life: Culture and Dance in Latin/o America*, Durham: Duke University Press.

Walsh, Michael (1988) 'Shake your body', *Time*, 11 July: 50–2.

Watrous, Peter (1989) 'Celia Cruz takes Cuba to Harlem', *New York Times*, 29 October: 62.

2.

Louise Bennett in Performance
Pedagogies of Nation and Gender

| DONNA AZA WEIR-SOLEY

IN JAMAICA, THE NAME Louise Bennett, or Miss Lou, as she is fondly called, is almost a metonym for humour and folk culture. In the Jamaican diaspora at large, and arguably, throughout the anglophone Caribbean community, Louise Bennett's name is metonymic with Jamaican national identity, second only to Bob Marley (whose name is metonymic with reggae music and the Jamaican brand internationally and transculturally). Bennett has become a household name in Jamaica since the early 1950s for her poetry and dramatic monologues, which were written and performed through various media in Jamaican Creole. She began performing in the Jamaican National Pantomime in 1943, frequently appearing alongside the talented comedian Ranny Williams (affectionately called Mass Ran).[1] The *Lou and Ranny Show* was the first radio sitcom in Jamaica and was popular island-wide from its inception in 1959 – it was the first programme aired by the Jamaica Broadcasting Corporation (JBC) – until its finale in 1964.[2] From 1968 to 1980, Bennett hosted the popular children's television show *Ring Ding*. The show got its name from a line in the folk song "Moonshine Tonight"; it was modelled on the traditional Jamaican custom of sitting or standing in a ring on moonlit nights, telling stories and playing games.[3]

Bennett died in July 2006 in Toronto, Canada, where she had lived for the last two decades of her life. But Bennett, who held several honorific titles including the Order of Jamaica, two honorary doctorates, one from the University of the West Indies, Mona, Jamaica, and the other from York University in Toronto, continues to be one of the most recognized Jamaican personalities. Not only was she a cultural ambassador for Jamaica in her lifetime, but she was also a vehicle through which Jamaicans in the diaspora could reconnect with their past, celebrate their Jamaican folk identity and reinforce their pride of nation. Jamaicans loved her for her cultural critique through humour, knowledge of folklore, sympathetic portrayal of the common folk, matchless comedic timing and obvious pride in her Jamaican language and identity. According to Rex Nettleford, who wrote the introduction to Bennett's third volume of poetry, *Jamaica Labrish,* Bennett captures "the spontaneity of the ordinary Jamaican's joys and even sorrows, his ready poignant and even wicked wit, his religion and his philosophy of life".[4] She was able to accomplish what very few Jamaican writers had done before her precisely because she wrote and performed in the Jamaican vernacular. By writing her verses in the language of the Jamaican people, Miss Lou was able to directly represent experiences and give voice to feelings on various issues without compromising shades of meaning that often get lost in translation.

As a public figure, Bennett was one of the foremost non-politicians to instil Jamaican national identity into its citizenry. In Bennett's obituary, published in the online journal *Roots Outta Control,* then prime minister Portia Simpson-Miller describes Jamaica's most famous daughter as follows: "the very essence of our Jamaicanness – larger than life, earthy, humorous, warm, good-natured, highly creative and full of wisdom".[5] For the purpose of this chapter, I will analyse her recorded performances to show how she purposefully undertook a very nationalist agenda as preserver and transmitter of Jamaica's cultural traditions to Jamaicans at home and, furthermore, how her dedication to her role as cultural preserver extended beyond Jamaica's borders into the Jamaican diaspora. Though I am in no way suggesting that Bennett can or should be solely credited for branding the Jamaican image abroad, I want to argue that she played a major role in helping Jamaicans in the diaspora maintain their pride of nation and their connection to Jamaican culture. She also helped transmit Jamaican culture to the non-Jamaicans in her audience, some of whom were of Caribbean background and could no doubt recognize and appreciate the Afro-Caribbean cultural practices – shared across the region – that were in Bennett's repertoire.

Reading Bennett's poetry and dramatic monologues on the page can be a delight and/or a challenge, depending on your level of literacy in the Jamaican vernacular. For, as Mervyn Morris explains, "the words on the page suggest recognizable noises and nuances of meaning" if one is on intimate terms with Bennett's Jamaican Creole language.[6] Morris argues against situating Bennett primarily as a performance poet; in fact she started writing poetry before she started performing and made every effort to ensure that her work appeared in print.[7] Nevertheless, having only seen her perform once in person, I can attest to the fact that seeing her in the flesh is the ultimate Bennett experience. Seeing a video of her in performance is a close second, and hearing an audio recording still captures some of the magic of Bennett on stage. This study of Bennett's work is based on two recordings of her in performances that included songs, monologues and dialogues with her audiences.

In addition to recording many of her live performances, Louise Bennett collaborated with other musicians and record labels on several albums and singles. In 1953 she recorded *Jamaica Singing Games*. Then, in 1954, she recorded an LP, *Jamaican Folk Songs* on the Folkways Records label, which include many songs that are part of the mento tradition. Songs on this album include "Day Dah Light" (later made popular by Harry Belafonte as "Day-O"), "Linstead Market", "Chi-Chi Bud", "Hosana", "Dip Dem", "Under the Coconut Tree", "Dry Weather Houses", "How You Come Over (De River Ben Come Dung)", "Hol' 'im Joe" and "Towns of Jamaica". Also released in the 1950s was a single of dance-band mento on the UK label Melodisc which includes "Linstead Market" and "Bongo Man". Other songs such as "Cudelia Brown", "Matty Rag", "Hog Eena de Cocoa" and "Dis Long Time Gal" were released as singles on the Tri-Jam-Ba label in the 1950s. In 1957, she recorded the LP *Children's Jamaican Songs and Games* on the Folkways Records label accompanied by acoustic guitar, backing vocals and hand clapping. *Mis' Lou's Views* was another LP released by the Federal label in 1962 – this contains dramatic monologues with musical interludes (instrumentals) by Byron Lee and the Dragonaires. In 1968, she recorded *Listen to Louise* – an LP combining music and performance poetry, also on the Federal label. In 1980, she released a folk and mento LP, *The Honorable Miss Lou*, on the BOONOO label, backed by Peter Ashbourne on piano. *Yes M' Dear: – Miss Lou Live* was recorded in London in 1983. In 1999, Bennett also recorded a live performance, *Lawd, di Riddim Sweet*, in Scarborough, Ontario, which was jointly produced by Joan Andrea Hutchinson and Marjorie Whylie and published by Sangster's Bookstore. In 1987, she recorded the folk tale "Ribba Muma" on the cassette collection with an introduction by Olive Lewin entitled *Jamaican Folk Tales and Oral Histories*. This cassette accompanied Laura Tanna's *Jamaican Folk Tales and Oral Stories*.[8] During the 1960s and 1970s Louise Bennett's performances were frequently recorded on cassette tapes for the Library of the Spoken Word Collection, under the auspices of the Radio Education Unit at the University of the West Indies, Mona, Jamaica. Additionally, Louise Bennett and her performance partner, Randolph Samuel Williams, were the headliners in the Jamaican pantomime for many years. They also performed regularly on Radio Jamaica Radiofusion (RJR) as "Miss Lou and Mass Ran" and became household names in Jamaica as comedic figures and social commentators.

Bennett's popularity in Jamaica set the stage for the role she was to play in helping to shape Jamaican national identity in the post-independence period.[9] She did so through the use of folklore, poetry, songs, music, riddles, parables, lectures and performances – all laced with her particular brand of humour. Miss Lou was Jamaica's favourite performer, comedienne and writer because she appealed to the Jamaican masses. As Nettleford reminds us, "It must not be forgotten that Louise Bennett wrote many of her poems for performance and even those published weekly in the *Sunday Gleaner* throughout the forties were read in tenement yards all over the country – probably by the one literate person in each yard."[10] Nettleford's quote situates Bennett as a favourite performer and folklorist, and a beloved national figure long before Jamaica became independent in 1962. By the time she created the children's show *Ring Ding*, which aired on the Jamaican Broadcasting Corporation television station every Saturday morning from 1968 to 1980, Bennett had been a household name for decades, and her agenda extended well beyond entertaining. On that show and beyond, Bennett was waging a deliberate nationalist campaign to ensure that Jamaican children would know their cultural heritage and that national identity would be transmitted to the post-independence generation.

The rest of this chapter will analyse Bennett's 1983 performance in London (*Yes M' Dear: Miss Lou Live*) and her 1999 album *Lawd Di Riddim Sweet*.[11] These two recordings of live performances help to capture Bennett's style, sense of comedic timing, ease with the audience and role in helping to shape Jamaican national identity in the diaspora. The 1983 and 1999 performances are somewhat similar in content, but the context of these recordings is very different. The 1983 album is recorded from a live show in London while Bennett was still touring. However, the 1999 version was performed to a more intimate audience (primarily the Heritage Singers), specifically for the purpose of recording the album. On the 1999 recording, Bennett performs and explains the meaning and contexts of various Jamaican folk songs and some of her poems.[12] In both recordings, Bennett uses various techniques to include her audience in the performance: call and response, question and answer, parables, riddles, proverbs, and her own brand of infectious humour. Her performance is punctuated by humorous commentary, jokes and riddles which put the audience at ease and effectively draw them into the dramatic moment, including them as participant-observers. Bennett's charisma and ease with the audience can be felt through the recordings and the reciprocity of this engagement is transparent. Both the 1983 and the 1999 performances feature live audiences in the Jamaican diaspora, and both highlight Bennett's larger role as cultural ambassador, cultural preservationist, nation-builder and self-appointed salesperson for Jamaica in the diaspora.

In both the 1983 and the 1999 performances, Bennett's discussion of *Ring Ding* highlights the self-consciously nation-building initiatives she had developed for Jamaica and Jamaicans in the 1970s, which she continued to promote way into the twenty-first century. Explaining that the show's title was taken from a traditional folk custom of playing ring games outdoors during moonlit nights, Bennett sings the song "Moonshine Tonight" on both recordings to demonstrate how she used folk music to teach Jamaican cultural heritage to children born after independence. She sings the lyrics in the first stanza:

> Moon shine tonight
> come mek we dance and sing
> moon shine tonight
> come mek we play ring-ding
> yuh de rock so
> mi de rock so
> under a banyan tree
> you de rock so
> me de rock so
> under a banyan tree.

She then sings the lyrics from the second stanza, "then we join hands and dance around and round", to underscore that it was a children's game and that she thought it efficacious to use this mode and whatever else would work to get and keep the attention of young children. Based on my own remembrance of Bennett in performance, I assume she also used movement to show the dance steps of the children's ring-game to her rapt audiences.

In the 1999 recording, Bennett can be heard repeating the following phrase quite often: "It was important, yuh know, that they learn about the tings that belong to them." She also explains that she used to set aside some time in the programme to teach the children riddles, proverbs and traditional folk songs. She recounts humorous stories of how the children related to her. From one little boy: "Miss Lou, a thought yuh was a picture!" From another: "Miss Lou, is de fus time I see yuh in colour" (at the time, Jamaica had one television station, JBC, and it still aired in black and white). She recounts teaching the children lullabies so they would know that Jamaica also had its own lullabies: "Clap Hand", "Bi-yah, Bi-yah, Mi Baby", "Done Mi Baby Done", "Carachee, Carachee" – most of which the children know, but do not recognize as lullabies. She also demonstrates how she used to teach riddles to the children by challenging the audience with riddles. For example: "Riddle mi dis, Riddle mi dat / Guess mi dis Riddle, and perhaps not: One piece a yellow yam serve the whole world." Someone in the audience yells out the answer: "Moon!"

Listening to the audience's response to Bennett's stories, one cannot help but make the connection between the children Bennett reminisces about and the adults in her audience, many of whom also grew up on those stories, songs and riddles either by watching Bennett on her television show (*Ring Ding*), and/or participating in these games in their own Jamaican communities. Bennett's influence on these people when they were children, and her shaping of their identities, is underscored by the emotional tenor of their responses to her as adults. This is made even more poignant when one considers how many Jamaicans have lived for years abroad without benefit of legal status and are, therefore, not free to travel back and forth between Jamaica and their host countries. Through Bennett they are affirmed in the Jamaican "tings that belong to them": intangibles that are vulnerable to time and distance, but are preserved through memory, and through Miss Lou's performances. The songs in these recordings also include selections from the mento and folk traditions, including the following: "Dis Long Time Gal Mi Never See Yuh", "Carry Mi Ackee Go a Linstead Market", "Chi-Chi Bud-O", "Sammy Dead" and "Manuel Road". Bennett explains the origins of each of these songs to her eager diaspora audience. Bennett situates "Sammy Dead" and "Manuel Road" as digging songs or work songs, used in the fields or in other forms of manual labour such as breaking rocks or building roads, and so on. She identifies the mento section in "Dis Long Time Gal Mi Never See Yuh" for the audience. She interrupts her rendition of "Carry Mi Ackee Go a Linstead Market" to explain that it is written in the Dinkie Minnie tradition, which means that the song's lyrics recount a misfortune, but it must be sung in an upbeat, cheerful manner.

The album *Yes Mi' Dear – Miss Lou Live* was recorded live in London in 1983 complete with eight piece band, acapella riffs and poetic renditions from Bennett's own repertoire.[13] Bennett is in rare form during this performance. Linton Kwesi Johnson makes a guest appearance on the recording and, as he comes on stage, he can be heard on the recording playfully admonishing Bennett to take a drink of water to "cool" herself down. Bennett responds, "But see yah . . . alright . . . mi drink it." Even this commonplace exchange engenders hilarity from the crowd. When she finishes and pronounces "No watah no sweet like Jamaican watah", there is another burst of hilarity. They perform two songs together. Johnson "talks" the male parts of "Under the Coconut Tree" (the parts sung by Bennett's husband, Eric Coverly, in the 1999 recording). Bennett and Johnson also perform the fast-paced "Morning Buddy" together, with Johnson keeping perfect pace, matching Bennett's pitch-perfect performance on this recording.

Bennett's 1983 performance is punctuated with good-natured storytelling laced with jokes. The audience responds with relish. Her gentle ribbing of Johnson provokes even more laughter from the audience, and light rejoinders from Johnson himself. Johnson's reverence for her, her delight in him, and their charisma on stage is easily transmitted through the 1983 recording.

Similarly, the London audience is captivated with Bennett, and she uses this occasion to perform many of her poems and to sing folk songs, with frequent breaks in between sets to educate and to entertain. Bennett begins her performance with the Jamaican welcome song, "Dis Long Time, Gal" and the audience appears to be fully participating in the chorus. Bennett interrupts her performance to warn the audience good-naturedly: "I don't want to hear anybody say 'Come let me hold your hand' " – this is meant to caution the audience against using standard English in a Creole folk song, and it provokes much merriment, especially after she adds, "please don't *'pwile* [spoil] up the culture!" When she sings the stanza: "Peel-head John Crow siddung pon treetop, Pick off de blossom / Mek me hold your han, gal / Mek me hol yu han",

Bennett stops to explain it to the audience. She tells them that a John Crow is a vulture and that vultures do not eat blossoms. The stanza is therefore meant to convey the rareness of the occasion and the speaker's surprise and delight at having met this old friend: "What an unusual thing, what an impossible thing. I never knew we would meet again."[14] In true Bennett style, these "teaching moments" are laced throughout with good humour: "Jamaican people will know it [the song], but Barbadian people won't know. Some Barbadian people did come to Jamaica and when they see the John Crow, hear dem now: 'Jamaica turkey does fly *high*!' " This is delivered with an exaggerated elevation of the word "high" as Bennett mimics Barbadian speech, amid peals of laughter from the audience.

Although they appear engaged, the setting for the 1983 performance seems to be quite formal, and the audience does not frequently interrupt Bennett's performance to join in the folk songs (unlike her more intimate 1999 recording) but, at her invitation and prompting, those who know the songs eagerly participate in the call and response segments of songs like "Dis Long Time, Gal", "Day-O" and "Chi-Chi-Bud". One can but assume that since this is England, the audience is comprised of Jamaicans, Caribbean people born in England, Caribbean nationals and, possibly, white British people, East Indians and others. Bennett uses this occasion to explain that in Jamaica, "we have a lot of heritage songs and proverbs and, of course, our language which we have been speaking for over 300 years. Yes, mi dear."

Anti-Colonial Theories in Louise Bennett's Performances

In *Noises in the Blood*, Carolyn Cooper insists that Bennett's creation of Auntie Roachy as a mouthpiece to voice her resistance to Eurocentric hegemony is a deliberate political intervention. Cooper argues cogently as follows: "Bennett's choice of subject matter and language is an affirmation of what one might call naygacentric/nativist aesthetic values, rooted in the particular contradictions of Jamaica's history."[15] Bennett's linguistic resistance stands side by side with many of the better-known critiques of colonialism such as those proffered by Ngũgĩ wa Thiong'o, Frantz Fanon and Albert Memmi. Ngũgĩ, in his book *Decolonizing the Mind*, reveals that corporal punishment was administered to any child who was caught speaking Gĩkũyũ (sometimes written "Kikuyu") in Kenya after the British regime took over the school system in 1952. Ngũgĩ writes, "the unfortunate victim was made to carry a metal plate around his neck with inscriptions such as I am stupid or I am a donkey".[16] The Martinican Fanon, in *Black Skin, White Masks,* also demonstrates the effects of French education on Antillean consciousness: "The Negro of the Antilles will be proportionately whiter – that is, he will come closer to being a human being – in direct ratio to his mastery of the French language."[17] Albert Memmi insists that in a colonial situation, the ruthless attack that is often levelled at the language of the colonized has a devastating impact: "The colonized's mother tongue, that which is sustained by his feelings, emotions and dreams, that in which his tenderness and wonder are expressed, that which holds the greatest emotional impact, is precisely the one which is the least valued."[18] Deriving from different nationalities and linguistic spaces, what these critics share is a colonial history whose common denominator is the perpetuation of Western hegemony through the privileging of European cultures and languages, and the concurrent debasement of languages (and attendant value systems) of colonized groups.

Although she does not mention the Jamaican motto (which is "Out of Many One People"), Bennett makes use of its ethos in her explanation of Jamaican cultural identity in her 1983 performance in London. She explains that "[a]ll this folklore and this culture that we have come from all the different people who have lived in this country [Jamaica]. And we just use it and now we have a real West Indian, a real Jamaican culture." Bennett explains the process of creolization in her own inimitable fashion:

> When the Asian culture and the European culture
> Buck up on de African culture
> We wheel dem and we tun dem to we flava
> We shake them up and move them to we beat
> We wheel dem and we turn dem
> And we rock dem and we sound dem
> And we temper dem, and lawks de rhythm sweet!

However, unlike the Jamaican motto, Bennett gives more weight to the African presence. She explains to her London audience that African culture is responsible for many of the proverbs, riddles and folk songs that she shares with them, and it is also the foundation of the Jamaican language that she uses. In this performance, Bennett revives her alter-ego Aunty Roachy, a mainstay of her dramatic monologues done in Jamaica, loved and recognized by Jamaican audiences as much as Bennett herself. Feisty, intelligent, politically knowledgeable and well-versed in the Jamaican language, parables, riddles and folklore, Aunty Roachy is the one responsible for dressing down anyone who speaks ill of Jamaican language or tries to belittle the African roots of Jamaican folk culture.[19] Bennett explains to the London audience that her "Aunty Roachy" told her that Jamaican language evolved when the English slave masters were trying to "mus' and bound" the African slaves to speak English, but these African ancestors "pop dem" (tricked them) by "disguising" the African word in the English language, so that the English slave-masters still could not understand what they were saying. Bennett's comedic delivery of this message elicits laughter, but the gravitas in her message comes across clearly. The African ancestors of modern Jamaicans were intelligent and subversive, so modern Jamaicans must also be crafty and intelligent.

In the London performance, Bennett further presses the notion that the Jamaican vernacular most Jamaicans know as "patois" (pronounced "pat-wa") or Jamaican nation language, should be valued as the legitimate language of the Jamaican folk.[20] She makes favourable comparisons between the Jamaican vernacular and the English language to a diaspora audience that appears to be listening very eagerly to her pointed political intervention into this issue. Bennett uses her alter ego, Aunty Roachy, to explain why it vexes her so to hear English people say that English is *derived* from the Norman French, Latin and Greek, while the Jamaican language is a *corruption* of English. She asks the following questions: "Why dem mus *derive* and we *corrupt*? We derive tuh! Jamaica derive!"[21]

Again, the London audience erupts in laughter, but the point is made. Bennett explains that the Jamaican language is derived from English and a "good-good" African language called Twi. She relates this crucial information with just the right amount of humour to get the audience interested and to mark the lesson indelibly upon their minds. For example, in pronouncing the word "Twi" Bennett places a softer emphasis on the syllabic word-sound combination, both to give the audience the correct pronunciation (the "w" in the word being a sound in between "r" and "w") and to demonstrate the elegance of the word and language called Twi. She laughs, the audience laughs with her, and in that laughter they get her true meaning – African languages are beautiful and "good-good". Jamaicans should be proud, and not ashamed, of their linguistic heritage. She provides examples of "good-good" Twi and Jamaican words: *bankra* (basket), *nyam* (to eat), *putto-putto* (mud), *dutty* (ground), *pala-pala* (messy), *fenky-fenky* (weak), and *pya-pya* (inconsequential). These examples drive home her point that the Jamaican vernacular is not corrupt or bastardized English, but actually is derived from a legitimate African language: Twi. To underscore her point she assures the audience: "So we no haffi shame a nutting at all, no mi dear."

Pride of ancestry and pride in much-maligned African heritage is an important step in the decolonizing process for Jamaicans, as for New World blacks at large. In post-independence Jamaica (even as early as the 1970s, when I attended elementary and high school) efforts were made to teach children from a curriculum that included Afro-Jamaican writers such as Claude McKay and Una Marson. Bennett's poetry, though not officially taught in my classrooms, had a ubiquitous presence in school recitals. Like Memmi, Fanon and Ngũgĩ, Bennett recognizes that for Jamaicans to embrace their folk roots they must first reject the colonial misrepresentations of indigenous/folk and African culture as backwards and inferior.

In this way, albeit through a much lighter medium, Bennett is aligned with more recognized critics of colonialism and with more radical Jamaican thinkers such as Marcus Garvey and his ideological successor, Bob Marley. Marley's beloved freedom anthem "Redemption Song" borrowed its most salient lines from a 1937 speech given by Marcus Garvey in Nova Scotia, Canada, and later printed in 1938 in Garvey's magazine *Black Man: A Journal of Thought and Opinion*. Garvey's version is as follows: "We are going to emancipate ourselves from mental slavery because whilst others free the body, none but ourselves can free the mind. Mind is your only ruler, sovereign. The man who is not able to develop and use his mind is bound to be the slave of the other man who uses his mind."[22] Marley's definitively anti-colonial stance is evident in the urgency with which he captured and disseminated Garvey's message in "Redemption Song". The line from the song, "how long shall they kill our prophets", is a clear reference to the mistreatment of Garvey, who was called "the Black Moses" in his time, as well as a possible reference to Marley's own imminent death from cancer – the song was recorded after Marley was diagnosed and ailing.

Marley and Garvey both admonish New World blacks to "emancipate" themselves "from mental slavery"; Bennett delivers the same message in her own fashion. This is an important lesson for the Jamaicans in Bennett's diasporic audience and helps them to cultivate and nurture national pride, even though (and perhaps, especially because) they no longer live in Jamaica. For the non-Jamaicans in her audience, Bennett's teaching moments help to shape how they see Jamaican culture and people: knowledgeable, possessing a rich cultural heritage, proud of their African ancestry, nationalistic, but yet relaxed enough to not take themselves too seriously – frequently laughing at their cultural foibles and at themselves. In this manner, Louise Bennett inaugurated and reinforced her own brand of Jamaican transnationalism contiguous with the transnational identification with reggae and Rastafarianism credited to Bob Marley and metonymic with the black pride message promoted by Garvey.

Louise Bennett and Harry Belafonte

As with the 1983 album, the 1999 recording is also laced with humorous interludes, storytelling, riddles, parables, and gentle ribbing of the audience who dissolve into peals of laughter at Miss Lou's comedic interjections. The 1999 performance sounds more intimate and more laid back than the 1983 recording. The audience appears largely Jamaican, based on their familiarity with the songs in Bennett's repertoire and the fact that they join in without prompting when Bennett does a set. Bennett clearly has the audience eating out of her hands. When she relates that her favourite digging song is "Chi-Chi Bud-O", the audience responds "Aaaawwww!" On several other occasions they empathize with and/or indulge her nostalgic reminiscences with the same exclamation: "Aaaawwww!" In full participant-observer mode they join raucously in the folk songs, shout out answers to the riddles and laugh with abandon at Bennett's humorous commentary and jokes. They constantly interrupt her. When Bennett explains how her husband Eric Coverly courted and married her, one person shouts: "Was it under the coconut tree?" This is a clear reference to the folk song "Under the Coconut Tree" that was a staple in their repertoire when Bennett and Coverly performed together. On this recording, Bennett and Coverly sing "Under the Coconut Tree" together, to the delight of the audience who clearly knows the song very well and can anticipate the humorous moments.

There is a shared worldview, and common cultural framework that lends intimacy to the 1999 recording. Explaining the origins of Jamaican Creole seems to have been a staple part of Bennett's repertoire as well. In the 1999 recording, she re-invokes Aunty Roachy's counter-hegemonic responses to the belittling of African and Afro-Jamaican language and culture, and recounts the same jokes as she did in the 1983 recording (the discussion of derivation as opposed to corruption of language, and so on). One noteworthy difference in the 1999 recording, however, is what Bennett reveals about Harry Belafonte, a performer who gained international fame as a Jamaican folk-singer when Bennett was still not widely recognized beyond Jamaica and, to a lesser degree, in some circles in England. Without malice or rancour, Bennett explains to her 1999 audience that she taught the banana loading song "Day-O" to Belafonte. According to her, Belafonte made a crucial error, singing "six-foot, seven-foot, eight-foot bunch" instead of "six-hand, seven-hand, eight-hand bunch!" Bennett laughs and remarks that after he became famous they met again and she took him to task for the error: "But what about this foot business, Harry. Bananas don't have toes, you know. Bananas have fingers!" The audience laughs, but the irony cannot fail to register with some: as someone who lives in North America, and without even a traceable Jamaican accent, Belafonte is able to achieve worldwide fame as a Jamaican folk-singer, even after muddling the lyrics. The fact that it is Belafonte who became famous for that folk song, symbolizes the global currency of the Jamaican cultural heritage, the challenges faced by the artist in a developing nation like Jamaica, and the gender disparities in society at large. Bennett sings the song to the audience, and one cannot help but wonder what kind of impact it would have had if she had been given the opportunity to present that song to the world instead of Belafonte. For example, when Bennett sings the line (left out of Belafonte's sanitized version): "nuh gi me so-so bunch, mi no horse wid bridle", her comedic timing is so unbelievably accurate, I could hardly contain my own hilarity. On reflection, I recognize that it was funny to me not only because of my familiarity with Jamaican humour, but also because it invoked the words of another black woman folklorist and novelist who, like Bennett, was a tireless champion of the folk: Zora Neale Hurston. In *Their Eyes Were Watching God*, Hurston character's Nanny cautions her granddaughter against the drudgery of poorly compensated and unappreciated manual labour: "De nigger woman is de mule uh de world so fur as Ah can see."[23] To dramatic effect, Bennett channels the rebellious black woman in that song, emphatically resisting the role of work horse and demanding to go home from a hard night of loading bananas, so she can get the rest that is her due. One cannot fail to see the irony in the fact that Bennett, herself a hard worker who tirelessly promoted Jamaican culture for so many decades, never achieved the success and the international recognition that Harry Belafonte was able to claim after popularizing the folk song that was taught to him by Bennett herself.

Representations of Working-Class Jamaican Women in Bennett's Work

Included in Bennett's repertoire in this 1999 performance are poems like "South Parade Peddler", "Dutty Tough", "Uriah Preach", "Dry Foot Bwoy", "Noh Lickle Twang", "Pedestrian Crosses" and "Cuss-Cuss". Bennett delivers each poem pitch-perfectly, singing some of the lines instead of merely reciting them. It is through these poetic renditions that Bennett's creative genius finds true expression: her command of every linguistic inflection, every nuance in folk expression, every dramatic pause, and every clever turn of phrase reveals someone who, beyond being a true professional who is really attentive to her craft, actively listens to and delights in the Jamaican folk from whom she draws her material.

In her introduction to the poem "Cuss-Cuss", Bennett explains that it is not to be confused with *kas-kas* (gossip). She states the following: "Cuss-Cuss is when yuh leggo tongue pon smaddy." This draws much laughter from her audience. In an interview with Bennett, critic Leleith Bailey accuses her of reinforcing stereotypes of women as "nagging, gossipy bitches" in poems such as "Cuss-Cuss" and "Kas-Kas". Bennett responds with a theory of her own, offering a counterpoint to Bailey's reading of her poems: "I wouldn't say they are nagging. They are not afraid to speak if they feel that a thing is not right. Because a lot of times, you know, in Jamaica, it is the woman who really carries the burden of the family, mostly."[24] Bennett continues in staunch defence of the strength of Jamaican women, portraying them as the backbone of the extended family structure. Bennett emphasizes the importance of women, especially older females, in providing support for the younger generation of both sexes. In essence, Bennett's counter argument makes it clear that as long as Jamaican women are carrying the family, they have a right to speak up and this should not be read as "nagging" or "gossiping". She posits Jamaican women as rich repositories of advice, financial assistance and productive dialogue, and foregrounds the importance of experience, good listening skills and good oral communication that women use to sustain their families and communities.

Bennett's observations about the role of female communication stand in clear contrast to the way Bailey and others construct Bennett's use of women's talk. To emphasize the negative aspects of gossip is to reduce the importance of female communication styles, since conversation among women can so easily be relegated to gossip, despite the topic and/or the purpose behind the talk. As Cooper effectively argues in "That Cunny Jamma 'Oman", Bennett's representation of the Jamaican female sensibility is a recuperative act whose aim is to affirm and reposition Jamaican women in their proper role as *tallawah* (meaning "powerful" in Jamaican Creole) nation builders without whose agency and resourcefulness the entire project of Jamaican nationhood would have remained stillborn. Furthermore, Bailey and others miss the dramatic significance of these poems and the way they underscore the linguistic prowess of competent Jamaican Creole language speakers. Clearly, poems like "Cuss-Cuss" and "Kas-Kas" also highlight the value of Jamaican Creole, its ability to convey complex, graphic, biting commentary, as well as infectious humour and somber reflections.

Anthropologist Roger Abrahams opines that public speaking in the Caribbean is mostly done by men, while women's speech takes place in the private sphere of the house or the yard and is relegated to gossip. Abrahams states, "[f]or the most part, speaking is associated with men, and most of the social types and events are regarded as appropriately male activity . . . it is assumed that women primarily speak in their yards and house and therefore engage in the kinds of two-person interactions of commess [gossip]".[25] In her essay "Riddym Ravings: Female and National Identity in Jamaican Creole Poetry", Elizabeth Wheeler notes that Bennett's poetry seems to provide some notable exceptions to the binary paradigm that Abrahams sets up. Wheeler, who comments that Bennett's women "speak and act confidently [*outa road and inna yard*]",[26] reminds us that terms such as "house" and "yard" take on different meanings when viewed through culturally specific lenses.

Bennett's poetry celebrates the audacity of working-class Jamaican women who, denied the privileges of respectability and gentility associated with middle-class women, choose to use their voices in service to their own needs as women and as active participants in Jamaican society. As Cooper observes, "the proverbial cunning of the Jamaican woman is one manifestation of the ambiguous craftiness of Anansi, the Akan folk hero, transmuted in Jamaican folklore into Brer Nansi, the archetypal trickster".[27] As Cooper and Wheeler argue, Bennett's decision to use the language of these marginalized women as her poetic medium is indeed subversive. As a middle-class woman, educated in the best schools in Jamaica and the recipient of a British Council scholarship to study at the Royal Academy of Dramatic Art, Bennett is supposed to know better than to write in a language that has no status and carries with it a stigma associated with the disenfranchised people who speak it. Her insistence on writing in the people's language, despite the criticism and dismissal of many in her class, coupled with her dedication to proving the worth of the language of the Jamaican masses, is truly heroic.

Humour as a Modality of Resistance in Bennett's Performance

Despite Bennett's middle-class upbringing, and despite the critique that can be levelled at her ventriloquism, it is understandable why working-class Jamaicans love her as much as they do.[28] They love her because she teaches them how and why they should be proud of themselves, and how to laugh at themselves, at the forces that oppress them, and transcend (if only temporarily) life's hardships by being able to see the humour even in the pain. The quote "(wo)man alone suffers so excruciatingly, that (s)he was compelled to invent laughter", is a feminist revision of Friedrich Nietzsche's quote in reference to man's invention of laughter as a coping device.[29] Similarly, in his study of black culture and consciousness, Lawrence Levine writes about the black community's reasons for choosing laughter as a response to oppression:

> Central among them is the desire to place the situation in which we find ourselves into perspective; to assert some degree of control over our environment. The need to laugh at our enemies, our situation, ourselves, is a common one, but it often exists the most urgently in those who exert the least power over their immediate environment; in those who have the most objective reasons for feelings of hopelessness.[30]

Bennett offers her audience a poetics of resistance that is made more authentic by the location of the poetic/dramatic voice within what Bakhtin would call the "heteroglot"[31] of the folk, the articulation of a collective consciousness emanating from one source (such as Bennett's character Aunty Roachy) or from several sources such as the female personas in many of her poems. It is fitting that Bennett credits her use of humour to these working-class Jamaican women who were her mother's clients. Morris observes: "She remembers noticing from them that laughter was very important, and that sad or tragic information might be communicated without solemnity."[32] In Bennett's work, one cannot separate her use of irony, satire and parody from the vernacular of her language: it is as much her use of humour, as well as her skilful manipulation of the language spoken by competent Creole speakers, that makes Miss Lou such a popular figure in the island of Jamaica and in the metropolitan centres such as the United States, Canada, England and wherever Jamaicans are to be found.

Bennett's invocation of humour as a survival strategy is evident in many of the poems she recites on the 1999 recording. For example, "South Parade Peddler" (quoted above by Wheeler) and "Dutty Tough" both employ speakers who, though clearly undergoing economic hardships, are also defiant, feisty, rebellious and transgressive. "Uriah Preach", which is about a son who uses the pulpit to get back at his enemies and his mother's critics, and "Cuss-Cuss", which celebrates the art of "tracing" (using harsh insults to diminish one's opponent), both testify to the artistry, dexterity and effectiveness of the Jamaican language. The Jamaicans in the audience laugh uproariously because they recognize their cultural characteristics – warts and all – in these poems. They also recognize that Bennett is celebrating these characteristics, even as she forces the audience to see the truth about themselves. Humour represents a defiant declaration of humanity in the face of structures of dominance, economic disparities, and systematic violence that characterize the experiences of working-class Jamaicans.

Laughter as an act of resistance is predicated on a lived theory of resistance that refuses to allow misery to take over. In "Laughter in *Crick Crack, Monkey*: An Exploration in Comic Discourse", Jennifer Rahim informs us that "within the culture of the colonized, laughter can be identified and indeed celebrated as a strategy for survival, a weapon for resistance and defiance, a means of self-affirmation and empowerment, a signal of triumph".[33] The ability to view humour as transcendental ("tekkin' bad tings mek laugh") and to recognize and accept duality as a fact of existence – rather than an unresolvable contradiction – becomes clear in Louise Bennett's dramatic renderings of Jamaican folk subjectivity. Clearly the Jamaican diaspora audience, who laugh uproariously to Bennett's songs, poems and jokes, are cognizant of (and often participating in) the art of "tekkin' bad tings mek laugh". But for them laughter is more than an adaptation and/or resistance to the hegemony of the dominant culture. Laughter is a way of reconnecting with their Jamaican roots, celebrating their Jamaican identity and even feeding their nostalgia for home.

In the 1983 London recording, Bennett jokes that if you say the word "mango" too hard to some Jamaicans in London, "dem bus out a bawling". Bennett seems to have the opposite effect for these Jamaicans in her audience. Everything she says provokes a burst of hilarity that is at once a testament to her effectiveness as a comic, and a result of their nationalist identification with her material. Like the mango, Bennett's presence, and her dramatic repertoire, evoke a strong sense of Jamaican nationalism and reminds these voluntary exiles of what they are missing: home. This is true for both sets of audiences despite the fact that Bennett is herself living in Canada at the time of the 1999 recording, and had been living outside of Jamaica since the 1980s. Bennett has the predominantly Jamaican audiences eating out of the palm of her hand. However, Bennett herself becomes the consumable Jamaican product that feeds their nostalgia and nationalist identity better than any mango. The inimitable Miss Lou becomes a substitute for Jamaica – the audience simply cannot get enough of her.

In poems like "Noh Lickle Twang" and "Dry-Foot Bwoy", Bennett uses humour to critique Jamaica's obsession with "foreign" and render transparent the contradictions of the colonial mindset. In setting up these two poems, Bennett explains to her audience that Jamaicans believe that when you go abroad, you should always return with something new. However, if you change too much, those same people will find reason to criticize you, to say that you are only pretending. She introduces the above two poems as different sides to the same coin: in one, a young man travels to America and returns just as he left (no new fashion, no American accent); and in another, a young man goes to England and returns speaking with a heavy English accent. Both are heavily critiqued by the same female persona (the mother of one young man and auntie of the other). In her essay "Noh Lickle Twang: An Introduction to the Poetry of Louise Bennett", Cooper writes that Bennett's poetry "depicts and attempts to correct through laughter the absurdities of Jamaican society".[34] In the 1999 recording, Bennett recites these two poems to much laughter from the audience. In "Noh Lickle Twang", which means "not even a little accent", a Jamaican woman berates her son for having returned from a six-month stay in the United States without having acquired the requisite American accent:

> Bwoy yuh noh shame? Is soh you come?
> Afta yuh tan so lang!
> Not even licke language bwoy?
> Not even lickle twang?
> An yuh sista wat work ongle
> one week wid 'Merican
> She talk so nice now dat we have
> De jooce fe undastan?

In using irony to expose the speaker's reverence for American culture and language, Bennett comments on the society's glamorization of "foreign" at the expense of national identification and cultural pride. Although the poem states that the son has earned decent wages and, arguably, has improved his lot economically, his mother's primary concern is that he shows no superficial improvement but, "come back ugly same way". The son's lack of American trappings of success – "drapes trouziz", "gole teeth", "gole chain" – deglamorizes his travels and frustrates his mother's bragging rights. Most significantly, his lack of Americanized speech – which would render him "better", meaning more intelligent, more sophisticated, more beautiful and more valuable than Creole speakers, completely subverts her agenda to lord her son's American experience over her neighbours. This mother's views represent the then prevailing viewpoint of many Jamaicans who uncritically accepted the assumption of first British, then American, cultural superiority. Even more significantly, the mother's views in this poem represented the views of many Jamaicans who, despite being Creole speakers themselves, had very little regard for the legitimacy of Jamaican Creole. To show the fallacy and political immaturity of these assumptions, Bennett relies on bathroom humour, usually associated with children, to solve the dilemma of the son who must somehow impress upon his father that he has been positively transformed by his trip to America:

> Ef yuh want please him mek him tink
> Yuh bring back something new.
> Yuh always call him "Pa" dis evenin'
> Wen him come say "Poo"

Bennett's use of bathroom humour perfectly renders the political immaturity of a people who would denigrate their own culture and elevate the culture of another. Although the son has been the butt of the joke all throughout the poem, the poem ends in an inversion that makes mother, father ("Poo") and son all comedic figures. The audience laughter is directed at the son who, in attempting to sound American, would call his father "Poo", and also at the mother who would give such foolish advice. They also laugh at the father, who is being unflatteringly renamed as excrement. Though her choice of bathroom humour could be perceived as unsophisticated, it is actually quite expedient. Bennett exposes the mother's uncritical acceptance of American cultural superiority as "excrement", thereby undercutting the speaker's abatement of Jamaican Creole language and Jamaican culture.

Before performing "Dry Foot Bwoy", Bennett explains that this same mother mocks her nephew who returns from England speaking the queen's English and acting as if he no longer understands the Jamaican language:

> What wrong wid Mary dry foot Bwoy?
> Dem gal got him fe mock,
> And wen me meet him tarra night
> De bwoy gi me a shock!

Bennett's diaspora audience begins laughing even before she gets to the funny parts of this poem. Clearly, they have heard or read it before and know what is coming next:

> Mi tell him sey him auntie
> And him cousin dem sen howdy,
> And ask him how him getting 'awn,
> Him sey, "oh, jolley, jolley!"

One has to hear Bennett's guttural mimicry of a deep male voice imitating an English accent in the phrase "oh, jolley, jolley" to understand why her audience would erupt into uproarious laughter at this point. The poem continues in that vein, only getting more and more humorous:

> Same time me las' me tempa, an
> Me halla, "bway kir out!
> No chat to me wid no hot pittata
> Enna yuh mout!"

> Him tan up like him stunted, den
> Hear him noh, "How silley!
> I don't think that I really
> Understand you actually."

Bennett's audience laughs along with her and with the female speaker in the poem, but there is a cautionary tale to this poem and there has to be some self-reflection, despite the laughter. Many of those laughing in the audience are Jamaicans living in the diaspora, and the poem cautions them about the danger of losing one's culture. It is an imminent danger, if not for these immigrants, then for their children, many of whom will not speak the Jamaican vernacular and may not like certain Jamaican foods and practice Jamaican customs. Miss Lou's poem elicits more than laughter – she makes her audience think about what it means to live outside of one's country, in voluntary exile, especially for extended periods of time. Certain customs begin to be replaced by new ones, even one's language can become unfamiliar, as the language on the home front (in Jamaica) is constantly growing, changing, replenishing itself.

Louise Bennett and the "Good-Good" Jamaican Brand

Contemporary debates over dual citizenship in Jamaica have revolved around the holding of political office.[35] Jamaicans who live in Jamaica, and particularly those in positions of power and authority, take centre stage in this debate. But, truth be told, even working-class Jamaican nationals in the diaspora, who have no intention of ever holding political office in Jamaica or elsewhere, have long been concerned with these issues. Many live in North America for decades, and raise children and grandchildren in these countries without becoming naturalized citizens. Pledging allegiance to another country may entail renouncing one's allegiance to Jamaica and surrendering the Jamaican passport.[36]

Despite the advantages to be accrued from American citizenship, many die-hard Jamaican nationals (who only migrate because they cannot survive in the economic climate of Jamaica) refuse to renounce their country of birth. Besides the concern over the probable loss of full citizenship rights in Jamaica, they have other less tangible, but personally meaningful, concerns having to do with national and nationalistic identity such as the following: "Can you still be a true *Yaardie* if you no longer have a Jamaican passport?" or "Which line do you stand in when you arrive at customs at Norman Manley airport – the line for Jamaican citizens or the line for foreign nationals?" Of course, there are clear advantages to American citizenship – scholarship opportunities, positions in some government agencies (CIA, FBI and so on) and, significantly, protection from deportation (later compromised by the Patriot Act).[37] Nevertheless, giving up one's Jamaican citizenship is not an easy decision for most. Jamaicans in the diaspora take their Jamaicanness very personally.

In some cases, deportations could have been prevented had these Jamaican/Caribbean nationals, many of whom have lived in the United States, Canada or the United Kingdom since they were children, deemed it expedient to become naturalized citizens. When they run afoul of the law, the full legal protection due to the American, Canadian or British citizenry is denied them because, for one reason or another, they (or their parents) did not choose the option of naturalization. One may safely assume that there are many Jamaican deportees who, in hindsight, do regret not having become naturalized citizens in their host countries. However, one cannot as safely assume that their reasons for not doing so are due to oversight, negligence or ignorance. Identities are subject to becoming unstable in exile – be it voluntary or forced exile. The majority of Jamaicans living abroad are not well versed in the Jamaican constitution. Many have never really been clear about what, in fact, they would be giving up if they surrendered their Jamaican passports. In the current debate surrounding dual citizenship it has become increasingly clear that, indeed, many of these fears were not unfounded. It can be argued that one reason it appears that the Jamaican diaspora audience identifies so completely with Bennett is because she reassures them of their Jamaicanness, even as she nurtures their nostalgia for home and fans the flames of Jamaican cultural and national pride.

For the non-Jamaicans in her audience, Bennett brands Jamaica as a land replete with a rich cultural heritage, and a proud but "cool" or easy-going people who can be seriously talented with international acclaim, like Marley, or deliriously funny and also seriously talented, like Miss Lou. In this sense, Bennett's message may, at times, mirror the hackneyed view of Jamaica popularized by the following slogan from the tourism industry: "Jamaica. No problem, mon!" What's not to love about these people who can make us laugh, and can laugh at themselves, all the while showing us how beautiful they are? Undoubtedly, this image of Jamaica as non-threatening explains some of the attraction Jamaica holds for many non-Jamaicans. As I argue above, the opposite (though, arguably, equally clichéd) view of Jamaica as a dangerous place with dangerous people, also has its uses, and can be equally compelling for Jamaicans and non-Jamaicans alike.

On its current website, Jamaica Promotions Corporation (JAMPRO) advertises a "brand building" campaign in an effort to expand Jamaican's profile from a tourist destination, "celebrated for its cultural icons and athletes, to one where business plays an even greater role".[38] Similar efforts to rebrand Jamaica revolve around trade and investment opportunities in the business sector geared at attracting foreign investors and at protecting the Jamaican image from outsiders who would seek to profit from the saleable aspects of the country's profile. However, as blogger Denise Campbell argues cogently in "Smile Jamaica: Branding Beyond Sand and Sea", Jamaica has long enjoyed a paradoxical, somewhat schizophrenic "branding". Campbell asserts that this dual image that Jamaica embodies is a result of the Bob Marley, reggae, sand and sea schmaltz promoted by the Jamaica Tourist Board, coupled with the media's emphasis on Jamaica's poverty, inner-city violence and government corruption.[39] Jamaicans in the diaspora have not been immune from the effects of their country's dual image in the global community. Their responses to this duality mirror the complexity of the brand itself. Some take full advantage of both sides of Jamaica's dual personality as shaped by the media. Others distance themselves from the negative associations and take full advantage of the positives.[40] Still others have manipulated one or the other side of this duality to serve specific agendas.[41] It is safe to conclude that Jamaicans in the diaspora have both benefitted and suffered from this two-sided Jamaican brand. Nevertheless, the slipperiness of the global Jamaican image no doubt adds to a crisis of identity (among some Jamaicans in the diaspora) that is a corollary of the immigrant experience for so many groups. For this reason, one salient point argued by proponents of local branding in Jamaica – namely, that there are intangible benefits to be gleaned from "branding", benefits such as the consolidation of national identity and cultural pride that are as important as branding for profit – is no less true for Jamaican communities abroad.[42] These intangibles are so important when one lives outside of Jamaica (but still identifies strongly as a Jamaican), and this chapter seeks to address them with respect to Bennett's role in shaping and affirming Jamaican identity at home and abroad.

Significantly, the popularity that Jamaicans have enjoyed in the diaspora in some historical periods and places – a partiality that has sometimes drawn envy and resentment, but also elicited admiration and respect – can be attributed to the duality evidenced in the "branding" of Jamaica. Granted, a reputation for danger is a different form of being "cool" than the folksy, down-to-earth, laughing, easy-going persona that Bennett projects. However, for Jamaicans (and, arguably, for Americans and lots of other people in the world) brought up on American Western films, and other popular forms that designate dangerous men and women as cultural heroes, to be dangerous is indeed to be cool. This branding of Jamaica as both forms of "cool" – usually attributed to Marley (who is himself dually constructed, both dangerous and easy-going: big spliff hanging from his mouth, guitar in hand, shirt half-open, singing about love and war with equal stridency) is both consistent and in contestation with the tourist board's branding of Jamaica. For in some tourist ads Jamaica is beautiful, tropical, sexy and folksy, but also passive and consumable. In others, the African presence is dressed up in polite servility (as a butler or maid in uniform serving a tourist), with a broad smile for good measure. Others project Marley's image and/or his music as the sexy, cool aspect of Jamaica that tourists would find enjoyable.

Miss Lou's representation of Jamaica involves a careful balancing of images and ideologies. In Bennett's work Jamaica is "cool" and consumable, folksy but also proud. Her representation of the African presence in Jamaica is not passive, but strident, subversive, confident and ubiquitously dominant in all cultural forms. Bennett, however, carefully avoids positioning Jamaica as violent. Even during the late 1970s, and into the 1980s and 1990s, when crime in Jamaica rose to alarming levels and garrison communities shaped the lawless image that lent authenticity to the negative branding, Miss Lou's representation of Jamaica on stage was devoid of this lived reality. Bennett migrated to Canada, leaving the violence and instability behind her as so many middle-class Jamaicans had done. But Bennett continued to preserve the "brand Jamaica" as safe, even as she asserted a liberatory poetics that positioned African identity at the centre of Jamaican cultural representation. It is interesting to note that, unlike the Rastafarian philosophy that espoused repatriation to Africa, the Bennett philosophy never called for a physical return to

Africa.⁴³ In fact, in her poem "Back to Africa", Bennett pokes fun at the ideology of repatriation.⁴⁴ In the second stanza, the speaker says to the disgruntled Miss Mattie who wants to return to Africa: "Me know seh dat you great, great, great / Granma was African. But Mattie, doan you great, great, great / Grandpa was Englishman?" In a later stanza she tells Miss Mattie that besides these two foreparents who were from Africa and Europe, respectively, everyone in Mattie's family were born and raised in Bun Grun, Jamaica. Clearly, Bennett's agenda in this poem is to promote nation building and its antecedents: identification with and loyalty to Jamaica as home. Jamaica is posited as Mattie's real home, and the place to which she owes her allegiance: "Go a foreign, seek you fortune / But no tell nobody say / You dah go fe seek you homeland / For a right deh so yuh deh!" Bennett's engagement with Africa had absolutely nothing to do with a physical return. Her interest was purely ideological, subversive, and interventionist – a deliberate attempt to persuade Jamaicans to resist the allure of European cultural superiority. Cooper observes that Bennett "has long recognized the evocative power of Jamaican proverbs as the locus of folk philosophy".⁴⁵ Bennett's persona, Aunty Roachy, posits Jamaican proverbs as metonymic with Jamaican philosophy: "Dictionary seh dat philosophy mean 'the general principles governing thoughts and conducts' and 'a study of human morals and character'".⁴⁶ Jamaican proverbs, derived from African sources, serve a twofold role in Bennett's nation-building agenda: they show that the African culture, which is the basis of Jamaican folk philosophy, is as complex as the European one, and they promote positive identification with the Jamaican brand. The proverbs themselves are full of cautionary tales that promote sound character, good judgment and exemplary citizenship. For the people in the diaspora who attend Miss Lou's performances their identification with the Jamaican brand is complete. Encouraged by Miss Lou, they see themselves as the right kind of Jamaicans – proud of their African heritage, loyal to Jamaica as homeland, fully possessing the positive attributes of the right Jamaican brand, regardless of class, colour or gender.

An Epilogue: Louise Bennett and Bob Marley

"Emancipate yourself from mental slavery!" chants Marley. Bennett shows us that Jamaican language and folk identity are crucial steps in the process of self-determination as well as spiritual and political emancipation. We recognize that they are both "telling the truth", but somehow we see Marley as visionary and strident, but Bennett as funny and folksy. When we take the time to look at Marley and Bennett critically, we can easily read both of them as revolutionaries, tricksters and subversives, but we do not use a common language to talk about these two Jamaican icons. Does gender have anything to do with this tendency to elevate Marley to the level of prophet, and enclose Bennett in a language of domestic relations, "a true daughter of Jamaica" always existing within a framework of cultural nurturance, rather than cultural transgressiveness and radical cultural transformation? Such dichotomizing is perhaps not intentional, but we have to police our own language. Even as I raise these bogeys, I ask myself, am I also guilty of the charge I am levelling? Significantly, is Bennett also complicit in this gender bias by virtue of the modalities of self-expression that she chooses, for example, to deploy humour and drama to relay significant messages? Most readers might say no. Comedy has long been deployed to express cultural critique and to promote cultural transformation. Shakespeare does it, why not Louise Bennett?

Cooper notes that "[i]n the Jamaican context, class rather than gender is the functional determinant of power".[47] I cannot argue against the veracity of Cooper's statement. Everything I know about Jamaican culture confirms it. Everything, however, save for the issue of how Bennett and Marley are treated in the Jamaican imaginary. The fact that Marley's image has long been rehabilitated from that of *rude-bway* to that of international reggae icon is, perhaps, a statement that can be made without risk of censure. Co-opted in service to the Jamaica tourist board, Marley, Rastafari and reggae have been used to sell Jamaica as a counterculture slice of paradise, where one can be a little bad and still have a jolly good time.[48] Marley is now unabashedly claimed by the Jamaican middle class, especially middle-class Jamaican men. If working-class Jamaicans do not stand their ground, they will soon find themselves unable to stake any claim in Marley's legacy, especially in academic circles. Presently, it appears that only a select few can credibly discuss Marley in a public forum. So perhaps talking about class disparities between Marley's reception and Bennett's makes little sense. Marley is, after all, no longer seen as belonging to working-class Jamaica.

Marley's gender, on the other hand, has never been under dispute. Despite the truth of Cooper's claim above with respect to class, sexism, like colonialism, has a very strong foothold in our Jamaican subconscious. Much as we claim to love Bennett, I do not believe we take her as seriously as we do her male counterparts. Aisha Spencer argues that, from its very beginnings, Jamaican nationhood has been shaped by patriarchal and masculinist formulations that effectively excluded woman, except when it was necessary to use her as mere symbol.[49] Similarly, in *From Nation to Diaspora*, Curdella Forbes establishes that although the Caribbean was unsure about how exactly nationhood was to be constructed during the various independence movements across the region, in public discourses it was made very clear that these representations were to be "uncompromisingly male/masculine".[50] It therefore makes sense that if we have to imagine a figure to stand in for the Jamaican nation, we would choose Marley, who is not only male, but is also larger than life. But in doing so, we run the risk of further relegating the Jamaican woman to the sidelines. This does not in any way reflect the reality of the role Jamaican women play in the society. As Bennett made clear in her interview mentioned above, Jamaican women are not marginal in Jamaican culture, neither at home nor abroad. Jamaican women are *tallawah* and in the middle of everything. As the country folks in my part of St Catherine would say, "If is egg, dem in the red, if is butter, dem in the pat, and if it is salt, dem in the pack." In the Jamaican imaginary, if Marley is front and centre as an icon, Miss Lou must be as well – they both did their part to shape Jamaican nationhood. I contend that Bennett did it more self-consciously, more systematically and, significantly, more deliberately than Marley. For, in many respects, Bennett succeeded in doing exactly what she set out to do when she became a cultural worker in the 1930s: make Jamaicans proud of being Jamaican.

How does class further complicate this dialectic? Given that both Marley and Bennett are now seen as belonging to the middle class, does class always trump masculine privilege in Jamaican society? Are there ways in which being female (of any class, even in Jamaica) necessitates more strategic Anancyism in order to move along the path of self-empowerment, which is the stepladder to effective leadership and serious nation-building? In the Jamaican context, masculinity is primarily defined through sexual conquest, sexual dominance and aggression, not exclusively through material wealth and external manifestations of power. So what happens to a potential Bennett who is actually from the working class? Can such a figure be allowed entrance into the serious arena of nation building via the traditional channels dominated by the Jamaican middle class: attending the right schools, using family connections and having friends in high places? For surely working-class Jamaican women have also helped to build the Jamaican nation, often without recognition of these efforts. What is the key to access and visibility for these women who rarely attend the right schools and have neither family connections nor friends in high places? Is it education, hard work or marriage?

We know that working-class men are allowed entrance (at least in the public imaginary, if not in the private spheres of social engagement). Better put, they can cut their own road through with sharpened machetes of sound and fury, blazing trails and reinventing themselves, redeveloping language, reshaping the contours of culture, and transgressing traditional channels of social visibility. If they are bold enough and hungry enough and talented enough, they can transgress political and social boundaries confidently, with force, determination and true masculine, working-class grit.[51] At first we may call them *rude-bway, rhygin, stamina-puppa*,[52] but in time they become cultural heroes, prophets, iconoclasts. But there are very few female equivalents, and none (or a paltry few) allowed outside of the music industry. No *stamina-mumma* of politics, nor *rude-gyal* of high social standing and political cache, whose very name evokes worshipful, celebratory declamation. For a working-class Jamaican woman to achieve this level of recognition, she first has to shed the rude-girl image, clean herself up, and become respectable – and even then there is no guarantee that the taint of impropriety and the assumption of inferiority will not follow her like a bad smell.[53] The true equivalent of *rude-bway* is not *rude-gyal*, but *bad-gyal*, with the host of improprieties this term evokes – sexual impropriety, social ineptitude, *sketel*,[54] ghetto, wrong for the nation state, inappropriate as a role model, the very antithesis of an icon.

Although a middle-class female, Bennett's iconoclastic presence gives hope to working-class Jamaican women. Because so many working-class Jamaican women at home and abroad identify with Bennett, her effectiveness as an icon resides in her symbolic value. If Marley is the *sufferah* elevated to national iconoclast, the *rhygin* rehabilitated, redeemed and conscripted into service for brand Jamaica, and for the repackaging of reggae and Rasta as non-threatening, infinitely consumable, and internationally palatable, then Bennett as representational "daughter" for all classes of Jamaicans, transnationally, is similarly complex. Certainly, within the Jamaican framework (at home and abroad) her representation is equally resistant to simplistic binary configurations. Bennett is the prodigal daughter of the middle class, who foraged into the lean-to kitchen of the folk, ate their common *bickle*,⁵⁵ licked her fingers and inelegantly spat, regurgitating their words to recast their untutored worldview as African philosophy, their "bad-talking" as legitimate Jamaican language, and their superstitions, old wives tales and bush medicine, as folk wisdom. After several incredibly productive decades during which she was at first spurned for her elevation of folk culture and language, and then celebrated for the same, Bennett (symbolically) returns home to the bosom of middle-class propriety to assume her rightful place as honoured daughter, builder of the nation, Griot of the culture. But that is not all. For in rehabilitating the culture of the folk, she also hands the Jamaican centre of power its own authentic culture, complete with a language of its very own in which to articulate and promote its liberation from mental slavery and colonial serfdom.

Self-described as someone who "tek kin teeth kibber heart-bun", Bennett is a clever trickster figure who can couch her radically subversive messages in folksy humour. She is an interstitial figure who is not "of the folk", but is "for the folk". She can maintain the sexual propriety demanded by her class and gender, but remain desirable across gender and generational divides with her bright smile, infectious laughter and boundless amplitude – suggesting enough to go around, a little something for everyone. Traditionally, big women are the objects of male desire in Jamaica.⁵⁶ By the time Bennett left the island in the 1980s, that standard would not have changed as much as, arguably, it has today – with the ubiquity of American and European standards of beauty fast becoming global. Undoubtedly, Bennett's appeal to Jamaicans of a certain generation would not exclude sexual desire, especially during an era when the terms "fat" and "sexy" were mutually constitutive of each other, and mutually constitutive of feminine allure in Jamaica and in much of the Caribbean.

In most of her photographs, Bennett is portrayed as a big, beautiful, fair-skinned woman with a smile that lights up her entire face.⁵⁷ Very often she is photographed wearing the bandana print – the national dress of Jamaican folk singers. For Jamaicans *a yaard*, as Jamaicans call the country, and abroad, the name "Louise Bennett" symbolizes uproarious belly laughter, but it also evokes and invokes images of Jamaican national identity. Big and beautiful in an era when those two words together were not yet oxymoronic, Miss Lou's image was both non-threatening and affirming. Her smile, like those of the Rastas and other Jamaicans in service roles found within the tourist brochures, was part of her uniform, just like the bandana. However, Bennett transcended that non-threatening image, perhaps becoming much more than was intended. Her positioning of humour as a viable modality through which to articulate cultural and political resistance to the denuding of Jamaican folk values, Jamaican language and culture was, arguably, more effective and reached a wider audience than more formal political and academic treatises on the subject.

Jamaicans have certainly come a long way since Bennett first began insisting that Jamaicans take their culture seriously, but not too seriously. The immediacy and accessibility of her humour has to be credited for getting the message across so clearly. Today, comedians like Oliver Samuels, Joan Andrea Hutchinson and others owe much of their successes to Bennett's pioneering work in programming the Jamaican people to accept social critique through humour. Everywhere in the Jamaican diaspora that she performed and lectured, Bennett criticized the colonial mindset, elevated the language and cultural forms of the oppressed, and celebrated folk culture as *real* Jamaican culture. And, in doing so, she helped to create a brand for Jamaica nationally and transnationally. Today, to every person who is familiar with her work, Bennett's very image says: Jamaican pride, Jamaican humour, Jamaican folk culture, Jamaican language, *Jamaica! Jamaica nice, yuh see!* So, in the words of one precocious little Jamaican boy who was impressed with Bennett's dance moves on *Ring Ding*, "Go deh, Miss Lou!"[58] We should all join this little fellow in celebrating the audacity of Miss Lou, and ensure that as we "brand" Jamaica, we do not forget her importance in helping to shape this very same brand.

Notes

1. Marcia Davidson, "Jamaicans.com Exclusive Interview with Miss Lou", 1 July 2001, http://www.jamaicans.com/culture/people/misslouinterview.shtml.
2. Ibid.
3. See *Yes M' Dear: Miss Lou Live*, recorded in London, 1983.
4. Rex Nettleford, introduction, *Jamaica Labrish*, Louise Bennett (Kingston: Sangster's, 1966), 16.
5. "Obituary: The Honorable Louise Bennett-Coverly aka Miss Lou", 28 August 2006, http://www.rootsouttacontrol.de/modules.php.
6. Mervyn Morris, *Is English We Speaking and Other Essays* (Kingston: Ian Randle, 1999), 21.

7. Ibid., 3.
8. "Mento Music", accessed 1 October 2011, http://www.mentomusic.com/edric Conner.htm.
9. Aisha T. Spencer, "Interrogating Conceptualizations of Gender in the Shaping of a Nation, as Presented in Miss Lou's Monologues", *Journal of West Indian Literature* 18, no. 1 (November 2009): 73–85.
10. Nettleford, introduction, 16.
11. Louise Bennett, *Lawd Di Riddim Sweet* (Kingston: Sangster's, 1999).
12. See the website for Sangster's Bookstore at http://www.sangstersbooks.com. Website information about *Lawd Di Riddim Sweet* reveals that the *Heritage Singers* were Bennett's primary audience for the 1999 CD.
13. "Mento Music".
14. Bennett, 1983 recording, London.
15. Carolyn Cooper, *Noises in the Blood: Orality, Gender and the "Vulgar" Body of Jamaican Popular Culture* (Durham, NC: Duke University Press, 1993), 40.
16. Ngũgĩ wa Thiong'o, *Decolonising the Mind: The Politics of Language in African Literature* (London: Heinemann, 1981), 11.
17. Frantz Fanon, *Black Skin, White Masks* (New York: Grove, 1967), 18.
18. Albert Memmi, *The Colonizer and the Colonized* (Boston: Beacon, 1967), 107.
19. Louise Bennett, *Aunty Roachy Seh* (Kingston: Sangster's, 1993).
20. Edward Kamau Brathwaite developed the "nation language" to describe the creole languages of the Caribbean region. It enjoys wide usage among literary critics who write about language and the Caribbean. See Brathwaite, *History of the Voice* (London: New Beacon Books), 1984.
21. The emphasis is Bennett's.
22. Paul MacDougall, "Marcus Garvey and Nova Scotia: Birth of a Movement, Birth of a Religion, Birth of a Church", February–March 2000, http://www.shunpiking.com/bhs/Marcus-gar.htm.
23. Zora Neale Hurston, *Their Eyes Were Watching God* (New York: HarperCollins, 1990).
24. Leleith Bailey, "We Are All Contributing to Life: A Chat with Louise Bennett (1992)", *Caribbean Writer* 12 (1998): 165.
25. Roger Abrahams, *The Man of Words in the West Indies: Performance and the Emergence of Creole Culture* (Baltimore: Johns Hopkins University Press, 1983), 124.
26. Elizabeth Wheeler, "Riddym Ravings: Female and National Identity in Jamaican Creole Poetry", in *Imagination, Emblems, and Expressions: Essays on Latin American, Caribbean, and Continental Culture and Identity*, ed. Helen Ryan-Ranson (Bowling Green, OH: Bowling Green State University Popular Press, 1993), 140.
27. Cooper, *Noises*, 47–48.
28. In an interview with Ifeoma Nwankwo, I argue that Bennett's often touted "ven-

triloquism" bears further interrogation, especially by current academicians who were born and raised among the most marginalized segment of Jamaican society. This is not intended to demonize Bennett or to discredit her in any way, but instead to offer a critique of her work and agenda from the perspective of those she claims to speak for, some of whom may finally have a platform to address these issues in their own words. For more detail see Nwankwo, "Interview with Donna (Aza) Weir-Soley (Author of *First Rain* and *Eroticism, Spirituality and Resistance in Black Women's Writings*)", *Journal of West Indian Literature* 18, no. 1 (November 2009): 26–59.

29. Jennifer Rahim, "Laughter in *Crick, Crack Monkey*: An Exploration in Comic Discourse", in *The Woman, the Writer and Caribbean Society*, ed. Helen Pyne-Timothy (Los Angeles: Center for Afro-American Studies Publications, University of California, 1998), 209–19.

30. Lawrence W. Levine, *Black Culture and Black Consciousness* (New York: Oxford University Press, 1977), 300.

31. Mikhail Bakhtin, "Discourse in the Novel", *The Dialogic Imagination: Four Essays*, trans. Michael Holquist and Caryl Emerson (Austin: University of Texas Press, 1981), 259–422.

32. Morris, *Is English We Speaking*, iii.

33. Rahim, "Laughter in *Crick, Crack Monkey*", 18.

34. Carolyn Cooper, "Noh Lickle Twang: An Introduction to the Poetry of Louise Bennett", *World Literatures Written in English* 17 (April 1978): 317–27.

35. See, for example, Alicia Dunkley's article "JLP Strategy: Warmington Quits House Over Dual Citizenship", *Jamaican Observer*, 9 March 2011. See also "MPs Clash in Debate Over Dual Citizenship", *Gleaner*, 19 January 2011. In the *Gleaner* article, American-born member of parliament Sharon Hay-Webster came under fire for dual citizenship and attempts were made to silence her as a "stranger in the House". Hay-Webster countered that the Jamaican constitution did not prohibit dual citizenship, but states that "no person can be elected to serve in Parliament who is by virtue of his own act under acknowledgement of allegiance or adherence to a foreign state or country". Hay-Webster argued that being born in the United States did not in itself constitute a deliberate act on her part that should make her ineligible for political office, as she had never taken an oath of allegiance to any other country but Jamaica. The fact that people have to resort to splitting hairs over this issue further highlights the complex dynamics of this controversy, the heated debate that it has generated and the high stakes that are at play over dual citizenship. The same article states that Prime Minister Bruce Golding suggested that the matter be referred to a committee for further discussion.

36. For example, I had to renounce allegiance to all other countries when I took the oath of citizenship in the United States.

37. For more details see David Rowe, "The Patriot Act and the Caribbean", http://constitution-and-rights.com/patriotsAct.htm. Rowe, a Jamaican-born, Floridian lawyer, raises the question of whether Caribbean nationals have lost their constitutional rights under the Patriot Act. Rowe cites examples of naturalized citizens and American-born people of Caribbean descent who are harassed and terrorized for unsubstantiated charges or mere suspicion of terrorism because they have Muslim-sounding names, and so on.
38. See http://www.jamaicatradeandinvest.org/.
39. Denise Campbell, "Smile Jamaica: Branding Beyond Land and Sea", *Occasionally Clever: A Semi-regular Blog on Public Diplomacy*, 12 April 2011. http://628pd4.blogspot.com/2011/04/smile-jamaica-branding-beyond-sand-and.html.
40. For example, when the television programme *In Living Color* used to air in the 1980s, many respectable Jamaicans in the diaspora enjoyed the segment that mocked Jamaicans for being industrious and hard-working. The Jamaican character was often portrayed chiding folks who had only three jobs and calling them "lazy" because he himself had up to ten jobs. It was meant to poke fun at Jamaicans, but was seen by many as a positive stereotype. This was a period in which Jamaicans were not being represented on American television shows. When we made the news in New York where I lived, it was often in relation to some drug posse or other drug/gang related issue. Consequently, rather than being offended by the skit, many Jamaicans took pride in being portrayed as industrious and hard-working people. Many were disappointed when that segment of the show was pulled from *In Living Color*. I distinctly remember discussing the show with my very conservative uncle who thought the segment was pulled because it showed a positive image of Jamaicans that some Americans were not comfortable with – this was one occasion where we agreed on something.
41. According to one of my sources, Jamaicans in prison frequently use the negative aspects of this image to protect themselves from becoming targets of gang violence and/or harassment from other inmates. When tested, they are ready to back up the image with action. In so doing, they develop a formidable reputation in the prison system, on the streets of New York, and in inner-city public schools. The negative image of Jamaicans garners respect among offenders and leads some Caribbean nationals who are not of Jamaican parentage to identify themselves as Jamaicans (for protection from violence and for street credibility) on the streets and in the prisons. These observations are drawn from the notes of my unpublished interview with a former inmate of a New York state correctional facility.
42. See Robert Buddan's "Branding Communities and Community Entrepreneurship", *Gleaner*, 13 August 2006.
43. Stephen A. King, *Reggae, Rastafari, and the Rhetoric of Social Control* (Jackson, MS: University Press of Mississippi, 2002), 34.

44. See Bennett's "Back to Africa" in *Jamaica Labrish*, 214–15.
45. Cooper, *Noises*, 46.
46. See Bennett, *Aunty Roachy Seh* (Kingston: Sangster's, 1993), 7–8.
47. Cooper, *Noises*, 54.
48. King, *Reggae, Rastafari*, 122–30.
49. Spencer, "Interrogating Conceptualizations".
50. Curdella Forbes, *From Nation to Diaspora: Samuel Selvon, George Lamming and the Cultural Performance of Gender* (Kingston: University of the West Indies Press, 2005), 41.
51. In 2004, Mutabaruka was one of the invited speakers for the Haitian Bicentennial Celebration held at the University of the West Indies, Mona. If memory serves, I believe he was barefoot as is characteristic of Muta. Could a non-conformist, working-class Jamaican woman gain this kind of access? No disrespect to Mutabaruka, who was as eloquent and informed as anyone else on the programme. But my question is, can Muta's female equivalent be allowed to exist, and to have equal access to the hallowed halls of academia? Similarly, on 10 March 2011, Adidja Palmer, otherwise known as Vybz Kartel, was invited by the Department of Literatures in English and the Institute for Gender and Development Studies to give a lecture at the University of the West Indies, Mona. In the lecture, entitled "Pretty as a Colouring Book: My Life and My Art", Kartel discussed his views on skin bleaching. No doubt Vybz Kartel is an expert on the subject – he has effectively transformed himself into a fair-skinned man, ostensibly to highlight his many tattoos. My only question is this: do working-class women have similar access and, if so, how come their appearances do not make global news? An article on the Vybz Kartel lecture can be consulted: "Vybz Kartel guest lecturer at UWI today", last modified 10 March 2011, http://urbanislandz.com/2011/03/10/vybz-kartel-guest-lecturer-at-uwi-today-pretty-like-a-coloring-book-my-life-my-art/.
52. In Jamaican Creole the terms *rude-bway* and *rhygin* are often used interchangeably to connote a rebellious male figure. Both have working-class associations, but can be used in reference to middle-class males who operate (with impunity) outside of a given perimeter. The term *rhygin* is derived from a Jamaican outlaw from the 1940s (Ivanhoe Martin) who escaped from prison, formed a gang, and managed to evade the police while committing numerous crimes. He was regarded as a cultural hero of sorts and was nicknamed "Rhygin". His story is immortalized in the film *The Harder They Come*. *Stamina-puppa* is a Creole term that connotes sexual and social potency.
53. Take the Honorable Portia Simpson-Miller, for example, who has done everything required of the men in power (and more), and everything required of middle-class women (and more), to achieve her success. Yet she has strident and very vocal detractors, and the language some of them use to criticize her is so sexist and downgrading

that it has forced sharp public responses in the Jamaican media. See, for example, Petre Williams, "Gordon-Webley Under Fire", *Jamaica Observer*, 29 April 2007. See also Horace Hines, "Portia Lashes Out at Character Assassins", *Jamaica Observer*, 19 June 2006. The body type for this "global" standard is generally slender, but subject to change with the fashion trend – depending on whether it is Beyoncé's week to sell jeans and make-up, or Taylor Swift's.

54. A *sketel* is a sexually promiscuous female, and is usually applied to working-class Jamaican women.
55. *Bickle* is a Jamaican Creole term for food, specifically the type of food usually eaten by poor people.
56. Bennett is also a "brown" Jamaican and is therefore already constituted as "pretty" in the Jamaican aesthetic framework. Today, she would definitely be considered overweight in Jamaica. At the height of her popularity, to Jamaican men as well as women, Bennett's size was part and parcel of her likeable, relatable image.
57. King, *Reggae, Rastafari*, 125.
58. As told to Bennett's 1999 audience by Bennett.

3.

Between La Habana and Veracruz
Toña la Negra and the Transnational Circuits of *Música Tropical*

| B. CHRISTINE ARCE

IN THE SMALL TOWN OF Coyolillo in southern Veracruz on the Gulf Coast of Mexico, "cubano" is one of the many racial taxonomies used to refer to black or dark-skinned Mexicans.[1] This chapter discusses the impact of Cuban music and culture on Mexican cultural production and identity, focusing on the figure of Toña la Negra, a famous singer of boleros and Cuban *son* from the Gulf region of Veracruz, Mexico. The concept of Afro-Mestizo[2] has been circulating for some time and is central to the *jarocho* culture (*jarocho* refers to the inhabitants of Veracruz and means "mixed blood"; the mixture to which it refers is precisely the African and Amerindian, and is a matter of great civic pride).[3] However, it is after the Revolution that the cultural life of the city actively sought to establish cultural links with the Caribbean, particularly Cuba. It is through this cultural exchange that Veracruz's Afro-Mexicanity marks its lasting contributions to Mexican culture and the national imaginary through its appropriation of *danzón*, *son*, *boleros*, and of course the creation of the *son jarocho*, a musical genre whose very name and unique sound point towards a pan-Caribbean imaginary in a distinctly Mexican fashion.

I will engage the figure of Toña la Negra as not only a practitioner of Caribbean music, but also an embodiment of the musical, historical and cultural tensions that inhabit the assimilation and naturalization of tropical music in Mexico. Through an analysis of the figure of Toña la Negra, I will discuss the ways in which Mexican musical culture reflects the influence of African-inspired Caribbean music while deflecting the autochthonous Afro-Mexican presence. The centrality of Toña as a figure, as well as the insistence on her blackness evidenced by her stage name, points to the fractures of *mestizaje* as a Mexican discourse. The triangulation of a racialized Caribbean identity with the strong African presence in Veracruz is the larger subject of this chapter. Contrary to other Mexican *mulata* figures, she is not marginalized in the popular imaginary, but rather is a positive and fundamental figure in the creation of a national culture. What is interesting is the paradoxical elision of her blackness: she is the *prima donna* of Mexican music that just "happens" to be black, thus making the paradox of the invisibility of blackness in Mexico painfully obvious because her name, body and music commemorate the Africanity of her heritage.

María Antonia del Carmen Peregrino Álvarez was born on 2 November 1912 in the barrio of La Huaca in the Port of Veracruz.[4] When she was ten years old she won her first prize and went on to become one of the most famous singers in Mexico. She started out singing *tangos*, but later sang *guarachas, sones, bambucos* and of course, *boleros*. She perfomed music written by Agustín Lara, Rafael Hernández, Pedro Flores, Sindo Garay, Gonzalo Curiel, Ignacio Piñeiro, Son Clave de Oro and even poet Andrés Eloy Blanco, who wrote "Píntame angelitos negros"[5] and formed part of the trio Uzcanga-Peregrino and later Son Clave de Oro. Innumerable rumours circulate regarding the way in which she and her counterpart, songwriter Agustín Lara, met: some say her brother introduced them, others that they met in the centre of town while hanging out in a bar or café, while still others claim that they met in a cabaret in Mexico City called El Retiro. One of the most folkloric versions of the story is that she arrived at the doorstep of Agustín Lara as a young mother, with her child in her arms, hoping he would give her an audition.[6] Another myth is that she was singing while washing clothes in Boca del Río, and Lara passed by and exclaimed at what a shame it was a poor laundress should waste her talent. This last myth seems to be the most unlikely of all, considering she was from La Huaca, a barrio in the centre of the port and somewhat distant from Boca del Río. Also, she came from a musical family of *soneros, treseros*, percussionists and singers, not poor laundresses. This is a problematic rumour as it supports a white, patriarchal mythology where the bohemian dandy "discovers" the poor black laundress.

The intersections of music, race and gender are important to understanding the figure of Toña la Negra because, as often happens with artists of colour, their nicknames become the racial markers that define them. In this case, she is a positive and an absolutely foundational figure in the creation and dissemination of a national culture. Unlike other fictive representations of *mulatas* in Mexico like the colonial legend of the *Mulata de Córdoba*, the revolutionary Coronel la Negra Angustias from Francisco Rojas González's novel (1944), or the various *mulata* figures from the film *Angelitos negros*,[7] she is not marginalized in the popular imaginary and she is not a victim or martyr; on the contrary, she is as both prominent and as *mexicana* as they come. She won innumerable awards and made countless records, thus making the paradox of the invisibility of blackness in Mexico that much more acute. Critic Frances R. Aparicio comments on the importance held by the strategic inscription of blackness into her name: "[h]er stage name – La Negra [The Black Woman] – reveals her strategic racial self-objectification or essentialization, a racializing gesture that exhorted Mexican audiences to accept the African heritage of the Caribbean coast as a central element of their culture".[7] Although she began her career as "la Peregrino", it is rumoured that Agustín Lara convinced her to take "la Negra" as her stage name.[9] Indeed, the performance of blackness through the creation of her very name, although not uncommon with black musicians (her nephew David also took on "el Negro" as his stage name) does perform the work Aparicio claims it does: it requires that Mexicans rethink their own conception of race, and, through the link to the Caribbean, allow race to enter in as central to the makings of their own cultural traditions and people.[10]

It is also curious that Agustín Lara, her counterpart, who was rumoured to have had countless lovers and bore a long scar on his face carved by a prostitute in a fit of jealousy, is, despite this tawdry past, one of Mexico's most beloved songwriters. Agustín is the king of the *bolero*, who also wrote Cuban *sones*, but is not of mixed race. Nonetheless, he fashioned his identity based on having been born in the heart of the musical hub of Veracruz, Tlacotalpan, home of the finest *jaraneros*, *decimeros* and, of course, *rumberos*. As such, it was the musical centre of the "Afro-Mestizo universe" that musicologist Rafael Figueroa claims has been forging itself since at least the seventeenth century.[11] Agustín is the maker of his own myth, practically fancying himself a child of that *herencia negra* (black heritage) although his actual birthplace is disputed, with some records indicating that he was in reality born in Mexico City. Regardless, he claims Veracruz as his home and inspiration, having been lulled to sleep by the sound of the river Papoloapan – "the river of the butterflies" – with Toña la Negra as his muse. He thus appropriated the Afro-Mestizo culture of Veracruz as part of his own musical heritage and birthright.

Despite the glaring lack of recognition of black cultural contributions in Mexico, Toña is the quintessential Mexican diva and icon; no one would ever deny Toña her Mexicanity, and yet her blackness is inscribed into her very name and sound. Aparicio underscores the maternal tenor of her voice as well as the stunning impact of her persona as an important element in Mexican culture; "the modulations of her voice and her almost matriarchal presence contributed to the inclusion of the Caribbean cultural heritage among Mexican listeners".[12] Aparicio astutely notes that she was "almost" like a maternal figure, not quite the sultry tragic mulatta of the North American tradition, but recalling a sort of "mother Africa" symbolism in a maternalizing gesture that is not unfamiliar to Mexican culture.

Yet this "almost matriarchal" presence is significantly muted by the sexuality that is invoked by her throaty voice with its low timbre; the sensuality implicit in the music she sings challenges the maternal presence highlighted by Aparicio. Her music clearly reflects and invites the tropicality of the Caribbean, and it is her relationship to the Caribbean that both sanctifies and legitimizes her music while simultaneously legitimizing her blackness. It is as if the Cuban *son* were strangely responsible for her *mulatez*, hence explaining why blackness still does not figure into the national narrative of mestizo subjectivity. Despite the claim by the Veracruz Institute of Culture that Veracruz forms part of the greater Caribbean,[13] many nationalists looked critically at the "invasion" of Cuban art forms because they introduced music and dance that was propitious to what they considered relaxed moral standards while also introducing Afro-Cuban artists. In this way, paradoxically, Toña created and embodied the domesticity of Caribbean music while critics simultaneously signified it as a pernicious foreign element.

Caribbean as Foreign

The impact of the Mexican film industry on Cuban music is impressive, as the golden era of Mexican cinema is marked by a whole genre of melodramas that were almost excuses for musical numbers featuring Cuban music and acts. In his article on the relationship between the Mexican film industry and Afro-

Cuban music, Francisco J. Crespo states that "[b]esides providing a simple musical framework that marked the different sequences of the film, Cuban music was used by filmmakers to represent cosmopolitanism, prosperity, and decadence brought on by the urbanization and modernization, reinforcing the new sets of urban sexual mores".[14] Crespo underscores that these musicals suggest not only a change in social mores, but the modernization of a traditional society in the postwar era. This modernization was viewed sceptically by conservatives and left little doubt as to the role that would be occupied by women should they leave the home.

Carl J. Mora also remarks on the integral role that music played in the creation of the genre called the *cabareteras* (cabaret girls) showcasing films such as *Aventurera* (1949) that usually featured poor women fallen from grace or prostitutes with hearts of gold. These films, in their own way, were commenting on the destruction of traditional rural values that were epitomized by the *comedias rancheras* (country comedies) through the introduction of a foreign music that operated within a specifically decadent libidinal economy as "the cabareteras dramatized the breakdown of those [traditional] values".[15] Mora remarks on what was perceived to be the foreignizing influence of Afro-Cuban music on Mexican cinema by stating that most of the music "was Afro-Cuban – danzones, rhumbas, congas, mambos, cha-chas – musical forms with a high level of erotic suggestiveness, which in turn highlighted the freer sexual standards of postwar urban life".[16] Lest we forget that *danzón* had been around since the turn of the century (and was actually introduced at the end of the nineteenth century) in addition to the fact that *son, rumba, conga* and *danzón* were all practically formalized as traditional musical forms with the institutionalization of *carnaval* in Veracruz in 1925, we might reconsider how truly "foreign" this music was. We should also recall that Toña's renditions catapulted many of the title songs from these films to the top of the charts: *Aventurera* is among the most famous films of the *cabaretera* genre and it is also the name of one of Toña's (and Lara's) most popular songs.

However, this is not so different from the kind of warning Mexican women received at the turn of the century with novels like *Santa* (1903) by Federico Gamboa (Agustín Lara wrote the title song for the film version of this novel and Toña la Negra sang it) and films like *La Mujer del Puerto* (1934) which, not surprisingly, takes place in Veracruz. In fact, narratives about prostitutes in literature and film are almost a cliché. But what makes this particular genre so remarkable is the way in which this fall from grace is racialized; or rather, the particular link that is made between *mulato* bodies, tropical music – or what Ángel Quintero Rivera has called "música mulata" – and a perceived excessive eroticism that allows the filmgoer to enjoy the cinematic experience with the scantily clad *rumberas* and *cabareteras*, many of whom are white, while the musicians are often black or mulatto. These films also send a social message to the Mexican women who might get seduced by this tropicalized, glamorous representation of nightlife in the big city, rife with infectious music, but also with danger. Although melodramatic and formulaic, they brought Cuban music to the international stage and further contributed to the naturalization of tropical music in Mexico. Despite the warnings, Mexicans continued to consume these "foreign" cultural products voraciously.

Crespo further emphasizes the importance of the Mexican film industry for Afro-Cuban dance and music as he claims that it strategically incorporated Cuban music into the quotidian listening practices of people around the globe, and that "Afro-Cuban dance music has enjoyed continued international popularity, in part because Mexican films opened the door to the world market".[17] The point here should not be missed: not only was Mexico appropriating Caribbean music (as well as actors and actresses), but Cuban music was becoming internationalized through its cultural and economic triangulation with Mexico. This relationship created a cultural partnership and artistic mutualism that continues even today. But we must not neglect that the cultural, artistic, economic flows of people and things have been going on for centuries between Veracruz and Cuba.

Caribbean as Proper: "Veracruz, por fortuna, es y seguirá siendo Caribe" (Veracruz, fortunately, is and will always be the Caribbean)[18]

Caribbean music has a long history in Mexico, starting with the old *son* "El Chuchumbé", to the introduction of *danzón* in the late-nineteenth century. Some colonial documents claim "El Chuchumbé" was brought to Mexico by *mulato* sailors from the port of Havana, which caused such a ruckus that it was twice banned by the Inquisition's authorities in the eighteenth century. To this day *danzón* reigns supreme in Veracruz as part of Mexico's cultural patrimony and is played a couple times a week for free by the local government. It is even taught in the primary schools as a traditional dance. Roberto

González Echevarría comments on the relationship between *danzón* and its black roots in Cuba: "Faced with the peninsular scrupulousness of the late nineteenth century, *danzón* was something dangerous, exotic, decadent and entirely too Cuban. It was about the open incorporation of the African to the social lives of the upper classes; an incipient mulatization of the powerful people."[19] The connection González Echevarría makes between African identity and its incorporation into upper-class musical forms provides a critical lens through which we can appreciate its ardent acceptance by the populace of Veracruz. The *mulatización* of the powerful Cuban elite seems to have struck a chord among those who performed and consumed *danzón* in Mexico; it may have begun as *demasiado cubano* (extremely Cuban) but it also ended up as entirely Mexican.

Furthermore, the existence of *carnaval* in Veracruz, among the largest in Latin America outside of Brazil, seems to be one of the main cultural events that has officially consolidated the primacy of *son cubano* and *música tropical* in Veracruz since 1925, having begun unofficially decades earlier. The *comparsas* (popular dance troupes) are the heart and soul of *carnaval* in Veracruz, typically dancing to *son*, *guaracha*, *rumba*, *conga* and now *salsa* and *reggaetón*, thus playing a key role in the explosion of tropical music in the port city. Finally, there is the *son jarocho*, which is a product of the Afro-Mestizo universe that has been forging itself in Veracruz since the seventeenth century. As contended by many ethnomusicologists, the *son jarocho* has distinct Cuban and African elements, such as syncopation, poly and cross rhythms, call and response and percussive strumming of the *jarana* and other stringed instruments.[20] I believe *son jarocho* fits perfectly into what sociologist Ángel Quintero Rivera, in his book *Salsa, sabor y control* defines as "música mulata" (mulatta music): a genre that combines both European melodies and instruments with African rhythms through a musical *cimarronaje*.[21] It is one of Mexico's most traditional musical genres, and songs like "La bamba" have, in a sense, globalized this brand of cultural Mexicanity, ironically placing the Afro-Mestizo musical legacy at the heart of one of Mexico's most commercialized songs.

Some musicologists declare that the Afro-Caribbean presence left its mark on the *son jarocho* in the southern countryside where there was a Cuban immigration in the mid- to late-nineteenth century. Beginning in the 1870s, Cubans skilled in tobacco and sugar harvesting began to migrate to the Sotavento where the *son jarocho* was born. Other ethnomusicologists claim that the Afro-Cuban *son de oriente* (the *son* from the eastern region of Cuba) from the early colonial period was instrumental in the creation of the *son jarocho*. In either case, the Afro-Caribbean presence had its hand in the formation of this unique genre. Moreover, the presence of these *sones* marks a space where, through music, and specifically *son* as a transcultural musical genre, the politically subversive attitudes of these early Afro-Mestizos were manifested, carving out an aural space from where their voices would be heard. Songs such as the proto-*son* "El Chuchumbé" bear witness to the tangled strands constituted by race, music and regional identity: the relationship between the masses *de color quebrado* (of broken colour) and the sexual explicitness of this song should be underscored as part of the way in which Afro-Mestizos were signified early on by both themselves and the religious authorities of the colonial regime. The insistence on the ties to Cuba later gave Mexican nationalists a place to blame the "exceptional" black presence. In light of this, we can begin to see how Afro-Mexicans were categorically erased from the national narrative by official history, and how traces of this culture have been fetishized as a product of Caribbean tropicality by both popular culture and high art.

Toña la Negra: "La Sensación Jarocha"

As mentioned, the term *jarocho* refers to people born in the state of Veracruz, and it originally meant "mixed breed". Bernardo Rivera claims it was Pedro de Lille who named Toña "The Jarocha Sensation" after a series of concerts because "Toña was the voice of the creoles, mestizos, blacks and *mulatos* from the barrio of la Huaca in Veracruz".[22] Rivera's claim allows us to appreciate how, despite Toña's singularity as an exceptional black figure, she was metonymically identified with a larger, invisible community and the irony of her almost immediate success. Toña's first hit with Lara was "Enamorada", and on New Year's Eve of 1932, she appeared at the Esperanza Iris Theater singing "Lamento jarocho", a song Agustín Lara wrote especially for her. Jesse Varela writes that "[h]er exciting and passionate voice tore the place apart with seven triumphant encores. The club management quickly hired her for 24 additional evenings."[23]

Toña's repertoire also includes a few Afrocentric songs. She sang a musical version of the poem "Píntame angelitos negros" by Andrés Eloy Blanco, which rebukes the church for not representing blacks in its religious iconography. There is also "La negra Concepción", which is a paradigmatic song about a *mulata rumbera* (*mulata* party girl) who gets all the men folk ecstatic, as well as "Yo soy mulata", which manifests a veritable pride in her black body. This particular song reflects a strong claim to her black ancestry as it fully and loudly recognizes her black physicality, and states that "si no tengo nada, soy mulata de verdad" (I may have nothing, but I am a true *mulata*). Toña's voice literally sings that she may have nothing, but she knows who she is because she is black. This song, unlike the others that sound a lamentation or cry for justice, stakes a firm claim in her black heritage despite the empty place holder that registers the contributions of blacks to Mexican history and culture.

Toña's voice operates almost as an intermediary between the Caribbean and Mexico, and the instant popularity of her music speaks to the resonance this relationship has for her pluricultural Mexican public. The lyrics in the songs written for her by Lara reflect this tension; "Lamento jarocho" ("Jarocho Lamentation") is a lamentation directed to those "bronzed jarochos" who "suffer" and "cry" their misfortune:

> I sing to my race
> the race of bronze, the jarocho race
> who the sun has burnt
> ...
> The soul of a jarocha who was born dark
> The stalk that moves like the sway of a hammock
> ...
> The mouth that utters the moan of the pained protest
> Of an entire race full of bitterness
> The soul of the jarocho who was born valiant
> in order to suffer her misfortune.[24]

This song is written as an homage to the black soul of the *jarocha* singer who was born "valiant" in order to suffer her "misfortune", which in this case is the misfortune of being born black. The female figure metonymically represents the "bitterness of a people", while her body is simultaneously signified as a sensual and tropical object: her torso moves like the sway of a hammock, a beautiful metaphor that points to the sway of her voluptuous body, an image typical of the sexualized descriptors that are used to describe *mulatas*.

Despite the "matriachal modulation of her voice", Toña's blackness inevitably operates within the libidinal economy of *mulatez*; her racial hybridity and the lower timbre of her voice beckon the listener to imagine her body. In addition to providing the image of her swaying, it also describes burned skin that has been perfumed by the kisses of the sand. All of these metaphors recall images of tropical beauties waiting listlessly, in a sensual anticipation, on the shore while suffering the burden of their poverty. Many of the *mulatas* in Mexican and Caribbean art forms are similarly sexualized with references to their dark skin and voluptuous bodies, titillating readers and spectators, or in this case, listeners. Vicente Riva Palacio's poetic rendition of the Mexican legend "La Mulata de Córdoba" similarly constitutes its protagonist through her phenotype and signifies Veracruz (where the drama unfolds) as a heady, tropical space that begets the same sort of listless sensuality described in the lyrics by Lara.[25] However, the poem also emphasizes the "African rays" that emanate from her eyes in addition to the voluptuous sway of her body, thus constituting her sensual tropicality as other at the same time it is autochthonous. In this way we can see how the link to the Caribbean figuratively passes through Africa, and in this triangulation of desire exists a continual fetishizing of tropical spaces, making the role performed by Veracruz as its intermediary, and the gateway to the Caribbean, a place of racial and cultural contestation.

"Oración Caribe" ("Caribbean Prayer") is another one of Lara and Toña's greatest hits; it is written as a prayer offered to the Caribbean Sea, which, in the Santería and Candomblé spiritual traditions is embodied by the deity Yemanjá. The prayer tells of suffering and plaintive blacks who plead for mercy and light in their lives: "Caribbean prayer / that knows how to plead / psalm of the blacks / prayer of the sea".[26] Both "Lamento jarocho" and "Oración Caribe" are like parallel homages to the latent Africanity, *mestizaje* and *mulatez* within the Caribbean and Veracruz. These twin "prayers", if you will, herald and even exhort their audiences to recognize and honour this "raza de bronce" (bronzed race), as the lyrics in "Oración Caribe" plead for a little "heat" (as in love) and a little "light" (as in recognition and illumination) for the black race. Toña's voice sounds a mournful lament to the sea, honouring those blacks who ask for mercy. These songs, in addition to others like "Veracruz", "Vereda tropical" and "Noche criolla" extol the beautiful tropicality of Veracruz through its ties to a black past. However, this blackness seems to always be mitigated by its relationship to the Caribbean. The tropical inflection in all of these songs does not invoke the image of a "Madre Africa" (mother Africa) as much as it summons the fetishized tropicality of a Caribbean *mulatez*.

Racialization of Sound and Voice

Blackness is inscribed in Toña la Negra's voice as well as into the musical product she creates and that is written for her. While her voice proclaims the beauty of her native Veracruz, she equally offers "prayers to the Caribbean". As discussed, Afro-Cuban musicians were renowned for their talent and were particularly in demand in Mexico, evidenced by the fact that Mexican cinema's golden era starting in the mid 1930s through the 1960s was rife with racialized Cubans and Puerto Ricans. However, it is as if only through this call to the Caribbean that black culture could be summoned, and more importantly recognized, gesturing towards the performance maintained by the inscription of blackness in Toña's moniker. She somehow needed to be "la Negra" in order to sell her product through the fetishizing of the tropicalized black woman, but paradoxically needed this identification of blackness so that, like blackface, it simultaneously might be elided in the same gesture. As Saidiya Hartman reminds us in *Scenes of Subjection*, "[t]he fungibility of the commodity, specifically its abstractness and immateriality, enabled the black body or blackface mask to serve as the vehicle of white self-exploration, renunciation, and enjoyment".[27] That is, blackface serves to disassociate the reality of the black body from the performance of blackness, in this way providing a safe place for white reflection of racial purity. Toña's strategic naming operates in much the same manner; she is "la Negra" only because she is an exception and because blacks do not register within the nation's official history, leaving the sanctity of the mestizo identity (and its own problematic privilege of the European component) intact.

Ángel Quintero Rivera explains the role performed by music: "Music represents, then, a way in which people interact with their world and attempt to exercise control over their materiality, over their biology, collectively re-signifying one of the essential elements of their existence. It has, therefore, in all societies an enormous importance: the decisive function of the symbolic configuration of social reality."[28] Music allows for people to "symbolically configure their social lives" and even their very bodies. This theoretical intervention illuminates the way in which we might think about the role of Toña la Negra in the history of Mexican culture and music. If, by giving Veracruz its material tropicality in the form of her body, she also symbolically signified this tropicality with an inherent blackness both through her name and her voice. Consumed at this level, it remains aurally felt: at once symbolic, ephemeral and intangible. Figueroa poignantly describes the power of the duet formed by Toña la Negra and Lara: "The strength and beauty of her voice and personality – linked to the ingenuity of Agustín Lara – provided us with the warmth and aromas proper to a Port city that is always open to the musical and cultural flows that emanate from the Caribbean."[29] This description of her voice is marked by a gendered and sexualized image of the way in which Toña's voice and person, both as an intermediary and as instrument, allowed for the Caribbean and Veracruz to intermingle, each leaving behind an aromatic taste, or *sabor* in the mouth of the other.

Moreover, her low timbre reflects and even creates an expectation for a particular kind of body. Nina Edsheim discusses the performativity of racialized voices, claiming that "[v]ocal timbre is not the unmediated sound of an essential body. Instead, both body and timbre are shaped by unconscious and conscious training practices that function as repositories for cultural attitudes toward gender, class, race, and sexuality."[30] Thus blackness becomes produced through the content of the music that is written for her specifically (by Lara and others), through the association with a racialized Caribbean identity, but also, as suggested by Edsheim, through the performance of timbre. Edsheim posits that while timbre is not an exclusive to any race, it is nonetheless bound up with certain physical and cultural expectations of racialized bodies. This notion proves to be a provocative but not tidy theoretical intervention in the case of Toña la Negra because blacks simply do not register in the Mexican national imaginary in the same way their presence undergirds North American and Caribbean identity politics. However, the identification of timbre with a specific racialized body could perhaps be part of a dormant repository of cultural attitudes reactivated by the ubiquity of North American and Caribbean musical forms which have always had a specific history of racial politics defined predominantly in terms of blackness and whiteness. Therefore Toña's la Negra's naturally throaty timbre, whether "produced" or not, becomes a performative element of her blackness, and it is therefore interpreted as such by the composers, songwriters and consumers of her music.

Furthermore, Quintero highlights the salience of reception in music, especially *músicas mulatas* where the role of the cultural consumers or "receptors" who interact and communicate with the composer and musicians is of paramount importance. That is to say that music is not just the result of a composer or musician's arbitrary artistic volition; it is the public who, through its *usage, consumption* and *communication* in the form of improvisational interventions such as *gritos* (yells) or a collective social will also contribute to the music that will be produced.[31] In other words, Lara's tropical fetish and Toña's sultry voice are not the only reasons why they were so admired by their Mexican public; they reflected a deeper and more profound collective will, a sort of immanent popular aesthetic that created a mutual identification between the artists and the consumers.

Quintero also discusses the camouflaging of Africa within what he calls "músicas mulatas".[32] I believe this point to be critical because although it is a visual metaphor, it is specifically speaking to the disguised sonic renderings of an African past. In the music of Toña la Negra there exists a cultural acoustics full of tropicalized ambient sounds; yet there are moments, usually at the beginning and the end of her songs, when it is as if she were singing for you. This sonic significance titillates the listener but also constitutes what Edsheim calls a "sonic color-line" that racializes and eroticizes her voice, exemplified by the sensual description by Figueroa. As with the lyrics of Agustín Lara, the black voice is constituted as melodic and melancholic, part and parcel of what makes Veracruz a "tropical" space through the invocation of a black past that made its way to Mexico through the Caribbean.

Sound and "sones" are powerful media for expressing the qualities of a specific time and place. Quintero beautifully explains the power of music and sound to capture time and organize human existence as an element that is both physical and invisible. He maintains that unlike the other senses, the impact of sound is determined by the intensity of its physical vibrations in a specific temporal space.[33] It can register a particular historical moment as well as its prominent metaphors. Sound creates the possibility to feel and to organize; it can trap its producer (as is the case with the racialization of Toña's voice), but it can also release itself from its corporeal cast (the vibrations exist outside of the body and subsequently dissipate). In her book *Into the Vortex*, Britta Sjorgren explains the power of sound in the context of film. Despite referring to a very different artistic medium, she illuminates the role that aural recognition plays in the creation of an alternative paradigm or subjectivity that is not defined by an optic logic:

> The notion of consciousness as proposed by both Vasse and Rosolato relative to the voice provides just such a possible alternative paradigm. According to these theorists, the voice is both of the unconscious and the conscious, of the body and of the Other's body (anterior to the placing of a sexualized value on that body). The recognition of these differences "in" the voice, I argue, may remind of a state in which consciousness of self and Other does not imply dissolution for the subject. Such a voice may enable or incline the spectator to sustain difference, rather than to deny or punish (with a sadistic gaze) the images that accompany his or her sense of heterogeneity.[34]

Here, as suggested by Sjorgren, aurality defies the specular or optic logic that orders our sensorial universe. The voice, as part of the conscious and unconscious, of the body but eerily outside of it, creates this possibility for recognition that within a specular libidinal economy is rendered impossible. Images do accompany sounds, like the ones that have been created through Lara's sexualizing lyrics, or the ambient tropical sounds that racialize the sound of the music, thus creating a visual context for the eruption of the voice. But sound, nonetheless, can elude its materiality, as its vibrations are felt but then dissipate.

Much contemporary theory (and of course psychoanalytic theory) is heavily influenced by a scopic desire that is predicated on the visibility of the phallus. But what happens when you cannot see, when the metaphorical night takes over? The voice takes its place and appropriates space; although voice can still be racialized and inflected, it maintains more open spaces that, according to Sjorgren, deflect the "sadistic gaze". These open spaces are like uninscribed vacuums, silences that simultaneously fill and do not fill. In Mexico, you cannot always "see" blackness, but does that mean it is not there? Does that mean it does not have a place in the making of modern Mexico? There are other forms of "seeing" and "knowing". What prevails in Mexico, at least in my reading, is the aural – the voice.

In the case of Toña la Negra, the medium of sound becomes the mechanism for entertaining and for creating a specifically Mexican product; although as a figure she is sexualized she is simultaneously maternal, a concept not incompatible with Mexican culture. Indeed, critic Roger Bartra theorized on the paradox of the mother/whore dialectic in Mexican society when he coined the term "Chingadalupe".³⁵ Nonetheless, can sound possibly grant agency, or, as is suggested by Sjorgren in her discussion of the "voice-off" in film, can it be a liberatory medium by sustaining difference? I am not sure if Toña la Negra as a cultural practitioner is really effecting that, but she *is* pointing towards another Mexico: one that is present and absent, a Mexico that is nominally black. Toña's name does not allow her to escape this, yet it is through this performance of blackness that she helps to catapult Mexican music to its apex. Aparicio highlights this idea in her claim that tropical music has Toña "sing to the geo-cultural spaces of an Afro-Caribbean Mexico that has remained marginal to an historical social reality invested in its indigenous, pre-Columbian past and in its very rigid European mestizaje".³⁶

Although mestizaje and a museological indigenous legacy have provided the discursive markers for discussions of racial identity in Mexico, this supposed investment in the indigenous past needs to be unpacked, as indigeneity in Mexico has been memorialized as part of a romanticized yesterday, but not part of the living, vital present.³⁷ In any case, like other *mulata* figures, Toña is paradoxically central as a cultural figure who both reflects the relationship between Mexico and blackness as a part of the circum-Caribbean, but deflects it through her status as an exception. The inscription of blackness into her name and voice, although intended to pay homage to her mixed-race ancestry, paradoxically erases it through this status as exception. In other words, despite her racialized subjectivity, Toña, as a black woman, is not the rule. Nonetheless, I would argue that although her blackness may be eclipsed by this idea of exceptionalism, her voice and aural presence prevail.

Son Como Son

The dialectic between *son jarocho* as homegrown and *son cubano* as foreign reproduces itself in Toña's voice, a voice that sings both to the Caribbean and Veracruz as paradoxically and simultaneously the same and other, as a part of her and her nation. Yet the African presence in the Americas, both in the Caribbean and in Mexico, is what curiously links them together, although mediated through their distinct musical trajectories. Tropical music is racialized and sexualized, but Mexican music is considered autochthonous, even though ethnomusicologists have long studied the African antecedents of the *son jarocho*. Nevertheless, Quintero Rivera reminds us, in the case of salsa as well and other "músicas mulatas" in the Americas, that it is not as important to trace the link to Africa as it is to critically recognize the eruption, creation and dissemination of music that is uniquely American, Caribbean, Mexican and, finally, "mulata". He argues that they are not musical traditions created in Africa, brought over and replicated, but rather they are instruments, sounds and rhythms that in their transcultural form generate their own *mulato* style.

On an extremely popular album, *Lamento cubano*, Toña sings an old *son jarocho* entitled, "El cascabel" in a Cuban arrangement by her nephew Pablo Peregrino.[38] The entire album is composed of Cuban music, yet she includes a *son jarocho* and not only riffs off her *jarocha* identity through an appropriation of its quintessential music form, she refashions it. This particular arrangement, although completely Cuban in its rhythm while using the *jarocho* melody and lyrics, ends in a curiously Mexican way. Her prolonged last note jumps up an octave; a style which, although present in *son jarocho*, is common in *sones jalicienses*, or what in the Bajío they call *huapango* (a kind of falsetto). This song symbolizes what I call the dialectics of *son*, as well as its relationship to Toña as its practitioner. It incorporates and appropriates, fearlessly, a traditional *son jarocho* proper to the countryside of Veracruz and combines it beautifully with the rhythm of a Cuban *son*. The back-up vocals in this song are also Cuban in style; perhaps the facility with which this classic *son jarocho* was appropriated is proof of the limits of geopolitical borders and testament to the transcendent possibilities of music through the fluidity of aural movement. The antagonistic musical forces of *son jarocho* as thesis and *son cubano* as antithesis result in this song as its synthesis, as the product of historical movement and change, of a people's musical reaction to different social forces, and of the power of music to not only reflect what socially already exists, but to configure it as well.

I believe the history of music in Veracruz and its relationship to the Caribbean, the contexts and vicissitudes of *son*, whether that be *son cubano*, *jarocho*, *montuno*, *huasteco* or *jaliciense* is fundamental to understanding the importance of music in negotiating the black presence in Mexico: *todos son como son*. It is critical in understanding the prominence of Toña la Negra and her status as the "Jarocha Sensation", diva of the *bolero* and the lone black figure in the twentieth century who represents the contours of Mexico's relationship to blackness. Blackness reaches far back, beyond the immigrations of

Cubans to Mexico in the eighteenth and nineteenth centuries, yet it exists only as residue, as phantasm, or in triangulation with the Caribbean. Her relationship to music, both Cuban and Mexican, reverberates this odd combination of proper and other, the ebb and flow, the comings and goings, the reciprocity and transculturation of Caribbean and Mexican music. In a nation that suffers historical amnesia with regards to its black presence, it allows for *veracruzanos* to appropriate *mulatez*, to become proud of blackness. In the eyes of some nationalists, however, it is always in relation to the Caribbean, and not homegrown. But we should remember that *jarochos* consider themselves part of the greater Caribbean, as is evidenced by the words of the former director of the Institute of Culture: "Veracruz, fortunately, is and will always be, the Caribbean."[39] Perhaps this deflection, and simultaneous tropical inflection, permits them to forget the painful memory of slavery, ignoring the reality of the black presence in order to proclaim them as welcome "guests". The negotiations of Cuban *son* with blackness as well as Tona's identity as "La sensación jarocha" help create Veracruz's identity as port city with an African past. Furthermore the *son jarocho* as an autochthonous musical expression with distinctly African and Caribbean components and the *son cubano* as somehow foreign and proper created this sublimated, mediated, phantasmatic blackness that through movement, transition, aural and oral exchange with the Caribbean becomes simultaneously proper and other, foreign and Mexican.

Conclusion

In many of the representations of *mulatas* in Mexico, as well as in other national traditions, the trope of unknown origins forms a critical element in the construction of the *mulata* subjectivity. This same trope continues to circulate, weaving its way in and out of the narrative fabric surrounding the contributions of blacks to Mexican music. The lost Afro-Mestizo universe that begat "the Chuchumbé" and the *son jarocho* as a musical form testifies to this because there is a fundamental ambiguity surrounding the origin of the Chuchumbé; its arrival with Cuban sailors may just be one of the many myths regarding *mulato*-inspired musical forms. The effect of this proto-son throughout the vice-royalty points to the connection the authorities made between Afro-Mexicans and vice, while its origin in Veracruz or Cuba would explain the "exotic" elements of this nefarious song. The persistence of oral poetry and the spontaneity necessitated by the call and response of the *jarocho* poet is also testament to this long tradition. Finally, the ardent integration of *danzón* and *son cubano*, and the persistence of the former for the last one hundred and twenty years, winding its way back to its place of origin as a part of Cuban culture, speaks to the immanence of Afro-Mestizo culture in Mexico.

The resolution of Mexican society to maintain the invisibility of their African past through the exceptionalization of its *mulato* figures is also part of this narrative of disappearance, despite the towering figure of Toña la Negra, whose paradoxical sultry voice and matriarchal presence constitute her as the quintessential Mexican diva, notwithstanding her claim to blackness. The trope of blackness in Mexican arts is marked by these constant disappearing acts and sudden emergences; the sonic and visual flickers of Africanity belie these supposed cloudy origins as part of a magical, mythical past. Although blackness has been submerged in the post-revolutionary rhetorical construction of Mexicanity, the black voice, with its multiple textures and myriad articulations, has remained through myth, legend, sound and, most importantly, music. Music is one of the nation state's most prized assets; it registers a claim to cultural authenticity and is a source of national pride. Toña's music, sound, voice and figure reflect, almost metonymically, a region deeply marked by racial, social and cultural heterogeneity. This region is a product of the violence, conquest, movement and polyphony that results when diverse peoples come together. The *jarochos* (whether they be boorish men, wild pigs or stick-wielding militiamen) today exhibit a pride in their origins, music and culture, which is both Native and African. However, the case of the African is also mitigated through yet another middle passage: that which passed through the Caribbean in order to land on Veracruz.

Notes

1. For an interesting discussion of how black identity is sometimes explained by a mythified migration of "Cubans" after the Mexican Revolution of 1910 in the town of Coyolillo, Veracruz, see Alfredo Martínez Maranto, "Dios pinta como quiere: Identidad y cultura en un pueblo Afro-Mestizo en Veracruz", in *Presencia africana en México*, ed. Luz Montiel (Mexico City: Consejo Nacional para la Cultura y las Artes, 1997), 525–70.

2. Some important Afro-Mexican scholars have rejected the usage of Afro-Mestizo in favour of Afro-Mexican. Although compelling arguments have been made for this substitution, rather than enter into the debate I will continue to employ both terms interchangeably.
3. According to the eminent anthropologist Gonzalo Aguirre Beltrán in his book *La población negra de México* (Mexico City: Ediciones Fuente Cultural, 1946), *jarocho* was the term that was used to describe the racial mixture between blacks and Amerindians. He declares that the etymological origin of the word stems from the epithet "jaro", which in Muslim Spain meant wild pig, to which they added the pejorative ending "cho". The Spanish supposedly applied this term to those Veracruzanos who were "*mulatos*" and "pardos", intending to call them wild pigs due to their multiple racial combinations. According to the twenty-second edition of the *Real Academia Española*, *jarocho* refers to a person with "boorish and insolent mannerisms". Additionally, the *Real Academia* and some scholars claim the word "jara" denotes both plants and pigs that are a "pardo rojizo" or "reddish-brown". Finally, the historian José Luis Melgarejo Vivanco claims that the term refers to *mulato* militiamen because the origin of the word in this rendition referred to a crude wooden weapon, thus spawning the name "jarochos" to describe the poorly armed *mulato* militiamen (47).
4. The barrio of "La Huaca" is known as a traditional black/*mulato* working-class neighbourhood. Interestingly, it is the barrio where the first samba schools emerged to perform in Veracruz's annual carnival celebrations.
5. This poem, written by Venezuelan poet and politician Andrés Eloy Blanco, was posthumously published in *La Juanbimbada* (1959), but made famous by the musical adaptation sung by Mexican artist Pedro Infante.
6. Rafael Figueroa Hernández, "Rumberos y Jarochos", in *La Habana Veracruz/Veracruz/La Habana*, ed. Bernardo García Díaz and Sergio Guerra Vilaboy (Veracruz, Mexico: Universidad Veracruzana; Havana, Cuba: Universidad de La Habana, 2002), 388–99.
7. Dir. Joselito Rodríguez (Producciones Rodríguez Hermanos, 1948; Cinematográfica Roma, 1970). This film was based on the play by Félix B. Caignet, which in turn was inspired by Fannie Hurst's *Imitation of Life*.
8. Frances R. Aparicio, *Listening to Salsa: Gender, Latin Popular Music, and Puerto Rican Cultures* (Hanover, NH: University Press of New England for Wesleyan University Press, 1998), 175.
9. "Peregrino" is Toña la Negra's surname, which was associated with a successful family dynasty of Mexican musicians from Veracruz. Hence, "La Peregrino" roughly translates to "Ms Peregrino".
10. Figueroa Hernández maintains that the family patriarch, Severo Peregrino, emi-

grated from Port-au-Prince, Haiti, in the nineteenth century ("Rumberos", 388). I have read no other accounts that make this claim.

11. Rafael Figueroa Hernández, *Son Jarocho: Guía Histórico-Musical* (Mexico City: Programa de Apoyo a las Culturas Populares y Comunitarias, 2000).
12. Aparicio, *Listening to Salsa*, 175.
13. This statement was pronounced by the director of the Instituto Veracruzano de Cultura (IVEC) Rafael Arias Hernández in the 1997 anthology of events from the "Afro-Caribbean Festival" in Veracruz. *Fiesta Internacional Afrocaribeño Veracruz* (Veracruz: Instituto Veracruzano de Cultura, 1997).
14. Francisco J. Crespo, "The Globalization of Cuban Music through Mexican Film", in *Cultures of Latin America: Global Effects, Past and Present*, ed. Steven Loza, Jack Bishop and Francisco J. Crespo (Los Angeles: Department of Ethnomusicology and Systematic Musicology, University of California, Los Angeles, 2003), 226.
15. Carl J. Mora, *Mexican Cinema: Reflections of a Society, 1896–2004*, 3rd ed. (Jefferson, NC: McFarland, 2005), 85.
16. Mora, *Mexican Cinema*, 85.
17. Crespo, "The Globalization of Cuban Music", 229.
18. Rafael Arias Hernández, *Fiesta Internacional Afrocaribeño Veracruz*, 1997.
19. Roberto González Echevarría, "Literatura, baile y béisbol", *La Jornada Dominical*, 26 March 1995 (author's translation). The original Spanish is as follows: "Frente a la pacatería peninsular de la última década de XIX, sin embargo, el danzón era algo peligroso, exótico, decadente y demasiado cubano. Se trataba de la incorporación abierta de lo africano a la vida social de las clases acomodadas; una incipiente mulatización de la gente pudiente."
20. Rolando Antonio Pérez Fernández, "El son jarocho como expresión musical afromestiza", in *Cultures of Latin America: Global Effects, Past and Present*, ed. Steven Loza, Jack Bishop and Francisco J. Crespo (Los Angeles: Department of Ethnomusicology and Systematic Musicology, University of California, Los Angeles, 2003), 39–56. In this article, Pérez engages in an extensive discussion of the importance of African rhythms in the *son jarocho*, pointing to the presence of cross-rhythms as seminal.
21. Ángel G. Quintero Rivera, *Salsa, sabor y control* (Mexico City: Siglo Veintiuno Editores, 1998), 34. Author's translation. The original Spanish is as follows: "La música representa, pues, una forma en que las personas interactúan con su mundo; un intento de ejercer cierto control sobre su materialidad, sobre su biología, resignificando colectivamente uno de los elementos consustanciales a la existencia. Tiene, por lo tanto, en todas las sociedades una importancia enorme: una función decisiva en la configuración simbólica de lo social."
22. Figueroa Hernández, "Rumberos", 389. Author's translation. The original Spanish is as follows: "La fuerza y belleza de su voz y su personalidad – aunadas a la genialidad

de Agustín Lara – nos brindaron la calidez y los aromas propios de una ciudad portuaria abierta siempre a los efluvios musicales y culturales provenientes del Caribe."
23. Jesse Varela, "Toña la Negra", *Latin Beat Magazine* 11, no.2 (February 2001), online edition.
24. Agustín Lara, "Lamento jarocho" (1932), *Las 15 Consagradas* (Orfeon Videovox, 2000), author's translation. The original Spanish is as follows:

> Canto a la raza
> raza de bronce, raza jarocha
> que el sol quemó
>
> . . .
>
> Alma de jarocha que nació morena
> talle que se mueve con vaivén de hamaca
>
> . . .
>
> Boca donde gime la mujer doliente
> de toda una raza llena de amarguras
> alma de jarocho que nació valiente
> para sufrir toda su desventura.

25. Vicente Riva Palacio and Juan de Dios Peza, "La mulata de Córdoba", *Tradiciones y leyendas mexicanas* (New York: Thomas Nelson and Sons, 1927).
26. Agustín Lara, "Oración Caribe", *La Sensación Jarocha* (Warner Music Latina, 2002), author's translation. The original Spanish is as follows: "Oración Caribe / que sabe implorar / salmo de los negros / oración del mar."
27. Saidiya Hartman, *Scenes of Subjection* (New York: Oxford University Press, 1997), 26.
28. Quintero, *Salsa*, 34.
29. Figueroa Hernández, "Rumberos", 389.
30. Nina Eidsheim, "Synthesizing Race: Towards an Analysis of the Performativity of Timbre", *Revista Transcultural de Música/Transcultural Music Review* 13 (September 2009), http://www.sibetrans.com/trans/a57/synthesizing-race-towards-an-analysis-of-the-performativity-of-vocal-timbre.
31. Quintero, *Salsa*, 338.
32. Ibid., 16.
33. Ibid., 35.
34. Britta Sjorgren, *Into the Vortex: Female Voice and Paradox in Film* (Urbana: University of Illinois Press, 2006), 14.
35. A term coined by Roger Bartra in *The Cage of Melancholy* (New Brunswick, NJ: Rutgers University Press, 1992) which discusses the importance of the mother/whore dialectic in Mexican society where women are expected to be at once passionate

lovers and consoling, virginal saints. The impossibility of reconciling these contradictory expectations that regulate female behaviour result in the following neologism: "Chingada" (meaning "fucked women" and of course referring to Malintzín, Cortés's consort and mother of the "first" *mestizo* child) and "Lupe" (the Virgin of Guadalupe, the patron saint of the Americas).

36. Aparicio, *Listening to Salsa*, 175.
37. See Analisa Taylor's book, *Indigeneity in the Mexican Cultural Imagination: Thresholds of Belonging* (Tucson: University of Arizona Press, 2009) for a detailed discussion of how indigenous people have been signified in the national imaginary as a product of the paternalistic, state-run project of *Indigenismo*.
38. Toña la Negra, *Lamento Cubano* (Tumbao Cuban Classics, 2004). This song and the first two-thirds of the music from this album were recorded in 1958 with the *conjunto* of Pablo Peregrino. The rest of the music was recorded between 1950 and 1953 with other orchestras, such as that those led by Rafael de Paz, Chamaco Domínguez, Avelino Muñoz and Juan García Esquivel.
39. Rafael Arias Hernández, *Fiesta Internacional Afrocaribeño Veracruz* (Veracruz: Instituto Veracruzano de Cultura, 1997), 12.

Discography

La Negra, Toña. "El Cascabel". *Lamento Cubano*. Perf. Conjunto de Pa lo Peregrino, Avelino Muñoz. Orq. Rafael de Paz, Chamaco Domínguez, Juan García. Tumbao Cuban Classics, compact disc, 2004.
———. *Cenizas*. Orfeon, compact disc, n.d.
———. *Colección Bolero*. Orfeon, compact disc, 2001.
———. *La Sensación Jarocha*. Warner Music Latina, compact disc, 2002.
———. *Las 15 Consagradas*. Orfeon Videovox, compact disc, 2000.
———. *20 Éxitos*. BMG, compact disc, 1995.
Lara, Agustín. "Oración Caribe". *La Sensación Jarocha*. Warner Music Latina, compact disc, 2002.

Part 2.

PERFORMING/CONTESTING IDENTITIES

4.

Guadeloupean Women Performing *Gwo Ka*
Island Presences and Transnational Connections

| KATHE MANAGAN

Introduction

Gwo ka (big drum) is a style of traditional music from the island of Guadeloupe, an overseas department (*Département d'Outre Mer*, or "DOM") of France, located in the Eastern Caribbean. *Gwo ka* music, centred on a type of traditional drumming, accompanied by singing, percussion and dance, has become a symbol of Guadeloupean identity as distinct from French identity, mobilized in independence and cultural revalorization movements on the island and in the metropole (mainland France) since the 1960s. Although this genre of music is envisioned by many as a cultural form that is uniquely Guadeloupean, its symbolic meaning within the Guadeloupean community is more complex and at times ambiguous when investigated in detail. Moreover, this icon of Guadeloupean identity is a largely male-dominated art form, in which women's roles are circumscribed.

It is important to note that Guadeloupean women play a significant role in Guadeloupean society. They are considered the *poto mitan* (centrepost) of the family and of society more generally. Guadeloupean women also enjoy a prominent place in other Guadeloupean musical genres, such as biguine and zouk (made internationally popular by the group Kassav', led by the Martinican singer Jocelyne Béroard). The fact that the independence movement focused on *gwo ka* as the primary icon of Guadeloupean identity, and not one of these other musical genres or some other facet of culture, has the consequence that the central role of women in Guadeloupean society is not highlighted in the symbolism that has been developed around Guadeloupean identity. Had the independence movement focused instead on traditional cuisine, for instance, as the primary icon of Guadeloupean identity, the contribution of women to Guadeloupean identity would have been underscored since most cooking is done by women in Guadeloupe. As we will see in this chapter, however, Guadeloupean women have struggled to have their voice heard in the milieu of *gwo ka* and to actively contribute to the elaboration and revalorization of Guadeloupean identity and transmission of Guadeloupean culture through the practice of *gwo ka*, whether as singers, dancers, drummers, teachers or as event organizers. Women have also been particularly impacted by the forces that have led to transnationalism and thus have important insights to contribute to any discussion of Guadeloupean identity.

This chapter does not make claims to be an exhaustive study of the role of women in Guadeloupean *gwo ka* music and dance, nor is it a detailed discussion of one artist. Instead, it is based on my own personal experiences and discussions with those in the *gwo ka* milieu in Guadeloupe since 1998 and on interviews conducted with women who are part of the *gwo ka* scene in Guadeloupe today, specifically those who have some type of transnational experience. In what follows I discuss what exactly *gwo ka* is, then briefly outline Guadeloupe's history, focusing on its relationship with France. I then discuss a selection of interviews with female *gwo ka* singers, dancers and drummers. And finally, I examine transnational connections in terms of the relationship that Guadeloupeans have with France, and their affective and ancestral connections with Africa, as seen in *gwo ka*, noting how the lives of the women I interviewed exemplify and illustrate the complexities of these transnational connections.

Gwo Ka and Its Image in Guadeloupe

Gwo ka is the term that, in contemporary Guadeloupe, refers to a type of music based on the sounds of a drum made from a large barrel and covered with a goatskin. Historical documentation reveals that this type of drumming and the dance and singing that goes along with it, has existed in some form from early in the colonial period.[1] At times, the drum has been referred to as tam-tam or *gros tambour* (large drum), but today it is almost exclusively called *gwo ka*.[2]

Gwo ka is most often heard and performed in a traditional *swaré léwoz* (or simply *léwoz*) or *kout tambour*. These types of performances, once disparaged because they were seen as uncivilized, now take place all over the island on weekend nights. The audience gathers in a semi-circle around a group of drummers, singers and musicians who play other percussion instruments. Most often, lead singers, drummers and many musicians playing other percussion instruments are men, while women tend to be back-up singers in the chorus. As the musicians play, audience members, men and women, may come to the centre of the circle, one at a time, to dance to the drumming. *Léwoz* is also the name of one of the seven primary rhythms played on the *gwo ka* drum. The other rhythms are *toumblak, woulé, kaladja, padjambél, graj* and *menndé*. A soloist, almost always a man, improvises on these main rhythms. When audience members get up to dance, they dance to the soloist's rhythm. Or, more accurately, the dancer lets the soloist know which rhythm she or he would like to dance to by their movements. During a *léwoz*, each song begins with the singer, generally male, who calls out the refrain, repeated by the chorus in the style of call and response. The singer also indicates when the drumming should begin, and often calls out which rhythm should be played. The audience, made up of men, women and children of various ages, is often encouraged to clap along, as they are seen as an integral part of the *ronde* (circle) that makes up the *léwoz*.

As the evening wears on at a *léwoz*, the audience, sometimes inspired by shots of rum, gets more and more animated and the dancers' gestures more and more sexually suggestive. The ambience of this type of event is typically *chaud* (hot). The rhythms draw the audience in and it is difficult not to at least clap along. It is common for these concerts to go on until late in the night, even until dawn. These aspects of *gwo ka*, the fact that the *léwoz* takes place late at night, involves sexually suggestive dancing and the consumption of alcohol, are what some point to as uncivilized aspects of Guadeloupean society. *Gwo ka*'s image within Guadeloupean society is tarnished by its association with all that is seen as not French, not respectable, and associated with plantation slavery, the past and Africa. Women in particular are expected to uphold notions of respectability, and any association with *gwo ka* is much more detrimental to a woman's status and reputation than is the case for men. As we will see, this is one reason that women's roles in *gwo ka* have been constrained.

Gwo ka suffers from its association with the past and with slavery, as much as it benefits from it. A term used to refer to older practices viewed as unrespectable and uncivilized is *vyé nég* (old black). In this derogatory usage, it is used to refer to people or things connected with an earlier period of Guadeloupe's history when Guadeloupe was less developed, such as traditional *gwo ka* drumming, rum drinking and basilectal Kréyòl (the variety that has the least influence from French and is viewed as the most pure by most Guadeloupeans). As Schnepel notes, *vyé* may also mean lazy, dirty, bad or ugly.[3] This term also has rural connotations. I never heard it used to refer to people living today. Thomas discusses the ideology of blackness in Jamaican national and everyday ideology, arguing that that popular images of black identity are distanced from reminders of slavery and the past, as Jamaicans would prefer to see themselves in images of modernity.[4] Similarly, Guadeloupeans today value their traditions and heritage, but prefer to see themselves as modern and on par with the metropole.[5]

Although *gwo ka* was once looked down on by many Guadeloupeans, it was later held up by the independence movement as an icon of a distinctive, separate Guadeloupean identity, as I shall discuss. This is because of its connotations of agricultural labour and also because it is frequently seen as local rather than French ("local" meaning being associated with African derivation). *Gwo ka* music has been the focus of major efforts to preserve it as part of Guadeloupe's *patrimoine* (cultural heritage). Today it has been embraced by a wider range of the population, in large part due to the efforts of women, such as Jacqueline Cachemire-Thôle, who has transmitted *gwo ka* dance skills to a wide range of students in her school, Akadémiduka. *Gwo ka* does appeal to certain segments of the young population even though it is not as popular among youth as zouk, rap or jump up. Some *gwo ka* songs are played on the radio and one sees children and adolescents at the *léwoz*. Many young Guadeloupeans also are learning to dance or play the drum. There are several different schools, many run by women, and there are also individuals in Guadeloupe who offer *gwo ka* drumming and dance classes, which have become quite popular. The *léwoz* tradition, long associated with drunkenness and indecency, has been brought back, developed and transformed into a practice many Guadeloupeans now value and respect. As I will explain, women have played an important role in maintaining and revitalizing *gwo ka*, even though it has come to be dominated by men. Nonetheless, many Guadeloupeans still feel it is inappropriate for women to practice drumming. And some even feel that women have no place singing either, as we will see.

My Research and Experience with *Gwo Ka*

I first became familiar with *gwo ka* while attending a music festival in Lafayette, Louisiana. The Festival International de Lafayette is one of many international festivals that *gwo ka* groups may perform at. While *gwo ka* is not as well known internationally as zouk, many Guadeloupean artists I've spoken with over the years have played at festivals in the United States, France, Africa and other Caribbean islands. In 1998, I began conducting ethnographic research in Guadeloupe, focusing on language and identity. While conducting my dissertation research from 1999 to 2001, I signed up for a weekly *gwo ka* drumming class. I took these classes for my own pleasure, but it enabled me to collect data about a traditional practice mobilized as an icon of Guadeloupean identity. Class members were mainly in their teens or early twenties, although there were those in their thirties or forties as well. The class members, particularly those who continued taking the classes and attended regularly, were predominantly male, although there were three other women in my class, and our participation was never discouraged in my observation. My friends and research consultants outside of the drumming class often commented on the fact that I was learning to play the drum. Several people suggested that this made me *plus guadeloupéen qu'un guadeloupéen* (more Guadeloupean than a Guadeloupean), because this practice is seen as closely linked with Guadeloupean identity, and few Guadeloupeans actually know how to play or even dance. Aside from these positive comments I received, I was also often asked if I was taking dance classes as well, or why I was not. It became clear to that for many (especially men) my learning to play the drum made little sense, since women are expected to learn to dance *gwo ka*, not drum.

A Brief History of Guadeloupe

The French established settlements on Guadeloupe in 1635; their interest in Guadeloupe centred on plantation-based sugarcane cultivation made possible through the forced labour of enslaved Africans. Slavery was abolished twice in Guadeloupe. It was first abolished in 1794 during the French Revolution, but, in 1802, after Napoleon Bonaparte came to power in France, a delegation was sent to re-establish slavery. The arrival of French troops prompted a revolt in Guadeloupe, which was eventually put down by French forces, resulting in the death of many. Today, some of those killed fighting against the French are considered heroes in Guadeloupe, including a woman referred to as La Mulatresse Solitude. Solitude has emerged as a crucial figure in the Guadeloupean imaginary and is used as an example to explain the significant role that women play in Guadeloupe today. *Gwo ka* is also often times linked to this history of resistance and is considered by many to have been a means by which enslaved Africans and maroons in Guadeloupe communicated with each other and organized revolts.

Slavery was eventually permanently abolished in all the French colonies in 1848.[6] Following emancipation, all Guadeloupeans were granted French citizenship; Guadeloupe remained a French colony though and maintained close ties to France. Guadeloupe became an overseas department of France in 1946, acquiring nearly the same administrative status as the mainland departments.[7] The French constitution adopted clauses (articles 72 and 73) that allow for different measures to be instituted in the DOMs to account for their local specificities.[8] For example, it was not until 1996 that French law required the minimum wage in the DOMs to be same as in the metropole.

The period after the Second World War brought about many changes in Guadeloupe besides a shift from colonial to departmental status. After the War, sugar plantations on the islands began to close for economic reasons.[9] The closure of the sugar mills and the decrease in sugarcane production drastically affected the island's economy, motivated some urban migration and led to social unrest. After departmentalization, the French also instituted measures to bring the living conditions in the DOMs in line with those of the metropole. In the post-war period, Guadeloupe also experienced a demographic boom, linked to improvements in health care and the institution of a social security system. This period was thus a time of rapid development, but also of social upheaval.

In 1962, as a means of reducing social tensions associated with the unemployment caused by the closure of sugar plantations, as well as meeting metropolitan labour needs, the French government created a bureau for overseas migration, BUMIDOM (*Bureau pour les Migrations Intéressant les Départements d'Outre-Mer*), which encouraged migration between Guadeloupe and the metropole.[10] Migration between Guadeloupe and France has historically been regulated in part by the metropole. With BUMIDOM, the migration of labourers, and later family members, was specifically encouraged, through recruitment and incentives including job training and paid, one-way airfare. At the outset, BUMIDOM facilitated the migration of more men than women, but by 1967, women and men migrated in relatively equal numbers.[11] BUMIDOM, along with private businesses and individuals, recruited Antillean migrants for specific employment sectors, and these followed cultural expectations of a sexual division of labour. Antillean women were recruited as domestic servants and hospital workers.[12] Between 1963 and 1981, 35,785 Antillean women (from Guadeloupe and Martinique) migrated to France with the help of BUMIDOM.[13] Many more migrated on their own or with the help of family or employers. Although BUMIDOM organized this labour migration and offered some training to migrants, not all migrants ultimately stayed on in the positions they were recruited for. Many migrants chose to join family and friends in the Paris area after they had been trained elsewhere. The academic literature notes that some migrants had difficulty finding work or housing after their training, but one must turn to popular anecdotes and music to hear of the darker side of migration, stories of those who dropped out of official documentation. The song "A Kòz Don Biyé San Fwan" by *gwo ka* singer Erick Cosaque (who himself lived in the metropole for many years), for instance, sings of the BUMIDOM migration and how some were exploited and even turned to prostitution.[14] During one of my interviews for this chapter, Josie Balzamont described her own experience that demonstrated the truth in Cosaque's song. She went to France to be with her mother, who had left Guadeloupe with the help of BUMIDOM, only to find that her mother was working as a prostitute. I have no idea how common or representative Mme Balzamont's experience may be, but it suggests that Cosaque sang the truth in that song.

When the Left came to power in France in 1982, they changed the official policy on Antillean migration. To discourage migration, they enacted a plan of economic stimulation in the French West Indies and instituted additional measures to facilitate the integration of the Antilleans in France. To this end, BUMIDOM was replaced by ANT (*l'Agence nationale pour l'insertion et la promotion des travailleurs d'Outre-Mer*), which was similar but it also emphasized the preservation of Antillean culture among immigrant groups in France, promoted return to the islands and served to reunite families.[15] In more recent years, the ANT budget has not been sufficient to continue many of these initiatives and thus it has scaled back its overall activity.

Since Guadeloupeans are French citizens (and the French government does not keep records based on its citizens' ethnicity or race), their movement between the island and the metropole is difficult to track. Marie suggests that 40 per cent of the Antillean population lives in the metropole. Whereas early migrants to the metropole, prior to BUMIDOM, were mostly elites, students or government employees, today migrants represent a broader spectrum of the population, including many women.[16] In my observation, migration touches all segments of the population of Guadeloupe, from the youngest to the oldest, the wealthy as well as those of more modest means, women and men. Given the difficult employment situation in Guadeloupe, many Guadeloupeans still see migration to the metropole as the only way to secure a decent job. Guadeloupeans living in France are able to maintain close ties with friends and family through communication technologies as well as visits. During the summer months, the island population swells with the return visits of these *vacanciers* (these are "vacationers", as opposed to "tourists", meaning non-Antilleans who visit the island). Since the early 1980s, there is a growing trend toward return migration.[17] Also, today young adult Guadeloupeans are choosing more often to study and work outside of France, especially in the United Kingdom and the United States.

Despite French government efforts to quell social unrest in the French West Indies in the 1960s, an independence movement emerged, calling for autonomy of Guadeloupe and Martinique from France. Radical calls for independence first emerged among Antillean student groups in the metropole. These students were influenced by the student movements in France during the late 1960s (for example, the student protests of May 1968). Later, as students returned home, French West Indian groups arose calling for independence from France, such as *Groupe d'Organisation Nationale de Guadeloupe* in Guadeloupe. During the 1970s and 1980s these groups concentrated on attracting the support of agricultural workers and took over control of the local trade unions. The independence movement focused on social practices associated with peasant farmers – practices envisioned as in danger of being lost as Guadeloupe assimilated into France – as emblems of a distinctive Guadeloupean identity.[18] Along with the local creole language, called Kréyòl, *gwo ka* served as a primary icon distinguishing Guadeloupean identity from French identity.[19] In 2009, the unions allied with many local cultural and social groups to speak out against the high cost of living and other injustices and to proclaim their distinctive identity. This alliance was called the LKP (*Lyannaj Kont Pwofitasyon*, meaning "the alliance against exploitation and harassment"). A general strike mobilized large segments of the population, lasted for forty-four days, from January to March, and made international news.

As a central icon of Guadeloupean identity, *gwo ka* has played a crucial role in union activities. *Gwo ka* drumming is often heard at protests and picket lines, and a *léwoz* is organized each year by the UGTG union (*Union Générale des Travailleurs de la Guadeloupe*, meaning "the general union of Guadeloupean workers"). For example, *gwo ka* drumming was heard outside of meetings when French officials met with the LKP. As well, a women's group created during the strike called *Fanm Debout o Ka* (Women Standing Up with Ka) put out an album of songs in support of the LKP. But, until the recent general strike, independentists and other pro-autonomists have remained fragmented and never achieved sufficient popular support to present significant opposition to departmental status.[20] Their occasional violent tactics, moreover, contribute to a lack of widespread public support for the independence movement and its icons, *gwo ka* and Kréyòl.

Women in *Gwo Ka*

As I mentioned in the above section on Guadeloupean history, women have played an active role in many of the defining moments of Guadeloupean society. In the next sections I will discuss interviews I collected that give some indication of the range of experience of women who are part of the *gwo ka* milieu today. The interviewees were selected in part because I knew they had experience living in France or elsewhere, so as to uncover transnational connections. Their stories have a lot to say about individual experience in *gwo ka* for women and about experiences with migration to France and Africa. These interviews thus illustrate the lived experience behind the historical facts I included above.

Lanmou Famn Ka et Mme Dancher

Mme Dancher is a founding member of the group *Lanmou Famn Ka* (Love, Woman, Ka), a group that was formed in 2007. Their first performance was at a commemoration of the abolition of slavery. During the ceremony, different groups representing the diversity of Guadeloupean society played the seven rhythms of *gwo ka*. Their group represented women, and they played a *graj* rhythm. Today this group consists of sixteen women.

Mme Dancher explained that the women in the group were all of a generation when *gwo ka* was disparaged, and girls, in particular, were discouraged from playing, dancing or having anything to do with *gwo ka*. Even simply tapping a rhythm on a table would bring reproach. The members of the group were born between 1954 and 1965, after departmentalization and around the time of BUMIDOM. As Mme Dancher described, this was a time when there was an effort to "erase Kréyòl, traditional music and anything that reminded them too much of pain, of Africa, of slavery". Girls were prevented from singing, or even worse drumming, because of *gwo ka*'s association with *vyé nég*. In their group specifically, members have all been the daughters of *fonctionnaires* (civil servants and those in administrative jobs, who are mainly from the middle class). But, as she said, "*sa ka taw (sé taw)*", a proverb that means "that which is yours (is yours)", and thus you cannot take it away. In this case, "it" refers to *gwo ka*, viewed as something that belongs to all Guadeloupeans.

She learned to play the drum on her own, like most of the members of the group. Presently, there are two women in the group who learned through their brothers who play. But, she stressed, for her and for their group, playing *gwo ka* was not an act of vengeance, but rather a reclaiming of their rightful place. She acknowledged the work of older women like Margritte Dupuy and Man Soso who resisted social pressure and made it possible for women today to have a role in the world of *gwo ka*. That being said, Lanmou Famn Ka was not easily accepted. Their group has played in various open air spaces in the town of Moule. Mme Dancher said that many times men came up and did not hesitate to make comments about women playing. In one instance, she let one young man play her drum, as a way to learn from him, but then he did not want to give her back her own instrument, as he believed women should not play.

She told me several anecdotes about how their group was initially not accepted by well-known male singers and musicians, but they later managed to win them over. For instance, they were invited to play at an homage to Erick Cosaque, a singer whose views on women in *gwo ka* are well known. He has famously spoken out against women sitting on or merely touching a *gwo ka* drum. They were invited by the event organizers, and not Cosaque, in order to provoke him, but in a gentle, joking way. Lanmou Famn Ka performed, playing an old song of his. In addition, they made a point of stating that they did not sit on the drums, as *boula* drummers (those who set the rhythm for a song) normally do (playing the drum while sitting astride it), but that they played anyway. When they finished, he told them to keep up their work because they had done a good job with a difficult song. He said they were *bien hardies* (very courageous, daring, audacious).

Some of the members of the group have lived in France, returning to Guadeloupe after retirement. Mme Dancher herself only returned to Guadeloupe in 2006 after living for a time in West Africa and spending fifteen years on the Canary Islands. She said she went to Africa because of her husband, which means that she was not going there to search for her roots. When she returned to Guadeloupe, she took *gwo ka* dance classes. For all her time spent living in Africa and the Canary Islands, though, she did not have much good to say. She mentioned, for instance, that she was not happy living in Africa and resented particularly the fact that several people called her the "daughter of slaves", thus highlighting the differences between her and them. She did not experience her time in Africa as a homecoming, as many African Americans and Afro-Caribbeans frame a trip to Africa, but rather felt out of place and suggests she was treated as though she were, in fact, out of place. In my own experience, when speaking with a Congolese friend visiting Guadeloupe, he often highlighted the differences between himself and Guadeloupeans by referring to them as the sons and daughter of slaves, which suggests that this expression and the beliefs that underlie it may be somewhat widespread. In my interview with Mme Dancher, she only mentioned her time living in Africa briefly, but in her comments she stressed the cultural differences between Guadeloupeans and Africans, often describing African practices in a negative light.

Mme Dancher stressed that her group makes efforts to maintain their femininity. They play in traditional dresses, and wear high heels and jewellery. In this, they see themselves as distinguishing themselves from some other women's *gwo ka* groups. Mme Dancher suggested that this is perhaps a reason they have eventually been accepted. They also set themselves apart from some other women's *gwo ka* groups by playing the drum while seated in chairs. Normally, drummers – all but the soloist – sit astride the drum. Although Lanmou Famn Ka only recently began playing together, and in most cases only recently learned to play, they have performed at many events, usually playing on stage or opening up a *léwoz*, for other (male) performers.

Kamodjaka et Raymonde Thorin

Mme Raymonde Thorin is the artistic director of Kamodjaka, a dance school, youth organization and dance troupe. Mme Thorin explained to me that in the 1980s, she took part in the first women's *gwo ka* group in Guadeloupe. The *gwo ka* master Marcel Lollia, known as Vélo (credited as one of the musicians responsible for keeping the tradition alive), taught her and others to play. At the time, her mother owned a store that Vélo frequented.

Based on what she said about her own experience and what I'd heard from others, I asked Mme Thorin if she thought that women had a more significant role in *gwo ka* in the past that has since been downplayed, especially by men. She mentioned some important female figures in *gwo ka*, such as Loulouse (mother of Napoléon Magloire), Man Simone and Man Geoffroy (the mother of the Geoffroy brothers and sisters in the group Kan'nida).[21] She also mentioned Man Soso, who was more of a dancer than a singer, but who played an important role in the *gwo ka* milieu by organizing *léwoz*.[22] Mme Thorin argued that *gwo ka* is still alive today not because of the implication of independentists, as one often hears, but rather because women appropriated *gwo ka*. She noted that women such as Man Soso and Man Geoffroy had organized *rondes a léwoz*. Women such as Man Adeline and Man Dota created folkloric dance troupes, and they are often criticized for being *doudouiste* (a derogatory term meaning "to folklorize", especially for an external tourist market). But Mme Thorin stressed that earlier women's efforts, including those today viewed as *doudouiste*, may have served to keep *gwo ka* alive. And, more recently, women such as Jacqueline Cachemire-Thôle have kept the artistic side of *gwo ka* alive by creating schools of dance. Indeed, Mme Cachemire-Thôle was the driving force in the creation of the Akedémiduka school, which teaches drumming and dance and has a professional troupe. The Akadémiduka has launched the careers of others, such as Mme Thorin.

Mme Thorin notes that, while she began playing in the female orchestra under the guidance of Vélo, she almost never plays the drum today. Instead, she has dedicated herself to singing, dancing, choreography and teaching others through Kamodjaka. She points out that women who do play the *ka* rarely do so at *léwoz*. This is because the *léwoz* is viewed by many as a site where experts perform – including singers, drummers and dancers. In my own experience, however, I have seen many male singers, dancers and drummers who lack expertise get up and perform without hesitation. They do sometimes encounter negative feedback, but not to the extent that women do, no matter what their level of skill. Mme Thorin pointed out that women also rarely play at *léwoz* because others make it difficult for them. If a woman is playing the base rhythm (*boula*), others will try and wear her out. *Boula* drummers play one of the seven rhythms during an entire song, which may last ten to fifteen minutes while dancers enter the circle, and this requires endurance, especially for the faster and more complex rhythms. By calling drummers to play such rhythms in songs back to back during a *léwoz*, a singer may try to wear a drummer out. If she is playing solo (*maké*), improvising on the *boula*'s rhythm, often following a dancer's movements, others will try to trip her up. Women play at *léwoz* usually only under special circumstances. For instance, Mme Thorin drummed for a few songs at a *léwoz* organized by her own group Kamodjaka. She felt that there were a few women who could play at a *léwoz*, based on their skill level. In my own experience, women do sing at *léwoz*, but I have only seen women play *léwoz* organized by and for women (for example, at the *léwoz* organized in the honour of Man Soso which I will discuss in more detail later).

Mme Thorin mentioned that women have difficulty being accepted as singers of *gwo ka*, in part because of the expectations of the local audience. Guadeloupeans prefer *gwo ka* singing in a lower pitch and even appreciate rough voices over refined ones. Thorin's singing voice approaches this aesthetic, which has been to her advantage.

Like most of the other women I interviewed, and very many Guadeloupeans, Mme Thorin lived for a period of time in the metropole; she spent four years living in Rheims, a city that lies eighty miles to the northeast of Paris. For her, *gwo ka* and the *gwo ka* artists living in the metropole at the time, including Erick Cosaque, served as "a lifesaver, a breath of fresh air". Other women I interviewed expressed this same sentiment. It seems that their interest and participation in *gwo ka* was reinforced because of their experience of living in the metropole or elsewhere. Thus, migration may be a factor in *gwo ka*'s resurgence, and especially women's participation in it. *Gwo ka* is also a key element serving to maintain transnational ties. Mme Thorin noted that *léwoz* were organized in France and attract large numbers of people (around one to six thousand people), although they are a bit different than in Guadeloupe, being played inside buildings rather than in open air and including some mixing with Martinican *bélé* music.

With her group, she has organized workshops to introduce Guadeloupean traditions of *gwo ka* to the metropole. This was for her a way of maintaining the tradition. But, in her choreography and dance classes, other influences are embraced. Her dance includes hip-hop elements, for instance. Kamodjaka has also used their performances to comment on the relationship between Guadeloupeans in France and on the island. In 2006, they produced an end of the year performance, entitled "*Nou ka sanm san sanm men nou ansam*" ("We are alike without being alike/resembling each other, but we're untied"). The performance theme was "*notre diversité et nos différences sont notre force, que l'on soit natif natal ou guadeloupéens vivant en France métropolitaine: solidarité*" ("our diversity and our differences are our strength, whether one is a native Guadeloupean or living in metropolitan France: solidarity").

When I asked her about other links outside of the island, she noted that there are indeed ties. For instance, Kamodjaka is working on an exchange programme with Louisiana and has participated in cultural activities with other Caribbean countries. She felt, however, that women in Guadeloupe have invested in their traditional music (here, she seems to be referring to drumming in particular) more so than in other Caribbean countries or in Africa. Likewise, she stressed the importance of Guadeloupean women in politics, arguing that there are more Guadeloupean women in politics than in the other departments of France or in other Caribbean countries. She mentioned the names of politicians Gerty Archiméde, Michelle Lucette-Chevry and Marie-Luce Penchard. She also noted that, during the general strike of 2009, journalists commented on the fact that so many women participated. She noted that it is not a coincidence that the *marraine* (symbolic patron) of the group is Solitude, the woman who was made a heroine for resisting the 1802 reestablishment of slavery. This image of the Guadeloupean woman as strong, defiant pillar of Guadeloupean society is a trope that can serve to enable women to carve out a place for their own expression, even in a context like *gwo ka* that is dominated by men.

Kalindika et Marie-Line Dahomay

For Marie-Line Dahomay, the introduction to *gwo ka*, and Guadeloupean music more generally, came through her family. Her sisters were politically active and often brought her with them to events in Pointe-à-Pitre, where *gwo ka* was played in independentist gatherings. Her brother was also a singer in the group Kafé. In the early 1980s, Mme Dahomay began singing in the group Ka Touré while living in the metropole. This group played a style of *gwo ka* known as *gwo ka évolutif*, a modern style that draws on other musical genres and breaks with some of the more rigid traditions of *gwo ka* (by including other instruments, for example). It was while living in the metropole that Mme Dahomay also began composing her own songs. While her music falls within the wide genre of *gwo ka*, she is influenced by other musical genres as well, such as jazz, Indian music and bossa nova. Between 1987 and 1993, she was a central member of a women's *gwo ka* group in Guadeloupe called Kalindika. At one point, there were six women in the group. This group is still in existence, and Mme Dahomay is its lead singer, but today this group does not have an exclusively female membership. In the different groups with which she has sung, Mme Dahomay has travelled and performed in many other countries, including the United States, Canada, France and Cuba. She also participated in the women's group that recorded an album in support of the LKP, as did Mme Thorin.

In addition to her work with Kalindika, Mme Dahomay has been involved in the promotion of women in the milieu of *gwo ka* through the *association* Aka Soso (meaning "at Soso's house"), which has organized women's *léwoz* in honour of Man Soso. Man Soso, she points out, helped to keep *gwo ka* alive by organizing *léwoz*, but also by dancing and singing *gwo ka*. *Léwoz* in Man Soso's honour were organized in 2005, 2006 and 2007. Unfortunately, the association has become less active, and the annual *léwoz* was not organized since 2007.

Like Mme Thorin, Mme Dahomay noted the fact that, in her previous experience, local expectations of *gwo ka* singing voices have not allowed place for different women's voices. She complained about the fact that often in public performances, the sound system is not well regulated, which makes it difficult to sing, and then, on top of that, accompanying musicians and singers try to get her (and other women) to sing in a lower pitch. She feels that this practice damages her voice. She believes that the different qualities and harmonies of women's voices need to gain appreciation in Guadeloupe in order for female singers to be successful.

Transnationalism and Guadeloupe: Complex Ties to France

Since the early 1990s, scholars have increasingly turned their attention to changing notions of space, time and community. For example, Manuel Castells speaks of a space of flows, David Harvey refers to "space-time compression" and Gupta and Ferguson discuss the impact of globalization on notions of space and place (specifically, the social construction of space into meaningful places).[23] The dominant trend in this multidisciplinary body of work is the notion that new technologies have resulted in a situation where people and capital more easily cross and link together geographical boundaries that were once seen as separate and more easily defined. In this context, the logic of the nation-state, or at least the definition of long-established nation-states, has evolved, and some would suggest waned or even disappeared. At the same time, groups throughout the world are reclaiming their specific identities, often times using new technologies to enable transnational linkages.[24]

As scholars have begun to examine these new relationships between space, culture, nation, identity and society, their research has focused on borderlands, interstitialily and hybridity. Thomas and Slocum have argued that this trend has brought to the forefront of anthropological theorization the Caribbean region, long ignored in anthropology because of its complexity.[25] As Trouillot notes, the Caribbean, marked by globalization and transnationalism from early days of European colonization, is quintessentially modern, or even postmodern.[26]

The Caribbean has, since the colonial period and perhaps before, been characterized by contact and linkages that extend beyond geographically contiguous boundaries. Those studying the Caribbean must recognize the significance of ties between European metropoles and their colonies, ties that include language, transportation, trade, cultural practices and beliefs, and feelings and imaginings of community. Still, despite the fact that migration has always been a fact of life for Caribbean peoples, in the Caribbean one also feels the effects of postmodernity, transnationalism and the concomitant increase in discussion of identity politics.

Transnationalism and Guadeloupe: The Image of Africa

Just as ongoing links to the metropole must be recognized, one must also take into account ties between the Caribbean and Africa. Although links of transportation and trade have been severed, linguistic, cultural and emotional links remain. Some scholars, such as Melville Herskovits (1941), have sought to uncover African retentions as a way of explaining the complexity of Caribbean language, culture and society.[27] At the very least, ties with Africa are maintained through imaginings of community, and African-inspired religious and cultural practices, such as Rastafarianism or Kwanzaa, have been created throughout the African diaspora to embody this sense of shared identity.

It is noteworthy that Guadeloupeans I spoke with rarely mentioned the African contributions to Kréyòl or other cultural practices.[28] Those who did tended to be better educated, or activists familiar with academic writing on African retentions. For example, the lyrics of a *gwo ka* song written by the band Kan'nida attempt to reclaim the roots of *gwo ka* music and make the genre more popular, explaining,

> Kréyòl is a Congo soup [a local okra soup with many ingredients]
> A bit of English, a little pinch of Spanish
> A little bit of French
> A big spoonful of African
> It gives you the Kréyòl language,
> it gives you the creole culture.[29]

Most often, though, the origins of creole culture and creole practices and attitudes in general were imaginatively located in the slave period, as those of (African-descended) slaves, not as those of Africans living in Africa.

The one arena where reference to Africa is frequently made is in *gwo ka* songs as well as comments made by singers between songs during *léwoz*. The *menndé* rhythm, for instance, is widely considered to be a rhythm that was introduced into the *gwo ka* repertoire after slavery was abolished, when indentured workers from the French Congo were brought over (along with indentured workers from India and China). This rhythm is sometimes referred to as "the African rhythm". These indentured workers who came from the Congo have maintained a community in the town of Capesterre-Belle-Eau, providing tangible traces to an African past. This Congolese-descended community is best known for the *grap a kongo* ritual for the dead that takes place on All Souls Day, where members of the community sing in Kikongo.[30] Younger generations and members of the audience do not necessarily understand what is being sung. We find reference to the *nég kongo* (Congolese) in song lyrics, comments made during performances, as well as in day-to-day conversations. The term *nég kongo* thus refers specifically to this population, although in some uses it seems to refer more broadly to those who have come directly from Africa, as opposed to local creoles. One also finds the image of Africa in *gwo ka* lyrics. A traditional song, with some variations, talks about "nég kongo, nég kongo, i pa ka palé kréyòl, i pa ka palé fwansé, i ka palé (yenki) wani wani, i ka palé charabiya" (the Congolese, she or he does not speak creole, she or he does not speak French, she or he speaks only gibberish). In one version I heard, the singer also sang "i ka palé lingala" (she or he speaks Lingala), demonstrating some knowledge of languages actually spoken in Congo. At a *léwoz* in summer 2009, I heard a singer begin talking, before requesting a *menndé* rhythm to sing to, about how we (the audience) are all Congolese. As an aside, a Congolese friend I was with, once I translated that statement from Kréyòl, did not find that statement very amusing or feel this same sense of connection. Other songs refer to Africa and Africans. At the Gwo Ka Festival in Sainte Anne in summer 2009, the group Voukoum sang a song with lyrics that contained the words "Afriken pa pléré ba mwen . . . gwadloupéen asé pléré" (Africans do not cry to me . . . Guadeloupeans have cried enough). A well-known song by Zagalo, entitled "Nég la", speaks instead about black people having been discriminated against because of their race and refers both to himself and his own pride in being black, as well as to conditions of poverty and starvation in Africa.[31]

At *léwoz*, you sometimes see performers and audience members dressed in African dress. While it is most common for Guadeloupeans to wear a more European style of dress (with a definite Caribbean twist), those who are closely aligned with the independence movement or with language and cultural revitalization sometimes proclaim their connections with an African past by wearing clothing made of African material and in African style. African dance music, especially *soukous* and *coupé décalé*, is popular in Guadeloupe, and several dance schools and gyms offer African dance classes. But for many, this popularity seems more to come from simply appreciating the music and dance than from any seeking of roots or a sense of shared identity. After all, salsa music and dance are also quite popular. Thomas notes in her research on Jamaica that the image of Africa and a sense of imagined community with Africans is a contested image.[32] The same is true in Guadeloupe. In my own experience, while Guadeloupeans recognize that they have ancestors who came from Africa, feelings about Africa and its people today are more ambiguous, and at times quite negative. But in *gwo ka* music and performance, it is most common to find positive images and expressions of a shared sense of identity with Africans. Indeed, *gwo ka*, more than Kréyòl or other local cultural practices, is viewed as being directly linked to African practice. As we saw in the song lyrics above, Kréyòl is viewed as that which distinguishes local creoles from Africans, but *gwo ka* drumming and dance are considered to be more of a pure African retention, an embodiment of Africa in contemporary Guadeloupe.

Actual ties in the present with Africa are generally very limited in Guadeloupe. I have met only a few African immigrants living in Guadeloupe. There is a much larger community in France, oftentimes living in the neighbourhoods and interacting with French West Indians.[33] Some of the women I interviewed had actually lived in Africa, as I will discuss. Although in my research I have met a few Guadeloupeans who have travelled to Africa or even lived there, it is hardly the most common destination for Guadeloupean travel. But *gwo ka* musicians in better-known groups do have opportunities to travel to Africa to perform in festivals, which may be a site where transnational connections are made in terms of music.

Les Ballets Briscantes et Josie Balzamont

Mme Balzamont left Guadeloupe to go to France in search of her mother when she was seventeen years old. Mme Balzamont's mother became pregnant at a young age, and following the customs of the time, Mme Balzamont was raised by her grandparents and told that her biological mother was simply a cousin. Once she got older and learned the truth, she decided to seek out her mother, who had moved to the metropole with the help of BUMIDOM. Mme Balzamont did not, however, find a mother anxious to take her in. Instead, she discovered that her mother had turned to prostitution and could not, or did not want to, take care of her. Mme Balzamont's mother abandoned her and went to live in Switzerland. Left on her own (her family in Guadeloupe refused to help since she had made the choice to leave herself), Mme Balzamont continued her studies and did her best to survive. One night, she was discovered by Henri Duchel, who was the director of Les Ballets Briscantes in France. This troupe performed folkloric Antillean dance, not traditional ballet, in a Parisian restaurant and also travelled around the world.[34] With this troupe, she travelled and performed in Togo, Benin, Greece, Switzerland, Italy and Corsica. She also danced with the Ballet Kodia (a dance company in the Republic of Congo which performs traditional Congolese dance) and performed with Guadeloupean artist Moune de Rivel.

An amazing part of her story is that she went from being abandoned in Paris, "a child of the streets" in her words, to being a successful dancer, travelling the world. She was involved in a crucial period of *gwo ka*'s history in the metropole: during the years of migration, when *gwo ka* gained popularity for an audience outside of the island. She performed in opening acts for artists such as Bob Marley and Johnny Hallyday. She also performed for spare change in the metros of Paris with other Guadeloupeans, like singer Erick Cosaque. In many ways, her story parallels the movement of Guadeloupean women between the island and the metropole. Her mother went to Guadeloupe with BUMIDOM, and, like many, did not succeed as hoped. Mme Balzamont, in following her mother to France, thus was pulled in by this same force. She later returned to Guadeloupe, as is the case with many Guadeloupeans.

But her story also reveals much that is uncommon. She has travelled much more extensively than most Guadeloupeans. In addition, she spent years living in Africa. She seemed happy living in the Republic of Congo, noting it was the one African country that reminded her of Guadeloupe. Indeed, from her story, I got the impression that she would have stayed in Congo had it not been for the civil war in the late 1990s, when her partner and his family were killed.

Conclusions

Many Guadeloupeans describe the local society and culture as *créole* (creole), *métissé* (culturally and racially mixed) or *mélangé* (mixed), but essentializing images of identity based on notions of purity exist as well. Efforts to define a distinctive Guadeloupean identity often focus on cultural, linguistic and racial mixing that occurred in the past and define the pure creole culture and language that resulted from this mixing against the ongoing hegemony of French culture and language (also defined in purist terms). In these representations, particular cultural elements are given priority. For example, independentists and cultural activists have singled out *gwo ka* drumming as one of the icons of a distinctive Guadeloupean identity. *Gwo ka* is associated with the non-elite masses and with African retentions. Other local musical forms, such as *quadrille*, *raga* and zouk, do not receive the same attention.[35] Given that women's role in *gwo ka* has been circumscribed, this choice to focus on *gwo ka* has significant implications.

The symbolism of *gwo ka* within Guadeloupean society and the differential implications it has for women and men may be analysed using the concept of the dual value system, associated particularly with the work of Wilson.[36] Wilson asserts that there are two value systems which mediate social actions in the Caribbean: first, the imposed, colonial system of hierarchy; and second, the local system of egalitarianism. These are reflected in concerns over respectability (adherence to colonial values) and reputation (adherence to the value of egalitarianism and to cultural practices not derived from the colonial power), which are said to exist in a continual dialectic and be unevenly dispersed across race, gender, class and generational lines. According to Wilson, in Caribbean society women must be especially concerned with maintaining respectability, whereas men may seek status through the system of reputation as well. In this way, men may engage in practices not associated with the colonial power and derive status from them, whereas women must adhere to colonial values lest they lose status. The division of these dual values along gender lines has been critically examined by scholars such as Sutton, Besson and Young.[37] While I agree with these criticisms, it is true that *gwo ka* is associated with practices seen as uncivilized and unrespectable, especially for women, and this is due in part to the fact that such practices are viewed as being distanced from that which is French, as inculcated by the French educational system.[38]

Guadeloupeans' increased interest in local traditions could also be seen as an effect of increasing globalization. Daniel points out that, while the assimilation of the DOMs into France and then into the European Union has resulted in their increased economic and political dependence, assimilation has also given rise to an increase in local cultural manifestations, as cultural ties with France and Europe are weakened by transnational flows.[39] Like Jamaica, Guadeloupe grapples with the problem of developing a collective identity that recognizes not only an African heritage and a connection with both the past and tradition, but also the place of these islands and their people in the modern world.[40] Nonetheless, efforts at promoting a distinctly Guadeloupean identity – a creole identity – has had an impact on the islands. Scholars such as Khan caution that ethnographic data from "creole" societies reveals that rather than being a model of the harmonious melding of cultures and peoples, the concept of creolization has been used in certain contexts to create lines of social division in societies marked by asymmetries of power. Furthermore, Khan points out that not all people in creole societies "participate in equally meaningful . . . and equally empowering ways" in the creolization process and its elaboration as a guiding image for collective identity.[41] While Khan points to the exclusion of certain religious and ethnic groups from creole identity movements, in this chapter I have stressed the ways in which women may be ideologically erased from key symbols developed in identity movements.

As I have argued in this chapter, we must recognize that women in Guadeloupe have had to fight to take part in one of the most potent symbols of Guadeloupean identity: *gwo ka*. Moreover, the important work they have done to maintain *gwo ka*, specifically by organizing *lèwòz*, has not received ideological focus. In fact, the folkloric troupes such as Ballets Briscantes have been criticized by certain Antillean intellectuals as representing a negative folklorization of tradition that played on the exoticization of Guadeloupean culture for an outside audience, thus reflecting the colonial gaze. There is a monument to the solo *gwo ka* drummer Vélo, and everyone knows the Geoffroy brothers of Kan'nida, but what of Man Soso and Man Geoffroy? Were it not for women such as these, the tradition of the *lèwòz* may not have survived to be revalorized and to serve as a symbol of that which is most Guadeloupean. Furthermore, with the increasing commercialization of *lèwòz*, women's traditional role as organizer has shifted to radio stations and municipalities. My interviews have demonstrated that women, as the *poto mitan* (centreposts) of Guadeloupean society, have been involved in all of the major events that mark Guadeloupean history, including the revolt of 1802, the migration of BUMIDOM and the recent general strike. Women like Raymonde Thorin, Marie-Line Dahomay, Mme Dancher and Josie Balzamont are fighting to make sure that female contributions to Guadeloupean society – and to *gwo ka* in particular – are recognized. As Mme Dancher said to me, *gwo ka* is as much theirs as anyone else's in Guadeloupe. These women feel they have a right to actively participate in its development and deployment as a symbol of Guadeloupean unity. I hope that this chapter contributes to their struggle, bringing their stories to an international audience.

Notes

1. Jacqueline Roseman, *La Musique dans la Société Antillaise 1635–1902* (Paris: L'Harmattan, 1986).
2. Marcel Mavouzny, *Cinquante Ans de Musique et de Culture en Guadeloupe: Mémoires 1928–1978* (Paris: Présense Africaine, 2002).
3. Ellen Schnepel, "The Politics of Language in the French Caribbean: The Creole Movement on the Island of Guadeloupe" (PhD diss., Columbia University, 1990), 244.
4. Deborah Thomas, "Emancipating the Nation (Again): Notes on Nationalism, 'Modernization', and Other Dilemmas in Post-Colonial Jamaica", *Identities* 5, no. 4 (1999): 501–42.
5. Cf. David Beriss, *Black Skins, French Voices: Caribbean Ethnicity and Activism in Urban France* (Boulder: Westview, 2004), and Richard Price, *The Convict and the Colonel* (Boston: Beacon, 1998).
6. When slavery was abolished, indentured workers from India, as well as China and Africa, were brought in to work on the plantations.
7. Pierre Pluchon, ed., *Histoire des Antilles et de la Guyane* (Toulouse: Privat, 1982).
8. Fred Constant, "Les nationaux d'outre-mer; des citoyens comme les autres?", in *Citoyenneté et nationalité: Perspectives en France et au Québec*, ed. Dominique Colas, Claude Emeri, and Jacques Zylberberg (Paris: Presses Universitaires de France, 1991), 243–59; Fred Constant, *1946–1996: Cinquante Ans de Départementalisation Outre-Mer* (Paris: L'Harmattan, 1997); Claude Emeri et al., *La question statutaire en Guadeloupe, en Guyane, et an Martinique: Elements de réflexion* (Pointe-à-Pitre: Editions Jasor, 2000).

9. Lucien René Abenon, *Petite histoire de la Guadeloupe* (Paris: L'Harmattan, 1992).
10. Beriss, *Black Skins*.
11. Stéphanie Condon and Philip Ogden, "Emigration from the French Caribbean: Origins of an Organized Migration", *International Journal of Urban and Regional Research* 15, no. 4 (1991): 505–23.
12. Jean Goosen, "The Migration of French West Indian Women to Metropolitan France", *Anthropological Quarterly* 49, no. 1 (1976): 45–52.
13. This is in comparison to 50,078 men. Stéphanie Condon, "Travail et genre dans l'histoire des migrations antillaises", *Travail, genre et sociétés* 2, no. 20 (2008): 67–86.
14. Erick Cosaque, "A koz don biyé san fwan", *Musique, Voix, Percussions: Génération Culturelle de la Guadeloupe* (Erick Cosaque Productions, 1998).
15. Hervé Domenach and Michel Picouet, *La Dimension Migratoire des Antilles* (Paris: Economica, 1992).
16. Condon, "Travail et genre", 67–86.
17. Domenach and Picouet, *La Dimension Migratoire*; INSEE, *Tableaux Economiques Régionaux de la Guadeloupe, édition 1998* (Paris: INSEE, 1998).
18. Yarimar Bonilla, *A Striking Past: Labor and the Politics of History in Guadeloupe* (PhD diss., University of Chicago, 2008).
19. Lambert-Felix Prudent and Ellen Schnepel, eds., "Creole Movements in the Francophone Orbit", special issue, *International Journal of the Sociology of Language* 102 (Berlin: Mouton de Gruyter, 1993); Kathe Managan, "Language Choice, Linguistic Ideologies and Social Identity in Guadeloupe" (PhD diss., New York University, 2004).
20. Richard D.E. Burton, "The French West Indies à l'heure de l'Europe", in *French and West Indian: Martinique, Guadeloupe and French Guiana Today*, ed. Richard D.E. Burton and Fred Reno (London: Macmillan, 1995), 1–19.
21. *Man* is the Kréyòl equivalent of *Madame* or Mrs.
22. For more discussion of how *léwoz* were organized and the role they played in mutual aid in Guadeloupe, see Luciani Lanoir L'etang, *Réseaux de solidarité dans la Guadeloupe d'hier et d'aujourd'hui* (Paris: L'Harmattan, 2005).
23. Manuel Castells, *The Rise of the Network Society* (Cambridge, MA: Blackwell, 1996); David Harvey, *The Condition of Postmodernity* (Cambridge, MA: Blackwell, 1990); Akhil Gupta and James Ferguson, "Beyond 'Culture': Space, Identity, and the Politics of Difference", in *Culture, Power, Place: Explorations in Critical Anthropology* (Durham, NC: Duke University Press, 1997), 33–51.
24. John Comaroff, "Ethnicity, Nationalism, and the Politics of Difference in an Age of Revolution", in *The Politics of Difference: Ethnic Premises in a World of Power*, ed. Edwin N. Wilmsen and P.A. McAllister (Chicago: University of Chicago Press, 1996).

25. Karla Slocum and Deborah Thomas, "Rethinking Global and Area Studies: Insights from the Caribbean", *American Anthropologist* 105, no. 3 (2003): 553–65.
26. Michel-Rolph Trouillot, "The Caribbean Region: An Open Frontier in Anthropological Theory", *Annual Review of Anthropology* 21 (1992): 19–42.
27. Merville Herskovits, *The Myth of the Negro Past* (Boston: Beacon, 1941).
28. Compare to the argument about the problematization of African contributions to contemporary Jamaican culture in Thomas, "Emancipating".
29. Kan'nida, *Kyenzenn* (Amiens: Label Bleu, 2000).
30. Dany Bebel-Gisler, "The Incomplete Past of Slavery: The African Heritage in the Social Reality, Subconscious and Imagination of Guadeloupe", in *From Chains to Bonds: The Slave Trade Revisited*, ed. Doudou Diene (New York: Berghahn Books, 2001).
31. Kan'nida, "Nèg la", *Véyé* (MIS, 1992).
32. Thomas, "Emancipating".
33. During a showing of a documentary about *gwo ka* in France (during the Gwo Ka Festival Sainte-Anne, summer 2009), producer Franck Salin mentioned that some of the musicians and dancers were in fact from Martinique or Africa and that there is some mutual influence between *gwo ka* and Martinican *bèlé* as well as styles of Congolese drumming in the metropole.
34. The term "ballet" in the name of the troupe does not indicate that the group performed ballet dance.
35. For a discussion of zouk, see Joselyne Guilbault, *World Music in the West Indies* (Chicago: University of Chicago Press, 1993).
36. Peter Wilson, *Crab Antics: The Social Anthropology of English-speaking Negro Societies in the Caribbean* (New Haven, CT: Yale University Press, 1973); Daniel Miller, *Capitalism: An Ethnographic Approach* (Oxford: Berg, 1997).
37. Constance Sutton, "Cultural Duality in the Caribbean", *Caribbean Studies* 14, no. 2 (1974): 96–101; Jean Besson, "Reputation and Respectability Reconsidered: A New Perspective on Afro-Caribbean Peasant Women", in *Women and Change in the Caribbean*, ed. Janet Momsen (Bloomington: Indiana University Press, 1993), 15–37; Virginia Heyer Young, *Becoming West Indian: Culture, Self and Nation in St. Vincent* (Washington, DC: Smithsonian Institution Press, 1993).
38. See also Patricia Blafan-Trobo, "La place de la femme dans le gwoka. De la stigmatisation à la transmission", online dossier, http://www.lameca.org/dossiers/femme_gwoka/index.htm.
39. Justin Daniel, "The Construction of Dependency: Economy and Politics in the French West Indies", in *Islands at the Crossroads*, ed. Aarón Gamaliel Ramos and Angel Israel Rivera (Kingston: Ian Randle, 2001), 61–79.
40. Thomas, "Emancipating".

41. Aisha Khan, "Journey to the Center of the Earth: The Caribbean as Master Symbol", *Cultural Anthropology* 16, no. 3 (2001): 273.

Discography

Cosaque, Erick. *Musique, Voix, Percussions: Génération Culturelle de la Guadeloupe*. Erick Cosaque Productions, compact disc, 1998.
Kan'nida. *Kyenzenn*. Label Bleu, Amiens, compact disc, 2000.
———. *Véyé*. MIS, compact disc, 1992.

5.

Celia's Shoes

| FRANCES NEGRÓN-MUNTANER

Shoes can tell us where a person has been and where she wants to go.
— Erin Mackie[1]

I HELD A PAIR OF CUBAN singer Celia Cruz's most famous shoes long enough to marvel at the seven-inch razor-thin platform that had lifted her up in the air for decades. I had barely touched the shoes when I felt compelled to put them down as fast as possible, to not completely erase the awe of the object, the fact that they belonged to a queen. Hand-carved by Mexican artisan Miguel Nieto, known as *el zapatero de los sueños* (the shoemaker of dreams),[2] the one-of-a-kind shoes felt heavy, as if in their long stage life they had carried not only the memories of salsa music's most important female star but also of Cubanness itself.

Since 1997, Celia's shoes have been part of the permanent collection of the Smithsonian National Museum of American History in Washington, DC. The shoes found their way there at the initiative of Marvette Pérez, the Smithsonian's Latino history and culture curator. Early on, Pérez became interested in acquiring Caribbean music artefacts for the museum, which, despite having a rich collection of objects belonging to African-American music greats, such as the Supremes and Ella Fitzgerald, had few Latino items. While at the Smithsonian, Celia's shoes have been exhibited four times to large and appreciative audiences. To find her shoes off season, however, I had to be led through the Smithsonian's back rooms by Marvette's hand, a hesitant if generous Virgil, who could not help but to continuously ask, "Why do you want to see Celia's shoes?"

The year that I made the journey into the singer's displaced closet, in 1998, I was not entirely sure of the answer. But it came to me soon enough. Shortly after returning home, I mentioned my impulsive visit to a distinguished Cuban who had been a diplomat under Fidel Castro's government and still considers himself a socialist. To my surprise, the former ambassador held only the deepest contempt for what he called the Smithsonian's "pedestrian" taste. Insisting that the museum's exhibition of Celia's finery was a way of humiliating Cuban exiles in the United States, he asked, "Couldn't the Smithsonian choose something more *elevated* to represent the Cuban people? . . . A poem by patriot José Martí? A portrait of Father Varela, the nineteenth century priest called the 'first Cuban'? A uniform worn by the pro-independence general Antonio Maceo?"

Although depending on how you look at it, the difference between Maceo's pants and Celia's shoes might be only a matter of accessories, the Cuban diplomat did see one thing straight. In displaying Celia's shoes, the Smithsonian was choosing to represent Cuban exiles through the lowliest of cultural and corporeal signs as imagined by elite culture, whether in the Caribbean or on terra firma. For how much "lower" can one possibly go, socially speaking, than under the feet of an old, salsa dancing, Afro-Cuban woman?

Seen from below, however, Celia's shoes are so much more than footwear. They bear the mark of endless negotiations with the trappings of upward mobility, *Latinidad*, the eternal feminine and the body's inevitable decline over time. Furthermore, that some of us may be inexplicably drawn and others passionately repulsed by Celia's shoes implies that these are part of a larger signifying web, one which, to paraphrase psychoanalyst Jacques Lacan, "catches" spectators in their desire to be seen and identified in a specific fashion. This is why, with (if not entirely in) Celia's shoes it is possible to walk through her career as a Cuban female singer in the nearly all Puerto Rican male club of salsa, and thread the ways that shoes told stories of hardship and triumph differently enjoyed – and sometimes disowned – by Latinos as part of their public "ethnic" body in the United States.

Oye Como Va (Hear How It Goes)

Born Úrsula Hilaria Celia Caridad Cruz Alfonso on October 21, 1924, the singer began her unlikely rise to stardom in Santos Suárez, one of Havana's poorest neighbourhoods. Although Celia's class origins prompted official biographer Ana Cristina Reymundo to suggest that "nothing in her background gave any indication of the heights she would reach",[3] a sense that this girl had a special gift became evident early on. According to Cruz lore, reproduced in countless published accounts in the popular press, young Celia began to sing to put her siblings to bed, attracting the attention of her neighbours and cousins, one of whom registered her to participate in an amateur singing contest called *La hora del té* (*The Tea Hour*). Already a university student, the twenty-three-year-old Celia won the competition by singing the tango "Nostalgia", a prophetic choice in light of her eventual and permanent exile from Cuba.

Before considering a career in music, Celia studied to be a schoolteacher, a relatively low-paid profession that nevertheless connoted a certain level of respect for blacks in Cuba, who had historically been excluded from educational opportunity. But it was not meant to be. By 1951, and only four years after her debut on the radio, Celia had become the lead singer for La Sonora Matancera, Cuba's most popular orchestra. Even if fans initially rejected Celia because she was virtually unknown and had replaced the wildly popular Puerto Rican singer Myrta Silva, she quickly consolidated her own following, eventually earning the first in a succession of cultural titles: *la guarachera de Cuba*.

After more than a decade of touring and recording with La Sonora, Celia responded dramatically to the 1959 Cuban revolution and its swift restructuring of the entertainment industry. She first moved to Mexico and then settled permanently outside New York City. This turn of events was to have contradictory consequences. On the one hand, Celia experienced exile as a great loss: she would never see her parents or set foot in Havana again. On the other hand, exile provided the conditions for her to ascend from the nationally bound musical identity as *la guarachera de Cuba* to a pan-Latino and global one as the Queen of Salsa. While Celia seems to have rationalized this loss of identity by arguing that salsa was but a variation of the Cuban *son* (a long and exhausted debate among musicians and scholars), she had little trouble incorporating the new accents that came to define "Latin" music over the next forty-three years. True to form, the last major hit of her career, "La negra tiene tumbao", combined elements of salsa, reggae and hip-hop.

In retrospect, Celia's legendary ability to fuse a wide range of sounds undoubtedly contributed to her longevity as a star. Yet, in an era where looks and not vocal ability tend to sell records, Celia had to also creatively *resolver*, that is, deal with a small problem to ensure long-term success as a salsa diva: that of not "looking good" as a performer.

At the height of her global fame, for instance, Celia was not beautiful in a conventional sense, slim or young. She was also hailed as a "nice" person in a context in which gossip sells newspapers and a racy personal life defines iconicity. "The collective question", declared television producer Cristina Saralegui after she pitched Celia's story to Hollywood studios, was: "How do you write a compelling screenplay about somebody whose life had no apparent Tina Turner tragedy, no *Behind the Music* crash and burn, no tabloid-worthy scandal?"[4] What Hollywood executives may have missed, however, was precisely what her fans saw in her, and, I would argue, was the open secret of the *salsera*'s long-term success. For whatever Celia may have lacked in typical celebrity ways, she made up for by other means, through what many came to refer to as the "unique and unmistakable Celia Cruz look".[5]

Different from other Latina singers, Celia's most recognized performative excess was not how she moved her body – the queen was at times as regal as her title – but how she fashioned it. From the start of her career, Celia showed a great interest in style, and as a starving young singer in Havana, admittedly "spent all her money on clothes".[6] Yet it was in exile, living in a racially polarized country where Latinos remain expendable, that Celia became as famous for her distinctive voice as for her shoes, wigs and gowns. In the words of music critic Ramiro Burr, Celia wore lavish dresses made up of "feathers, spangles, lace, and yards upon yards of multi-colored fabrics".[7] Topping the dresses were often outrageously designed wigs, complemented by hands "featuring long painted nails and expensive jewelry" that, according to one observer, made it "quite obvious that she's never had to do the dishes".[8]

But although wigs, gowns, and nail polish constitute an important part of the singer's public anatomy, shoes were considered "Celia's signature"[9] and bear the greatest weight in narrating her public persona. Eveningwear designer Julian Asion was perhaps the most succinct when he wrote, "On top of these heels, you have this voluptuous body moving around, dancing around. Those heels are her."[10] The question that remains is why did this load fall so heavily on Celia's shoes and to what effect?

Esa Negrita Que Va Caminando (That Black Girl Walking By)

As has been noted by journalists and other observers, Celia had a formidable collection of shoes. The collection included thousands of pairs kept at home and in New Jersey warehouses that were worn "for photo shoots and to perform on stage or on the red carpet".[11] Significantly, despite the collection's size, the vast majority of these shoes were of only one style: high heels, a type of footwear originally linked to the aristocracy since it was considered to be "highly impractical for women who had to perform menial labor".[12] Although Celia may or may not have been aware of this historical detail, the fact that her shoes were often made of glittery, simulated diamond or ruby materials references the style's origins. It also seeks to confirm her status as a queen – *la reina de la salsa* – at the same level with, if not a cut above, that other voracious collector of high-heeled shoes, the French queen Marie-Antoinette.[13]

Celia's signature shoes, however, went beyond being elaborately decorated high heels. They were *very* high heels, some standing as high as nine inches off the ground. Perhaps because shoes worn by the poor tend to be ill fitting due to coarse material and design,[14] Celia's shoes were handmade, too costly to mass produce and fitted exclusively for her. These attributes not only point to affluence and luxury, but also uniqueness and difference, a way to, in the words of journalist Colin McDowell, "signal clearly who and what their wearer is and why he is different from (and superior to) the rest of mankind".[15] Even further, Celia's footwear seemed to defy gravity itself, as they did not rest on a conventional heel but on the thinnest of soles. By appearing physically unfeasible, Celia's trademark shoes offer the illusion of walking on air, a magical attribute that again elevates the queen above mere mortals.[16]

Part of the explanation therefore rests on the ways that the shoes themselves connoted wealth, luxury and enchantment. Given the singer's "undistinguished" class origins and membership in a racial and ethnic group rarely afforded the dignity of individuality, Celia's shoes insisted on her uniqueness as a person and a performer – a one of a kind brand. Moreover, if as theorist Maureen Turim has written, feet are the "most abject part of the body . . . the body part in direct contact with the dirt and assigned the role of support",[17]

Celia's heels literally raised her from the soil – away from her lowly social origins – onto a stage where reality appears to be free and self-fashioned. In this regard, Celia's "wildly stylish"[18] shoes "dressed up" her struggle of upward mobility while insisting that a black woman born in poverty on a small Caribbean island can reach the heights of a transnational star.[19]

Accordingly, in her hagiographic story of upward mobility, Celia's social location is almost always narrated in relation to shoes. For instance, Celia was one of thirteen children "as shoeless as her" who managed to finish her education by going to school with "torn shoes".[20] This state of poverty only began to change when as a teenager "Celia got her first pair of quality shoes singing for a tourist on the street".[21] Toward the end of Celia's career, it was said more than once that no one, including her handpicked successor La India, could possibly fill her shoes.[22] And even when her high place in popular music history was completely assured, Cuban journalist Norma Niurka wrote that, after finally recording an album with a major label in 2000, Celia felt as "a girl with new shoes".[23]

Although on various occasions Celia disputed the anecdote that she sang to tourists for shoes, saying, "I was very poor but never a beggar",[24] this tale with *ribetes de leyenda*[25] (streaks of legend) stands as her founding myth. "Not only had my singing made them happy", Celia recalls in her autobiography, "but those white patent-leather shoes, which meant so much to me, initiated my lifelong fascination with fashion".[26] Shoes, then, refer to and incorporate what literary scholar Erin Mackie has called an "originary event", one that "fixes together previously disparate, heterogeneous elements into a novel identity",[27] in this case, that of an Afro-Cuban female star. A step further, they made Celia not simply a singer of humble origins who became famous, but a "Black Cinderella", a girl who, like in a fairy tale, went from a "poor neighborhood of Havana to a queen's burial in New York".[28]

De Cuba Vengo (I Come from Cuba)

The idea that shoes denote social status is evident across many cultural contexts, including the United States and Latin America. In this regard, Celia's shoe fetishism – that is, her tendency to invest shoes with non-inherent meanings – was widely shared with her Caribbean and Latino peers. Since the (sometimes shoeless) native peoples encountered the (often well heeled) Europeans, shoes have become a significant social concern for everyone who lives in the Americas. As Turim reminds us, "The opposition of shoes to bare feet is central . . . to significations of wealth, public space, and civilization itself."[29]

Puerto Rican history, for example, is full of references to shoes as a means to narrate national life. The Spanish priest and historian Iñigo Abad y Lasierra described the eighteenth-century *criollos* or "native-born" as not only promiscuous and lazy, but also prone to going barefoot.[30] Over a century later, US President McKinley requested an 1899 report on the state of Puerto Rico that measured the island's poverty in part by the size of its shoeless population: "child labor was common practice, unemployment was widespread, and out of a population of nearly a million people some seven hundred thousand were without shoes".[31] Not surprisingly, when after the Second World War the Puerto Rican and US elites embarked on a modernization effort to curb extreme poverty on the island, the project was known in English as "Operation Bootstrap". And this is probably why, toward the end of the 1980s, writer Luis Rafael Sánchez concluded that since Bootstrap could only deliver on higher levels of consumption by setting off mass migration and excessive debt, Puerto Ricans still belonged to *la América descalza* (barefoot America) of the south and not the wealthy North America exemplified by the United States.[32]

Among Cubans, shoes are also tied to national narratives, and perhaps with a tighter bow. In his memoir from the independence war of 1868, *A pie y descalzo, de Trinidad a Cuba, 1870–1871 (Recuerdos de campaña)*,[33] Ramón Roa measures the *mambises'* enthusiasm for the war in terms of their willingness to fight without shoes, and urgently defines his own situation – shoeless and horseless, *a pie y descalzo* – as the most abject and dehumanizing of all social conditions.[34] In Roa's words, "[with] my feet cracked and swollen due to the stones and bushes . . . I began for the first time in life to suffer the moral horrors that can only be suffered when one sees oneself, above all, barefoot and hatless, something like abandoned by mankind and at the enemy's mercy."[35]

Even though writer and pro-independence advocate José Martí harshly criticized Roa's book in his speech "Los pinos nuevos" because it could discourage Cubans from embracing the cause, several of his texts further elaborated on the relationship between shoes, class and national struggle. In his 1891 classic essay "Our America", Martí represents US imperial power as "giants in seven-leagued boots",[36] and authentic Latin Americans as those who wear not "epaulets and professor's gowns" but "hemp sandals and headbands".[37] Arguably, Martí uses shoes as a trope to maximum effect in his broadly anthologized modernist poem "Los zapaticos de rosa" ("The Little Pink Shoes"), in which a well-off girl offers her pink shoes to another who is ill and poor in order to temper the shame of class privilege.[38]

Far from ending with the nineteenth century's independence struggles, the allusion to shoes in Cuban cultural production continued well into the twentieth century and without ideological distinctions. While pro-revolutionary writer Lourdes Casal criticized those who left Cuba during the Mariel exodus and ridiculed Western "democratic normalcy" as an "office full of shoe boxes",[39] the dissident writer and *marielito* Reinaldo Arenas, who once called Casal's journal *Areíto*, "the official organ of the Cuban state police in New York", launched his own career with a short story titled "Los zapatos vacíos" (The Empty Shoes). Here, Arenas alludes to a peasant boy's pair of torn shoes left unfilled on Three Kings' Day, to suggest that despite living in great poverty, the child had access to something grander than mere presents: the infinite wealth of nature's bounty.[40]

In the United States, high heels have also been linked to Latina feminine identity. As literary critic Tace Hedrick has observed, "the connection of heels with the exotic beauty of certain Latin American and Hispanic American women has been part of the United States' collective imaginary for decades".[41] For Cuban-American women of the post-war period, high heels were explicitly associated with ethnic difference, autonomous sexuality and validation of a different body type presumed to be below "average" height, meaning "inferior" to (white) Americans. According to Cuban-American columnist Liz Balmaseda, during the 1970s "it was the heels that distinguished the Latinas from the Americanitas. We were the chicks in the seven-inch, custom-designed platforms, the ones unconcerned by details such as dwarfing our dates."[42]

Since Celia would never have been confused with the white girls Balmaseda calls "Americanitas", her fashion choices were more linked to a desire to be seen as a Latina rather than as an "American" black woman, a common response for Afro-Caribbean people living in the United States who reject the country's rigid racial binary and overt exclusion of blacks as full citizens. Yet, while stepping up her *Latinidad* did not imply a denial of her black identifications, evident in her recordings of African diaspora rhythms and her display of pan-African style, Celia's "Latin thing" tended to rule over her "black power" in public discourse. Her success in using style as a means to assert Cubanness and *Latinidad* above other identities is evident when designer Julian Asion makes Celia's shoes the litmus test of Latino identity. Referring to a pair of Celia's signature shoes, Asion states: "If you don't know whose shoes these are, you're not Latino."[43]

Celia's shoe fetish was therefore not just a personal choice or private affectation. If, for Celia, shoes stand in for her achievements as a black working class woman, a Cuban exile and a Latina icon, for her fans, many of whom were female, black, Latino, poor and/or queer, they offered the possibility of reaching a similar stature and of unsettling the social hierarchies that keep them down. This partly explains why, despite the extravagance inherent in Celia's shoes and the affluence implicit in acquiring a sizable collection, fans did not resent these displays of wealth. On the contrary, Celia's overt love for shoes struck a chord with many fans (including those in the mainstream media), who saw in the popular singer a person who, despite adversity, "never allowed her dreams of liberty and dignity to be stepped on".[44] The importance of Celia's shoes to telling her story makes evident that, in contrast to the common definition of fetishism as an individual sexual perversion, a fetish is, as psychoanalyst Robert J. Stoller once put it, "a story masquerading as an object".[45]

Caballero y Dama (Gentleman and Lady)

Celia's buying into the stereotype of the high (and well) heeled Latina helped her to maintain ethnic and national specificity, and accentuate a different way to be a black star, not to be confused with African-American divas. But to the extent that in Western culture shoe styles are gender coded, and high heels in particular signify "universal" femaleness and sexuality,[46] Celia's love of shoes is also about standing up for femininity itself. In fact, Celia pointed to shoe style as a fundamental marker for gender differentiation, irrespective of ethnicity and race. In responding to her husband, Pedro Knight, on the subject of stars who wear sneakers along with tuxedos, Celia vehemently argued, "[T]hey're men, Pedro . . . Women can't do that."[47]

At the same time, while high heels made Celia a woman, she did not want to be just any kind of woman. She wished to be seen as a Cuban, Latina and Afro-Caribbean woman, but also a *mujer decente*, a decent woman. Celia, for instance, rarely failed to tell interviewers about the contrast between her and the singer she replaced at La Sonora Matancera, the Puerto Rican Myrta Silva, who was known for projecting a sexually unconventional and mischievous public persona captured in nicknames such as *la gorda de oro* (the golden fat lady) and *la vedette que arrolla* (the vedette that will run you over).[48] In Celia's words, "[Silva] would come out in *Bohemia* magazine wrapped in just a towel. I was very serious."[49]

Celia's need to be perceived seriously and as a serious woman reached panic levels in 1949. During an engagement in Venezuela, one of the women dancing in the troupe that accompanied Celia, Las Mulatas del Fuego, became ill. On a whim, Celia offered to replace the fallen dancer on the show. Although Celia dressed in the customary *mulatas* bikini and made it to the edge of the curtain, she could not go forward: "I froze: I couldn't go on. I just couldn't . . . I felt naked. There were so many people out there looking at us."[50]

In Celia's narrative, the resistance to expose herself in this way was explicitly linked with the shame of being looked upon as an "easy" woman by her father, who viewed her entry into show business as tantamount to declaring that she was a prostitute. "When he saw the path that I was on as an entertainer," recalled Celia, "he feared that I would disregard my teaching aspirations and fall prey to the *mujeres de la vida* (prostitute) culture . . . My father was ashamed of me and he wouldn't even tell anyone I even existed. Fortunately, all of that changed one day."[51] The fear of being taken for a *mujer de la vida* may also explain Celia's confessed inability to dance or move her body while she lived in Cuba. At times, Celia's physical stiffness was so pronounced that her Aunt Ana repeatedly advised her to loosen up and "shake a little": "You have to understand that you have to let the public feel everything you're carrying inside through your entire body. Not just your voice."[52]

Whereas Celia eventually loosened up as she became increasingly successful, a second, and more pervasive, bodily shame came to constitute her public persona: the shame of being "ugly". In fact, "ugliness" appears in Celia's narrative of self as the one major liability that she had to deal with, rather than those explicitly associated with race, ethnicity, sexuality or gender. For example, when things got rocky early on at La Sonora, Celia stated that she compensated by hard work and good values: "God may have not given me a pretty face, but He gave me many gifts."[53] Celia further claims that, during her early years, she was unable to hire an agent because, "I was ugly. Yes, I did have a pretty voice, but I didn't have the look many agents wanted to represent."[54] In a succinct declaration, Celia described herself as "fea de cara pero bella de alma"[55] (having an ugly face but beautiful soul) underscoring the height of spirituality over the lowliness of her body.

In this regard, Celia's shoes carried the burden of a shamed femininity, one that dare not be revealed in the flesh. Accordingly, Celia fashioned her body away from "natural" conceptions of beauty. Apart from her spectacular shoes, most of her wigs were dyed with colours not found in nature. Even though Celia argued that wigs were good because they were practical and easy to use since the natural hair did not have to be worked on,[56] the kind of hairstyle (straight), colour (blue, red), and other features of most of her wigs underscore that Celia's general aesthetic was against regimes of representation that signified beauty as part of a woman's "nature". And while it is true that Celia experimented with a spectacular "Afro" style in the 1980s, not only was this look equally unnatural, but her own hair was rarely seen and when it was, it was in the chemically "relaxed" style. Not surprisingly, the wig she donated to the Smithsonian was blonde, and so was the one that she was buried in.[57]

That Celia bore masks, however, did not mean that she did not want to be seen. On the contrary, Celia wanted the audience to both listen and take note of her body, particularly as she aged. "If I can't call attention on my own", Celia asserted, "I will do so through my clothes."[58] In this sense, it is important to underscore that Celia did not hide but rather covered up to avoid being perceived in ways that black women are assumed to signify available and "hot" sexuality. This move protected Celia against two discriminating looks, one that consumed her as a vulnerable object – female and dark – as well as one that may not have found her to embody black "beauty" in acceptable terms.

To cover up was then more than a simple matter of accessories. It was also a style of struggle, deployed by a woman who was aware of the forces that aimed to limit her possibilities as an "unattractive" black female singer. This may be why Celia threw a big mantle over all details about her life. She always insisted, for example, that she had an idyllic sentimental life with her husband and manager, Pedro Knight, and avoided the spectre of scandal at all costs.

She linked her body's hard fought ability to dance not as a sign of her sensuality, but as part of the "joy of singing", an offering and a plea not to be excluded from cultural exchange because of race, class, sexuality or gender. As Celia observed on more than one occasion, "Music is the only gift that God has given me. Unless he takes it away from me, I will continue to share that gift."[59] With great skill, Celia protected this gift – and her hard won social privilege – by always appearing as a "black Latin woman, who achieved greatness through a lot of hardships that she always kept to herself".[60]

Celia's strategy of looking good of course had a price: accepting the stereotype of the maternal and asexual black woman. She has been called charming, generous, affectionate, motherly and gracious by many musicians, writers and television personalities, but in very rare instances as sexy or attractive.[61] According to novelist Oscar Hijuelos, "Celia was the kind of gracious lady that we would love to have for an aunt, a fairy godmother whose tender-heartedness works a healing magic on even the most troubled souls."[62] Celia was also frequently represented as a guardian angel, not unlike the matronly black nannies and cooks that populate canonical hemispheric American fiction, characters that exhibit, in novelist Toni Morrison's words, great "benevolence, harmless and servile guardianship and endless love".[63]

Yet, it was the fusion of *seriedad* (seriousness) and extravagance that allowed Celia to be seen both as a spectacle worth looking at and as a decent woman, impossible to confuse with the *mujeres de la vida* her father worried about.[64] In this way, Celia was able to become an icon without engaging in the sexual ambiguities of her hand picked successor, La India, nor proclaiming the erotic disconformity performed by her relative contemporary, the Queen of Soul, Guadalupe Yoli Raymond, also known as "La Lupe", who took off her shoes and threw them at the audience.[65] If Celia was going to sing salsa – that is, black music – and was not deemed beautiful enough to be appreciated by the eyes of strangers, her unique style allowed her to project an illusion of abundance, dignity, talent, Cubanness, beauty, femininity and, toward the end of her life, eternal youth.

Mi Vida Es Cantar (Singing Is My Life)

There is, however, a second important reason why Celia required a style that accentuated her femininity: the kingdom of salsa – like the nation – is almost universally associated with men and male ideologies of gender.[66] Salsa's virility is reiterated in multiple ways, including the fact that, as scholar Wilson Valentín-Escobar has commented, top *salseros* are often baptized with names calling attention to their particular kind of masculinity. In this canon, the mellow Gilberto Santa Rosa is "el caballero de la salsa" (meaning "salsa's gentleman") and the *muy macho* Tito Rojas is "el gallo de la salsa" (meaning "salsa's cock"). Moreover, the salsa that Celia was part of was considered *salsa dura* (hard) versus more recent incarnations such as the *salsa sensual* or *monga* (limp), that is characterized by the bolero's "feminine" discourse of courtly love[67] and a softer sound that "contain[s] little or no brass and percussive sounds and/or improvisational swing".[68] Within this context, any woman that attempted to crown herself as the queen of salsa had to artistically situate herself on the genre's hard side without losing her feminine look. And this is precisely what Celia did.

From a musical point of view, Celia always succeeded in being perceived by critics, audience members and peers alike in the best of terms, that is, in masculine terms. For instance, Celia is frequently represented as a woman who "entered" the salsa world and "had the gallantry of incurring in this genre".[69] In addition, Celia's voice itself was repeatedly described with adjectives that underscore its masculinity: "tough", "raspy",[70] "powerful contralto"[71] and projecting "a mature *marimacho* punch".[72] Her impressive talent to *sonear*, an improvisational skill that is assumed to separate not only the men from the women but the boys from the men, also earned her the admiration of other singers. As *salsero* Cheo Feliciano famously observed, Celia was different from other female singers because, unlike most women who were confined to singing boleros and ballads – "girl stuff" – she "understood and assimilated the masculine way of singing and feminized it . . . that is why there will be never be any other woman who can wear her shoes and do what she did".[73]

At the same time that Celia was widely praised for her masculine "way" of singing salsa, her male peers also valued her feminine "discretion" in personal matters. In Feliciano's terms: "[s]ince she was the only woman in the group, she was always very discreet touring. You know . . . men things, she never said a word."[74] Equally important, Celia never crossed the line that distinguished singers from true musicians. She followed the "feminine" tradition of interpreter, and did not participate in arranging, producing or distributing her music. A clear example of the ways that musicianship is gendered in salsa can be appreciated in the filmed 1989 Fania concert in Zaire, available on DVD and currently marketed as *Celia Cruz and the Fania Allstars in Africa*.[75] Whereas Celia opened the concert, sang and was arguably the most compelling performer to the audience, she was clearly different than the rest of the participants. In contrast to every other musical or vocal performer on stage – which included Santana, Ray Barreto, Hector Lavoe, Johnny Pacheco and Roberto Roena – that Celia was literally not a boy in the band underscored the fact that the business of salsa essentially remained a Latin and male thing.

The importance of successfully managing gender codes for women aspiring to stardom in Caribbean music can be confirmed by comparing Celia to other major female stars. The Puerto Rican Ivy Queen, otherwise known as "the queen of reggaeton",[76] has also been able to stay on top of a male-dominated musical genre. In contrast to Celia, Ivy Queen initially became famous for a hard masculine look of oversized jackets, caps and overalls. But once reggaeton went global, she polished her hard gender edges with a formula similar to that of the Cuban queen. Known for her "raspy vocals"[77] that according to journalist Gavin Mueller sound "less feminine than a lot of male reggaeton MCs",[78] Ivy Queen reminded fans that she was a real woman through a "flaming style" that includes high heels, long hair, nails up to four inches long, platinum accessories and plastic surgery to enhance bust size. Furthermore, she insisted that "in contrast to other divas she does not come to sell her *nalgas* [buttocks] but her lyrics".

Ivy Queen's and Celia's successful incorporation into their respective genres contrasts to other female stars in Latin music. Despite her importance, La Lupe continues to be ignored in the salsa canon due to her excessive "feminine" performance style – desiring, hysterical, impossible to contain – even if, as Frances R. Aparicio argues, she also "gave voice to the urban, warlike, and male-gendered modulations of salsa".[79] Similarly, La India's voice is often described in gendered terms as having an "androgynous style rather than a soft, melodious tone",[80] and her ambiguous sexuality has made many see her as not a lady in the midst of a male world but as "the industry's Tomboy, who likes to play with the big boys and knows how to hold the pants better than they ever will".[81] Although La India's women-centred lyrics and self-fashioning have won her hardcore fans among women and gays, who claim her as the

"Princess of Salsa and underground dance music",[82] the fact that she has been rumoured to be a lesbian – even if her publicists counter that she is married and is the mother of two children – marginalizes her in relation to the salsa family. The difference then lies in what kind of masculinity is invoked and to what ends. While La India's imagined lesbianism and La Lupe's feminine irreverence make some uncomfortable, Celia's masculine vocal range and feminine sensibility constituted the perfectly gendered arrangement for salsa success.

In other words, given the likely dire consequences of a style misstep, Celia's hyper feminine costuming can also be understood as a means to both "hide anxieties about being perceived as masculine"[83] and insist on her image as a "real" (decent) woman. In this sense, it is revealing that although in some classic studies about Latin music such as *The Latin Tinge* by John Storm Roberts and *Salsa, sabor y control* by Ángel Quintero Rivera she is largely neglected, when Celia is addressed at length, the excessive style of her star persona takes precedence over her male relationships. Perhaps because she was aware that style was an important strategy to hold her place, Celia encouraged female impersonators and drag queens to "perform" and never forget her. In doing so, Celia seemed to know that her immortality – a critical concern for any queen – came from being constantly remembered as a public woman, bound by the "feminine" discourse of fashion while singing "like a man".

Epilogue: *Yo Viviré* (I Will Survive)

Even if unthinkable to many salsa fans, *la reina de la salsa* passed away at her home in Fort Lee, New Jersey, on 16 July 2003 after a relatively short battle with brain cancer. News that Celia had died travelled fast throughout Latino communities in the United States. In Miami, the capital of Cuban exiles and the home of over a million Latinos, emails, phone calls and street chatter celebrated the singer as a dignified representative of Latino America. For several months before her death, as she struggled with illness yet continued to release hit songs, one could spot scribbled messages on cardboard on the front entrances of *cafetines* and other modest gathering places. One in front of the Latin American Restaurant in Coral Gables said: "Celia te queremos" ("Celia, we love you").

But while many fans cherished her, Celia's popularity among Latinos, including Cubans, was far from universal. If the donation of her shoes to the Smithsonian had provoked a rumble of discontent from those who felt that the shoes did not adequately represent Cuban culture, perhaps no other event of her public life brought to light so many internal racial and national tensions among Cuban exiles as her funeral.

Envisioning her funeral as a grand finale, Celia herself desired nothing short of making a spectacle of her dead self. "Laid out in a platinum-blonde wig, a sequined gown and flashy jewellery, her nails painted white, her lips hot pink", Celia had requested public viewings in Miami and New York.[84] In her own words, "I want a wake and a funeral home where a lot of cars can park and everybody attends."[85] And they did – over half a million people stood in interminable lines to get a last glimpse. But, as is often the case, the wake revealed as much – if not more – about the mourners than the departed. If New York was to be the final resting place in lieu of Cuba, Miami was the showcase, the surface upon which Cubans contemplated the state of their transnational selves.

Respecting her wishes as communicated to her family and circle of influential friends, Celia occupied the signs of Cuban exile politics as well as those of the New York elite. Her viewing was held in Torre de la Libertad, a processing centre in Miami for Cuban exiles during the 1960s. In New York, the city closed Fifth Avenue so she could be carried along before her mass at St Patrick's Cathedral. Then she was flown to Frank E. Campbell's funeral home, where viewings for both Jacqueline Kennedy and Judy Garland were held, although according to "funeral directors who handled the historic Judy Garland wake in 1969 . . . it could not compare to Celia's".[86] She was buried at Woodlawn Cemetery; her mausoleum rests between the tombs of music legends Miles Davis and Duke Ellington.

Yet, if in Miami and New York, Celia's funeral was televised by the Spanish language media and her life heralded as a symbol of Latino achievement in the United States, another story was unfolding on the pages of Miami's newspapers. Scores of angry letters to the editor indicated that the bitterness that I had originally encountered with the Cuban diplomat was neither idiosyncratic nor isolated. In the words of Efraín Hernández, a reader of *Street*, a Miami cultural weekly, Celia did nothing useful in this society except jiggle around on stage and scream. She is an embarrassment to all Cubans who are trying not to be the laughing stock of the American community . . . Did you ever take the time to listen to her talk? She was dumber than two boxes of rocks, and she represents the Cuban people? No way! We have many successful Cuban doctors, educators, politicians, businessmen . . . Thanks to Celia Cruz, every person in the modern world thinks Cubans are nothing but Salsa dancing, banana eating idiots . . . Let's move on.[87]

At this moment, after death, it became clear that if Celia played it safe as a "good" black, a "good" wife and a "good" exile, she had her reasons. For Efraín was not alone.

In the letters section of Miami's main cultural weekly, the *Miami New Times*, mail poured in in response to an article by Celeste Fraser Delgado in which the journalist underscored how race played a role in Celia's life and death. During the first week, two letter-writers expressed offence at Delgado's "foolishness": "What an idiot Celeste Fraser Delgado is . . . as a Cuban woman I was quite offended by her constant mention of Celia Cruz being black. First and foremost, Celia was Cuban."[88] But the real fireworks went off a week later. In the 14–20 August edition, five letters were printed. Of these, three found the suppression of a discussion on race and racism to be the insulting part. "What I find offensive," wrote Maggie Urrely, "is to hear cries of racism, and once backs are turned, hearing racist remarks blurted out."[89] And from Doris Fernandez: "I know from firsthand experience that white Cubans are just as bigoted as their American counterparts, so they can try that rhetoric on other Cubans because we Americans know better."[90]

The crudeness of the racism of some exiles seemed to contrast with Celia's standing with the white Cuban elite. In writing about the virtues of the past versus a mediocre present, historian Luis Aguilar León, for instance, commented that Celia herself was a symbol of better times, specifically times of "mulatta laughter", "the narrow streets of Havana", "the smell of coffee". In sum: "Celia Cruz is living Cuba, present, flaming, seminal and eternal", a performer capable of offering "class, hierarchy, elegance".[91] Significantly, this type of assessment was not limited to those Cubans of Celia's own generation. For Richard Pérez-Feria, the "ñ generation" editor of *People en Español*, "Celia Cruz . . . always made herself felt in my home. Not so much her music, to be honest, but her spirit, her energy, her cubanía, which was [what] my parents wanted me and my siblings to emulate."[92]

In addition to her status as one of the most famous bodies of exile – "estandarte del pueblo cubano y del exilio patriótico" (banner of the Cuban people and its patriotic exile)[93] through which "vibra en ella Cuba entera" (all of Cuba vibrates)[94] – Celia's acceptance also rests in her having the right line concerning Fidel.[95] According to popular accounts, the only topic that made Celia lose her habitual composure and dignified stance was her hatred of Castro, who she once allegedly called, "hijo de la gran . . . pura y sincera" ("son of a . . . pure and sincere", that is, son of a bitch).[96] If in private Celia was in constant communication with relatives in Cuba and sent money to them, in public, she was represented as a queen who was never seduced by the tyrant, and was made to suffer when Fidel did not allow her to bury her mother in Cuba. For influential segments of the exile community, Celia was an acceptable symbol, one who never embarrassed them politically, cherished pre-socialist Cuban culture, preached the importance of hard work and success so essential to the myth of Cubans as a model Latino minority, and, although "proud of being black",[97] sang to harmony and good humour in the face of adversity.

In this sense, publicly loving Celia was a way to camouflage the pain of exile itself. While most of her fashion choices had pan-Latino appeal, some elements of style, such as dresses inspired by the traditional *bata cubana* and *rumbera* outfits, directly evoked Cuba and spoke to exiled Cubans. An example of this is the much-photographed Cuba flag outfit that Celia wore in a May 2002 concert in Miami to commemorate Cuban Independence Day. The idea that by dressing up as Cuba one could literally remain there was a strategy to minimize the political defeat of Cuban exiles and never accept exile as final or definitive. In other words, if being an exile is to suffer a break between time and space, to be suspended, Celia lived for (and on) the stage, a trope for home and a site for memory. "The stage, my performances, and my audience," Celia noted, "have always been my refuge."[98]

The defence of exile as an in-between space is also evident in that Celia never attempted to cross over into the English-language market. Her famous refusal to speak English because her *inglés* was not "very good-looking",[99] articulated not only a resistance to accept exile as permanent but a rejection of "Anglo" ways of fashioning the public self in the United States. By always insisting that she had left her heart in Havana, her feet took her all over the world in a frenzied pilgrimage to not lose her place.

Celia's final crossing, which paradoxically underscored to what extent and in what ways many Latinos have become part of America, likewise heralded the end of the *Cuba de ayer* that Celia represented to so many, as well as the Cuba of Fidel, its necessary inverse. In the words of Marta Cabrera, a Cuban exile employed as a domestic worker in Washington: "Cuba is leaving us. The good ones are leaving us and Fidel doesn't even fall off the bed."[100] Meantime, Celia's passing in style left all salsa lovers with a complex icon who navigated the treacherous constraints of subalterity with caution, creativity and intelligence. Perhaps a significant part of Celia's legacy is precisely her particular style of *taconeo*, the distinct way that she clicked her heels while moving through deep waters. For, as her curator Marvette Pérez once said, "The men, when they have died, have left behind other men who could take their place. But Celia left no woman who could step into her shoes."[101]

Acknowledgements

In writing this chapter, I was fortunate to receive the support of colleagues and friends. I would like to thank writer Celeste Fraser Delgado for her editorial acumen, Marvette Pérez for her scholarly generosity, and Kairos Llobrera and Katerina Seligmann for their exceptional research assistance. I would also like to thank Myra Mendible, Ifeona Fulani, James McGirk and Erin MacLeod for their editorial suggestions.

Notes

1. Erin Mackie, "Red Shoes and Bloody Stumps", in *Footnotes: On Shoes*, ed. Shari Benstock and Suzanne Ferris (New Brunswick, NJ: Rutgers University Press, 2001), 233.
2. Juan Soto Meléndez, "Pelucas y vestidos", *PROFROGUI*, http://www.prfrogui.com/caribenet/celiatributo2e.htm.
3. Celia Cruz with Ana Cristina Reymundo, *Celia: My Life* (New York: HarperCollins, 2004), 3.
4. Lydia Martin, "Adiós to the Queen of Salsa", *Miami Herald*, 17 July 2003, http://www.puertorico-herald.org/issues/2003/vol7n29/AdiosQueen-en.shtml.
5. Cruz with Reymundo, *Celia*, 5.
6. Marvette Pérez, telephone interview with author, 25 September 2003.
7. Ramiro Burr, "La primera en su clase", *El Nuevo Herald*, 28 December 2000, 39D.

Original Spanish: "Celia generalmente usaba trajes con plumas, lentejuelas, encajes y yardas y más yardas de telas de colores."
8. Julian Asion, "Style by Celia", *Latina*, September 1997, 85.
9. Ibid.
10. Ibid.
11. Dario Mendez, "Celia Cruz, ¡Unica!", http://www.mipunto.com/foros/foros.jsp?forum=266&start=51.
12. Toby Fischer-Mirkin, *Dress Code: Understanding the Hidden Meanings of Women's Clothes* (New York: Clarkson Potter, 1995): 196.
13. Shari Benstock and Suzanne Ferris, introduction, in *Footnotes: On Shoes*, ed. Shari Benstock and Suzanne Ferris (New Brunswick, NJ: Rutgers University Press, 2001), 1.
14. Colin McDowell, *Shoes: Fashion and Fantasy* (New York: Rizzoli, 1989).
15. Ibid., 118.
16. Asion, "Style by Celia", 85.
17. Maureen Turim, "High Angles on Shoes", in *Footnotes: On Shoes*, ed. Shari Benstock and Suzanne Ferris (New Brunswick, NJ: Rutgers University Press, 2001), 62.
18. Cruz with Reymundo, *Celia*, 181.
19. Dick Hebdige, *Subculture: The Meaning of Style* (London: Routledge, 2003), 78.
20. "Una guarachera con aché", *Letralia,* no. 96 (21 July 2003), http://letralia.com/96/ar02-096.htm.
21. "Adiós Celia", *People*, 4 August 2003, 71.
22. Marla Friedler, "India Upon Her Grammy Nomination", http://www.salsaweb.com/features/indianew.htm.
23. Norma Niurka, "Celia Cruz: La armada invencible de la salsa", *El Nuevo Herald*, 26 October 2000, 27D. Original Spanish: "se siente como niña con zapatos nuevos".
24. "Biografía no autorizada de Celia Cruz", 11 November 2003, http://cronica.com.ar/article/articleprint/1060646710/1/27/.
25. Javier Zerolo, "Adiós a la ceniciente negra", 27 September 2003, http://diariodeavisos.com.
26. Cruz with Reymundo, *Celia*, 19.
27. Mackie, "Red Shoes", 236.
28. Zerolo, "Adiós a la ceniciente negra".
29. Turim, "High Angles", 62.
30. Hugo Rodríguez Vecchini, "Foreword: Back and Forward", in *The Commuter Nation: Perspectives on Puerto Rican Migration*, ed. Antonio Carlos Torre, Hugo Rodríguez Vecchini and William Burgos (Rio Piedras: Editorial de la Universidad de Puerto Rico, 1994), 75–76.
31. Thomas Aitken Jr, *Poet in the Fortress* (New York: Annual World Book, 1994), 38.
32. Luis Rafael Sánchez, *La Importancia de llamarse Daniel Santos* (Hanover: Ediciones del Norte, 1988), 3.

33. Ramón Roa, *A pie y descalzo, de Trinidad a Cuba, 1870–71 (Recuerdos de campaña)* (Havana: Establecimiento Tipográfico de O'Reilly, 1890). Reproduced as part of Ramón Roa, *Pluma y machete* (Havana: Instituto del Libro, 1969).
34. Roa, *Pluma y machete*, 55. Original Spanish: "se dirigían hambrientos, casi desnudos y descalzos a la ambicionada meta".
35. Ibid., 33. Original Spanish: "agrietados los hinchados pies por las piedras y zoquetes de los arbustos . . . empecé a sufrir por primera vez en la vida los horrores morales que sólo se experimentan cuando se ve uno, sobre todo, descalzo, y luego sin sombrero, algo así como abandonado de los hombres y a merced del enemigo".
36. José Martí, "Nuestra América", in *Nuestra América* (Venezuela: Biblioteca Ayacucho, 1977), 26. Original Spanish: "los gigantes que llevan siete leguas en las botas . . . charreteras y togas . . . alpargatas en los pies y la vincha en la cabeza".
37. Ibid. Translation, Jeffrey Belnap, "Headbands, Hemp Sandals, and Headdresses: The Dialectics of Dress and Self-Conception in Martí's 'Our America' ", in *José Martí's 'Our America': From National to Hemispheric Cultural Studies*, ed. Jeffrey Belnap and Raúl Fernández (Durham, NC: Duke University Press, 1998), 198.
38. Jose Martí, "Los zapaticos de Rosa", in *Páginas escogidas*, ed. Roberto Fernández Retamar (Havana: Editorial de Ciencias Sociales, 1971), 124–29.
39. Lourdes Casal, *Palabras Juntan Revolución* (Havana: Ediciones Casa de las Américas, 1981), 25.
40. Reinaldo Arenas, "The Empty Shoes", *Mona and Other Tales* (New York: Vintage, 2001), 3.
41. Tace Hedrick, "Are you a Pure Latina? Or, Menudo Every Day: Tacones and Symbolic Ethnicity", in *Footnotes: On Shoes*, ed. Shari Benstock and Suzanne Ferris (New Brunswick, NJ: Rutgers University Press, 2001), 135.
42. Liz Balmaseda, "Seduction by Spikes", *Latina*, September 1997, 82.
43. Asion, "Style by Celia", 85.
44. Dario Mendez, "Celia Cruz, ¡Unica!", http://www.mipunto.com/foros/foros.jsp?forum=266&start=51.
45. Robert J. Stoller, *Observing the Erotic Imagination* (New Haven: Yale University Press, 1985), 15.
46. Benstock and Ferris, introduction, 5.
47. Lydia Martin, "Salsa Queen Celia Cruz Is Praying for a Special Heeling", *Miami Herald*, 31 October 2001, 2E.
48. Frances R. Aparicio, *Listening to Salsa: Gender, Latin Popular Music, and Puerto Rican Cultures* (Middleton, CT: Wesleyan University Press, 1998), 177.
49. Martin, "Adiós".
50. Cruz with Reymundo, *Celia*, 47
51. Ibid., 50.
52. Ibid., 34.

53. Ibid., 62.
54. Ibid., 67.
55. Merce Beltrán, "Azúuucar", *La Vanguardia: Cuba News*, http://64.21.33.164/Cnews/y01/dec01/1707.htm.
56. Leila Cobo, "Azúcar para toda una época", *El Nuevo Herald*, 28 December 2000, 31D.
57. Hebdige, *Subculture*, 3.
58. "Sin Celia", *People en español*, October 2003, 81. Original Spanish: "Si yo no llamo la atención, que la llame mi vestuario."
59. Cited in "Celia Cruz", 27 September 2003, http://geek.musicasdelmundo.org.
60. Lydia Martin, "Salsa Star Celia Cruz Is Recuperating in N.Y. from 'Delicate Surgery'", *Miami Herald*, 6 December 2002, 4A.
61. One such instance is Ernesto Montaner's song, "Un son para Celia", where he calls Cruz "muñequita de café" ("coffee-coloured doll") and "negra linda" ("beautiful black woman"). In Cruz with Reymundo, *Celia*, vii, viii.
62. Oscar Hijuelos, "A Song of Love for Cuba", *New York Times*, 23 August 2003.
63. Toni Morrison, ed. *Race-ing Justice, En-gendering Power: Essays on Anita Hill, Clarence Thomas, and the Construction of Social Reality* (New York: Pantheon, 1992), 207.
64. Martin, "Salsa Star Celia Cruz", 4A.
65. *People*, 4 August 2003, 69–78, 75.
66. Aparicio, *Listening to Salsa*, 144.
67. For further commentary on this distinction, please see Frances R. Aparicio, "La Lupe, La India, and Celia: Toward a Feminist Genealogy of Salsa Music", in *Situating Salsa: Global Markets and Local Meanings in Latin Popular Music*, ed. Lise Waxer (New York and London: Routledge, 2002), 135–60.
68. Wilson Valentín-Escobar, "Nothing Connects Us All but Imagined Sound", in *Mambo Montage*, ed. Agustín Laó-Montes and Arlene Dávila (New York: New York University Press, 2001), 207–33.
69. Javier Santiago, "Celia: La perseverante de la salsa", *Claridad/En Rojo*, 22–28 June 1990, 25. Original Spanish: "se distingue como una de las pocas mujeres que se han atrevido a cantar salsa . . . [que] han tenido la gallardía de incursionar en este género".
70. Jon Pareles, "Celia Cruz, Petite Powerhouse of Latin Music, Dies at 77", *New York Times*, 17 July 2003.
71. Martin, "Adiós".
72. Celeste Fraser Delgado, "Over Her Dead Body", *Miami New Times*, 24 August 2003, http://miaminewtimes.com/issues/2003-07-24/music.html/l/index.html.
73. Estela Pérez, "Celia Cruz triunfó en un mundo de hombres", http://holahoy.com/lunes/internet.nsf/All/pg003798.htm.
74. Ibid.

75. *Celia Cruz and the Fania Allstars in Africa*, director Leon Gast (Geneon Entertainment, 2001, DVD).
76. http://www.musicofpuertorico.com/en/queen_ivy.html.
77. Patricia Meschino, "Ivy Queen", *Miami New Times*, 18 November 2004.
78. Jonpito, "India", http://www.stylusmagazine.com/feature.php?ID=1326.
79. Aparicio, *Listening to Salsa*, 179.
80. Aparicio, "La Lupe", 148.
81. "India", http://www.freestylemusic.com/Interviews/india.htm.
82. Howard Perez, "India Loves the Nightlife: The Princess of Salsa Talks about Her Music and Her Love for the Gay Community", *qvMagazine*, www.qvmagazine.com/qv6/latinospotlight.html.
83. Lorraine Gamman, "Self-Fashioning, Gender Display, and Sexy Girl Shoes: What's at Stake – Female Fetishism or Narcissism?" in *Footnotes: On Shoes*, ed. Shari Benstock and Suzanne Ferris (New Brunswick, NJ: Rutgers University Press, 2001), 98.
84. "Adiós Celia", *People*, 4 August 2003, 70.
85. Ana Cristina Reymundo, "Celia Cruz: La bella época de una diva", *Nexos* (January-March 2003): 73. Original Spanish: "Yo quiero que me velen y quiero una funeraria donde quepan muchos carros y que todo el mundo vaya."
86. Lydia Martin, "Queen of the People", in *Presenting Celia Cruz*, ed. Alexis Rodríguez-Duarte (New York: Clarkson Potter, 2004), 79.
87. "Not His Queen", *Street*, 8 August 2003, www.miami.com/mld/streetmiami/entertainment/6480646.htm.
88. Rebecca Díaz, "We Cubans Found It Offensive", *Miami New Times*, 7–13 August 2003, 7.
89. "Celia: I'll Tell You What's Offensive", *Miami New Times*, 14–20 August 2003, 7.
90. "Celia Racial Rhetoric", *Miami New Times*, 7–13 August 2003, 7.
91. Luis Aguilar León, "Hay que refugiarse en Celia Cruz", *El Nuevo Herald*, 8 October 2000.
92. Richard Pérez-Feria, "Mi tía cubana", *People en español*, October 2003, 12. Original Spanish: "siempre se hacía sentir en mi hogar. No tanto su música, para serles sincero, sino su espíritu, su energía, su cubanía, que era lo que más mis padres querían que mis hermanos y yo emuláramos."
93. Olga Connor, "Tributo a Celia Cruz: de Santos Suárez para el mundo", *El Nuevo Herald*, 23 July 2003.
94. Ernesto Montaner, "Un son para Celia", in Cruz with Reymundo, *Celia*, v.
95. For further analysis concerning Celia Cruz's politics, see Frances R. Aparicio's essay, which is chapter 1 of this book.
96. Beltrán, "Azúuucar".
97. Cruz with Reymundo, *Celia*, 211.
98. Ibid., 211.

99. Ibid., 102.
100. Francisco Ayala-Silva, "De Celia, Compay, Cuba y otras hierbas", *ElSalvador.com*, 19 July 2003, http://www.elsalvador.com/noticias/2003/07/19/escenarios/escen1.html.
101. Lydia Martin, "Capital Museum Mounting Show on Celia Cruz", *Miami Herald*, 30 October 2004.

6.

Calypso Rose's Phallic "Palet" and the Sweet Treat of Erotic Aurality

| LYNDON K. GILL

> A woman can be a bridge . . . A way to cross over.
> – Dionne Brand[1]

CALYPSO IS THE ORIGINAL Trinbagonian leitmotif.[2] It is difficult to imagine an investigation of cultural production in the Republic of Trinidad and Tobago that turns a deaf ear to Trinbagonian music. Generations of scholars have had not only to include Trinbagonian music in their ostensibly non-music-oriented studies, but also to rely upon that music – at least in part – as a means by which to understand Trinbagonian culture.[3] If it has remained the case for centuries that "in Trinidad [as well as in Tobago], music is an important means for making and contesting cultural claims about identities" and more than this that "music is also an important means for *thinking* and generating *feelings* about such claims", then calypso stands always in a spotlight on the Trinbagonian epistemological stage.[4] This intellectual responsibility to address calypso music is less a burden than an opportunity to listen more closely to the music and the artists who create it.

The calypsonian to whom I propose we give a close critical listen is by many accounts the grande dame of calypso music: McCartha Sandy-Lewis, better known by her delicate (though thorny) sobriquet "Calypso Rose".[5] Lewis's 1968 song "Palet" provides the sonic focal point for the following analysis.[6] Over the course of this chapter, I give a brief listen to the echoing history of calypso music, introduce Lewis as an artist and foreground the enticing work her song does as part of a particular sex-gender politic that is as inflected with female same-sex desire as it is with spirituality.[7]

Through her song and her person, Lewis is instrumental to my elaboration of "erotic subjectivity" as an epistemological proposition. This proposition, which provides my interpretive infrastructure, is deeply indebted to Caribbean-American, lesbian feminist, poet, novelist and essayist Audre Lorde. It is Lorde's re-conceptualization of the sensual as a bridge between the political and the spiritual in her classic essay "Uses of the Erotic: The Erotic as Power" that has set the tone for the present intervention.[8] I propose extending Lorde's political-sensual-spiritual triad into not merely a broadened sense of the erotic – still mostly synonymous with the sensual – but rather into a new conceptualization of the erotic altogether. An epistemic trinity, erotic subjectivity recognizes the political, the sensual and the spiritual as part of an interlinked way of experiencing and interpreting the world. This perspectival trinity – at its most abstract – attends to various formal and informal power hierarchies (the political); sexual, as well as non-sexual, intimacy (the sensual); and sacred metaphysics (the spiritual).[9] Erotic subjectivity provides a particular means by which to recognize the mutually constitutive relationships among these seemingly separate, but actually linked, epistemologies in the life and work of an exemplary artist.

By imagining herself as "Rosie-the-*palet*-vendor" chanting through the streets of Barataria, Trinidad – summoning customers (or perhaps the occasional sweet tryst) – Lewis puts calypso to work in the tradition of the genre, without forcing the pleasure out of her play. This play holds the quotidian "real" and imaginatively re-crafts it so effectively that it pointedly calls into question that selfsame reality as a means by which to challenge the listener's own imagination.[10] In this respect, calypso sings the challenge that one finds in most artistry, but to fully appreciate that challenge in this particular artistic genre, one must first return if only briefly to the troublesome beginnings of calypso's utterance.

A Very Brief History of Calypso: Echoes of a Shifting Origin

Calypso is an aural pastiche. A mischievous laugh in the face of questions of origin, this quintessential Trinbagonian music genre is the sonorous chorus for a culture composed of harmonious dissonance.[11] Well over three centuries old by most scholarly accounts, modern calypso's earliest form likely combines two vocal traditions – the *lavway* and the *calipso* – both closely associated with the Trinbagonian *kalinda* (also *calinda*), or stickfighting tradition, of the early eighteenth century.[12] A call-and-response challenge song led most often by *chantuels* (typically the very stickfighters who were soon to engage in physical combat), the *lavway* was a means by which to lure an opponent while boasting of one's stickfighting prowess.[13]

Although stickfighters and *chantuels* are almost invariably considered to have been male, there is a well-documented history of formidable female *bâtonnieres* and sharp-tongued *chantuelles*.[14] In fact, the *calipso* (also called the *cariso* or *caliso*) – the song and accompanying dance tradition to which the modern calypso most likely owes its name – was performed predominantly by women during the rest periods of stickfighting matches.[15] These derisive banter songs would have had more elaborate compositional structures and addressed a wider breadth of themes than the male-dominated *lavway*. Nevertheless, the *chantuelle* and the *calipso* singer have been so closely aligned in calypso scholarship that *calipso* song or dance are seldom mentioned at all, obscuring the distinctiveness of the largely female vocal tradition about which little thus far has been written. The British colonial government's repressive legislation against stickfighting in the late-nineteenth century would result in the increasing transfer of aggression from the contest of the *bois* (French for "wood" and used to describe the stickfighter's dreadful tool) to the tongue-lashing. As male *chantuels* and stickfighters took refuge in song, they adopted elements of what, for well over a century, had been a predominantly female song of playful ridicule.[16] As the aural distinctiveness of the *calipso* song and the *lavway* began to fade, female *calipso* singers were nearly flooded out of the Trinbagonian singing tradition. The principal elements of a new syncretic vocal art form were in place; the dawn of the twentieth century witnessed the birth of calypso, a new genre of music characterized by a mixture of musical elements inherited from the *lavway* and the *calipso*: a driving 2/2 or 4/4 rhythm, leader-and-chorus cooperation, consistent syncopation and a predominance of the minor mode.[17] But this unique new form was largely reserved for men due to the severe repression of female public performance mandated by an unduly gender-biased Trinidadian Victorianism.[18]

McCartha Linda Sandy-Lewis: A Rose by Any Other Name

Four decades into the twentieth century, women were still overwhelmingly excluded from the calypso music genre. However, a girl child born on 27 April 1940 in the hilltop village of Bethel on the island of Tobago would soon sing a sonorous challenge to that exclusion.[19] Although Lewis herself acknowledges that she was not the first woman to sing calypso in the tents, she is the first female calypsonian to garner significant recognition and reap the rewards for the mastery of her craft.[20] The fourth of eleven children born to the Spiritual Baptist Altino Sandy and his wife Dorchea Sandy (née Ford), McCartha Linda Sandy wrote her first calypso in 1955 and began her professional career in Trinidad's capital, Port of Spain, in 1963.[21] By 1977, Lewis became the very first female calypsonian to win the national Road March title (with her hit song "Tempo").[22]

Later that same year, anticipating that Lewis (or perhaps another female calypsonian) could potentially win the highly coveted national "Calypso King" competition during the upcoming 1978 carnival season, the Carnival Development Committee introduced the newly renamed national "Calypso Monarch" competition. The name change marked a new possibility in the predominantly male calypso arena, returning women – almost a century after their near exclusion from the genre – to centre stage in the art form that calipso singers, *chantuelles* and female stickfighters had in large part helped to midwife. During the 1978 carnival season, Lewis reclaimed this legacy, becoming the very first female national Calypso Monarch (singing "Her Majesty" and "I Thank Thee") while again winning the national Road March title (with her song "Come Leh We Jam").[23] The first calypsonian – female *or* male – to simultaneously win both titles in a single year, Lewis had successfully executed a calypso coup.[24] *Her* Majesty (the new reigning monarch in the kingdom of song) had made a way – her own. As she put it, "I am like a river overflowing its bank. You try to stop me, I'm going to find room to pass."[25] A river can be a bridge – a rippling way between two shores. A swollen river, ravenous and bankless, does not cease to be a bridge, but the rushing water has another way in mind. This is precisely the unfathomable path Dionne Brand brings to life when she insists in this chapter's epigraph that "A woman can be a bridge . . . A way to cross over."[26] If Lewis is a flooded path, which I entreat you here to follow, then all that has preceded this invitation has been intended to reassure you for the journey.

Coming to "Palet": Calypso Masculinity and the Scholar who Refuses

In his article "I Lawa: The Construction of Masculinity in Trinidad and Tobago Calypso", Gordon Rohlehr provides the only scholarly treatment – though brief – of Lewis's 1968 calypso that I have yet seen.[27] And it is Rohlehr's analysis of the song that has prompted, in part, the present close engagement. I do not intend to re-present Rohlehr's arguments in full here, but his handling of phallic symbolism in calypso, and its correlative import for Trinbagonian masculinity, opens an irresistible space for intervention into the gendered politics of what might be called "calypso masculinity".[28] Although Rohlehr quite accurately identifies the calypso music genre as one of the most elaborately articulated archives of Trinbagonian masculinity,[30] he stops short of being able to recognize this masculinity anywhere but in the male body. If, for him, masculinity is always already confined to the male body, then it comes to function as little more than a euphemism for maleness.[29] This troublesome conflation of sex (maleness) and gender (masculinity) severely undermines Rohlehr's ability to accurately read the "phallus" and its relevance for his interpretive approach to Lewis's "Palet". In fact, this sex-gender conflation is matched by an equally troubling correlative conflation between the phallus and the penis that I must first address in order to recuperate one of the principal leitmotivs for masculinity – the phallic symbol – that Rohlehr uses (to tell an origin narrative of calypso masculinity) and refuses (just when it seems that Lewis too might possess it).

A Working Definition of the "Phallus": Risking Unnatural Synecdochism

Without getting lost in psychoanalysis – the sub-discipline that has "gifted" us the phallus as a theoretical concept beyond its original Greek etymology – and yet mindful still that the very act of attempting to define the phallus is invested with its own highly charged philosophical and psychoanalytic implications, I nevertheless attempt here a working definition of the term.[30] The most effective means by which to explain this rather counterintuitive concept may be to begin by clarifying what the phallus is *not*. Despite its etymology, the phallus, as redeployed by Austrian psychiatrist Sigmund Freud and French psychoanalyst Jacques Lacan – who perhaps offers the most sustained psychoanalytic treatment of the phallus – is summarily *not* the penis.[31] I turn to Lacan as the only appropriate gesture in an attempt to clarify a term whose popularity is largely indebted to his elaboration of Freud in his 1958 invited lecture "The Signification of the Phallus" delivered at the Max-Planck Institute in Munich, Germany.[32] Neither imaginary apparition nor material object, I understand the Lacanian phallus – informed by Lacan's elaborate forays into the baroque science of semiotics – to be a symbolic ideal with no adequate direct object referent; in essence, an exclusively symbolic object to which a multitude of material objects refer, but none can ultimately fully contain. Following Freud, Lacan is ostensibly clear about the fact that the phallus is not the penis, and yet there remains an inherited slippage in his work that threatens the very conflation that both theorists claim to resist.[33] It is perhaps the case then that Rohlehr's phallus-penis slippage is an inherited one – inherent in the terms as long as one fails to clarify the distinction.

If, for the purposes of this analysis, the phallus is to be read as the whole constellation of associations ("the effects of the signified") that any particular society or culture invests in the penis either directly or indirectly, then the closest we can come to defining the phallus is as a web of meaning that includes but is not contained by the penis. In other words, through an elaboration ad infinitum about the penis, one approaches asymptotically a definition of the phallus. Therefore, the penis is better understood as a synecdoche for the phallus, a part representing a larger whole within which it is incorporated. Furthermore, I propose that masculinity is perhaps best defined as the whole constellation of associations that any particular society or culture invests in the phallus – either directly or indirectly – constituting a web of meaning that includes the web of meaning that defines the phallus but is not ultimately contained by it. In other words, the phallus is a synecdoche for masculinity. Therefore, the synecdochic relationships of penis-phallus and phallus-masculinity come not merely to mirror each other, but rather to form an interpretive chain in which the penis is a synecdoche for the phallus, which is in turn a synecdoche for masculinity.

Before this proposition begins to stiffen too comfortably, I turn to feminist theorist Judith Butler, whose critique of the slippage between phallus and penis is premised in part upon denaturalizing the very synecdochic chain that I propose.[34] Returning to critique Freud in her critique of Lacan, Butler emphasizes that there is nothing "natural" about this penis-phallus-masculinity linkage. These relationships are of course the result of social construction, but what is important about this social construction for Butler is that it is inevitably unstable and thus requires constant reaffirmation often through the repetition of precisely the slippage that Freud, Lacan and Rohlehr commit over and over again.[35] Butler contends that it is an impotence of the imagination that compels us to interpret the phallus always and only through the penis, naturalizing a link between the two that is the result of our association and not of nature. Although Butler concedes that materiality (where the penis resides as a morphological structure) and language (where the phallus resides as a symbolic element of discourse) are co-constitutive, fully embedded and implicated in each other, she uses this mutuality to refuse the presumption that the penis is the "real" phallus; in fact, for Butler, the phallus is fundamentally transferrable property.[36]

Perhaps what is most immediately relevant for this discussion is Butler's proposition (by evoking the possibility of a "lesbian phallus") that the imagination – or imaginative play with this transferrable phallus – can trouble that unstable link between the material and the ideal by disrupting the seemingly natural order precisely at its moment of repetitive reaffirmation.[37] Butler's rhetorical posturing with the "lesbian phallus" is intended to function as a discursive intervention that, through insisting upon the coherence of a seeming contradiction, actually opens up a site within which to identify implicit gendered presumptions. If the phallus is kept true to its symbolic form, there ought to be no reason why one could not imagine the phallus without men; this discursive re-territorialization erases the penis while simultaneously enacting the recuperative potential of "reiteration with a difference".[38] The phallus seemingly displaced is thrust into such high relief that it, in effect, becomes more clearly identifiable. Judith Halberstam has made a near identical case for masculinity, arguing that the notion and enactment of "female masculinity" actually provides the clearest picture of masculinity as such.[39]

If Butler's proposition is an invitation to see the phallus more clearly, then the present analysis hopes to focus that vision even further by proposing a particular cultural location from which to challenge the tacit politics of unsituated gender theory. If Butler is aggressively re-territorializing the phallus by emphasizing its transferability, I am here aggressively territorializing that attempt by calling for an attention to place, a mindfulness of cultural territory. A Trinbagonian cultural geography – like any specific cultural geography – contains its particular landscape of phallic objects, at once contributions to and reflections of a Trinbagonian phallic symbolism. It is by virtue of recuperating one such phallic object – the *palet* – that Lewis's playful gender politic becomes audible.

The Phallic *Palet* and a Gendered Politic of Representation

Unable to deny the seductive double entendre of "Palet", Rohlehr is nonetheless unwilling to recognize Rosie's *palets* as phallic objects; he insists, despite figurative incongruence, that Lewis's song is suggestive not of fellatio, but of cunnilingus.[40] Perhaps the most plausible explanation for this misalignment of a metaphor is to be found in Lewis's own female morphology; the spectre of her vagina appears to prevent Rohlehr from recognizing Rosie's phallic treats. If Rohlehr is unwilling to buy the phallic *palet*, this is only in part because of his inability to relinquish the phallus-as-penis conflation already dissected. There is a deeper refusal that Rohlehr enacts, perhaps not altogether consciously, which turns a deaf ear to an implicit critique that Lewis nimbly disseminates through the penis-phallus-masculinity synecdochic chain. Relying precisely upon an impotence of the phallic imagination, Lewis levies an indirect critique of the penis; this is a critique that simultaneously allows Lewis, as the character of Rosie, to repossess the phallus (a reminder of the long tradition of female stickfighters and the symbolism of this presence) while allowing Lewis, as calypsonian, to playfully critique the penis through an understated yet ribald mockery characteristic of the music genre.

If Rohlehr's history of masculinity in calypso foregrounds the stickfighter's *bois* as the symbolic object representing the penis and thus alluding (quite unnaturally) to a particular kind of Trinbagonian masculinity, then the historical presence of the formidable female stickfighter – a spectre that Rohlehr cannot avoid – inadvertently demonstrates the accessibility of the symbolic penis for the Trinbagonian woman willing to grab hold of it.[41] By replacing the *bois* with the *palet* (a truncated stick), Lewis is able to hold the penis in song just long enough to critique it by measuring it through a more palatable phallic object. Reading the *palet* as a phallic object does indirect work on the penis precisely because the penis occupies such a prominent place as the unnatural phallic object par excellence. The penis-phallus slippage that Rohlehr, Lacan and Freud allow, but which Butler critiques, is precisely the location in which Lewis inserts her intervention. This sung gender politic must be heard as part of a long Trinbagonian oral tradition resounding with "picong". From the French *piquant* meaning "pricking" (the pun is not only welcomed, but humourously instructive here), the word describes the exchange of stinging, biting and pointed humourous insults, usually between friends.[42] Lewis's loving mockery offers up the penis as a sweet treat at the same time as it snickers at its melting.

Lewis's melting phallic object – and in the tropics, the *palet* is perpetually melting – is a playful dissolution of the unforgiving hardness of even the most formidable erect penis. Lewis reminds us of the inevitable flaccidity of the penis, which metaphors like "wood" and "iron" – perhaps the most common indirect referents for the penis in Trinbagonian speech and song – would pretend to obscure. In essence, the erect penis is always vanishing, never able to be the mythic, perpetually erect, ithyphallus. The song's double entendre then is more than a mere mask for the penis, rather it takes the opportunity of the unimaginative association of all phallic objects to the penis as a means by which to critique the sex organ. This critique is able to trouble the penis-phallus link in the synecdochic chain by demonstrating – through association with the *palet* – the failure of the penis to be the phallus. This phallic object is returned to its rightful place, disallowed from materializing the symbolic. The restorative rupture, sung in a Trinbagonian key, alludes to a broader potential for Trinbagonian masculinity, unmoored to the penis or the phallus. Hearing "Palet", while reminded of the central female presence (in song, dance and fight) as part of Rohlehr's aggressively masculine, pre-calypso, kalinda tradition, only sweetens the gender picong, pointing to a long tradition of assertive Trinbagonian female masculinity.

The Pleasures of Giving Suck

Although the *palet* metaphor is a form of critique, its sweetness – its desirability – persists nevertheless. One of the long enduring gustatory tropes of Trinbagonian sexual discourse, the figurative "sweetness" of the penis is quite literally actualized by its competing phallic object. There is a sensuality to the *palet* as phallic object that ought not to be subsumed by the previous discussion of the *palet* as an intervention into a certain gender politics. It is mostly, after all, for the pleasure of giving suck that Rosie sells her *palets*. The shillings she earns from selling her popsicles are ostensibly the way that Rosie makes her living, but we learn by the last couplet of the song that successful business is not after all her motivation: "I don't care if meh business bust [if she goes out of business], I selling *palet* and a giving trust [credit]."⁴³ Even if it drives her out of business, the *palet* vendor is willing to give a bit of sweetness on credit.⁴⁴ It is this emphasis on sweetness for sweetness's sake that encourages a turn to a discussion of pleasure.

The easiest point of entry for this engagement with pleasure and desire is via *palet*'s most obvious and seductively apt homonym: the "palate" or the roof of the mouth. The repeated "palalalala lala lalet!" of the chorus requires a repeated delicate tap of the tongue against the palate that not only calls attention to the homonymic pair, but also quite intimately pin points the exact space the *palet* is called to fill. This flirtatious coaxing with sung speech emphasizes the highly sensual quality of vocality.⁴⁵ Though not a reproductive organ, the mouth is most certainly a sexual organ – in oral sex (when the mouth comes into direct contact with the genitals) as in *aural* sex when the voice is used to enhance arousal (or even replace actual physical contact).⁴⁶ The voice then as metonym for sexuality is saturated with the sensuousness of the space from which it flows and the uses to which it can be put; even outside of an explicitly sexual encounter, the resonance of sensuality still echoes in the voice. This voice, like the sensuality it summons, is nearly always marked by a whole range of subject-positions – gender being perhaps the first cue for which we listen intently.

In "Palet", four lines of its six-line chorus repeatedly call particular attention to the fact that both the singing mouth of the *palet* vendor and the desired mouth of the potential customer are decidedly female. Lewis sings: "*Palet, palet*, mama. *À la petite palet,* mama. *Palalalala lala lalet! À la petite palet,* mama. *Palalalala lala lalet! À la petite palet,* mama."⁴⁷ Echoing the pushcart vendors she grew up hearing seduce their customers with song, Lewis uses song to imagine herself as one such character, but with one substantial difference. Lewis recalls as follows:

> There used to be three people passing down 12th Street – well, [really] the whole of Barataria. [On Saturdays and Sundays] It's the nuts man, the pudding man and the palet man. I never saw a female [vendor]. It is only when I came to America that I saw females pushing their [cart] in the summer to sell snow cones. But [in Trinidad], it was men [who] used to be selling, pushing their carts and selling.⁴⁸

Lewis's own female body converts this simple French Creole refrain into a declaration of possibility for Trinbagonian female same-sex desire.[49] It is significant that Lewis does not imagine herself a male *palet* vendor – even in spite of never having seen a female vendor when the song was written – nor does she substitute a masculine vocative for the feminine "mama". The sensual pleasure of giving suck is here shared between women over the sticky, melting sweetness of a phallic symbol that critiques the penis's claim to the phallus while offering a pleasurable bridge for a female same-sex encounter. The *palet* as melting phallic symbol subtly vanishes the penis, which is precisely the tool (pun here intended) that is presumed to render female same-sex coitus, at best, unfulfilling (quite literally) and, at worst, simply impossible. At the throbbing centre of a potential female same-sex encounter, Lewis is able to brandish phallic symbolism without the penis getting in the way.

Rumour and the Dilemma of Vanishing Desire

By playfully encouraging the conflation of Calypso Rose and Rosie-the-*palet*-vendor, Lewis indirectly centres her own same-sex desire. And yet despite this and other quite explicit references to her same-sex desire in song or in conversation, Lewis's highly visible presence as a calypso icon has ironically rendered her largely invisible as a same-sex desiring Caribbean woman. The possibility of Lewis's same-sex desire has perhaps been most notably dismissed into the far reaches of malicious rumour by noted Caribbean feminist and literary scholar Carole Boyce Davies: "Calypso Rose had to survive through rumours of lesbianism and for years had a distinctly androgynous appearance; her stage performance was similar to some male Calypsonians like the Mighty Sparrow, including dancing and projecting the microphone as phallus. Singing songs of men, sex and satisfaction . . . Rose ably competed with her male peers."[50] Although Davies hesitates to make a definitive statement about Lewis's sexual orientation, she is still able to imply – without necessarily saying – that it is Lewis's (perhaps strategically) masculine stage performance that has caused her to suffer seemingly unfounded accusations of lesbianism, a veritable assault upon her unstated and thus presumed heterosexuality. Undoubtedly, Lewis's distinctly boyish appeal off stage – and here I directly contest Davies's reading of Lewis as "androgynous" as perhaps part of a refusal to see Lewis's alluringly handsome charm – has only contributed to the wide (hushed) recognition of her same-sex desire. This recognition has often to do with Lewis's on- and off-stage refusal of the trappings of "appropriate" Trinbagonian femininity – a femininity that is often assertive, forceful, gregarious and quite vocal, but still adheres to a very particular aesthetic that Lewis largely avoids. The artist's shortly cropped, unpermed hair, affinity for pants (flamboyant though they may be) and discomfort with high heels are by now not in the least surprising for her Trinbagonian audiences, who have come to normalize Lewis's "odd" gender expression as largely idiosyncratic. But this signature style would have early on set Lewis apart from femininity even if Lewis herself had not displayed a certain comfort with an ostensibly effortless Trinbagonian masculinity that comes across often as suave, colourful and rum-shop sociable.[51]

Davies does attend to the false premise that sexual orientation can be read through one's ability or inability to perform her gender "correctly". As it is most often the case that sex (as reproductive morphology or chromosomal make up) and sexuality (as sexual practice) are hardly seen in public spaces, gender becomes the cue for these other two categories that in actuality have very little to do with gender at all; Davies seems to align herself with feminist theorist Judith Butler's contestation of a *heterosexual matrix* that compulsorily aligns sex-gender-desire based primarily on gender's legibility.[52] And yet, Davies – by not explicitly considering the possibility that Lewis may in fact be a same-sex desiring woman even if she does not call herself a "lesbian" – indirectly perpetuates the very same *compulsory heterosexuality* that Butler contests, disallowing through silence Lewis's same-sex desire – which is indeed not directly correlated to her performance of a short-haired, boyish masculinity, but present nonetheless even in spite of her courting (or more often tenderly chastising) men in song.[53]

In an ironic turn that exposes one of the principal weaknesses of textual citatory practices in academe, Davies's oblique reassurance that the rumours of Lewis's lesbianism will prove false has taken on the infectious quality of rumour itself. Cited repeatedly in scholarly texts as *the* definitive (non) statement on Lewis's sexual orientation, Davies's attention to Lewis's sexuality might be read a bit more generously as an attempt to side step the matter altogether by noting that Lewis has had to confront rumours of lesbianism regardless of her actual, unstated sexual orientation.[54] However, as is the case with the most resilient rumours, the least generous or subtle readings have proven to be the most infectious. In the limited existing scholarly literature, as in the abundant popular media accounts of Lewis's life and oeuvre, the assumption of Lewis's heterosexuality has only been further justified by her 1966 marriage of convenience to Aubrey Lewis in Puerto Rico. Queer feminist writer Adrienne Rich reminds us that opposite-sex marriage does not a heterosexual woman make, emphasizing that same-sex desiring women who do choose to marry men may do so for strategic purposes and not in an effort to divorce themselves from their same-sex attractions.[55] However, Lewis's marriage of convenience proves inconvenient for an accurate reading of her same-sex desire.[56]

It is precisely this complexity of relationships that makes same-sex desire among Caribbean women so seemingly difficult to recognize, except perhaps when lives and love depend on it.[57] More often than not though, the surreal invisibility of Caribbean female same-sex desire is unconvinced by the materiality of flesh, palms pressed, thighs touched, chests breathing in unison or the flutter of kisses on her body's tender seams.[58] Yet, nearly drowned in a swirling silence that swallows like the sea, desire still speaks its name with tongues on fire.[59] Lewis had this to say about her same-sex desire:

> I am a . . . how you call the word? How you call the word? I have a friend or a lover and she always says, "Your work – because this is what you love – your work comes first." But I still divide [my time between] my work [and] my lover and we are domestic partners. This year will make it eleven years I've been married . . . September will make it eleven years. We were married in a church in California – a Catholic Church.
>
> I say, look, this is my life. I was raped when I was eighteen, so I have never had a man in my life. I was raped by three men when I was eighteen years of age. So, I never had any man in my life [and because of that] all the Calypsonians [would taunt Lewis by saying,] "She's a lesbian" [only] because I never slept with any of them. Thank the Lord for that!
>
> So, I made it final [by deciding to "marry" her long term partner] because this is my life. My family accepts me – my whole family knew . . . my aunt had known . . . [that same] aunt – the lady who raised me – accepted me. Everybody accepts me. And who can't accept me, chew them!
>
> [People in Trinidad and Tobago] do talk about me, but I don't care. [They may talk] But not in a negative way. Not in a negative way at all. If they saying negative, it's probably in their mind. But they still hug me, they still kisses me, they still bow to me. Oh yes! Every time I arrive home [to Trinidad and Tobago] they bow to me, man![60]

Lewis finds a way around using any particular language to describe her sexual identity; she offers instead a demonstration of the elaborate language of ellipses that Trinbagonians use as effectively as the spoken word. There is an entire vocabulary for silences, ways to indicate with different kinds of noiselessness what it is exactly that is going unspoken, ways to mention the unmentionable outside of language.

During the course of the interview, I dared not offer "lesbian" or "homosexual" or "queer" to fill the space that Lewis perhaps intentionally leaves unfilled. Instead of attempting a word to describe what she *is*, Lewis shifts quickly instead to describe who she *has*. Her sixteen-year domestic partnership with her female partner, consecrated by the Catholic Church, is a testament to Lewis's comfort with her same-sex desire, so her hesitance to name that desire comes from somewhere other than self-denial; perhaps the available terms are not as effective as the silence. A rape and breast cancer survivor,[61] Lewis holds as tightly to the love of her partner as she does to her love of life, a life lived her way to the tune of her own happiness, uncluttered by any voiced referent for her affections. The fact that her family acknowledges and accepts her bold resolve to live and love in a manner that brings her joy can only be a boon to Lewis. Later in the interview, upon asking her explicitly if she would describe herself as a "lesbian", Lewis quickly smiles at me and with all the ease of a breath says, "I am happy."[62] And as best as I can tell, she is happy; she is calypso royalty. She must have a sense of rumours circulating always just out of ear shot – the pests of all royals it seems – but she is comforted by knowing that her subjects still bow lovingly before her. She must be comforted too by the sense that rumour feeds upon secrecy and shame; this seventy-one-year-old woman, who has found love with another woman, suffers neither. What happens to a rumour once it is proven true?

Healing, Mourning and Prophecy: A Calypsonian's Spiritual Ascension

Spectral rumour – and the ritualized language of ellipsis that summons it – calls attention to the vanished in Lewis's "Palet". This attentiveness to the ghostly in turn summons a force that goes unmentioned explicitly in the song, but remains a haunting presence in her consciousness and thus also in her artistry: it is the spiritual.[63] The daughter of a Spiritual Baptist minister – a reverence for the unseen sown deeply in Lewis's consciousness from an early age – it perhaps seemed more likely that she might become a church leader than a calypso singer. Presumed diametrical opposites in the Trinidad and Tobago of the 1940s and 1950s, the lewd song of the calypsonian and the righteous song of the Spiritual Baptist were thought to serve opposing spiritual allegiances; one could not serve God and the devil at the same time.[64] And it seemed from her earliest days in the Tobagonian villages named for biblical cities that Lewis had been touched to serve God:

> Before I could have comprehended [it completely], my father [used to] tell me that I born with a gift. Because when I was small – before I went to Trinidad – many times they [would] miss me [not know where to find her]; and when they miss me, they [would] have to go hunting the whole of Bethel and Bethlehem looking for me ... Some spirit used to come into me and lead me away.
>
> ... One time when they found me, they found me in a house in Bethlehem – the whole yard was full of people. I was healing people ... I know that I have a sort of a spiritual gift within me.[65]

Whether a true child prophet laying hands on the people of a village aptly named or a precociously young girl anxious to minister like her father in a village longing for a Caribbean Christ, Lewis had indeed been led by a compulsion beyond her reckoning to the faith of her father.

Although she was baptized into the Spiritual Baptist faith, it would not be until adulthood that Lewis would formally begin her spiritual trials on a quest to deepen her faith:

> We – the Spiritual Baptists – when we go into the inner chamber to gain higher wisdom, we go into a room and [are] locked away for certain number of days – it depends: five days, seven days, two weeks or whatever ... I did it five times. I was mourned five times. We call it "mourning", when you seclude yourself from the carnal world and you go to the spiritual world. And all you do is pray. All you do is drink water and pray. You are fasting. There is light, but your eyes are banned. And the reason why your eyes are banned is as a symbol that you are banning yourself from the sight of the world.
>
> So, I mourned five times. The first time I mourned, I was a healer. The second time I mourned I was a Diver and Searching Warrior [spiritual roles in faith]. The third time I mourned, I'm a Mother. The fourth, I'm a Mother; the fifth time, I'm a Mother. [I ask for clarification] A "Mother" is at the head ... which means to say that I can put bands on my children [offer sacred protection and guidance to her own circle of followers]. I can baptize children, put seals and signs on them, and

> mourn them [initiate and offer spiritual counsel to newcomers in the faith]. I am very high up there.⁶⁶

Having mourned the death of her carnal self five times and each time experiencing a transfiguration of spirit, Mother McCartha cherishes her role as the religious leader she was perhaps called to become through various phases of enlightenment.⁶⁷ These phases are revealed to the fasting suppliant during the mourning ritual; devotees come to see themselves – their spiritual selves – more clearly as they journey towards higher planes in the religious tradition. First seeing herself as a healer, Lewis believes she has been given the ability to soothe pain with her touch; as a diver and searching warrior in her second journey into her sacred self, Lewis believes she was chosen to be a spiritual warrior tasked with scouring the sea floor in search of lost spirits in order to guide them home. One cannot help but imagine these diving warriors of this syncretic religion having been given the task of walking the watery underbelly of the Middle Passage looking for those unsettled souls, presumed to be roaming the fathoms of the Atlantic yearning for a way home. In her final three crosses into the realm of the otherworldly, Lewis is thrice called spiritual *Mother* though she has had no child of her own flesh. Lewis has reached a rarified height in the Spiritual Baptist tradition.

And yet, Lewis's ascension in her faith has not distanced her from her craft as a calypsonian; quite to the contrary, Lewis attributes her talent for reading music and writing music, as well as playing the piano and the guitar to divine intervention. A musical autodidact, Lewis has never taken a single lesson to augment her craft and yet her virtuosity with the calypso music genre amounts to little less than the miraculous outcome of finding a passion, hearing clearly the message to deliver and claiming a medium to deliver that passionate message. In fact, Lewis's spirituality is in many respects the nerve centre of her musical sensibilities; she is forthright about her devotion to the Spiritual Baptist faith *and* to calypso music.⁶⁸ It is impossible then, in Lewis's estimation, to imagine her or her artistry disconnected from her religious foundation:

> [A strong Spiritual Baptist rhythm is] in me, ah born with it (she laughs). As I told you, I born a Baptist . . . I am a Baptist from birth. I grew up with it and don't matter what I do, it's within me. And there is something that one has to know, you cannot hide from that fact – you may try to take me out of the religion, [but] . . . the spiritual aspect, they can't take that out of me because no matter what, it is here

in my singing, in my speaking . . . my spiritual background and who I am spiritually also help me to create . . . I believe my music does something for people. That's why I feel that I am a messenger.[69]

To be wary of essentialist presumptions about an ontological spiritual self, one might best hear Lewis's statement as a testament to the centrality of her spirituality even in the very sites that seem so far removed from conventional religious terrain. Lewis is quick to affirm the devoutly spiritual nature of even her "sex songs" in an effort to call forth the very recalibration of the sensual as spiritual and the spiritual as sensual that erotic subjectivity in part encourages.[70] If it is that the messenger offers her testament in song, then she conveys it via what is perhaps the most miraculous and sensuous (not to mention ancient) instruments yet known: the voice.[71] Voice acquires a mysterious sensuality here not merely because of its relationship to the mouth, but also because its very production is here defined as an intimate vibration that comes from flesh and air resisting or giving way, muscles tightening or relaxing, in the soft folds of the vocal tract. Lewis's voice carries within it – in speech or in song – the echoes of a harmonized sensual-spiritual that resonates beyond a false dichotomy between the sexual and the religious.

Hearing the Call: Erotic Aurality and the Evidence of Things Unseen

Although perhaps conventionally considered one of Lewis's "sex songs", "Palet" does not simply engage sex, but it is mindful of both a gendered politic and a spiritual consciousness that hears sensuality as contributing to a three-part harmony of the political-sensual-spiritual.[72] Erotic subjectivity functions here as a hermeneutic measure, an interpretive frame that prompts a particular listening technique. It is most certainly the case that Lewis's extensive musical oeuvre provides myriad opportunities to listen for erotic subjectivity.[73] In fact, if one were inclined to dissociate the political, sensual and spiritual in an interpretive approach to Lewis's oeuvre, a tempting tripartite taxonomy might be the result: political songs, sex songs and religious songs neatly separated just so. However, this severed taxonomy represents not only a less challenging – and perhaps less interesting – interpretive frame, but also reinforces the troubling distinctions that have made the erotic (not simply as a euphemism for the sexual) so difficult to recognize. The challenge undertaken here is precisely to hear the political, sensual and spiritual at once in (perhaps even through) each other as part of a single sonic landscape.

However, this critical challenge is only in part about hearing erotic subjectivity in an artistic work that seems confined to the sexual (a constricted "erotic"). Song also provides a different interpretive mechanism with which to contest any attempted primacy of the visual in the elaboration of the concept. This analysis of "Palet" encourages one to *listen* for erotic subjectivity as keenly as one might have looked for it in other contexts. A conceptual and interpretive frame, erotic subjectivity extends even beyond the expansive gaze of the mind's eye. McCartha Linda Sandy-Lewis's life, faith and artistry are a melodious testament to the gospel of erotic subjectivity. She asks us only to close our eyes and listen.

Notes

1. Dionne Brand, *In Another Place, Not Here* (New York: Grove Press, 1996), 16. A lauded Caribbean lesbian poet, novelist and immigrant rights activist living in Toronto, Canada, Dionne Brand sets the tone for this analysis. Although Brand's impressive oeuvre – especially the remarkable novel from which this quote is taken – deserves careful attention, I employ her here in the hopes that her words will not only infuse the discussion they precede, but will also inspire readers to seek out her words in their original contexts.
2. Since the early 1970s, soca music's rising popularity as a younger Trinbagonian leitmotif has only contributed to the century-old aural legacy of the calypso music genre. See Donald Hill, *Calypso Calaloo: Early Carnival Music in Trinidad* (Gainesville: University Press of Florida, 1993), 283. Although its etymology is as feverishly contested as its parentage, soca is reputed to have been one of the many children of the calypsonian Garfield "Lord Shorty" Blackman (who would later turn away from the genre almost completely – though not away from music entirely – and devote his life to Rastafarianism, changing his name to Ras Shorty I). Marrying the traditional calypso to various pulsing rhythmic patterns from the Indian subcontinent, music that had made its way to Trinidad and Tobago in the sure hands and resounding memories of Indian indentured labourers, this Afro-Trinidadian musician (mostly likely among others) stripped calypso to its rhythmic creole soul. The "soul of calypso" – soca – danced from her mother's womb. See Milla Riggio, *Carnival: Culture in Action – The Trinidad Experience* (New York: Routledge, 2004). Mother, child and even the percussive Indo-Trinbagonian abba are all very much alive and well in Trinbagonian culture.

3. For one of the most recent discussions of this genealogy, see Kevin Birth, *Bacchanalian Sentiments: Musical Experiences and Political Counterpoints in Trinidad* (Durham: Duke University Press, 2008), 5. This genealogy includes Melville Herskovits and Frances Herskovits, *Trinidad Village* (New York: A.A. Knopf, 1947); Daniel Miller, *Modernity, an Ethnographic Approach: Dualism and Mass Consumption in Trinidad* (Providence: Berg, 1994) and *Capitalism: An Ethnographic Approach* (Providence: Berg, 1997); Kevin Yelvington, *Producing Power: Ethnicity, Gender and Class in a Caribbean Workplace* (Philadelphia: Temple University Press, 1995); Kevin Birth, *Any Time Is Trinidad Time: Social Meanings and Temporal Consciousness* (Gainesville: University Press of Florida, 1999); and Viranjini Munasinghe, *Callaloo or Tossed Salad?: East Indians and the Cultural Politics of Identity in Trinidad* (Ithaca: Cornell University Press, 2001). Anthropologist and ethnomusicologist Alan Merriam expands this claim further by emphasizing the ability to hear all music, much like other arts, as a symbolic means by which to understand peoples and behaviours and thus as a necessary tool for all socio-cultural analysis. See Alan Merriam, *The Anthropology of Music* (Evanston: Northwestern University Press, 1964), 13.
4. Kevin Birth, *Bacchanalian Sentiments* (Durham: Duke University Press, 2008), 12. Italics in original.
5. Throughout the analysis that follows, I will refer to Lewis by her unhyphenated married name, in accordance with her professional and personal preference.
6. Referring to an iced lollipop or popsicle, *palet* is most likely a French Creole rendering of the French "palette" from the Latin "paleta/paletta" for a flat instrument or flat bladed tool with a handle that is used for a variety of purposes. The French *palette* would thus refer primarily to a thin flat board or tablet; these flat boards with holes for thumb grips that were often used by painters to mix their colours. So, the term *palette* would come to refer also to a range or selection of colours or any assortment of items from which one chooses. *Palet* may have been used to describe the frozen lollipop because of the flat wooden stick inserted into them, the assortment of colours or flavours from which to choose, or perhaps a syncretic mix of all of these. The *Oxford English Dictionary Online* provides the recipe for this etymological confection (Oxford: Oxford University Press, 2011), www.oed.com.
7. I offer here a transcription of the song's lyrics for the reader's reference:
"Palet"
Composed and performed by Calypso Rose
(Lyrics transcribed by author)

> Is *palet* I selling
> to make a shilling.
> Is *palet* I selling
> for meh living.

That is my occupation
to be a *palet* woman.
Stretch out yuh hand I bound to stop;
I selling meh *palet* from ten cents up.
If you hear me:

(*Chorus*)

Palet, palet, mama.
À la petite palet, mama.
Palalalala lala lalet!
À la petite palet, mama.
Palalalala lala lalet!
À la petite palet mama.

I going all about –
East, West, North and South.
All by the college
I have meh privilege.
I have all kind of flavour:
orange, pine, sour sop and vanilla.
I pushing meh cart all through the rain.
Coming down I singing the same refrain.
If you hear me:

(*Chorus*)

From Sunday to Monday
and public holiday,
I selling meh palet;
Me ent have no limit.
Any time that yuh thirsty,
you could suck a palet from Rosie.
I don't care if meh business bust;
I selling palet and I giving trust.
If you hear me:

(*Chorus*)

8. Audre Lorde, "Uses of the Erotic: The Erotic as Power", in *Sister Outsider* (Trumansburg: Crossing Press, 1984 [1978]), 56.
9. Much like this transfigured sense of the erotic, "subjectivity" itself also signifies multiply as part of this epistemological intervention: the agential actor (Lewis as subject

of her own life narrative) in this analysis also forms the analytic centrepiece (the subject at hand, if you will) of this engagement.

10. If – as V.S. Naipaul acerbically proposes – "it is only in the Calypso that the Trinidadian touches reality" (Naipaul's *The Middle Passage: Impressions of Five Societies, British, French and Dutch, in the West Indies and South America* [London: Andre Deutsch, 1962) quoted in Louis Regis, *The Political Calypso: True Opposition in Trinidad and Tobago 1962–1987* [Kingston: University of the West Indies Press, 1999], xi), then that reality is a cunningly carnivalesque one. We have here a reality that mockingly defies the realness of the "real" with an infinite series of masks each more – or less – believable than the last until an interest in the masque finally overcomes a desire to look behind it. For more on this reading of the mask see Donald Hill, *Calypso Calaloo* (Gainesville: University Press of Florida, 1993), 216–17.

11. There does exist substantive scholarly literature on the origin of the term "Calypso": see Daniel Crowley, "Toward a Definition of Calypso (Part I)", *Ethnomusicology* 3, no. 2 (May 1959): 57–66; Daniel Crowley, "Toward a Definition of Calypso (Part II)", *Ethnomusicology* 3, no. 3 (September 1959): 117–24; and Daniel Crowley, "Folk Etymology and Earliest Documented Usage of 'Calypso' ", *Ethnomusicology* 10, no. 1 (1966): 81–82; J.D. Elder, "Evolution of the Traditional Calypso of Trinidad and Tobago: A Socio-historical Analysis of Song-change" (PhD diss., Department of Folklore, University of Pennsylvania, 1967); Errol Hill, "On the Origin of the Term Calypso", *Ethnomusicology* 11, no. 3 (September 1967): 359–67; Raymond Quevedo, *Atilla's Kaiso: A Short History of Trinidad Calypso* (St Augustine, Trinidad: University of the West Indies, 1983). This etymological debate holds within it competing claims about the "true" geo-cultural origins of the music genre, claims which Trinbagonian culture has taken delight in confounding since its birth and continues to confound centuries on. Nevertheless, the scholarly treatment of etymology-as-origin is instructive – though far from definitive – in that it allows one to mark a few of the various music traditions calypso incorporates or perhaps simply resembles. Considering the layered history of settlement, colonization, immigration and indentureship in Trinidad and Tobago, it would be very difficult to imagine a Trinbagonian aural landscape absent the resounding musical cross influences from the fifteenth century up through the nineteenth and early twentieth centuries. These influences include Native American, European, West African, Indian, Chinese, American (North and South) and even Middle Eastern music.

12. Elder, "Evolution"; John Cowley, *Carnival, Canboulay and Calypso: Traditions in the Making* (Cambridge: Cambridge University Press, 1996). The Tobago-born, University of Pennsylvania–trained folklorist J.D. Elder has written what is perhaps the most thorough ethnographic description of the Trinbagonian stickfight in his 1966 article " 'Kalinda': Song of the Battling Troubadours of Trinidad", *Journal of the Folklore Institute* 3, no. 2 (August 1966): 192–203.

13. The term "chantuel/chantuelle" is perhaps a creolized version of the French *chanteur/chanteuse* (meaning "singer"). And "lavway" may be a creolized version of both the French *la voix* (meaning "the voice") and *le vrai* (literally meaning "the true"). These propositions are informed by Cowley's *Carnival* and John Mendes's *Cote Ci Cote La: Trinidad and Tobago Dictionary* (Port of Spain: Zenith, 2003 [1986]). *Lavway*'s translational double entendre may be indicative less of a linguistic imprecision than of a flexibility in the French Creole unmatched in the Standard French. In essence, the *lavway* is a voiced oath of challenge that immediately declares its own truthfulness.
14. See Andrew Pearse, "Mitto Simpson on Calypso Legends of the Nineteenth Century", *Caribbean Quarterly* 4, nos. 3–4 (1956): 250–62; Susan Campbell, "Carnival, Calypso and Class Struggle in Nineteenth Century Trinidad", *History Workshop Journal* 26, no. 1 (1988): 1–27; Elder, "Evolution"; J.D. Elder, "Cannes Brûlées", *Drama Review* 42, no. 3 (Autumn 1998): 38–43; Carole Maison-Bishop, "Women in Calypso: Hearing the Voices" (PhD diss., Department of Educational Foundations, University of Alberta, 1994); Maude Dikobe, "Doing She Own Thing: Gender, Performance and Subversion in Trinidad Calypso" (PhD diss., Department of African-American Studies, University of California, Berkeley, 2003); and Hope Munro Smith, "Performing Gender in the Trinidad Calypso", *Latin American Music Review* 25, no. 1 (Spring–Summer 2004): 32–56.
15. Elder, "Evolution"; Gordon Rohlehr, *Calypso and Society in Pre-Independence Trinidad* (Port of Spain: Gordon Rohlehr, 1990); Cowley, *Carnival*; Dikobe, "Doing She Own Thing".
16. Elder, "Evolution", 109; Rohlehr, *Calypso and Society*, 213; Smith, "Performing Gender", 35.
17. Elder, "Kalinda", 200.
18. This Trinidadian Victorianism was the result of Queen Victoria's new "moral" order, which had begun with the British queen's accession to the throne in 1837. As fiercely defended in Trinidad by the colonial government as it was by the local middle class, Victorian morality would discourage female performance while not actively discouraging the calypso genre. In fact, the bawdiness of calypso provided just the appropriate balance of restraint and hedonism so relished by the Victorian era.
19. The scant scholarly literature that has thus far directly addressed Lewis's life and artistry has only made cursory mention of her place of birth – if Tobago is mentioned at all. Many of theses texts have summarily baptized her a "Trinidadian" (Maison-Bishop, "Women in Calypso"; Cynthia Mahabir, "The Rise of Calypso Feminism: Gender and Musical Politics in the Calypso", *Popular Music* 20, no. 3 [October 2001]: 409–30; Dikobe, "Doing She Own Thing"; Smith, "Performing Gender in the Trinidad Calypso"). Undoubtedly, Lewis's time in Trinidad from the age of nine – when she was taken to live with her uncle and his common-law

wife in Barataria – well into adulthood must have had a lasting impact on her character and the character of her art; however, one cannot turn a blind eye to Lewis's first nine years in Tobago and over seven decades returning *home* to the island regularly for kin and kind. The consummate "Trinbagonian" for having lived significant portions of her life on both islands, Lewis is quick nevertheless to sing the praises of her Tobagonian roots as a figurative battle cry against the too frequent elision of Tobago and Tobagonian cultural specificities in the popular and official discourses about Trinbagonian culture.

20. Thelma "Lady Trinidad" Lewis sang "Advice to every woman" as early as 1937 and Edna "Lady Ïere" Thomas-Pierre – who McCartha Lewis meets in the Original Young Brigade tent singing alongside her husband – both preceded Calypso Rose by at least a decade (Dikobe, "Doing She Own Thing", 39–41; Geoffrey Dunn and Michael Horne, dir., *Calypso Dreams* [In For a Penny, In For a Pound Productions, 2008, DVD]). It is quite likely that there is still an entire chorale of female calypsonians thus far unacknowledged by calypso scholarship. All of these unknown voices resound in the mouths of the few whose names survive them.

21. Spiritual Baptism is an Afro-Caribbean syncretic faith thought to have originated in St Vincent and the Grenadines, but brought to Trinidad and Tobago by black American ex-slaves who were recruited by the British into the West India Regiment and Core of Colonial Marines and decided to stay in the region once the units were disbanded. For a more detailed engagement with the faith – also referred to as the Shouter Baptist faith, indicating the highly vocal nature of worship – please see George E. Simpson, "The Shouters Church", in his *Religious Cults of the Caribbean: Trinidad, Jamaica and Haiti* (Rio Piedras: University of Puerto Rico, 1980); Eudora Thomas, *A History of the Shouter Baptists in Trinidad and Tobago* (Tacarigua: Calloux Publications, 1987); Hazel Gibbs De Peza, *My Faith: Spiritual Baptist Christian* (St Augustine: University of the West Indies School of Education, 1999); Kenneth Lum, *Praising His Name in the Dance: Spirit Possession in the Spiritual Baptist Faith and Orisha Work in Trinidad, West Indies* (Amsterdam: Harwood Academic, 2000); and Frances Henry, *Reclaiming African Religions in Trinidad: The Socio-political Legitimation of Orisha and Spiritual Baptist Faiths* (Kingston: University of the West Indies Press, 2003).

22. The "Road March" is a people's choice award given to the artist whose song is played most frequently at certain judging stations all along the carnival parade route. This coveted title might be considered tantamount to a "People's Monarch" title, awarded based on the votes of dancing, revelling bodies.

23. Although Lewis migrated to New York City in 1974, where she still currently resides when not on tour abroad or at home in Trinidad and Tobago, she continued to participate quite actively in the national calypso competition in Trinidad during the carnival season. This diasporic participation is not uncommon even today in

the calypso competition; there is in fact a long tradition of calypsonians returning to Trinidad from various sites of the Trinbagonian diaspora – in Canada, the United States or even the United Kingdom for instance – for a chance at the calypso crown.

24. Over the course of her career, Lewis has accumulated a flood of other awards in Trinidad and Tobago, in the Caribbean region and internationally. An honourary citizen of Belize and an official ambassador-at-large for Liberia, Lewis has long championed a form of international "musical diplomacy" through which she introduces various aspects of Trinbagonian, Belizean and Liberian culture (to name only a few) to her global audiences in song.
25. Dunn and Horne, *Calypso Dreams*.
26. Brand, *In Another Place*, 16.
27. Before his retirement in 2007, Gordon Rohlehr was professor of West Indian literature at the University of the West Indies' St Augustine campus in Trinidad. A meticulous archivist of the calypso genre, Rohlehr is perhaps best known for his extensive writing on calypso music.
28. I am referring here to Gordon Rohlehr, "I Lawa: The Construction of Masculinity in Trinidad and Tobago Calypso", in *Interrogating Caribbean Masculinities: Theoretical and Empirical Analyses*, ed. Rhoda Reddock (Kingston: University of the West Indies Press, 2004). Although not the focus of Rohlehr's analysis, calypso music also proves correlatively to be quite an elaborate archive of Trinbagonian femininity as represented – for better or for worse – by men as well as women.
29. Unfortunately, Caribbean masculinity studies has yet to insist upon this sex-gender distinction, instead leaving unchallenged the presumption that masculinity is the rightful and "natural" domain of men only. Although a relatively new field of study, Caribbean masculinity studies has inherited this sex-gender blindness from its parent field, Caribbean gender studies, in which femininity (and perhaps even feminism) is always already confined to the female body and thus presumed to be the rightful and "natural" domain of women only. See Rafael Ramírez et al., *Caribbean Masculinities: Working Papers* (San Juan: University of Puerto Rico, 2002), and Reddock, *Interrogating Caribbean Masculinities*, for this sex-gender blindness in considerations of Caribbean masculinities.
30. According to the *Oxford English Dictionary*, the word *phallus* is a classical Latin word meaning "penis" (usually an erect *ithyphallus* from the Greek for "straight phallus") that is probably a derivation of the ancient Greek word *phallos* also meaning "penis". And yet, we owe a rather counterintuitive redeployment of this term – and generations of others – to the psychoanalytic school of psychology. Undoubtedly, the gifts psychoanalysis gives are frustrated gifts at best.
31. Judith Butler, "The Lesbian Phallus and the Morphological Imagination", in her *Bodies that Matter: On the Discursive Limits of "Sex"* (New York: Routledge, 1993), 60.

32. Jacques Lacan, "The Signification of the Phallus", in *Écrits: A Selection,* trans. Alan Sheridan (New York: W.W. Norton, 1977), 285.
33. For this point, I am indebted to Kaja Silverman, "The Lacanian Phallus", *Differences: A Journal of Feminist Cultural Studies* 4, no. 1 (1992): 96.
34. Of course I am referring here and in what follows to Butler's seminal essay ("Lesbian Phallus").
35. Ibid., 89–90, and Judith Butler, *Gender Trouble: Feminism and the Subversion of Identity* (New York: Routledge, 1999).
36. Butler, "Lesbian Phallus", 59–69.
37. Ibid. 73–74, 86, 89.
38. José Esteban Muñoz, *Disidentifications: Queers of Color and the Performance of Politics* (Minneapolis: University of Minnesota Press, 1999).
39. Judith Halberstam, *Female Masculinity* (Durham: Duke University Press, 1998).
40. Rohlehr, "I Lawa", 368.
41. Ibid. 328–30, 335.
42. Mendes, *Cote Ci Cote La,* 145.
43. A naughty double entendre here relies upon the word "business" also potentially referring to the genitals (male or female) and the word "bust" referring to either a literal breaking of the male sex organ or the figurative verb "to break" often used to describe male ejaculation (the noun "break" may also describe male ejaculate). Therefore, the thinly veiled reference here may be to both injury and orgasm at once.
44. I remind the reader here that the transcribed lyrics to the song have been provided in a previous note.
45. Richard Middleton, "Appropriating the Phallus? Female Voices and the Law-of-the-Father", in his *Voicing the Popular: On the Subjects of Popular Music* (New York: Routledge, 2006), 92–93.
46. Much like *palet* and "palate", "oral" and "aural" also share an intimacy highlighted through their homonymic association.
47. Calypso Rose, "Palet".
48. McCartha Sandy-Lewis, interview by the author, 18 January 2007. The interview was conducted at Lewis's home in New York City.
49. The lingua franca of black peoples in Trinidad and Tobago in the nineteenth century, French Creole was the expected language in which the *lavway* and the *calipso* were composed and performed (Cowley, *Carnival,* 231). It would not be until 1898 that calypso composers would first experiment with lyrics sung – in part – in English, leading verse by verse to the composition of the first full English-language calypso "Jerningham the Governor" in 1899 (Elder, "Evolution", 113; Errol Hill, *The Trinidad Carnival: Mandate for a National Theatre* [Austin: University of Texas Press, 1972], 59; Cowley, *Carnival,* 126, 138). However, even once English had

become the dominant language of calypso, a French Creole call-and-response was often retained in the refrains of songs for centuries still (Campbell, "Carnival", 18–19). Over the course of two centuries, calypso had undergone a significant language flip – English and French trading places near completely in the mouths of the calypsonian. This language change is perhaps indicative of a more fundamental tectonic shift in the topography of Trinbagonian linguistic affinities.

Interestingly enough, the chorus of "Palet" harkens back to the earliest bilingual calypsos of 1898, which were sung primarily in English, but retained French Creole for their choruses. This linguistic retention results from the persistence of French Creole in the everyday lives of Trinbagonians up through the 1950s. Still quite well preserved in speech as well as in song even in contemporary Trinidad and Tobago, French Creole words and phrases have survived as part of common parlance.

50. Carole Boyce Davies, " 'Woman Is a Nation . . .': Women in Caribbean Oral Literature", in *Out of the Kumbla: Caribbean Women and Literature,* ed. Carol Boyce Davies and Elaine Fido (Trenton: Africa World Press, 1990), 183.

51. Over the course of her career, Lewis has become well known for quite literally kicking off her heels rather early – often right after her first or second song – in her stage performance to the noticeable delight of especially her expectant Trinbagonian audiences. Although Lewis frequently sings and dances through most of her sets barefoot, it is interesting to note that she always steps out on stage first in high heels. Perhaps these heels are worn in anticipation of her entertaining ritual, or perhaps Lewis has found a way to compromise her own comfort on stage and socio-cultural expectations about feminine respectability that persist even for the female calypsonian – whose respectability is perhaps even more in question than that of her always potentially disreputable male counterpart.

52. Butler, *Gender Trouble*, 3–44.

53. Adrienne Rich, "Compulsory Heterosexuality and Lesbian Existence", in *Blood, Bread, and Poetry: Selected Prose 1979–1985* (New York: Norton, 1986), 23–75.

54. See Dikobe, "Doing She Own Thing", 112; and Jocelyne Guilbault, *Governing Sound: The Cultural Politics of Trinidad's Carnival Musics* (Chicago: University of Chicago Press, 2007), 109. Maude Dikobe's dissertation, "Doing She Own Thing", contains perhaps the most balanced (though brief: confined to only two sentences in the over two-hundred-page work) scholarly engagement with the question of Lewis's sexuality. Although Dikobe cites Davies's indirect refusal of Lewis's same-sex desire, she insists that Lewis – like the noted blues singer Gertrude "Ma" Rainey – "has refused to say whether she is lesbian or not" (p. 112). Perhaps the comparison of Lewis to Rainey is an apt one considering that neither woman had necessarily to call herself a "lesbian" in order to revel in her same-sex desire. By most accounts, Rainey was bisexual though there may be no telling how Rainey herself identified. I will shortly address Lewis's relationship to the word *lesbian*; for now, it is vital to

emphasize that refusing to say does not necessarily preclude same-sex desire.
55. Rich, "Compulsory Heterosexuality".
56. Recognizing the strategic importance of Lewis's marriage ought not to amount to discrediting it as a complete sham. Beyond her married name, Lewis has also maintained ties to the family into which she married; her de facto adoption of her husband's young daughter (from a previous relationship) as her own has kept Lewis to this day in close contact with the woman – now residing in the Bronx – and her five children, who Lewis showers with all the affection grandmothers reserve for their grandchildren.
57. Rosamond King, "More Notes on the Invisibility of Caribbean Lesbians", in *Our Caribbean: A Gathering of Lesbian and Gay Writing from the Antilles*, ed. Thomas Glave (Durham: Duke University Press, 2008), 194.
58. Makeda Silvera, "Man Royals and Sodomites: Some Thoughts on the Invisibility of Afro-Caribbean Lesbians", in *Lesbian Subjects: A Feminist Studies Reader*, ed. Martha Vinicus (Bloomington: Indiana University Press, 1992).
59. Rosamond Elwin's *Tongues on Fire: Caribbean Lesbian Lives and Stories* (Toronto: Women's Press, 1997) is the only book-length text that I am familiar with to date that directly addresses Caribbean female same-sex desire. Combining the oral histories and fiction of twenty-seven queer Caribbean women living in the region and the diaspora, *Tongues on Fire* serves as a peppery testament to the invisible made real.
60. Lewis, interview.
61. Lewis underwent surgery for breast cancer in 1996.
62. Lewis, interview.
63. Though not in reference to Lewis's calypso, Rohlehr stumbles upon a spiritual object imbued with potential phallic symbolism when he likens the penis to a *poteau mitan* (the "centre post" of the Voodoo religion), thereby inadvertently encouraging the alignment of a sensual and a spiritual object (Rohlehr, "I Lawa", 334). At the literal and figurative centre of Vodoun ritual and ceremony, this axis mundi – usually a wooden pillar or platform permanently lodged in the ground in the centre of a worship site and intended to provide a bridge between the spirit world and the mortal world – also appears in the Spiritual Baptist religion as the sacred centrepole (Lum, *Praising His Name*, 2000). This bridge provides a figurative way between the flesh and the spirit at the same time that it defies the presumed distance between them – a defiance corroborated by a belief in spirit-made-flesh (or the soul "housed" within the body). The shift here from sensuality to spirituality is always already tempted by a shift back of the order perhaps best represented by the connotative journey of the "fetish" from a spiritual object invested with supernatural force as described by early ethnographers to an object saturated with displaced sexual energy as adopted by psychoanalysis.

64. Lewis quoted in *Calypso at Dirty Jim's*, dir. Pascale Obolo (Paris: Maturity Music Limited and Dynamo Productions, 2005, DVD).
65. Lewis, interview.
66. Ibid.
67. In 1987, while still performing widely, Lewis became an ordained minister (Guilbault, *Governing Sound*, 109).
68. Dikobe, "Doing She Own Thing", 110.
69. Lewis quoted in Rudolph Ottley, "Calypso Rose", in *Women in Calypso: Part I* (Arima: Rudolph Ottley, 1992), 11–12.
70. Rohlehr, "I Lawa", 365–66.
71. See Don Randel, "Voice" and "Singing", in *New Harvard Dictionary of Music* (Cambridge: Harvard University Press, 1986), 926–27, 749–50; Elizabeth Wood, "Sapphonics", in *Queering the Pitch: The New Gay and Lesbian Musicology*, ed. Phillip Brett et al. (New York: Routledge, 1994), 27.
72. Even as a "sex song", "Palet" pushes far beyond the parochial implications of the phrase by earnestly – though no less playfully – calling easy sex-gender presumptions into question. In other words, if it is that sex is always pregnant with a double entendre that refers at once to sexual differentiation (male/female) and sexual intimacy, Lewis's "Palet", as a "sex" song, actually takes sex (and gender) much more seriously by attending to this double entendre than the categorization would at first imply.
73. The fact that Lewis has written well over eight hundred songs is an impressive accomplishment even considering that she began writing calypsos at the age of fifteen – over five and a half decades ago.

Discography

Calypso Rose. "Palet" (1968). *The Best of Calypso Rose: Calypso Queen of the World*. Caribbean Music Group Limited, Port of Spain, compact disc set, 2005.

7.

"Born in Chanel, Christen in Gucci"[1]
The Rhetoric of Brand Names and Haute Couture in Jamaican Dancehall

ANDREA ELIZABETH SHAW

> Tight pussy gal no fight over man
> An everybody know say we a name brand
> When me a wind me gi him de wickedest slam
> But me sorry fi di gal dem out deh weh no have no glam.
> – Spice, "Fight Over Man"[2]

THIS CHAPTER EXPLORES THE role of high-end designer fashion in the reggae dancehall arena and contemplates how fashion in general, but specifically designer wear, is invoked and fetishized within that realm.[3] Given the North American and European origins of high fashion, I am particularly interested in how performers employ their designer-wear discourse and how this discourse relates to the political and social tensions between the Caribbean and the developed world. In "Signal di Plane" Elephant Man sings: "Da dance yah make everybody a kick up a storm / Show Jack Sowah the brand weh you have on / If a Louis Votorni, Armani, Sean John / Enjoy yourself, nuh make nobody keep you calm."[4] In this quite celebratory tune, why does Ellie mention designer Louis Vuitton, whose name Ellie has himself transformed into Louis Votorni? What is it that accounts for the recent proliferation of references to designer name brands in dancehall – the addition of Gucci, Moschino and Dior, among others, to dancehall's lexicon? Perhaps your initial response to this question is the same as mine: an acknowledgment that Jamaicans may simply have too much of a "foreign mind", in this case a love for imported products, especially from North America and Europe. While this observation may be true and perhaps explains the underpinning of dancehall culture's appetite for designer brands, I'm not convinced the answer is quite so simple.

Jamaican dancehall fashion has become a distinctive visual signifier of the music after which it is named. This fashion aesthetic took shape in Jamaica during the 1980s, the decade which gave rise to the current epoch of dancehall music, a genre that continues to dominate the Jamaican musical landscape and influence musical styles worldwide. Women's dancehall fashion – often associated with explosive colour, sequins, and of course ubiquitous spandex – has been particularly conspicuous in the public visual arena, the clothing's salacious reputation the subject of numerous newspaper editorials and radio talk show discussions.[5]

In a 2008 *Gleaner* article titled "Slackness and More Slackness", the principal of a local high school engaged in a lengthy harangue about the corrosive qualities of dancehall music: "Dancehall dress leaves little of the women's bodies to the imagination. It is this mindset that is now affecting so many of our young people in school. They are following the dancehall culture of 'badmanism', 'hottie girls', 'nuff girls', 'nuff skin' and body parts exposed, 'nuff slackness', public wining and grinding, 'bling and more bling', and every thing else that the culture promotes".[6] As self-appointed arbiters of Jamaican propriety, the middle and upper classes have increasingly voiced "nuff" disdain for dancehall music, which defies and contests traditional notions of decency. Middle- and upper-class ideals also hold similar contempt for dancehall music's rough-and-tumble comrades, including the controversial "daggering",[7] street dances and their attendant "chaka chaka" noise, and, of course, dancehall's extravagant fashion.

Power struggles relating to dancehall fashion have also emerged *within* the dancehall. They play out in the 1997 film *Dancehall Queen* through the challenges facing Marcia, the film's leading character, as she tries to establish herself as a key contender in the dancehall arena.[8] Marcia is a street vendor and single parent struggling to earn a living. After seeing the reigning dancehall queen during the daytime when she is dislocated from the glamorous dancehall space, Marcia realizes that the queen looks quite ordinary without the aid of her elaborate clothing. This revelation regarding fashion's capacity to alter the wearer prompts Marcia to vie for the title of dancehall queen, so she can supplement her paltry street-vending income. However, she must compete against

numerous other women, and the film reveals fashion's crucial role in capturing attention within the dancehall and improving the opportunity of ascension to queen. Marcia designs her own outfits and begins to bedazzle the dancehall audience, which cannot tell that this queenly woman is Marcia the vendor. In fact, her own daughter can hardly recognize her mother once Marcia is festooned in her fashion creations. Marcia's dancehall outfits, like Cinderella's gown, transform her appearance, indeed her persona, and eventually transform her economic circumstances when she wins the dancehall queen title.

Sonjah Stanley Niaah defines the transformation enabled by dancehall

Guests at Jagga B's Dancehall Biggest Giveaway session, many of them in the latest designer wear, 2008. (*Gleaner* photographs.)

fashion as a form of "masking", associated with historical African cultural practices.⁹ In the context of the dancehall, masking is a ritualistic practice which disputes identities associated with the abject poverty faced by Jamaica's black underclass.¹⁰ Furthermore, Niaah argues that dancehall fashion "contests and rewrites historically biased religious, sexual, and class scripts".¹¹ Dressing in designer wear (the current fashion ideal in dancehall), or approximations of these types of clothing, allows patrons and performers to represent themselves in ways that challenge their social status as underprivileged. According to Niaah, "masks are aggrandizing tools for the self", and "within such practices as dress (new outfit and hairstyle), the wearing of a different mask at each dancehall event ensures readiness for the video light".¹²

Carolyn Cooper suggests that Marcia is fully aware of "the power of costume to enable the transformation" from vendor to dancehall diva.¹³ This transformation process takes on as fantastical an identity as the elaborate costumes themselves. This is because of the "magical" potential costuming provides for the economic transformation that becomes accessible to women who can attract attention in the dancehall as either performers or patrons. Donna Hope explains: "Dancehall's emphasis on costuming and public performance is organically linked to the development of what I call the 'video-light syndrome' in the dancehall dis/place. This powerful need to be seen, documented, photographed and, in particular, videotaped, has been an important part of dancehall culture since the introduction of video cameras as a regular part of activities in the dancehall."¹⁴ Hope further explains that a number of contests anchored in a dancehall aesthetic, similar to the contest portrayed in *Dancehall Queen*, have been developed (although some may no longer exist) such as Miss Buff Bay, Miss Healthy Body and Miss Go-Go Wine.¹⁵ The prizes and publicity associated with these contests play a pivotal role in propelling participants to dancehall fame. An actual Dancehall Queen contest, which attracts both local and international contestants, has thrived for well over a decade, and the 2010 winner, Kristal Anderson, took home J$400,000 (approximately US$4,600), a trophy and a variety of gift packages.¹⁶

Additionally, women who are not vying for specific dancehall-associated titles like Anderson's and are content with their role as dancehall patrons nevertheless actively compete for attention in the dancehall, and fashion plays a key role in their viability. Hope describes these women as "hidden queens of the dancehall" and explains that they are economically independent women

Luxury evening wear designed by Lex Perry, 2006. (Adrian Frater, *Gleaner* photograph.)

who "wear elaborate hairstyles and engage in conspicuous consumption of expensive liquor at dancehall events"[17]. One such woman Hope references is Sandra Lee, whose family background is in informal commercial trading. According to Hope, Lee frequents dancehall events, where her arrival is usually announced and her image recorded by videographers.[18] Surprisingly, funerals have become another venue where women compete for attention in their dancehall garb.

Over the past two decades, the flamboyance and performativity of the dancehall expressive complex[19] have had a distinct impact on funeral rituals practiced by some inner-city Jamaicans. These funerals have become increasingly conspicuous and exhibitionist, generating as much contempt and condemnation as the music and fashion that have influenced them. Annie Paul explains that "the coffin or casket in particular acquires the expressiveness of a status symbol signifying the importance both of the deceased and the bereaved family or community".[20] She further notes that families spend relatively large sums to acquire these elaborately adorned caskets. The dress and behaviour of funeral participants have also been implicated as elaborate, extravagant and unruly.

In the aftermath of the funeral of dancehall dance legend Bogle, journalist

Ian Boyne commented that the Seventh-Day Adventist church was reviewing its funeral policies and suggested that this was because of the behaviour of attendees at Bogle's funeral: "The wearing of outrageous dancehall fashion – a tautology – the smoking of ganja, drinking of liquor on church premises and general unruly behaviour at what is traditionally a solemn occasion where the dead is honoured, has been proving too much for the conservative Christian denomination."[21] Doyenne of the Jamaican fashion world Norma Soas proffered a similarly derisive critique of the inner-city don[22] Jim Brown's funeral in 1992, suggesting that the dancehall styles worn by the mourners were vulgar and indecent: "No mini was too short, no tights too tight, no chiffon too sheer, no lace too see through."[23] However, dancehall fashion, in all its extravagance, is also a locus of celebration and commercial success for some, including Soas's designer counterparts whose clothing graces the dancehall stage and floor.

Numerous dancehall fashion designers have become preeminent on the local fashion scene, including names like Earl "Biggy" Turner, Stanley "Lexxus" Bailey, Paul "Tu-Lox" Gaynor, Garfield Hussey and White Skyy Designs. Furthermore, designers such as Lexx Perry have taken dancehall fashion onto the global stage, designing for celebrities and showcasing clothing at international venues. Dancehall fashion is now routinely included in local fashion events, and organizers of the prestigious 2008 Pulse Model Search fashion show used the dancehall expressive complex as inspiration for their show's set. The backdrop featured zinc fences, ostensibly invoking the inner cities, inscribed with dancehall vernacular like "to the wurl'" and "gully creepa".[24]

Dancehall's impact on fashion is a notable one, and fashion itself is a powerful transformative force that betrays cultural desires to belong, escape and contain. The socio-political significance of dress within the new world is evidenced by the politics surrounding it that emerged during the European colonial venture. Perhaps the most foundational component of dress politics that affected Africans in the new world was the requirement that they wear European-styled clothing. In his insightful study *The Language of Dress: Resistance and Accommodation in Jamaica*, Steeve Buckridge explains that a 1696 law in Jamaica not only specified the items of clothing a slave should have but imposed a fine on slaveholders who did not provide their slaves with sufficient garments.[25] This requirement underscored the European colonizers' persistent presumption of a feral and primitive African nature in need of containment. European-styled clothing on the bodies of black slaves signalled white dominance and legitimated the oppressive enterprise of slavery because it in part resulted in the gentrification of black bodies that may otherwise have been irreverently exposed. In Jamaica and other parts of the new world, osnaburg was the favoured fabric for concealing the black slave body; it was cheap and durable but also extremely uncomfortable.[26] In light of this, Jamaican slaves sometimes sold their clothing allotments in order to trade up and purchase better quality garments.[27]

In fact, white men used clothing as currency to reward female slaves for "sexual favours".[28] This availability of fashion alternatives for slaves led to a range of new world anxieties, and, in some parts of the Caribbean, sumptuary laws were passed, prohibiting slaves from wearing fabrics such as silk.[29] This restriction reflects both the plantation hegemony's fears over slaves challenging their status in the plantation hierarchy at the nadir of that society's social ladder. In addition, it demonstrates the fluidity of race since physiology alone was not sufficient to permanently fix race, and its attendant class presumptions, in place. Similar dress restrictions were enacted in the Antebellum South, among these the South Carolina Negro Act of 1735. Leon Higginbotham explains: "when a slave managed to obtain clothing that might accord him some dignity or prestige, the act declared that when such clothing was 'above' that which a slave should wear, it could be taken from the slave by 'all and every constable and other persons' to be used for his or their own benefit".[30] This act limited slaves to clothing made from "negro cloth . . . osnabrigs . . . coarse garlix or calicoes . . . not exceeding ten shillings per yard".[31] These sumptuary laws were enacted based on hegemonic imperatives to deprive slaves access to the transformative power of fashion.

Clothing's ability to alter the wearer has long been recognized, and it is at the heart of several popular myths. Cinderella's conversion from a grimy chambermaid into a beautiful maiden is firmly anchored to the glamorous evening gown her fairy godmother conjures up. The Congolese folktale of Umusha Mwaice bears remarkable resemblance to the Cinderella story and tells of a slave girl who has exquisite clothing made from leaves. When one of her father's wives takes away her clothes, she climbs into the belly of a cow and emerges with even more exquisite fineries than those she had before.[32] Furthermore, when Dorothy becomes stranded in Oz,[33] in *The Wizard of Oz*, her ability to transform her surroundings and get back home to Kansas is facilitated by magical shoes. Indeed, the transformative effect of clothing is so potent that even the false belief that one is wearing clothes produces an alteration in persona, which occurs in the fairytale "The Emperor's New Clothes". The emperor marches through town completely naked but with great aplomb because of the confidence he derives from the clothing he *thinks* he is wearing.

References to clothing and designer fashion in reggae dancehall lyrics indicate a similar recognition of the transformative power of dress – its impact on the body of the wearer and on the nature of the gaze from the onlooker. Many reggae songs seem to offer up the black female body as the site of transformation and fetishize items of female clothing in response to a male onlooker. In their 1978 hit "Uptown Top Ranking" Althea and Donna sing the following: "See mi 'pon the road and hear you call out to me / True you see me in me pants and thing / See me in a 'alter back, / Say me gi' you heart attack."[34] The woman's halter back outfit threatens to give the male-constructed onlooker a "heart attack", reifying the potency of female dress.

Buju Banton's "Batty Rider" also celebrates the potency of dress, as he ecstatically acclaims the item of women's clothing after which the song is titled: "Gal you see you batty rider, murder / You must be waan the DJ charge fa . . . Shorts hitch up on you saddle, ride up on you back / Exposing you property, man a say it fat."[35] A "batty rider" is a very short pair of women's shorts that exposes the derriere of the wearer. Banton's lyrics imply that because the woman referenced in the song is so overwhelmingly appealing due to her shorts, the song's narrator could end up charged for an offence, presumably some sexually inappropriate behaviour. Reference to the woman's buttocks as "fat" is grounded in an African diasporic aesthetic that recognizes the fleshy woman's body as appealing.[36]

This privileging of the heterosexual male gaze and celebration of clothing that titillates the male gazer is popular in reggae and dancehall. Some songs even go as far as to warn against disappointing the male gaze by not appropriately dressing the female body. In "Deport Them" Sean Paul warns, "From a gal no up to date we deport them / Can't keep up with the trends we report them / If a no the modelling type we no court them / But if a the big beauty queen we support them."[37] Sean Paul's use of deportation as the metaphorical punishment for non-compliance with the current fashion trends seems severe, but it aptly reveals the real-life urgency attending the female pursuit of what my mother would call "up-to-date" clothing. Just as deportation from the cities of the United States and Great Britain is often preceded by a reduced access to the economic and educational opportunities represented by these locales, fashion deportation, such as what "Deport Them" calls for, is preceded by a decline in female access to the economic and social opportunities that men provide in exchange for sex. Fashion deportation, an inability to "keep up to the trends" as Sean Paul says, expels women from the realm of sexual viability into a chasm of sexual improbability.

In recent years, however, these lyrical references to clothing have taken on even more distinctive characteristics as attention has turned quite specifically to European and North American designer wear. Elephant Man's "Signal di Plane", Tifa's "Spell It Out" and Vybz Kartel's "Start Well" also tout designer brand names, including Armani, Moschino and Gucci, with a peculiar familiarity that disrupts the conspicuously Jamaican flavour of dancehall yet quite appropriately situates the music within its increasingly global context. Tifa sings "Woy, me body full a Armani / Me no wear town G-U-C-C-I / Me have to take first-class F-L-Y" (Whoa, my body is full of Armani / I don't wear town Gucci / I have to take first-class flights).[38] She revels in her designer garments, thumbing her nose at fake brand-name products from the local market (she refers to these as "town Gucci"), and suggests that her Armani-clad body is an equivalent status symbol to first-class travel.

The song "Fight Over Man" is performed by Spice, a female Jamaican deejay, and similarly celebrates designer fashion; furthermore, Spice situates fashion as a metonym for sexual dexterity. The song both applauds and mystifies female sexuality, attributing the narrator's bedroom prowess to her designer clothing and resultant erotic appeal. "Fight Over Man" quite specifically identifies its protagonist's "tightness" as the source of her appeal and labels this apparently desirable quality as a designer feature, in effect branding the woman's private parts just as clothing is branded. Girls lacking in "glam" are sentenced to the "deportation" process for which Sean Paul advocates in his song. Spice sings: "Tight pussy gal no fight over man / An everybody know say we a name brand / When me a wind me gi him de wickedest slam / But me sorry fi di gal dem out deh weh no have no glam."[39] The narrator in "Fight Over Man", however, need not fear being "dipped". Her "name brand booty" not only saves her from exile, but gives her access to wealth and social mobility. Unlike other women whose private parts bear a generic label, the narrator, with her designer brand booty, does not need to compete for male attention due to her superior talents in the bedroom:

> Mi know fi do me ting me know fi gauge an pace it
> Big buddy deh ya but some woman a waste it
> Gal a wind fast like a race she a race it
> Me put it on proper him say do make me taste it
> Me no have no time fi come a war with Susan
> She a fight fi man cause him would give her a two grand
> Whole heap a millionaire deh yuh fi pick and choose from
> An me know me keep me nooky tight like a clam.

In the chorus of "Fight Over Man" Spice sings "De whole a dem a dead over mi name brand booty / Cause me born inna Chanel an me christen in Gucci." These lines further underscore the song's branding motif and suggest that sexual desirability is conferred through designer wear. Being "born in Chanel and christened in Gucci" now sits alongside being born with a silver spoon in one's mouth, both signifiers of a prestigious social status.

Buju Banton's "Driver A" presents a masculinized perspective on brand-name fashion that reflects the sentiments in "Fight Over Man".[40] "Driver A" features a male protagonist who is ostensibly one of the millionaires the narrator of "Fight Over Man" can "pick and choose from" because these men are interested in acquiring sexual favours from her. The song opens with the narrator immersed in anxiety over the delivery of his illicit drug shipment. This "boss man" provides a range of strict "delivery" guidelines for his driver and implores, warns, begs and threatens him to make sure that, no matter what, the delivery arrives safely at its final destination. The boss lists various reasons why the success of this delivery mission is a must, and interestingly, but not surprisingly, among them is his woman's penchant for designer underwear. In the boss man's own words, "A business man a run me no inna no but nor because / My gal waan wear Victoria Secret drawers." This reasoning certainly reflects the sentiments in Spice's song and suggests that one of the aims of Caribbean male labour and its resultant economic benefits is to secure and maintain women who offer designer-brand sexual services.[41]

Like "Fight Over Man", "Hotter Than the Rest" from Lady G and Mr Vegas celebrates this transformative power of designer fashion and insists that the female narrator's "hotness" derives from the numerous items of designer clothes and accessories she is able to import.[42] "Hotter Than the Rest" illuminates the global context within which dancehall operates. It highlights the growing significance of imported brands as a legitimating agent for female sexual value, and perhaps nationalistic value as well. "Hotter" emphasizes these importations – the "Moschino and Versace we fling down / You know a Dolce and Gabbana we a bring down" – that comingle with the black Jamaican female body to alter it and to glamorize it in such a way that it becomes "hotter than the rest". Furthermore, the song enunciates a marginalization of non-brand-name fashion. According to the female narrator, "Me no wear no frilla frilla . . . that a sketel name brand fi make me favour fritters."

Classifying fashion that is not brand-name with the appellation of "sketel name brand" positions these garments and the bodies that wear them as underclass, unrefined and lacking sexual sophistication. "Sketel" refers to a promiscuous woman; this "sketel" class of goods ostensibly includes locally produced garments that do not have the designer-name recognition of, say, Moschino or Versace. The ordinary and unappealing quality of locally produced fashion is further implied when the song invokes fritters in association with "sketel" fashion. Fritters are a popular Caribbean food item, somewhat similar to pancakes. They are not usually perceived as a glamorous or sophisticated dish. In fact, because they can be made relatively cheaply – the main ingredient is flour – they are often associated with the poor and working class.

Dancehall enthusiasts who favour brand-name designer fashion that claims its origins in the metropoles of the United States and Europe mark their bodies as sophisticated and Westernized in contradistinction to wearers of "sketel" or "fritter" fashion. This dichotomy, with unsophisticated sketel clothing on one end of the continuum and Moschino or Versace on the other, suggests that the wearer of brand-name designer fashion is part of an expansive global fashion community in which membership is established and validated via one's degree of access to foreign designer clothing. Reinforcing colonially inspired notions that Eurocentric culture and ideals are more desirable than those originating in native, racialized spaces, "Hotter Than the Rest", alongside various other dancehall songs that reference designer fashion, devalues locally made clothing and the bodies that wear those clothes, rendering those bodies and the spaces they occupy unrefined and vulgar.

According to local dancehall fashion designer Earl "Biggy" Turner, this penchant for foreign clothing has had a damaging effect on the Jamaican

Right: A model wearing one of Earl "Biggy" Turner's designs at Caribbean Fashionweek, 2006. (Winston Sill, *Gleaner* photograph.)

fashion industry. In a 2006 newspaper article, Turner decries the influx of imported clothes turning up in the world of dancehall fashion. Of the past, he says, the clothing worn to the dancehall "was just the fashion of the people. The people would never be caught out without their specific dancehall fashion. They had something that defined them and that they could identify with."[43] Turner implies that the "fashion of the people" was clothing conceived and produced in Jamaica by Jamaican design talent. Another local designer, Paul "Tu-Lox" Gaynor, further elaborates on this perceived loss of originality: "We were more original, that is number one. The dancehall now is more geared towards the cable look . . . the whole cable thing take away from the dancehall designers."[44] Gaynor's comment implicates the global mass media as an agent of fashion, and by extension cultural, indoctrination. He also recognizes the ways in which this preference for "cable" fashion privileges the accompanying values associated with the global while disenfranchising those bodies and values associated with the local. He concludes by suggesting that the early dancehall styles have all but disappeared, a consequence of this disenfranchisement: "Dancehall now don't have a dress code, we only have some music. If we don't hold on strong we are not going to have dancehall again."[45] These fashions initially associated with the dancehall were bright and flamboyant, but they were, most importantly, created by local fashion designers, and despite the current fetishization of imports, some dancehall artists like Beenie Man remain faithful to locally designed fashion. According to Martin Miller of White Skyy Designs, "Dancehall image now is more about brand than fashion. Beenie is the only one right now who has maintained the image of what the dancehall is with his style."[46]

Some sectors of the reggae dancehall expressive complex echo Turner and Gaynor's perception of designer brands as an affront to dancehall, namely the "conscious" reggae performers whose music is tightly yoked to Rastafarian ideology. Capleton is one of these performers, and he addresses the fetishization of designer wear in his song "Bun Dung Dreddie", a diatribe against Rastafarian backsliders who flout Rasta principles. Capleton sings: "How you fi ras and then you still a eat pork / How you fi ras and then you still a smoke coke / Still all a sail pon Babylon boat / Nuff rent-a-dread a bow pon the north coast."[47] These lines admonish sexual behaviour by alluding to "rent-a-dreads" (dreadlocked male prostitutes who sell their sexual services to tourists) as well as non-Ital[48] dietary habits and drug use. Further in the song, Capleton includes fashion missteps among his list of infractions, celebrating traditional Rastafarian dress and dismissing designer garments: "Can't see the king if you no royal hot / Royalness a fi the royal flock / Robe and turban fi de royal flock / No Moschini, Versace and dress like ah ah." In keeping with the Afrocentric tenets of Rastafarian identity politics, Capleton rejects dancehall music's current embrace of Western designers like Moschino and Versace. He locates imported fashion as antithetical to Rastafarian principles. By touting a "robe and turban" as idealized garments, Capleton definitively anchors Rastafarian fashion principles in both an African and a religious aesthetic, since the image of a robe and turban evokes both traditional African dress as well as visual interpretations of biblical fashion.

In many respects, the colonial venture in Jamaica set the precedence for favouring imported fashion. According to Buckridge, female European settlers on the island initially ordered all their clothing from Europe. These garments were highly inappropriate given Jamaica's hot climate, but for several generations, European settlers refused to alter their dress customs.[49] This resistance reiterates the cultural function of clothing; it is an expression of the British colonizer's desire to not be subsumed by a Caribbean identity. Among slave women, there was a parallel preference for garments similarly identified as exclusive; consequently, "expensive and elaborate dress" was "often a way of achieving differentiation and social mobility".[50] Eventually "Creole" fashion emerged among the slaves, combining elements of both European and African dress. According to Buckridge, "Creole dress was fundamentally radical because it defied easy categorization" and resisted the white hegemony's efforts to employ fashion as a clear definer of race.[51]

The designer-brand references emerging from dancehall music suggest that the intermingling of designer clothing and the Caribbean female body result in a similar creolization, a blending of black Caribbean bodies and white-identified designer garments. This hybrid status of the dancehall diva who can acquire the appropriate clothing becomes a potent signifier of femininity that renders the wearer of these designer garbs "hotter than the rest", that is to say sexually superior to her counterpart clad in local fashion and deadly to her male conquests. Interestingly, the women who provided working-class Jamaicans with some of the earliest access to brand name clothing, and imitations of that clothing, themselves emerged from the same marginalized space occupied by the dancehall.

Higglers or, as they are more politically correctly referenced, informal commercial importers, are Jamaican, and indeed Caribbean, entrepreneurs who import products for resale. Women predominate in this industry, and during the 1970s became a conspicuous presence on the sidewalks of popular "uptown" shopping areas in Kingston. They sell a range of products, including clothing, fashion accessories and household goods. Commentary from Jamaican journalist Morris Cargill quite aptly represents the resistance of some of the middle class to their presence.[52] He also refers to these traders and their luggage full of the merchandise destined for Jamaica's sidewalks as a "menace" to other travellers, and comments that they "infest" the shopping centres where they sell their goods.[53] He further marginalizes them by implying that their bodies are physiological anomalies: "[F]ew [higglers] seem to weigh less than 250 lbs. They are also a special shape, sticking out back and front simultaneously: huge protruding bottoms and equally huge tops, both of which they use as battering rams."[54]

The shopping centres to which Cargill refers are popularly known as "uptown", a term also used in Jamaica as a distinguisher of class, with implications of race.[55] The price of the products offered for sale in Kingston's uptown shopping areas distinctly mark these venues as middle- and upper-class spaces. Higglers disrupt presumptions of who can legitimately occupy that space while also creating opportunities for "downtown" and other women to engage in "uptown" consumptive practices by giving them access to cheaper variations of previously inaccessible products. As such, higglers bear a very meaningful economic and symbolic relationship to dancehall.

Their forceful entrance into the class-restricted entrepreneurial spaces of Jamaica helped create the means by which inner-city women developed a style of dress that challenges uptown conventions of fashion and attendant values. After historical exclusions of the poor and working class from the opportunities to engage in middle-class consumption patterns, modern-day dancehall divas use dancehall fashion as a way of mirroring those consumptive practices while concurrently resisting them. With increased access to faux and authentic designer wear, inner-city women are able to redeploy middle-class styles in ways that transgress conventional fashion norms. Just as informal commercial importers have emerged as a part of Jamaica's ongoing forays into the commercial global arena, the sustained invocation of brand-name clothing in the dancehall expressive complex globalizes the dancehall space and is perhaps a response to global commentary on both dancehall and blackness – commentary from within and without that suggest the space is vulgar, undesirable and unrefined.

This commentary on dancehall also questions the spending ethics of inner-city women and implicates dancehall as the cause of many an unpaid school fee and empty kitchen cupboard. While it is true that the sartorial extravagance associated with dancehall may compromise some women's financial circumstances and limit their ability to cover other essential expenses, I do not see dancehall as the *cause* of this fiscal imprudence any more than I see the manufacturers of BMW motorcars as the cause of middle-class extravagance and attendant excessive debt, with which many professionals struggle. What the willingness to spend beyond one's means to buy Gucci and Armani demonstrates is that poor money management is an egalitarian ailment, and the attendant criticisms are perhaps informed by the impulse to legislate working-class values and are also a projection of the middle class's anxieties about its own irresponsible spending habits.

In fact, I imagine that some of the wives and daughters of the British colonizers who insisted on "keeping up with the trends" in Europe probably accumulated quite a bit of debt themselves. Just as these women would not have their British identity devoured by a primitive Caribbean space, the desire for exclusive foreign clothing on behalf of modern-day dancehall proponents may represent a similar impulse. By consuming these white-identified garments, the dancehall space and the bodies that operate within are creolized to produce a more palatable black body and perhaps even a more palatable black experience that is not the equivalent of a "sketel name brand" that "favour fritters".[56] Instead, the result is a Moschino, Versace or Dior body that is not subject to the "deportation" of which Sean Paul sings because the exclusivity and desire associated with that body due to the designer fashion in which it is clad is transformative.

Furthermore, the deportation metaphor helps to unravel and expose some of the gender dilemmas created by the Caribbean's dominant patriarchal hegemony, which has persisted from colonial times through to the present. Patriarchal and hegemonic aesthetic imperatives, which undergird hierarchical determinations about female sexual viability, prescribe specific physiological, behavioural, and sartorial standards. Ignorance about these prescriptive aesthetic norms or the inability to conform to them has always resulted in a type of metaphorical deportation from the realm of sexual viability. So, in many respects, the colonial white women who imported expensive and uncomfortable clothing from Europe along with present-day underclass black women who insist on sporting Gucci or Dior have formed a sisterhood of sorts, a sorority whose objective is to stand firm in a space where their heterosexual aesthetic appeal is affirmed and the perception of their sexuality as a "designer" brand is unquestioned. While dependency on imported fashion is rooted in patriarchal hegemonic efforts to sustain female anxieties over the value of women's bodies, diverting female attention from the numerous gendered inequities and abuses endemic to a patriarchy, women's collusive role in the entire scheme must be acknowledged. Because without women's ideological embrace of this hierarchical order to determine sexual viability and even more of the specific requirements (such as dressing their bodies in imported garments) that determine designation in that order, anxieties over being "born in Chanel and christen in Gucci"[57] would not be possible.

Notes

1. This is a line from the chorus of "Fight Over Man" by Spice.
2. Translation to Standard English:
   Girls with tight pussies don't fight over men
   Everyone knows that we are like a name brand
   When I am engaged in sex, I give him the utmost in pleasure
   But I'm sorry for the girls out there who are not glamorous
3. The fetishization of designer wear within the dancehall space bears some notable irony given that space's concurrent demonization and dismissal of homosexuality, metaphorical and otherwise, and the conspicuous presence of gay men in the cadre of North American and European designers. Another occurrence, well worth scholarly pursuit, is the increasing attention that men in the dancehall arena have been giving to their own appearance and the increasing flamboyance of male dancehall fashion. The feminized aesthetic that results from this amplified attention often features dyed hair, plucked eyebrows and hip-hugging, bright-coloured clothing.
4. Elephant Man, "Signal di Plane", *Good 2 Go* (VP Records/Wea, 2003).
5. While dancehall music and hip-hop music have both cross pollinated and influenced each other's development, arguably so have the associated clothing trends. Hip hop fashion, legendary for its exaggerated jewellery, exposed undergarments and revealing female dress, bears a distinct similarity to dancehall fashion in its subversion of propriety and conventional dress codes.

6. Esther Tyson, "Slackness and More Slackness", *Gleaner*, 6 April 2008, http://www.jamaica-gleaner.com/gleaner/20080406./cleisure/cleisure5.html.
7. "Daggering" refers to a dance style that involves very aggressive and suggestive sexual movements.
8. *Dancehall Queen*, dir. Rick Elgood and Don Letts (Palm Pictures, 2004, DVD).
9. Sonjah Stanley Niaah, *Dancehall: From Slave Ship to Ghetto* (Ottawa: University of Ottawa Press, 2010), 134.
10. Ibid., 132.
11. Ibid., 134.
12. Ibid., 132–33.
13. Carolyn Cooper, *Soundclash: Jamaican Dancehall Culture at Large* (New York: Palgrave Macmillan, 2004), 127.
14. Donna P. Hope, *Inna di Dancehall* (Kingston: University of the West Indies Press, 2006), 127.
15. Ibid., 71–73.
16. Adrian Frater, "Trelawny's 'Fluffy' Is Dancehall Queen", *Star* (Jamaica), 4 August 2010, http://jamaica-star.com/thestar/20100804/ent/ent6.html.
17. Hope, *Inna di Dancehall*, 63.
18. Ibid.
19. My term for the various creative components associated with dancehall, including the music itself, associated dance moves, fashion trends, hair styles, vernacular and so on.
20. Annie Paul, "'No Grave Cannot Hold My Body Down': Rituals of Death and Burial in Postcolonial Jamaica", *Small Axe* 23 (June 2007): 142–62.
21. Ian Boyne, "Easter and the 'Money Oh' Culture", *Gleaner*, 27 March 2005.
22. "Don" refers to inner-city area leaders who are often presumed to control their territory through illegal activities, including drug trafficking and blackmail.
23. Norma Soas quoted in Gina Ulysse, *Downtown Ladies: Informal Commercial Importers, a Haitian Anthropologist and Self-Making in Jamaica* (Chicago: University of Chicago Press, 2004), 223.
24. Krista Henry, "Dancehall, Fashion Took Centre Stage", *Star* (Jamaica), 9 September 2008.
25. Steeve Buckridge, *The Language of Dress: Resistance and Accommodation in Jamaica, 1760–1890* (Kingston: University of the West Indies Press, 2004), 29.
26. Ibid, 36.
27. Ibid.
28. Ibid, 43.
29. Ibid, 31.
30. A. Leon Higginbotham Jr, *In the Matter of Colour, Race and the American Legal Process: The Colonial Period* (Oxford: Oxford University Press, 1980), 173.

31. Ibid., 174.
32. Mary Jane Lupton, "Clothes and Closure in Three Novels by Black Women", *Black American Literature Forum* 20, no. 4 (Winter 1986): 410.
33. Frank Baum, *The Wonderful Wizard of Oz* (New York: HarperCollins, 2000).
34. Althea and Donna, "Uptown Top Ranking", *Uptown Top Ranking* (Frontline, 2001).
35. Buju Banton, "Batty Rider", *Mr. Mention* (Fader, 1993).
36. See my discussion of black beauty aesthetics in *The Embodiment of Disobedience: Fat Black Women's Unruly Political Bodies* (New York: Lexington Books, 2006), 6–7.
37. Sean Paul, "Deport Them", *Stage One* (VP Records, 2000).
38. Tifa, "Spell It Out" (Ward 21 Music, 2009), http://www.myspace.com/tifamusiq1.
39. Spice, "Fight Over Man", *Riddim Driven: Two Bad Riddims Vol. 3* (VP Music Group, 2006).
40. Buju Banton, "Driver A", *Too Bad* (Gargamel Music, 2006).
41. "Driver A" suggests that male capitalistic desire is fuelled by female consumerism and that women's bodies are culpable for men's risky and perhaps immoral and illegal capitalistic engagements. This seemingly disingenuous appropriation of responsibility bears a distinct similarity to arguments made in service to the European colonial project. In the article "Nabobinas: Luxury, Gender, and the Sexual Politics of British Imperialism in India in the Late Eighteenth Century", *Journal of Women's History* 18, no. 4 (2006): 8–30, Tillman Nechtman argues that nabobinas, the female relatives of British men employed by East India Company, became "implicated in domestic conversations about luxury, consumerism, and material opulence. They were suspected of harboring a passion for material consumption that verged dangerously on the edge of immorality" (p. 10). Could "Driver A" also seek to reduce the responsibility for questionable male behaviour by dislodging and relocating it on the site of the woman's body?
42. Lady G and Mr Vegas, "Hotter Than the Rest", *The Ultimate Dancehall Mix* (Jamdown Records, 1999).
43. Kavelle Anglin-Christie, "Dancehall's Flair Ladies", *Gleaner*, 12 February 2006.
44. Ibid.
45. Ibid.
46. Tanya C. Ellis, "Dancehall's Trends", *Star* (Jamaica), 5 January 2008.
47. Capleton, "Bun Dung Dreddie", *More Fire* (VP Records, VPCD1587, 2000, compact disc).
48. "Ital" is an idiom that derives from Rastafarian culture and refers to something wholesome and healthy. It is usually used in reference to food.
49. Buckridge, *Language of Dress*, 63.
50. Ibid., 93.
51. Ibid.

52. Morris Cargill, *Public Disturbances: A Collection of Writings 1986–1996* (Kingston: Mill Press, 1998), 28–29.
53. Ibid., 29.
54. Ibid. See my discussion of higglers in the context of their black and presumably fat bodies in *The Embodiment of Disobedience: Fat Black Women's Unruly Political Bodies,* chapter 3, "Bodily Abundance".
55. For a study of the identity politics affixed to the "uptown" and "downtown" dichotomy, see Gina Ulysse, *Downtown Ladies: Informal Commercial Importers, a Haitian Anthropologist and Self-Making in Jamaica* (Chicago: University of Chicago Press, 2004).
56. Lady G and Mr Vegas, "Hotter Than the Rest".
57. Spice, "Fight Over Man".

Discography

Althea and Donna. "Uptown Top Ranking" (1978). *Uptown Top Ranking.* Frontline CDFL 2023, 2001, compact disc.
Buju Banton. "Batty Rider". *Mr. Mention.* Fader 921 503-2, compact disc, 1993.
———. "Driver A". *Too Bad.* Gargamel Music GGML 004, compact disc, 2006.
Capleton. "Bun Dung Dreddie". *More Fire.* VP Records VPCD1587, compact disc, 2000.
Elephant Man. "Signal di Plane". *Good 2 Go.* VP Records 83681-2, compact disc, 2003.
Lady G and Mr Vegas. "Hotter Than the Rest" (1998). *Best of the Best Volume 1: Roots Culture Dancehall.* Jamdown Records, mp3 download, 2010.
Sean Paul. "Deport Them". *Stage One.* VP Records, VPCD1572, compact disc, 2000.
Spice. "Fight Over Man". *Eighty Five (Rhythm).* Mad House, compact disc, 2006.
Tifa. "Spell It Out". *Ward 21: The Brand New Riddims,* Ward 21 Productions, mp3 download, 2009.
Vybz Kartel. "Start Well". *Up 2 Di Time.* Greensleeves GRELCD 275, compact disc, 2004.

8.

The Rhetoric of Hips
Shakira's Embodiment and the Quest for Caribbean Identity

| NADIA CELIS

> Si alguien exigiera una explicación visual, una gráfica de lo que es el Caribe, lo remitiría al caos espiral de la Vía Láctea... cambio, tránsito, retorno, flujos de materia estelar.
> —Antonio Benítez-Rojo, *La Isla que se repite*[1]

> Articulation is not uniquely a function of the domain of writing or speech; rather the definition of articulation derives from the "flexing of joints." If literature speaks the illusion of national unity, might dance not articulate the struggle that belies the illusion?
> — Celeste Fraser Delgado and José Esteban Muñoz, *Everynight Life*[2]

Honest Hips

During an interview on MTV, Shakira declared that "Hips Don't Lie", her greatest hit to date, originated in a dream featuring an appearance from Wyclef Jean. The morning after her dream, she was informed that the Haitian musician, whom she did not know personally, had just called her manager to propose a joint project. Taking the dream as a "sign from heaven", Shakira decided to meet Jean immediately.[3] Their collaboration resulted in a fusion of reggae, rap, salsa and cumbia, interpreted in the song's video through a similar blend of dancing traditions and a carnival parade, which allowed Shakira to claim her Caribbeanness in an unprecedented way.

The title of the song came from a joke between the artist and her band.

Shakira had instructed her musicians to observe her hips while composing the musical arrangements for her songs: "Listen, my hips don't lie. If they are not moving this is not working. If they shake, we're in good shape."[4] Whether they lie or not, it is true that Shakira's hips and body speak and have always spoken with a voice of their own, at least since the time when, at the age of four, she began to belly dance spontaneously in a restaurant, revealing her unique talent to an astonished public. Today, her loquacious hips address global spectators in a rhythmic language that transcends linguistic and cultural barriers. But, what do Shakira's hips say? And what are the meanings embodied by this prodigious voice, undulating navel, voluminous curls, bare feet, defiant gaze and sensuality on which she herself confers metaphoric value?[5]

"Hips" and its video provide some clues to interpret Shakira's rhetoric. The video portrays Shakira dancing in front of Jean, who stares at her, amazed by the "unexpected" way she moves. With her unmistakable vibrato, the Colombian singer encourages him to "be wise" and "keep on reading the signs of my body", provoking a battle of words and movement that ends when the feminine voice declares her self-restraint defeated by the spell of the masculine dancing body. At this time, the scene moves into a circus-like theatre where two groups in carnival costumes gather in a parade that suggests a broad Caribbean alliance emerging from the kinetic power of the dancing bodies. Clapping the *clave,* the artists urge their listeners: "Baila en la calle, de noche, baila en la calle, de día" (Dance in the streets day and night).

The song simultaneously narrates Jean's realization of Shakira's Caribbeanness. His declaration of not having "the slightest idea" of this fact until he saw her dancing, echoes a trend in Shakira's reception. This trend is evident in the few academic articles on her career, which all neglect her Caribbean background, focusing entirely on her Colombian and Latina identities. Furthermore, by addressing this omission, the song reveals and challenges the racial and linguistic hierarchies that continue to preclude transnational alliances within the Caribbean, and it asserts the pan-Caribbean associations emerging from its diasporic experience. This connotation expands when the Haitian musician asks the *señorita* to move "like you come from Colombia". A clarinet bursts in with a cumbia tune that Shakira, leading a pyramid of women in white dresses,[6] interprets as she replies: "Mira, en Barranquilla se baila así. Say it!" (Look, this is how we dance in Barranquilla). Jean's repetition of the verse in Spanish voices his inclusion of both Shakira –"a refugee like me", and the

Hispanic continental Caribbean in the regional map. The song ends by celebrating the conquest of the United States by immigrants of the Third World. Placing musicians at the head of this movement, Jean raps his praise of the empowerment of the Caribbean diaspora, whose mobile subjects now "run the seas because they own their own boats".

Music and dance are claimed by these musicians as the means of what Josh Kun has called an "audiotopia", a transformative social and sonic space in which "transported by the technologies of transnational capital, music becomes an experiential network of connection and intersection that enables global simultaneity by juxtaposing the same with the different, bridging the near with the far, and confusing the local with the global".[7] Refugees, the voices claim, continue to be persecuted, due to a "musical transaction" whose invasive character is confirmed by the CIA's suspicion of them: "Why the CIA wanna watch us, Colombians and Haitians?" – the artists wonder. The opening and final verse with the phrase "No fighting", reiterates the peaceful character of their embodied rhythmical and linguistic invasion, whose most persuasive weapon is the alleged honesty of Shakira's hips in motion.

This chapter is, first of all, a response to Shakira's own suggestion of "reading the signs of my body". My point of departure is the shift in Shakira's deployment of her personal and cultural identity, culminating in the simultaneous emphasis on her Caribbeanness and on her corporeality in "Hips Don't Lie". I argue that many of the "unexpected" aspects of this artist's personality spring from her Caribbean origins, a cultural framework that she both recalls and re-creates through her performances and self-representation, making of her career's trajectory an embodied audiotopia of the Caribbean and its diaspora.

Shakira has carefully constructed her identity as a *bricolage* of simultaneous belongings – Barranquillera, Lebanese, Colombian, Latina – all of which meet and expand in her corporeality. In her words, she is "an ongoing contradiction. A mixture of elements that come from different and distant worlds . . . [and] do not fight but they coexist peacefully. I accept all the contradictions that there are in me and they accept each other."[8] Her identity also fluctuates between the personalities arising from her bilingualism and her multiple migrations through spaces and cultural codes. Shakira's capacity to carry the marks of her multiple identifications, to enact them and transmute them, points to a pillar of Caribbean cultural identity. While hierarchical distinctions linked to differences warn us against uncritical celebration of hybridity, the region is recognized for the ethnic, racial and cultural intermixing that nourishes its openness to accept and digest differences. The stage imagery and the artists' performance in "Hips" visually interpret several qualities that Shakira herself has repeatedly emphasized when explaining the naturalness with which her music and performance move across quite diverse traditions, including her multicultural descent and her upbringing in Barranquilla,[9] "a city of the Coast of the Caribbean . . . where people are perhaps a little freer".[10] Such freedom she situates in the communicative corporeality of *barranquilleros*, people who "learn how to dance even before walking . . . [and] function very much around the cult of dancing. There is a code there."[11] Therefore, when Shakira dances and sings "En Barranquilla se baila así. Say it!", she is extending a call not only to speak in her native language, but to search in her background for the source of that movable subjectivity asserted by her dancing hips. She is also claiming her belonging to the rich tradition of Caribbean musicians, united and distinguished, as pointed by Ángel Quintero Rivera, by a very particular way to make music that includes, among other features, the anticipation and fostering of bodily response.[12] Therefore, the song's proposed conquest and expansion of Caribbean culture through music and dancing, has also the potential to bring bodies back to mind.

I follow the embodied landmarks of the Caribbean mapped by Shakira's personal and musical journey: the multiethnic origin and simultaneous identifications; rhythm, dance and performance; desire and sexuality. Based on both the statements articulated bodily in Shakira's performances and her declarations about her own body, I read her corporeality as a text where she encounters and disputes the region's complex discourses and practices around bodies and sexuality. Her mobility across cultures also allows me to consider the issues of translation faced by Caribbean body languages in their relation to transnational networks of meaning and capital.

Moreover, my interpretation of Shakira's trajectory focuses on the agency and creative capacity that she adjudicates to her body, and the power she derives from such an understanding of her embodied selfhood. Building on previous accounts of Shakira's achievements, my reading emphasizes the role of dancing, performing and polyvalent body language in Shakira's success breaking with gender and ethnic categorizations, and enacting her uniqueness despite her negotiations with the expectations of the United States and the global market. Drawing from feminist theories of subjectivity, I read Shakira as a paradigm of a self-aware "embodied subject" whose qualities may be extended to an understanding of Caribbean subjectivities. In doing so, I attempt to dispel – at the risk of engaging in it – some of the "discursive cannibalism"[13] proliferating in representations of bodies in Caribbean aesthetics. The tendency to reduce Caribbean people's relationships to their bodies to the incarnation of repressive forces and the violence that rendered them "vulnerable"[14] is also evident in theoretical accounts of its place in the formation of postcolonial subjects. I read Shakira's powerful body as a testimony of the political potential of bodies in motion to trace new routes of Caribbeanness. I consider her performative ability, highly articulated body language and her "nomadism"[15] as distinctive features of Caribbean cultural identity that are emphasized in the context of the diaspora, making this artist an emblematic figure of the contributions the Caribbean can make towards the search of alternative ways of being and coexisting in a postcolonial world.

"A Hot Little Weirdo"

In the complex mosaic of information and opinions that comprise Shakira's public image today, along with the recognition of her intellect and her artistic and social sensitivity, her boldness and tenacity set her apart. Comments proliferate about the artist's inexhaustible energy, her singular sense of responsibility and chronic perfectionism that she applies to the production of her songs, videos and performances, as well as to the development of the social projects piloted by her two foundations – Barefoot and ALAS (América Latina en Acción Solidaria). Reviews also emphasize her musical and personal eclecticism, her unconventional worldview, the heterodoxy of her lyricism, and her straightforward manner. Of course, comments on the exceptional features of her body, the changes in her appearance and extraordinary sharpness of her movements accompany almost all of the media coverage, revealing a mixture of fascination and suspicion – desire and anxiety – that has marked Shakira's reception since the start of her career.

The negative affirmation implied in "Hips Don't Lie" exposes the tensions around the translation of language and differences evident since Shakira's incursion into the American market. The title also illustrates the increasing emphasis on authenticity, marking her self-representation to her non-Hispanic fans, a complex multilingual rhetoric in which her corporeality has been her most visible ally. However, Shakira's genuineness had been questioned since the beginnings of her career in her native country,[16] where the list of charges against her included accusations of forcing her voice and not representing her vernacular culture because she preferred rock.[17] Of Lebanese descent, but born and raised in the Colombian Caribbean, Shakira's reception has been marked by the regional tensions surrounding Colombian national identity, provoking mixed feelings about her simultaneous identifications. These mixed feelings have only increased since she moved to the United States, assumed her Latinidad, and became a global pop star. Hostilities against Shakira's "audiotopia" in her native country increased during the first decade of the new millennium under the authoritarian regime of Álvaro Uribe, whose neo-nationalistic rhetoric, supported by other pop artists, was threatened by Shakira's transnationalism.

Shakira has carried a mark of "excess" all through her journey. Her success in multiple genres, compositions in both Spanish and English, and eclecticism in performance, ranging from belly dancing to reggaetón, have merely added to the perception of Shakira as "A Hot Little Weirdo".[18] But the power that has allowed her to break with cultural and linguistic frontiers and challenge all the categories employed to simplify her lies precisely in the paradoxes that she embodies and her ability to negotiate and reconcile differences.

Shakira's entrance into the anglophone world synthesized the mixed perceptions that distinguish the musician's trajectory. She was then the idol of thousands of Latin Americans and Latinos/as who observed with distrust and disillusionment the discolouration of the hair, and the loss of weight in both her body and lyrics when she started to sing in English. Clearly, at first, Shakira simplified her image to become digestible to her new public and used her best strategies of seduction to conquer them. Years later, Shakira herself would confess what was happening at that moment: "I wanted to fit in, to be accepted, approved of . . . I was coming from where I already had a place, but this was different."[19] Shakira's exceptionality revealed itself even at that transition, when she left Emilio Estefan[20] – the brains behind the 90s Latin music boom in the United States – to compose and produce her own bilingual album with Freddy De Mann, former manager of Madonna and Michael Jackson. The resulting album, *Laundry Service*, dazzled Shakira's new public with the unconventional English lyrics of this Latin American *rockera*, whose compositions, voice and performance broke with the parameters expected of rock and pop stars. With her next project, her third concert tour, entitled "Tour of the Mongoose", Shakira would confirm her immunity to the comparisons that characterized her initial reception, as the coverage on MTV News of the tour's inaugural concert attests:

> In her nearly two-hour show . . . [she] showed so many sides to herself it was hard to believe it was the same Shakira all night long. Not only did she flirt like Britney [Spears], play the guitar like Sheryl [Crow], shake her hips like Elvis [Presley], hit the drums like Tommy [Lee], play the harmonica like John [Popper] and take a political stance like Rage [Against the Machine], she did them all and more, naturally and compellingly.[21]

Once inside this new world, Shakira insisted on teaching her followers across the globe to locate in her origins the source of her complexity, inviting them to open themselves up to the diversity that she incarnates and celebrates. By 2005, when she released her two parallel albums, *Fijación oral* or *Oral Fixation* volumes one and two, Shakira could afford to invite her new fans to hear her in Spanish. This turn marked the beginning of a new stage in her self-representation confirmed by the mention of Barranquilla in "Hips Don't Lie" and in the "Oral Fixation Tour" DVD, which features a documentary about the work of Shakira's Barefoot foundation with children of marginal communities in her native city.[22]

The evolution of her relation to the global market demonstrates Shakira's success in articulating contradictory forces and ambivalent tendencies within a single artistic project. "Hips" portrays a mature Shakira, who has managed not only to conform to the global market's rules but to propose her own, to stand for her uniqueness and become a model, turning seduction into an invitation to join her exploration of other languages and cultures. Discussing Shakira's conquest of the US pop market, Cynthia Fuchs highlights how her resistance to "the usual containment of 'ethnic' marketing", has fostered new understandings of what it means to be a Latina woman and artist: "Shakira offers multiply layered performances as object and subject, rock artist and pop star, as she works borders between masculine and feminine or national and ethnic identities, deploying conventions defining the pop and 'Latin' body to discover and attain new territories."[23]

Fuchs's account of Shakira's trajectory echoes Kun's definition of "audiotopias". These are contact zones created by music beyond the containments of national identities that, borrowing Michael Foucault's conceptualization of "heterotopias", Kun defines as "spaces of effective utopian longing where several sites normally deemed incompatible are brought together not only in the space of a particular piece of music itself, but in the production of social space and mapping of geographical space that music makes possible".[24] Shakira's capacity to produce new zones is confirmed by the effects on Colombian migrants' identity of her music and image, whose marketing, as stated by María Elena Cepeda, "has arguably 'reconfigured the meaning and value of contemporary citizenship' among colombianos".[25] Moreover, by assuming, strategically, a Latina identity, and superimposing her Colombian upbringing with the US Latino experience, Shakira has challenged dominant definitions of Latinidad itself.

Embodied Caribbeanness

Voice, words, rhythm and movement have combined in the music and language of this "tiny woman from Colombia shutting down the crossroads of the world", in the words of James Montgomery.[26] Shakira's music not only creates new social spaces but also promotes alternative ways of being, understanding and coexisting. I became aware of this power in a mall in New Jersey, watching a clerk of Indian descent singing and dancing while watching Shakira's "Objection" video. Having grown up an hour away from Barranquilla, I have followed Shakira's career since her first album, *Magia* (Magic), released when she was thirteen. Full of feminist objections about her bodily transformations, I was also one of those fans who abandoned her when she crossed over to the American market. Seeing that girl at the store made me suspect I had been hasty in dismissing Shakira, but it was not until three years later, with "Hips Don't Lie", that my confidence in her was restored. I had not paid attention to the song or watched the video until I came across "Hips Don't Lie: Fans Only Version" by chance. This video features men and women of varied ages and origins taking the stage in their houses and in the streets, shaking their hips and navels in the Caribbean, American or Eastern style. It portrays bodies that do not respect ethnic distinctions or aesthetic ideals, accepting the invitation on behalf of Shakira's hips to assume their corporealities, and their differences, celebrating them through dance. This appropriation of Shakira's statement regarding her body's "perfection" led me to the official video. It was at this time that I realized Shakira was not only using her body to seduce her way into a new world and gather new fans, but she was also embodying a way of life applicable to her followers' relationships with themselves.

It is impossible to separate Shakira's trajectory from the different facets of her corporeality: the uniqueness of her voice; the flexibility of her five foot tall body and her extraordinary talent for dance; the transformations in her appearance, including the slimming and whitening following her entry into the English-speaking market; the unfolding of energy, the passion and control over her performance; the sensuality of her movements; and even the temperance that she projects on her sentimental and sexual life. In her body, the confluence of physical, mental and emotional features becomes evident, as does the coexistence of her natural attributes with the conscious production of her corporeality.

The invitation the artist addresses "to read its signs" in "Hips Don't Lie" presents her body as a creative and communicative agent, suggesting the dissolution of borders and hierarchies between mind and body and subject and object that have dominated the definitions of the "Subject" in Western history and philosophy. Shakira's "lived body"[27] is, in the first instance, the ally of a multifaceted and complex personality[28] whose qualities echo the redefinitions of subjectivity proposed by feminist philosophers such as Elizabeth Grosz, Judith Butler and Rosi Braidotti.[29] Building upon accounts of power as embodied through practice,[30] these authors share an approach to bodies as the scenario for the encounter between the psychic, physical and social forces that give shape and unity to our subjectivity. They also characterize identity as the outcome of a constant performance of societal norms. Shakira's ongoing identifications and permanent reinventions enact the transitory quality of identity emphasized by these authors, while the visibility of her active corporeality makes her an emblem of the potential for individual and social transformations that these same authors situate in subversive practices of embodiment.

Nevertheless, as suggested by the lyrics and carnivalesque iconography in the video for "Hips", Shakira's capacity to negotiate norms, reconcile contradictions and embrace change needs to be traced back to her Caribbean origins. Bodies are a recurrent locus in Caribbean aesthetics, and the relationship between bodies and memory is pivotal to numerous critical and theoretical efforts towards understanding and re-writing both the colonial past and its recurrence in postcolonial subjects. According to Guillermina de Ferrari, the exhibition of bodies and their "vulnerability" is a common strategy across contemporary Caribbean writers, who situate in them "the conditions of possibility for reviewing the formation of colonial identities and contesting their essentialism".[31] The increasing scholarship on bodies in and beyond the Caribbean has also brought them to the spotlight while still emphasizing their role as receptacles of power both in society and in their fictional recreations. But as Myra Mendible states, "embodied selves rarely comply with the terms or theories that attempt to define them".[32] As suggested by Fraser Delgado and Muñoz in the epigraph to this chapter, it is in the motion of Caribbean bodies where we can find ongoing and perhaps even more effective ways to revise and contest colonial narratives of selfhood, and explore the negotiations that have allowed Caribbean subjects to continue to celebrate corporeality, enacting desire and joy.

Shakira's embodied audiotopia bears productive resemblances with the Caribbean "of the senses and sentiments", whose identity Antonio Benítez-Rojo defined as "a certain kind of way".[33] Rhythm, a dialectics between change and return, and a propensity for performance, all anchored in a particular relationship to bodies, are some of the features of Benítez-Rojo's Caribbeanness, which Shakira performs to paroxysm, underlining the potential of this culture for the study of embodied practices as the source of alternative subjectivities. Benítez-Rojo's definition of the Caribbean as flows of matter changing and returning also echoes Braidotti's figuration of the subject as "nomadic", a "movable diversity", who "has relinquished all idea, desire, or nostalgia for fixity".[34] A "political fiction" particularly enriching for understanding Caribbeanness from the diaspora, Braidotti's metaphor also describes Shakira's trajectory: "an identity made of transitions, successive shifts, and coordinated changes, without and against an essential unity", whose cohesiveness is "engendered by repetitions, cyclical moves, rhythmical displacement".[35]

Lost in Translation?

Let us return to Shakira's loquacious hips. Shakira invites her audience to complement listening with looking – *mira*, exalting the beauty of the dancing body and appealing to desire. Still, the iconography of the video limits access to her body, including shots of Shakira with her back turned, and of Jean following her across hanging veils but unable to touch her. The video illustrates both the increasing emphasis on her body and dance, as well as the ambiguity that is characteristic of Shakira's performance since her introduction into the multilingual market. The artist has consistently denied using sexuality as a marketing tool, although she has admitted to emphasizing dance and sensuality as a vehicle for both aesthetic pleasure and communication. In her words, "passion transcends language".[36] Therefore, Shakira's later emphasis on expressing herself through her body can be interpreted as a strategic shift aimed at communicating with a public that she could not address in her native tongue. Although the effectiveness of such a call is evident in the response of her fans, the messages transmitted by her hips are as complex as her simultaneous belongings and cultural crossings.

Shakira's body illustrates the "political fictions" with which both feminist and Caribbeanist scholars have attempted to account not only for identity but agency, revealing the possibilities of expansion and re-creation of a subject, and a culture, that embraces the complexity of corporeality, internal diversity and change. At the same time, Shakira's image – the hybridity resulting from both her efforts at self-representation and the construction of the idol on the part of her fans and the media – refers to a second meaning of feminine corporeality, its more traditionally assumed appraisal as "object". At this level, Shakira incarnates the difficulties of claiming desire and subjectivity "of one's own". These difficulties increased under the ubiquity of capitalism and mass culture, ever since female bodies evolved from being objects of exchange and appropriation to becoming objects of consumption.

Shakira's negotiations with the expectations of the United States and global market of a pop/rock and "ethnic" artist attest to the continuity of cross-cultural contradictions around female bodies, as much as to the effect of these contradictions on the formation of contemporary women's identities. Pointing to the "disproportionate amount of media attention" on Shakira's sexuality, Cepeda remarks upon the US market's incapacity to value young female artists independently of their physical appearance and sexuality, as well as "the well-entrenched acceptance of *marianismo* (or the 'Madonna/whore' complex) that informs the way Shakira is framed within transnational media".[37] Shakira's body is a media product, and she has profited from her exoticism, sensuality and rhythmical skills, all of which reaffirm dominant stereotypes of Latinas.

At the same time, Shakira's bodily statements problematize the reduction of women's bodies to sexual objects or products. The "routine seductions" displayed by her videos and performances are, as suggested by Fuchs, "also signs of warning: part teasing; part self-protective and part she is not so available as she seems. She has her own story to tell, her own interests extending beyond those of any possible spectator."[38]

Shakira has been exposed to these libidinal transactions from her very origins. One of the overlooked aspects of Benítez-Rojo's report on Caribbean peoples' celebration of their bodies is an account of the differences that mark embodied selves in Caribbean cultures. Regarding sexual difference, the "certain kind of way" conceals, perpetuates and even intensifies a double standard regarding women's sexuality. While according to which the display of female bodily sensuality for the gaze and enjoyment of men is stimulated, women's agency and desire continues to be restricted through sophisticated mechanisms of regulation. "Show it, but do not dare to use it" seems to be the Caribbean motto, except for those women whose sexuality is their means of survival.

Raised in a Catholic family and having attended Catholic school, Shakira played the "good girl" role all through her early career, and even during her crossover period, despite the increasing deployment of her sensuality in performance and the attention her sexuality elicited. Such apparent ambiguity responds to the Caribbean *marianismo*, which fosters the coexistence of the uninhibited public unfolding of sensuality and the negation of an active sexuality. The difficulties of translating these seemingly contradictory meanings across cultures are at the core of the misreading of US Latinas as sexually available, even if the stereotype would not apply to standards of femininity in other Latin American cultures, where the control over sexuality has equally proscribed the body's exhibition.

Shakira's transit into the United States and the global market did not only precipitate the translation of the Caribbean *marianismo* permissiveness towards bodies' exhibition, but it also exposed the artist to other imperatives on female bodies and subjectivities. The whitening of her image and her drastic weight loss illustrate Shakira's negotiations with a globalized model of beauty imposed by the increased emphasis on appearance demanded by contemporary paradigms of womanhood. Shakira herself admitted to a conflict with such paradigms, indicating her view that the preoccupation with feminine beauty has become pathological: "[there is] some kind of obsessive compulsion with becoming the perfect woman, not a 10, but an 11. It's about matching these images that pop culture puts in front of you . . . I feel like sometimes I've been both a victim of that and a victimizer, and it's not a good feeling, let me tell you."[39] Although upon reaching her thirties she affirms to having arrived at a stage of acceptance of her body, the energy and discipline invested in the improvement of her movements and in the perfection of her appearance are graphic manifestations of both the demands of her field and the anxieties that these provoke in the artist about her own relationship with her body. Still, what makes Shakira exceptional is not her immunity to the conflictive forces she synthesizes, but her audacity to negotiate them. This ability to play with the rules and to expand them, rather than to confront them, to *bregar*, is also a recurring theme in the theorization of Caribbean identity.[40]

Shakira's body rhetoric also reveals the transformations in the vision of herself and femininity that have resulted from her transit between cultures and her commitment to reinvention, including changes in her positions regarding love, sexuality and power. Her lyrical depictions of love, ranging from romantic odes to portrayals of abusive relationships, illustrate a transition from an idealized to a more complex and pragmatic vision. In a 2009 interview, the artist confirmed this shift when finally acknowledging her rejection of marriage, a decision that indicated her dismissal of the traditional model of femininity that she once seemed to embrace: "I want to say that I am no longer traditionalistic nor have I a classic vision of a couples' life," she clarified. "I believe that the institution of marriage did not always exist in society but it was invented much later. And it is part of the society in which we live."[41]

The English version of *Oral Fixation* provides evidence of the increasing detachment from social conventions implicit in the quote above, including her criticism of consumer society, voiced in her earlier albums in Spanish but now recalled with a deep disillusionment and an ironic rage that is unforgiving of governments, media, religions and herself.[42] Revealing her restlessness at the market's demands and her own transformations, her lyrics echo the anxieties that characterize her reception, recreating the way in which her nomadism has implied risks and compromises, in spite of her obvious achievements. The videos and lyrics of her songs, as well as the titles and covers of her recent albums, also demonstrate a more complex vision of desire and sexuality, under the influence of psychoanalytic exploration. A sample of this are the covers of both the English version of *Oral Fixation,* portraying a baby staring at an innocent Eve in the Garden of Eden, and the Spanish one, which plays with the medieval motif of the Virgin and the baby. The allusion to an Oedipal complex in both of these images furthers the enactment of psychoanalytic theories voiced by the album title. But it is in the rhetoric of her body, and especially her dance performances, where the continuities and changes in her worldview are best expressed.

Hip Talk

Given the fact that Shakira's physical appearance and her sexuality have been the major themes of the media surveillance and both her own and her audience's anxieties, choosing her hips as the speaker of the complexity and authenticity of her personality cannot be taken as an innocent synecdoche. In fact, hips have been historically charged with both derogatory and vindicating meanings. The "excessive" movement of hips has been a marker of "looseness" in many cultures, including the Caribbean itself. Hips are also closely linked to the evolution in the perception of Latinas in the United States, since the time when Carmen Miranda hipped her way into US stardom.[43]

Recent academic discussions illustrate the complex negotiations with power enacted in women's performances of sensuality as "ethnic" marker, conferring an attitude of defiance to body parts traditionally rendered as meaningless or sexually objectified.[44] Shakira's hips follow this tradition while adding a level of self-awareness that is remarkably articulated in her dancing and in the title of "Hips Don't Lie". Her carefully chosen and highly controlled movements, as much as her neat articulation of body-statements, and the sharpness of her hip shaking, compete in Shakira's dancing with the softness and roundness usually associated with strategies of seduction using the hips. Both her dancing and verbal statements expose an unusual relationship with her corporeality, displaying a consciousness of its power that conveys her body not only as a producer of meaning but also as a bridge in the relationship to her public.

It is likely that the reason Shakira had to state categorically that her hips don't lie is because they know and say too much. The responses of her followers, as expressed in the parodies of her videos or fan blogs, attest to the polyvalence and effectiveness of her body language in enacting that "certain Caribbean way", whose power, according to Benítez-Rojo, springs from its capacity to erase the distance between the performer and the spectator, and move him or her into another space dominated by paradoxes and bifurcations. From that space it is possible to promote an aesthetic of pleasure, "whose desire is nonviolence".[45] "No fighting" – Jean and Shakira sing. Shakira has demonstrated a singular awareness of the responsibility that is implied in this power, using it to articulate ideas on topics ranging from relationships and love, to explicit political commentaries. Perhaps one of the most suggestive results of Shakira's embodied paradox is the diffusion of Spanish engendered by her entrance into the English-speaking world, emblematized in the repetition of the verse "En Barranquilla se baila así" by the audiences at her concerts heeding the mandate of the artist to "Say it!" Her concerts, interviews and documentaries have been also a stage for discussing issues of social justice, the effects of war and the challenges of early childhood in Latin America. In 2011, she was invited by Oxford University to lecture on children's education, a central concern not only of her foundations' agendas but also of her increasingly intense and intentional political activity.[46]

Can these messages be transmitted or reinforced through dancing? Shakira's emphasis on her multiethnic background is clearly stated in the eclecticism of her choreographies, reassuring her position in regards to another of her recurrent themes: the celebration of human diversity. Although strongly anchored in the patterns of isolations, angulations and shakes of Middle Eastern dance traditions, her hips take much from Afro-Caribbean rhythms that she unapologetically mixes with modern dance and more aggressive gestures coming from rock, rap and hip-hop. Shakira's extraordinary talent as performer portrays dancing as a sophisticated form of expression both recalling and challenging the stereotype of Caribbean peoples and Latinos/Latinas as "natural" dancers. If the "unstated equation" behind this stereotype is, as Jane Desmond argues, that "Latinos are how they dance and they dance how they are",[47] Shakira's dancing rhetoric faces her audience with a subject whose complexity defies all other assumptions on how Latin people are. Moreover, Shakira's dance disputes claims of the primacy of the mind over the body that has supported every form of colonization and patriarchal power. Shakira and Jean's invitation to dance "in the streets, day and night" broadens this message, calling for a liberation from the limits of safe spaces to which dancing has been mostly confined through its expansion in the First World, such as in schools, ballrooms and Latin nightclub parties designed for middle-class American or European dance students.

It is not only through music, but also through its materialization in the space traced by the dancing body that the Caribbean "audiotopias" become effective. As Ángel Quintero-Rivera has argued exhaustively, Caribbean musical traditions are distinguished precisely by "a [certain] way of making music"[48] that implies, among other features, the fact of being composed with the body in mind, meaning the music is made to make bodies move. Therefore, through dancing, the global expansion of Caribbean music is not only creating new social spaces and retracing the region's map, but it is teaching the world, Quintero-Rivera would suggest, how to bring bodies back to the picture of the self.[49]

Powerful Hips

Academic articles, music reviews, press notes and comments from her fans register today the progressive acceptance of Shakira's irreducible complexity. Her reception also testifies to her extraordinary power to mobilize hundreds of thousands of people towards new meanings and perceptions of the world. After all, if massive change can be mobilized in our age, it may be more up to pop stars than philosophers to do so.

Shakira's body-mirror reflects the immense potential of listening to the language and the wisdom of bodies, rejecting their reduction to objects or the passive term of power. This is a statement of particular value for the Caribbean and its people. Shakira embodies and takes to paroxysm the contradictions and strengths that make this region a unique space for the production of meanings and ways of being. The language and the wisdom of bodies are a point of departure, but it is necessary to emancipate them not only from colonialism, but from the empire of both reason and patriarchy in order to listen to what they have to say. The audacity demonstrated by the artist in her negotiations with the expectations on her corporeality teaches Caribbean people that practices of embodiment do not need to be reduced to the exhibition of their bodies as local folklore, nor to the exaggeration of their rhythmical potential or sexualization to respond to the hunger of the exotic that lead the First World's perceptions of this region. In the inevitable negotiations that characterize the relation of the Caribbean with the world, it is urgent to assert the complexity and atavistic wisdom subjacent in *performance*, rhythm and that "certain kind of way" that makes Caribbean corporeality and geography so attractive to world tourism and foreign intervention. It is necessary, also, to dig into Caribbean inner contradictions in order to fight the distinctions of class, race and gender that make some bodies and subjects even more susceptible to "consumption" by both natives and foreigners.[50]

Finally, Shakira offers critics, readers, spectators and fans, from and beyond the Caribbean, evidence on the potential of ongoing embodiment: an identity open to transformation and reinvention, coherent with a subject who conceives of herself as an inherently diverse "I" in constant search of a self. Her trajectory is an open and unfinished book, full of possibilities and suggestions in which permanence and change through time, autonomy and intersubjectivity exist, and loyalty to national and cultural identities reconcile with an opennness to differences: "I think we come into this world dressed in many layers . . . and life is about tearing them off to hit the core of your essence. With every album I release and every year that goes by, I'm getting closer to who I am. And my fans accompany me in that process."[51] Shakira's songs and videos from her more recent albums, *She Wolf* (2009) and *Sale el sol* (2010), graphically enact this statement while continuing to assert the tendencies highlighted by this chapter: specifically, Shakira's bodily communication and corporeal subjectivity, and her transnational Caribbeanness. The latest is claimed through her trademark eclecticism and rhythmic hybridity. She combines pop, rock, electronic music, disco and Middle Eastern tunes with reggae, soca, cumbia and steel band instrumentation on the first, and the very Dominican merengue in the second album. However, *She Wolf* demonstrates a further shift in Shakira's performance. Inspired by a picture of the Jamaican pioneer Grace Jones posing naked inside a cage, the video of its opening single, also called "She Wolf", portrays Shakira dancing in two scenarios: a cage with bars from which she hangs while contorting herself in a skin-colour body suit, and a red tunnel, whose texture and colour resemble a vagina. The lyrics and the video play with the theme of the feline side of womanhood "in disguise", coming out when the moon is full to take over the "domesticated" life of a girl whose "body is craving". Shakira's body contortions and dancing proved their unsettling quality in the reception both in Latin America and the United States of her movements as "skanky". Not only does she invite this inner other woman to come out of the closet and set her desire free – while her partner is asleep – but she shows a control in her movements, defiant gaze and facial expression that is more disturbing than sensual. "She Wolf" demonstrates

Shakira's move from a display of sensuality to a straightforward account of female sexuality, and from seducing and inciting attraction to asserting and pursuing her own desire. Such intention is evident throughout the whole album, where Shakira steps out of her first-person autobiographic voice to play with different female roles, all of them characterized by a "she-wolf appetite" that the artist playfully, and with a certain ironic tone, enacts in different scenarios. No wonder she is read as aggressive; she is definitely showing off her power and encouraging other women to find and show their own. "Loca", "Rabiosa" and "Gordita", titles of three of the songs on *Sale el sol*, suggest the continuity of this playful embodiment of contemporary femininities – multiple and contradictory – through the vindication of non-flattering feminine qualities, translated as crazy, angry and chubby. Dressed in the most commercial and "sexy" of her costumes, with *She Wolf*, Shakira stripped down to her most feminist layer to date.

Notes

1. Translation: "If somebody demanded a visual explanation, an image of what is the Caribbean, I would refer to the spiral chaos of the Milky Way . . . change, transit, return, flows of stellar matter." From Antonio Benítez-Rojo, *The Repeating Island: The Caribbean and the Postmodern Perspective*, trans. James Maraniss (Durham: Duke University Press, 1996).
2. Celeste Fraser Delgado and José Esteban Muñoz, "Rebellions of Everynight Life", in *Everynight Life: Culture and Dance in Latin/o America*, ed. Celeste Fraser Delgado and José Esteban Muñoz (Durham: Duke University Press, 1997), 9–32.
3. Jennifer Vineyard, "No Lie: Shakira Says Wyclef Appeared to Her in a Dream", *MTV News*, 30 March 2006.
4. Ibid.
5. "I always try not to be graphic but to be metaphorical", Shakira said, commenting on her dancing performances. From Aaron Gell, "Love in the Time of Shakira", *Elle*, March 2006, http://www.elle.com/Pop-Culture/Cover-Shoots/Love-In-The-Time-Of-Shakira/Love-in-the-Time-of-Shakira.
6. The dance performed is a *bullerengue*, the only Colombian Caribbean dance interpreted exclusively by women. It welcomes puberty, menarche and the emergence of desire, represented by the dancers' hands rubbing the chest, belly and pubis. Men participate only as drummers.

7. Josh Kun, "Against Easy Listening: Audiotopic Readings and Transnational Soundings", in *Everynight Life: Culture and Dance in Latin/o America*, ed. Celeste Fraser Delgado and José Esteban Muñoz (Durham: Duke University Press, 1997), 289.
8. Ximena Diego, *Shakira: Mujer llena de gracia* (New York: Libros en Español, 2001), xxi.
9. Shakira's homage to her native Barranquilla in "Hips Don't Lie" is stated both in the lyrics and by the inclusion of several of its carnival characters and traditional dances in the video: the *marimonda*, the *garabato* and the *danza de los negros* (the dance of black people), among others. Despite Shakira's manifested national pride, and her conscious enactment of her multiple belongings, she emphasizes being *barranquillera* and from the Caribbean coast. The gesture responds to the problematic construction of Colombian national identity, whose representation excluded Caribbean cultural features until recent decades. Although the international reception of artists and writers from the region has propelled the revision of "national" symbols, the persistence of regionalist divisions is evinced in the remaining distinction between *música colombiana* (Columbian music) and *música costeña* (music from the coast). See, for example, David Sánchez Juliao, "Qué nombre le pondremos?", *El Heraldo* (Barranquilla), 16 September 2009; and Nadia Celis, "Entre cachacos y costeños", *El Universal* (Cartagena), 9 February 2009.
10. Ángel Quintero-Rivera, *Cuerpo y Cultura: Las músicas mulatas y la subversión del baile* (Madrid: Iberoamericana, 2009), 69–204.
11. Shakira, *Live and Off the Record* (Sony, March 2004).
12. "Creativity Is an Instinct, Music Is the Engine", *MTV News Raw: Shakira*, 21 April 2006.
13. M.M. Adjarian, *Allegories of Desire: Body, Nation and Empire in Modern Caribbean Literature by Women* (London: Praeger, 2004), 11.
14. Guillermina De Ferrari, *Vulnerable States: Bodies of Memory in Contemporary Caribbean Fiction* (Charlottesville: University of Virginia Press, 2007).
15. Rosi Braidotti, *Nomadic Subjects: Embodiment and Sexual Difference in Contemporary Feminist Theory* (New York: Columbia University Press, 1994).
16. Shakira was only thirteen when she got her first contract with Sony Music Colombia for her three first releases: *Magia* (*Magic*) (1990), *Peligro* (*Danger*) (1992) and *Pies descalzos* (*Barefoot*) (1996). The last beat all national and Latin American sales records, propelling her relocation to Miami.
17. Choosing rock implied also entering a predominantly masculine world. As María Elena Cepeda indicates, both rock artists and their critics are mostly men ("Shakira as the Idealized Transnational Citizen: A Case Study of Colombianidad in Transition", *Latino Studies* 1 [2003]: 217). Shakira herself has commented on the difficulties of leading her band, and composing her music in a world led by men: " 'I was always very sure of what I wanted to hear,' she said. But 'I had to fight to be heard: "Don't

play that melody in this part, play the other one." Guys don't like women telling them what to do. It reminds them of their mothers, or something like that. . . . I don't want to sound like a feminist saying this. But it's true it's a man's world' " (Jon Pareles, "The Shakira Dialectic", *New York Times*, 15 November 2005).
18. Robert Christgau, "Music: A Hot Little Weirdo", *Village Voice Music*, 6 January 2006, 1–2.
19. "Creativity", *MTV News Raw: Shakira*.
20. With Estefan, Shakira entered the Latino market in the United States, recorded "Dónde están los ladrones?" ("Where Are the Thieves?") (1998), and produced the *MTV Unplugged* (2000) that won her two Latin and one "American" Grammys. The *Unplugged* was also one of her first transcultural achievements, becoming the first programme in Spanish transmitted on American MTV.
21. Corey Moss, "Shakira Shows She's the Colombian Britney, Colombian Tommy Lee at Tour Kickoff", *MTV News*, 11 November 2002.
22. Shakira's Barefoot foundation currently sponsors the education of five thousand children through six schools in the Pacific and Caribbean regions of Colombia, the poorest areas of her native country. Shakira's global advocacy for children's education has received increasing attention over the last years, as is attested by her inclusion in the special edition "The World in 2010" of London's *Economist* (13 November 2009), where she shared the cover with Barack Obama, and was invited to write an editorial next to those of Dmitry Medvedev and Jacob Zuma, presidents of Russia and South Africa, respectively.
23. Cynthia Fuchs, "There's My Territory: Shakira Crossing Over", in *From Bananas to Buttocks: The Latina Body in Popular Film and Culture* (Austin: University of Texas Press, 2007), 169.
24. Kun, "Against Easy Listening", 289.
25. Cepeda, "Shakira", 213–14.
26. James Montgomery, "Shakira Says Her *Oral Fixation* Was Not Premeditated", *MTV News*, 9 June 2003.
27. Feminist philosophers owe this concept to Maurice Merleau-Ponty, *Phenomenology of Perception* (New York: Humanities Press, 1962).
28. Shakira's statements in several interviews confirm this perception of her body as an active being, whose creative character is implied in the mutually engaging relationship with her music: "When the music invades me and takes control of my body that is the best thing that can happen to an artist. When you don't have to think too much, you let yourself go and deliver yourself to the music. And the music rules" (Joe D'Angelo, "Shakira Strips Off Her Skins", *VH1 News*, 21 August 2002). Commenting on her preparation of the Oral Fixation Tour she also said: "I'm starting to get in touch with the songs from the performer's point of view: O.K., how am I going to interpret this with my body? How am I going to start to have now a physical

relationship with my songs?" (Pareles, "The Shakira Dialectic"). When asked what would be the thematic of her upcoming songs in *She Wolf*, the artist responded in a similar tone: "Ja, ja, ja, they will be consistent with a thirty-one-year-old woman. I am not going to talk about what politicians say. I will speak of the things that possess me today, of those things that inhabit my body and my sensations." Diego Giraldo, "Una charla con los pies descalzos", *Elenco* (Bogotá: Casa Editorial El Tiempo, 23 July 2008): 40–49; author's translation.

29. See Elizabeth Grosz, *Volatile Bodies: Toward a Corporeal Feminism* (Indianapolis: Indiana University Press, 1994) and *Space, Time and Perversion: Essays on the Politics of Bodies* (New York: Routledge, 1995); Moira Gatens, *Imaginary Bodies: Ethics, Power and Corporeality* (New York: Routledge, 1996); Lois McNay, *Gender and Agency: Reconfiguring the Subject in Feminist and Social Theory* (Cambridge: Polity Press, 2000); Judith Butler, *Bodies That Matter: On the Discursive Limits of Sex* (New York: Routledge, 1993) and *Gender Trouble: Feminism and the Subversion of Identity* (London: Routledge, 1999); and Rosi Braidotti, *Nomadic Subjects: Embodiment and Sexual Difference in Contemporary Feminist Theory* (New York: Columbia University Press, 1994).

30. They draw mostly from Michel Foucault and Pierre Bourdieu's works on power and bodies.

31. De Ferrari, *Vulnerable States*, 25.

32. Myra Mendible, "Embodying Latinidad", in *From Bananas to Buttocks: The Latina Body in Popular Film and Culture*, ed. Myra Mendible (Austin: University of Texas Press, 2007), 5.

33. Benítez-Rojo, *Repeating Island*.

34. Braidotti, *Nomadic Subjects*, 14.

35. Ibid, 22.

36. "Creativity", *MTV News Raw: Shakira*.

37. Cepeda, "Shakira", 222.

38. Fuchs, "There's My Territory", 179.

39. Ibid.

40. The aptitude to negotiate conflictive forces is implicit in theoretical accounts of Caribbean identities, such as Fernando Ortiz's concept of "counterpoint" and Edouard Glissant's "relational" poetics. In "De cómo y cuándo bregar", *El arte de bregar y otros ensayos* (San Juan: Ediciones Callejón, 2000), Arcadio Díaz-Quiñones examines the use and effects of the Puerto Rican verb for this aptitude, *bregar*, the action and the cleverness required to successfully operate within constricted limits, while avoiding confrontation. Considered, first, as a laborious work and the talent required to succeed in it, *bregar* also applies to sexual interactions. This second use, according to Díaz-Quiñones, attests to the Caribbean's "constant conscience of the subject being sexual" (29). Finally, *bregar* implies the necessary reflection and

negotiations for "finding solutions appropriate to create a bridge without making too much noise . . . to look for a midpoint, avoiding violence" (32–33), pertinent both to public and political, and to private and intimate struggles. Shakira's negotiations within the global market suggest her ability to "bregar" in all the senses of the word.

41. Diego Giraldo, "Una charla", 44.
42. See "Timor", "How Do You Do", "Animal City" and "Costume Makes the Clown".
43. Mendible, *Bananas to Buttocks*.
44. See Frances Negrón-Montaner, "El trasero de Jennifer López", *Nueva Sociedad* 201 (Enero–Febrero 2006): 129–44; and José Piedra, "Hips Poetics", in *Everynight Life: Culture and Dance in Latin/o America*, ed. Celeste Fraser Delgado and José Esteban Muñoz (Durham: Duke University Press, 1997), 93–140.
45. Benítez-Rojo, *Repeating Islands*, 21.
46. "Shakira Speaks at Oxford on Education", *Wall Street Journal*, 9 December 2009.
47. Jane Desmond, "Embodying Difference: Issues in Dance and Cultural Studies", in *Everynight Life: Culture and Dance in Latin/o America*, ed. Celeste Fraser Delgado and José Esteban Muñoz (Durham: Duke University Press, 1997), 58.
48. Ángel Quintero-Rivera, *Salsa, sabor y control: Sociología de la música tropical* (Mexico City: Siglo veintiuno editores, 1998).
49. Ángel Quintero-Rivera, *Cuerpo y Cultura: Las músicas mulatas y la subversión del baile* (Madrid: Iberoamericana, 2009), 326–57.
50. In *Consuming the Caribbean: From Arawaks to Zombies* (London: Routledge, 2003), Mimi Sheller traces the foundation of the Caribbean back to a variety of practices of "consumption" of bodies and their energies: abduction, forced labour, punishment, rape and even the confiscation of progeny, among other acts of "intimate violence" that inscribed imperial forces on the very materiality of native and African descendant men and women. Following the representation of Caribbean bodies from the conquerors' chronicles up to today's tourist brochures, Sheller brilliantly demonstrates that the struggle against the symbolic and material consumption of bodies continues to be at the centre of Caribbean people's identities.
51. D'Angelo, "Shakira Strips Off Her Skins".

Discography

Shakira. *¿Dónde están los ladrones?* Sony Latin, 82746, compact disc, 1998.
———. *Fijación Oral Vol. 1*, Epic, 5201623, compact disc, 2005.
———. *Live and Off the Record*. Sony, 515283, compact disc/DVD, 2004.
———. *Magia*. Sony Colombia, 14464663, LP/cassette, 1991.
———. *MTV Unplugged*. Sony Colombia, 83775, compact disc, 2000.

———. *MTV Unplugged*. Sony, 89338, video/DVD, 2002.
———. "Objection". *Laundry Service*. Epic, 4981202, compact disc, 2001.
———. *Peligro*. Sony Colombia, 51473102, LP, 1993.
———. *Pies descalzos, sueños blancos*. Sony International 81795, LP/compact disc, 1996.
———."She Wolf". *She Wolf*. Epic, 38188, compact disc, 2009.
———. "Timor", "How Do You Do", "Animal City" and "Costume Makes the Clown". *Oral Fixation Vol. 2*. Epic, 82200, compact disc, 2005.
———. *Tour Fijación Oral*. Epic, 0473, DVD, 2007.
Shakira ft. Calle 13."Gordita". *Sale el sol*. Sony, 777473, compact disc, 2010.
Shakira ft. Cata and Pitbull."Loca" and "Rabiosa". *Sale el sol*. Sony, 777473, compact disc, 2010.
Shakira ft. Wyclef Jean."Hips Don't Lie". *Oral Fixation Vol. 2*, Epic, 82876738952, compact disc (with bonus track), 2006.

Part 3.

AT THE DIASPORIC CROSSROADS

9.

The Black Diaspora North of the Border
Women, Music and Caribbean Culture in Canada

| LISA TOMLINSON

Introduction

A review of scholarly literature reveals that to date there is little research available on black popular music and Caribbean culture in Canada, especially as it pertains to women. A similar review of the music industry reveals that despite a number of very successful black Canadian female artists, both in Canada and the wider diaspora, black women continue to occupy a marginal position in the Canadian music industry. In this chapter I aim to challenge and close some of these gaps by examining the achievements of black Canadian women recording artists. In particular, this study focuses on black women artists of Caribbean heritage who work in the dub poetry, reggae and dancehall, and hip-hop genres in the Toronto area. I have chosen to focus on these three genres because of their creative overlap, as well as the significant impact each of them has had on black popular music in Canada. I will also consider how these female artists choose to integrate commentary on African-Caribbean gender issues in the Canadian context into their work, and how they strive to create a distinctive black diasporic sound, just as their male counterparts do.

In a 1988 article on hip-hop in Canada, Cameron Bailey argues that black Canadian youth have always incorporated and adapted black American culture to suit their own circumstances because the dominant white culture was either alien to their cultural experiences or simply not considered attractive.[1] Bailey, however, fails to recognize how black Caribbean youth in Canada have also always drawn upon their West Indian roots in articulating their cultural identities and lived experiences. This reality is reflected in the music of Canadian women recording artists with African-Caribbean origins or heritage. Indeed, their musical input has contributed to the strength of a Caribbean cultural presence in black Canadian music culture.

The Caribbean presence has long been a strong and dynamic force in black diasporic communities in Canada. A significant wave of migration from the English-speaking Caribbean to Canada in the late 1960s and early 1970s resulted in the importation of African-Caribbean cultural expressions, including music such as reggae and calypso, to cities like Toronto, Montreal and Vancouver. This same trend occurred in the Caribbean diasporic communities of New York and London, though it should be noted that Jamaican dancehall reggae in particular had a greater influence on black music in Canada and the United Kingdom than in the United States. The aesthetics of dancehall street style and reggae references are noticeable in almost every form of black Canadian popular music, and collaborations between Caribbean-Canadian artists and acts from Jamaica are common.

The alienation of African-Caribbean youth from the wider Canadian society contributed to their ongoing and close ties with reggae and dancehall and African-American hip-hop culture. While some youth immersed themselves in one form over the other for the purposes of cultural identification, many others merged these two influences. For African-Caribbean Canadian youth, black popular music as a cultural expression has typically taken on a hybrid sound that both represents the lived experiences of their disenfranchised communities and offers up an alternative space within the dominant white society. As is the case throughout the black diaspora, black popular music in Canada is a site from which African-Caribbean Canadian youth can contest negative stereotypes and forge new and meaningful identities.

However, this capacity of black popular music to function as an alternative space for disenfranchised African-Caribbean Canadian youth is one that has been largely occupied by men. While African-Caribbean male rappers such as Kardinal Offishall and Maestro Fresh Wes brilliantly contest notions of Canadianness and articulate narratives about African-Caribbean communities, they fail to include African-Caribbean women in their discourse. For instance, while Kardinal's popular rap song "Bakardi Slang" successfully offers an expression of black diasporic culture, and redefinition of Canadianness, via code switching from Standard English to Jamaican to a black Canadian voice, his use of visual imagery in the accompanying video is illustrative of male hegemony. In the video, Kardinal and his *bredrin* take centre stage as the representation of Canadian hip-hop while, as Maki Motapanyane points out, "ready to please women [fill] the backdrop, seductively co-signing the self-absorbed masculinity of the video's male star(s)".[2] Many black music videos in Canada reproduce this male centredness.

Historically, in North America and the Caribbean, black women's artistic involvements in cultural production, along with their voices in socio-economic and political spheres, have often been ignored, downplayed and overshadowed by male dominance. This is echoed in the Canadian context where black women have typically occupied a marginal space in society. As Charmaine Crawford notes, black Canadian women "have been marked by a sense of non-belonging due to the effects of gendered racism within their communities and wider society".[3] In response to such gendered racism, African-Caribbean Canadian female recording artists have had to stretch beyond just voicing the social and political realities of their communities to also include narratives about their lived experiences as black women in Canada.

Black diasporic culture has often been marked by marginality. However, while Caribbean and African-American cultures, and more recently black British culture, have had centuries and decades to develop, and in some cases assimilate, African-Caribbean Canadian diasporic culture is newer and remains largely underground both in and outside of the nation. With the exception of a few studies (see Walker[4] and Walcott[5]), there is little critical work on black popular music in Canada, and aside from the success of a small number of black Canadian recording artists, most of them male, the circulation of black popular music is primarily limited to community radio stations. In addition, popular discourses about Canadian black music are typically limited to a few alternative entertainment magazines with modest distribution. Given this situation, it is not surprising to find that black Canadian recording artists still find it difficult to attain critical and commercial success in the music industry either locally or internationally.

Ironically, it can be argued that non-black Canadian artists have achieved more success with the integration of black musical forms into their work than black artists themselves. Walker and Bailey both posit that limited access to record companies and mainstream radio are significant factors in the lack of success among black Canadian musicians. They also cite racism as one of the major factors hampering the accomplishments of black Canadian recording artists.[6] These realities have especially affected African-Caribbean Canadian women because they have had to deal with a male-dominated entertainment industry in addition to the factors mentioned above.

Even as she acknowledges the many difficulties African-Caribbean Canadian women recording artists in Canada face, Jamaican-Canadian reggae singer Nana McLean stresses that women generally confront such gender biases in the music industry regardless of where they're located, because, as she laughingly states, "de man dem have to always be up front". This reality, she surmises, is especially the case in the reggae music industry in both Canada and Jamaica. Elaborating on her argument, McLean recollects a specific incident where she was denied an opportunity to sing on a reggae instrumental "riddim" because it was reserved for male singers only.[7]

In spite of fierce competition for access to limited resources and the racism, sexism and marginalization African-Caribbean Canadian women face in the music industry, they have managed over the years to assert themselves against these multiple odds. Black women recording artists have managed to carve out artistic spaces from which to construct a uniquely black Canadian female diasporic identity within the growing field of black musical production in Canada. These efforts are explored in the following sections.

Dubbing North of the Border

Dub poetry has played a critical role in the emergence and growth of black popular music culture in Canada. The many dub performers in this country paved the way for the development of black Canadian musical forms. Lillian Allen can be credited not only for popularizing dub poetry in Canada, but also for the immense influence she has had on the development of African-Caribbean cultural expressions generally. Through Fresh Arts, a Toronto arts programme she started in the late 1980s, many young African-Caribbean Canadian rappers and performance poets were given the opportunity to hone their skills under her direction and leadership. Fresh Arts was a created under the umbrella of Jobs Ontario Youth. It was a part of a larger employment and training programme that the New Democratic Party government introduced to address the recession in the early 1990s. The programmes were targeted at black youth and it drew from the mentorship of established community artists; for example, Afua Cooper facilitated a creative writing class. Many of the youth involved in Fresh Arts (including performers such as Kardinal Offishall and Choclair) would later go on to pursue prominent careers in the music and entertainment industry.

However, long before Allen's involvement in Fresh Arts, she began her own career as a dub performer and released many successful recordings. Indeed Allen's work was critically received and she earned two Juno awards for her dub poetry albums *Revolutionary Tea Party* (1986) and *Conditions Critical* (1988). Like her counterparts in Jamaica, Allen used her work to speak about oppressive social conditions and injustice. Some of her poems included commentary about her native country of Jamaica while others addressed the realities of African-Caribbean communities in Toronto. Her lyrics were especially powerful for the way they named and decried the exploitive and oppressive conditions encountered by African-Caribbean women both within their own communities and wider Canadian society. For instance, in her dub verse "I Fight Back", Allen poignantly discusses the experiences of African-Caribbean women who are subjected to working in demeaning positions as nannies and domestic workers:

> ITT ALCAN KAISER
> Canadian Imperial Bank of Commerce
> These are privileged names in my Country
> But I AM ILLEGAL HERE
> My Children Scream
> My Grandmother is dying
> I came to Canada
> And Found the Doors
> Of Opportunities Well Guarded
> I Scrub Floors
> Serve Bakra's[8] Meals on Time
> Spend two days working in one
> And Twelve Days in a Week
> Here I am in Canada
> Bringing Up Someone Else's Child
> While someone Else and He in Absentee
> Bring up My Own
> AND I FIGHT BACK[9]

In addition to addressing the harsh experiences of black domestic workers in Canada, the track "I Fight Back" also engages in a theoretical discourse of "elsewhereness". This notion of "elsewhereness", as discussed by Carol Boyce Davies, signifies diasporic sensibilities about home and away, as well as belonging and non-belonging, that are central to black women's writing and black cultural politics in general.[10] In this case, Allen's "elsewhereness" is an allusion to Jamaica, the place from which she migrated to seek better opportunities in Canada. Ironically, however, upon arrival, Allen and other black women immigrants find they are given little access to the Canadian labour market, and in fact often find themselves exploited. As a wealthy liberal nation, Canada is also implicated in exploitation of Allen's native country of Jamaica through the reach of such financial institutions as the Canadian Imperial Bank of Commerce and Canadian corporate giants like ALCAN, KAISER and ITT.

Allen and many other African-Caribbean Canadian women dub performers helped to bring a black feminist aesthetics to the forefront of popular black music culture in Canada. Many of these artists also contributed to documenting forgotten Canadian herstory. Afua Cooper, for example, often focuses on political themes of race, gender and her native Jamaica, but as a historian, professor and dub poet, she also distinctively retells overlooked aspects of black Canadian and Caribbean herstory in many of her dub poems. In "Confessions of a Woman Who Burnt Down a Town", for example, Cooper draws on her native Jamaican Creole and reggae beats to recount the tragic story of Marie Josie Angelique, a runaway Canadian slave. She chants:

> Smoke, smoke, too much smoke
> Only intended fi one house fi burn
> Fire, fire too much fire
> But it done gone so already
> and I running
> My feet unshackled, unbound,
> free
> Running pass di city limits
> While behind mi di fire rage . . .[11]

Today dub poetry remains a vibrant musical art form within black popular culture in Canada. Jamaican-Canadian dub performer, playwright and actress d'bi young is a good example of the latest generation of dub poets in Toronto.

Young emerged as an important figure in dub in the early 2000s. Influenced by the traditions of her art form, young combines Jamaican Creole and English to articulate issues affecting the African-Caribbean community in Toronto and discuss universal themes of injustice. More distinctively, young infuses elements of punk, roots reggae, dancehall and Latin into her work, as well as underpinning it with a strong African sensibility. Like Allen and Cooper, young's thematic focus often centres on a feminist critique including commentary on female sexual identities, a theme which is hardly ever dealt with in black popular music. Additionally, young's feminist critique is expansive in that it is inclusive of the oppression of black male youth and men. Young's work, more so than the earlier dub artists, has had the tendency to focus on the racial problems that young black males face as well as acknowledging their efforts in joining the struggle against gender oppression.

Dub poetry in Canada has always enjoyed a strong and vibrant female presence. A strong case can be made that these women dub performers were instrumental in inspiring the participation of African-Caribbean women in the Canadian music industry. In addition, their legacy has contributed to the way black feminist discourse continues to be an important feature of the work of African-Caribbean recording artists.

Reggae and Dancehall Canadian Style

As with dub poetry, reggae music in Canada has also had strong female participation. Paradoxically, despite the large number of women working in reggae over the years, very few of them have realized the local or outernational success enjoyed by their dub poet peers. There has been little popular or scholarly literature available on Canadian reggae which may be one of the factors in keeping the music underground and not as commercialized as Canadian hip-hop. Unfortunately, the low profile given to Canada's reggae industry makes it even more difficult for African-Caribbean Canadian women to achieve success. Despite this lack of success, African-Caribbean Canadian women have, and continue, to actively contribute to the development of reggae music in Canada.

Reggae dancehall deejay Carla Marshal represents one of the few female deejays who have managed to garner substantial local and outernational success. As a seminal and popular dancehall deejay in the late 1980s and early

1990s, she realized greater success than many of her male counterparts. In 1995, Marshal won a Juno award in the category of best reggae recording for the song "Class and Credential", written by Donavan Jermaine. In a telephone conversation Marshal's former manager Denise Jones confirmed that Marshal was the second and only female deejay to win a Juno award in this category.[12] Since Marshal's win, no other dancehall artist has won a Juno.

Marshal's musical image echoed that of popular Jamaican deejays Lady Saw and Patra in that she was usually dressed in what some might refer to as "sexually provocative" outfits and she sang lyrics that were heavily coded expressions of female sexual desire. In her dancehall hit "Punny Punny",[13] for instance, Marshal, like her male deejay contemporaries, confidently boasts about the sexual "niceness" she possesses. In the chorus, Marshal declares, "Punny Punny mi have de sweetest punny. Punny Punny mi have de nicest punny. Punny Punny mi have de hottest punny."[14]

Marshal's provocative lyrics of having "de sweetest", "nicest" and "hottest punny" contrast sharply with the work of female dub poets who have tended to focus on challenging the sexual objectification and exploitation of the black female body and redefining black women in a less sexual and more holistic way. Indeed, some critics might argue that Marshal's "self-exploiting" lyrics reinforce stereotypes of the hyper-sexualized black woman, an image that has been controversial in black popular music and culture. Alternatively, Marshal's boldness could be read as a redefining of African-Caribbean Canadian women so that they stand in control of their own sexuality. Cultural critic Carolyn Cooper makes just such an argument pointing to Marshal's work as a subversive celebration of black women who assert their sexual freedom and celebrate their sexuality.[15] Andrea Elizabeth Shaw extends this argument to suggest that the representation of the black female body (particularly the larger body) in calypso and dancehall as "feisty" and "vulgar" is a "recasting of the hypersexualized large black female body [and] function as a subconscious retaliation to historical events like the dehumanizing exhibit of the Hottentot Venus's fat caged body, which was displayed across Europe in the nineteenth century".[16]

In my conversation with Jones she also maintained that Marshal's sexual candidness was not in any way derogatory to the image of African-Caribbean Canadian women. Jones suggested that Marshal's performances on stage should not be considered lewd but rather a model of sexual liberation, a liberation, Jones added, that in the past appears to have only been available to dancehall's male artists.[17] However, when one interprets Marshal's musical identity, there is no doubt she added a unique dimension to Canadian black popular music.

At the time of Marshal's reign as Canada's dancehall queen, other female reggae acts, such as pioneering singer Nana McLean, were also impacting the Canadian reggae industry. McLean has had a longer musical career than Marshal – her success in the music industry can be traced as far back as the mid 1970s. Like Marshal, McLean is one of the few female reggae artists who have managed to obtain local and national recognition. In 1997 she won a Juno award for her album *Nana McLean* and her music continues to receive considerable airplay on local community radio stations. To this day she remains a significant figure in Canadian reggae music.

A newer generation of female reggae singers including Sonia Collymore, Tanya Mullings and dancehall deejay Tasha T has emerged over the last few years to maintain the strong female presence in the Canadian reggae scene. However, in contrast to Marshal and McLean, these younger artists have not enjoyed the same level of success, with the exception of Sonia Collymore, who has won two Juno awards for best reggae recording – one in 2003 and the second in 2005. Incidentally, Collymore worked as a back up vocalist for Jamaican reggae singer Beres Hammond before launching her own solo career. Even though African-Caribbean Canadian women reggae artists continue to struggle for local and outernational recognition, they have become actively involved in the production and promotion of Canadian reggae music, a phenomenon I examine later in this chapter.

Northern Touch Hip Hop

Dubbed the first lady of rap, Jamaican-Canadian Michie Mee remains one of the most popular hip-hop artists to date in Canada. Even though Michie Mee has not had huge record sales, she enjoyed a large profile on Canada's premiere popular music channel, MuchMusic. As in the United States, hip-hop was very male dominated during the 1980s in Canada. Nevertheless, Michie Mee managed to break through this male-dominated space and find success. She became the first Canadian female hip-hop artist to be signed to a US record label, First Priority, which had also just signed two other women artists: Queen

Latifah and MC Lyte. Michie Mee's association with First Priority was a significant achievement because Canadian hip-hop struggled in the looming shadow cast by the US hip-hop industry, a situation that continues in the present era. Michie Mee was signed to First Priority on the strength of her talent, though her connections with prominent US hip-hop artists like Boogie Down Productions' KRS-One and Scott La Rock were also helpful.

In contrast to the earlier referenced dub performers, Michie Mee's lyrical content did not explicitly address the inequality that female rappers were facing in the music business nor did she speak directly to social issues affecting African-Caribbean Canadian women. Instead, like her male Canadian contemporaries, Michie Mee's lyrics showcased her unique linguistic blending of American hip-hop alongside reggae and dancehall culture. Her lyrics, coded in Jamaican Creole, did often reflect upon the African-Caribbean Canadian youth experience. Essentially, Michie Mee used her lyrics to distinguish herself culturally from US hip-hop rather than to separate herself from her male African-Caribbean Canadian hip-hop peers.

Michie Mee's commitment to musical hybridity was reflected in the title of her debut album, *Jamaica Funk: Canadian Style*. On the album she raps "I'm not mistaken, I'm Jamaican, / By the way that's my musical style", and further on, "Lookin' for Jamaicans? Toronto's got nuff / Yeah we eat curry goat and all that stuff."[18] Michie Mee's choice to showcase pride in both her Jamaican and Canadian identities can also be interpreted as a political statement in line with Canada's official multiculturalism policy that, in theory at least, permits the home and host culture to co-exist harmoniously alongside each other – in contrast to the melting pot ideology that defines the United States. In a similar vein, on "We're Coming to America", Michie Mee and her DJ LA Luv directly confront their American competition using Jamaican dancehall language to confirm that Canadian rappers spit lyrics in a uniquely linguistic and rhythmic way: "Some say we try to imitate many Americans, but like a true Canadian I know I can, I can, be original and mash up de dancehall."[19]

In interviews, Michie Mee has suggested that her use of Jamaican Creole may account for her lack of commercial success in the US market. In an interview with Canadian Broadcasting Corporation journalist Matthew McKinnon, Michie Mee maintains, "With me doing the reggae stuff, some of it was like another language. I didn't go in with a Canadian accent – I went there to make American hip-hop. Nobody understood what I was doing except for the hardcore street DJs."[20] Yet some Jamaican-American emcees were also using Jamaican Creole and reggae style and it did not hinder their success. In fact, the spreading of diasporic reggae into black US popular music culture began in the early 1980s. Jamaican-American rapper Shinehead, for example, successfully merged hip-hop and dancehall by alternating between Jamaican Creole and New York hip-hop, even rapping with a New York accent. Hip-hop acts such as the late Heavy D and KRS-One were also doing collaborations with well-known Jamaican artists like Super Cat, Patra and Shabba Ranks. In fact, KRS-One was blending dancehall with hip-hop even before his collaboration with Shabba Ranks. Heavy D, who is of Jamaican origin, recorded a reggae track called "Mood for Love" on his album *Big Tyme* before his collaboration with Super Cat on "Dolly My Baby". This suggests that the use of Jamaican Creole and reggae references in hip-hop may not have been a major factor in Michie Mee's lack of success in America. It is likely that US bias against Canadian rappers, coupled with gender discrimination, played a larger role in Michie Mee's lackluster commercial showing. Despite the unfair treatment Michie Mee received from American based record labels, she has remained an icon in Canadian hip-hop. During the late 1990s, Michie Mee was lead vocalist for the rock band Raggadeath, which allowed her to infuse hip-hop and dancehall vocal stylings into the band's metal sound.

It is safe to say that since Michie Mee there have been no major African-Caribbean women hip-hop artists coming out of Canada who match her stature. One might argue, however, that female spoken word performers such as Motion have, to some extent, bridged this gap. Born in Toronto to Antiguan and Barbadian parents, Wendy Braithwaite adopted the name "Motion" to reflect her fast progression into the growing art of spoken word and hip-hop. In 2002, Women's Press, Toronto, published her book of poems, *Motion in Poetry*, which includes accounts of black experiences in Toronto. These African-Caribbean Canadian female spoken word artists fuse elements of hip-hop rhythms, African-American vernaculars and African oral storytelling into their work. Much like Michie Mee, these female spoken word performers also incorporate Caribbean languages and an African-Caribbean Canadian sensibility as a way to distinguish themselves from their African-American spoken-word counterparts. And, like the dub poets, they use their lyrics as a platform for social critique.

Even though I have not included a review of R&B in this chapter, I think it is worth mentioning Jully Black, a Canadian R&B singer of Jamaican heritage. She is an important black Canadian female artist both because of her commercial success and the versatility that she brings to black popular music production in Canada. Canadian R&B is a musical genre that has clear roots in African-American culture. However, as reggae and cultural critic Klive Walker posits, rock steady and reggae also share a relationship, albeit a symbiotic one, with R&B. There are also links between dancehall and R&B. Walker gives the example of R&B artist Divine Brown who in a Canadian Broadcasting Corporation interview pointed out that reggae-soul[21] acts, such as John Holt and Dennis Brown, have had an equal influence on her music as R&B singers.[22] Therefore, like all the musical genres I have touched upon in this chapter, R&B in Canada often incorporates Caribbean rhythms, languages and references. Black's music successfully epitomizes this amalgamation of reggae, dancehall and hip-hop into R&B.

One last note of interest: both Black and Michie Mee were able to use their pop status to cross over into the television market. In the late nineties Michie Mee made her acting debut in her first film *In too Deep*. In 2000 she starred as a rapper Divine in the Canadian Broadcasting Corporation television series *Drop the Beat* and has made special guest appearances in the television shows *Metropolis* and *Da Kink in My Hair*. Jully Black has also made appearances on *Da Kink* as well as she was featured in the screenplay and has performed in the theatrical production *Dinner Mint*. Indeed it is through music that many African-Caribbean Canadian women have managed to gain greater access to Canadian television, film and other creative art opportunities, a trend that is not so true for their male contemporaries; this is an area that needs further exploration.

Black Music as a Voice of Belonging

African-Caribbean Canadian women recording artists have worked dynamically to create and shape a unique black diasporic sound in Canada. While black diasporic music is often tainted with male chauvinism and machismo, many African-Caribbean Canadian women have successfully used their music to challenge pernicious stereotypes of black women and/or underscore the struggles that African-Caribbean women face in their communities and wider society. Dub and recording artists Allen, Cooper and young have all used their work to critically address issues of racism and classism and to offer a black feminist perspective. Michie Mee, Motion and many others continue to use their music to articulate the distinctiveness of African diasporic youth culture in Canada. And as discussed above, Marshal's sex symbol image and "lewd" performances have, in some ways, subversively challenged notions of black female sexuality in Canada.

As well as taking on gender issues, these African-Caribbean women artists have, like their male counterparts, successfully reconstructed the notion of what it means to be Canadian. They have also counteracted misconceptions and stereotypes about African-Caribbean people and culture. Though much of their music is influenced by their Caribbean heritage, African-Caribbean women, as demonstrated in their lyrics, speak of the realities specific to the black Caribbean experience in Canada and assert their aspirations and desires for a sense of belonging in Canada. Rinaldo Walcott explains that "for Caribbean/black migrants and their descendents the problem of belonging to Canada is a significant and confrontational one", and it is only through black cultural expressions such as music, that this confrontation can be contested and scrutinized."[23] Thus, Cooper's lyrics in the poem "Confessions of a Woman Who Burnt Down a Town" boldly contest the erasure of black people's existence in Canadian his/herstory. And in "Canada Large" Michie Mee deliberately lists black communities and low income housing areas in Toronto so as to dispel negative images of the African-Caribbean communities who reside there and to firmly locate them in the context of Canada: "As you know, good things grow in Ontario / Like Mississauga, Thornhill, Brampton, and Scarborough / And Bad men to find them is a cinch / Jungle, Regent Park, Martingrove, Flemington, and Jane and Finch."[24]

Cooper and Michie Mee's efforts to locate black people in Canada present a challenge to Walcott's argument that Caribbean/black popular culture in Canada "can be and is only produced by those first and second generation descendants of the pre-and-post migration to Canada".[25] Walcott goes on to assert that "post 60s children of migrants have begun to articulate a belonging to Canada that allows for a cultural expressivity that is both uniquely theirs and simultaneously in conversation with an array of cultural expressivity of the black diaspora".[26] In spite of the generation gap Walcott speaks of, in both instances, Cooper and Michie Mee, who were both born in Jamaica, do use their cultural productions to affirm the presence of black Canadian bodies and identities. Walker gives us another example of a new Caribbean immigrant speaking to black Canadian belonging when he notes that Allen's dub poem "Rub a Dub Style" "represents an early example of Black music recognizing specific communities of African Canadians".[27]

Indeed, African-Caribbean Canadian musicians have a strong record of highlighting significant black Canadian people and events and asserting their own black Canadian identities in their work. For instance in his rap lyric "Quebec History X", Quebec based hip-hop artist Webster raps about forgotten historical figures such as Matthew Da Costa, a multilingual African who came to New France as Samuel de Champlain's interpreter.[28] And just as Michie Mee expresses pride in her Jamaican and Canadian identities in her rap "Jamaican Funk Canadian Style", in Nana McLean's popular dubplate[29] she includes verses of both the Jamaican and Canadian national anthems to signify her simultaneous belonging to Canada and embrace of her country of birth, Jamaica. Clearly African-Caribbean Canadian women have been instrumental in creating ways to reconfigure "the new belonging to Canada"[30] that Walcott discusses and they continue to use their music as a vehicle to express this belongingness by drawing on the expressive traditions of the African diaspora.

Conclusion

Even as African-Caribbean Canadian women artists continue to struggle locally and outernationally to gain recognition for their own work, they have gallantly taken on diverse roles to promote the production of black music in Canada. African-Caribbean Canadian women are no longer confined solely to recording roles as they were in the past. Today they are involved in the production and promotion of black music in Canada. This shift in role is especially evident in the Canadian reggae music industry and Tanya and Carrie Mullings serve as a good example of this transition. In addition to a singing career in reggae dancehall, Tanya Mullings, along with her sister Carrie Mullings (who is a community radio host of the popular CHRY weekly show *Reggae Vibes*), manages a number of other reggae artists. Other noteworthy women making their presence felt in the Canadian black music industry are Gunz'n'Rozez, a reggae sound system owned and operated by Tasha Rozez;

Woman Ah Run Tings, an all female reggae band; Masani Montague, a video and reggae recording producer; and Denise Jones, a pioneer reggae dancehall manager and previous promoter of reggae concerts in Toronto. Denise Jones must also be acknowledged for the leading role she played in the establishment of a reggae category in the Juno awards. Jones was the founding chair of the reggae category – she served in that role from 1993 to 2001 and still sits on the committee. With such an abundance of talented African-Caribbean Canadian women contributing to black popular music production, one can only anticipate that their creativity will continue to influence and impact the direction of black popular music culture in Canada.

Accordingly, the contributions of African-Caribbean Canadian female recording artists to popular black music production in Canada should be neither overlooked nor underestimated. Instead, their work must be seen as equally vital in the formation of an alternative cultural space that has given a new public voice to African-Caribbean communities in Canada, introduced a black feminist consciousness and raised a new sense of Canadian belonging among people of African descent. African-Caribbean Canadian women now have the opportunity to begin to use their changing roles in the industry to affect the overall production and promotion of Canada's black popular music culture and to change how the industry recruits, represents and supports women artists.

Notes

1. Cameron Bailey, "Hip Hop Inflects Toronto", *Fuse Magazine*, 12 (November–December 1988): 17–26.
2. J. Maki Motapanyane, "The Black Female Body and Artist in Canadian Hip Hop: The Question of Femini(st)ne Space", *New Dawn: Journal of Black Canadian Studies* 1 (2006): 40.
3. Charmaine Crawford, "Black Women, Racing and Gendering the Canadian Nation", in *Theorizing Empowerment: Canadian Perspectives on Black Feminist Thought*, ed. N. Massaquoi and K. Nathani Wane (Toronto: Inanna Publications, 2007), 125.
4. Klive Walker, *Dubwise: Reasoning from the Reggae Underground* (Toronto: Insomniac Press, 2005).

5. Rinaldo Walcott, *Black Like Who? Writing Black Canada* (Toronto: Insomniac Press, 1997).
6. Walker, *Dubwise*, 162; Bailey, "Hip Hop Inflects", 26.
7. Nana McLean, interview by author, Toronto, Ontario, 13 May 2009.
8. Commonly used for a white person of the planter class.
9. Lillian Allen, "I Fight Back", *Revolutionary Tea Party* (Verse to Vinyl, compact disc, 1986).
10. Carol Boyce Davies, *Black Women Writing, and Identity: Migration of the Subject* (New York: Routledge, 1994), 37.
11. Afua Cooper, *Utterances and Incantations: Women, Poetry and Dub* (Toronto: Sister Vision Press, 1999), 83.
12. Denise Jones, interview by author, Toronto, Ontario, 5 April 2009.
13. *Punny* refers to female genitalia in Jamaican Creole.
14. Carla Marshal, "Punny, Punny", *Class and Credential* (Chaos Recording, compact disc, 1994).
15. Carolyn Cooper, *Sound Clash: Jamaican Dancehall Culture at Large* (New York: Palgrave Macmillan, 2004), 17.
16. Andrea Shaw, " 'Big Fat Fish': The Hypersexualization of the Fat Female Body in Calypso and Dancehall", *Anthurium: A Caribbean Studies Journal* 3, no. 2 (2005), http://anthurium.miami.edu/volume_3/issue_2/shaw-bigfatfish.htm.
17. Jones, interview.
18. Michie Mee, "Jamaican Funk Canadian Style", *Jamaican Funk: Canadian Style* (First Priority Music, compact disc, 1991).
19. Michie Mee, "We're Coming to America", *Jamaican Funk*.
20. Matthew McKinnon, "Border Block: Canadian Hip Hop vs. America", Canadian Broadcasting Corporation, 25 March 2005, http://www.cbc.ca/arts/music/canadianhiphop.html.
21. I use the term reggae-soul to refer to the sounds of early reggae singers whose music was influenced by R&B.
22. Klive Walker, interviews by author, Toronto, Ontario, 2 December 2008; 7 February 2009 and 12 August 2009.
23. Rinaldo Walcott, "Caribbean Pop Culture in Canada; Or, the Impossibility of Belonging to the Nation", *Small Axe* 5, no. 1 (March 2001): 127.
24. "Good things grow in Ontario" was a commercial slogan that was used for advertising fruits and vegetables grown in Ontario to encourage consumers to buy locally.
25. Walcott, "Caribbean Pop Culture", 125.
26. Ibid.
27. Walker, *Dubwise*, 164.
28. Webster, "Quebec History X", *Sagesse Immobile* (Abuzive Muzik Inc., compact disc, 2007).

29. A dubplate is a one-of-a-kind recording performed by a reggae or dancehall artist.
30. Walcott, "Caribbean Pop Culture", 137.

Discography

Allen, Lillian. *Conditions Critical*. Verse to Vinyl, compact disc, 1989.
———. *Revolutionary Tea Party*. Verse to Vinyl, compact disc, 1986.
Kardinal Offishall. *Quest for Firestarter Vol. 1*. MCA Records, compact disc, 2001.
Marshall, Carla. *Class and Credential*. Chaos Recording, compact disc, 1994.
McLean, Nana. *Nana McLean*. Penthouse Records, compact disc, 1997.
Michie Mee. *Jamaican Funk: Canadian Style*. First Priority Music, compact disc, 1991.
Mullings, Tanya. *Breaking*. Rymshot Productions, compact disc, 2009.
Tasha T. *Hot Ya Now*. Ras Vibe Records, compact disc, 2010.
Webster. *Sagesse Immobile*. Abuzive Muzik, compact disc, 2007.

10.

Who Is Grace Jones?

| IFEONA FULANI

> I wasn't born this way. One creates oneself.
> – Grace Jones[1]

IN JULY 2009, GRACE JONES appeared on stage at New York's Hammerstein Ballroom to perform for the first time in twenty years in the city where she made her name as a singer. Clad in a zebra-striped cat suit with a headdress like a white flowing mane, she swaggered across a stage set up like a catwalk, growling at the stage hands and demanding the audience's attention. "Welcome me to New York!" she commanded, and the audience responded with a two-minute ovation. As Rob Tannenbaum succinctly stated in his review of the show: "How plebian to think a *concert* should be about songs."[2]

Tannenbaum's ironic comment draws attention to the audience's response to Jones's spectacular presence, a reaction not limited to those in the Hammerstein Ballroom. It is a paradox that despite Jones's remarkable career as *chanteuse* and recording artist, the few critics who have written about her – and their number is surprisingly small – focus on her physicality, her performance art, her experiments in collaboration with Keith Haring with Modernist Primitivism in costume design,[3] or the pantheon of on-stage personae created through costuming, all of which have contributed to the perception that she is "a self-made art object".[4] By her own admission, Jones is self-made, but she is a living, breathing performer. She may be eminently *objectifiable*, but she is not an object per se. One explanation for this focused attention to the aesthetics of Jones's exteriority and physical presentation may be that much of the critical work on Jones originates in the discipline of art history and thus aims to contextualize Jones's performance within that discipline's both postcolonial and postmodern *visual* aesthetics and discourses. Thus the visual and spectacular aspects of Jones performance are prioritized to the seeming neglect of the aural and musical: namely, Jones's songs, accompanying music, lyrics and vocalizations.

Splitting the visual and spectacular from the aural elements of musical performance results in exclusions that can lead to partial reading or misreading of the artist and her performance, for the visual element cannot be separated without loss of meaning from other important components. Music philosopher Stan Godlovitch defines musical performance as "a complex activity which focuses action, skills, traditions, and works in order to define and create musical experience".[5] Jeanette Bicknell extends Godlovitch's list of considerations by adding the artist's public persona, emphasizing its importance to the reception and interpretation of musical performance. According to Bicknell, an artist's public persona is comprised of her face, body, appearance and clothing, along with personality traits and quirks expressed publicly by word or gesture, as well as her known history, including information or gossip circulated by the media, in addition to factors such as gender and age, race and ethnicity.[6] Godlovitch underscores the importance of these aspects of the artist, emphasizing the need to look beyond image alone when interpreting and evaluating performance: "artist and artwork, performance and performer are quite as inseparable as people are from their histories, external and internal".[7]

Where Jones is concerned, one needs to consider her public personae, as over the course of her career she has demonstrated a shape shifter's ability to change and, at crucial stages, to radically transform her image. At any given time since her emergence as a singer on New York's disco scene in the 1970s, Jones's image, and the public's reading of it, has contributed to a myriad of fantasies about her life. Ramon Lobato, for example, suggests that, "[i]n Jones, a fantasy of experiential excess is embodied".[8] Others stereotype her as the tiger-woman, the "primitive" wild woman, a jet-setting hedonist given to deviant sensual and sexual excess, even a cyborg, a not-fully-human being.

Admittedly, aspects of Jones's performance on and off-stage support stereotypical and fetishistic notions of her as enigmatic, uninhibited and instinctual, and even the possibility of her being "a transvestite or even a transsexual".[9] Consequently, when I consider the plethora of images projected by Jones on and off stage, the question that arises insistently is, who is she? This chapter is the outcome of my efforts to "read" Jones's performance in its totality, and also to reach beyond it, not so much to arrive at a definitive answer to this question, which would be impossible, but to look beyond the fetishizing fixation with her image or her various personae. Thus my aim here is to examine Jones's evolution from her beginnings as a singer in the mid-1970s to the peak of her artistic maturity in the mid-1980s. Released in 1985, the video artwork *A One Man Show*, shows Jones at her most accomplished. The video presents Jones as a black and female artist of Caribbean origin, whose uniquely styled contestations of the boundaries of raced and gendered being, both engage and fall within traditions of African diasporic artistic radicalism. I argue that fantasy, stereotype and fetish have influenced critical response to Jones as an artist and thus have obscured important aspects of her artistic innovation. The result has been a lack of recognition the trajectory of her artistic development and the increasing complexity in her music and performance over time.

In referring to the act of fetishizing, I draw upon Nicholas Mizroeff's notion of "the fetishism of the gaze", a dynamic by which, he explains, "what is perceived is never actually the same as what is there in a material sense".[10] My intention is to move beyond fetishistic misconstruction of Jones's performance to a more nuanced understanding of "artist and artwork", by means of an exploration of Jones's history, both "external and internal". I review the arc of her career, her performances, songs and representations in *A One Man Show* to propose that, while Jones's career evolved in accordance with the professional opportunities available to her, her art, even in the various stages of its evolution, reveals subjectivity shaped by growing up black and female in postcolonial Jamaica. However, Jones's performance art and music also reveal a wide range of influences that combine, and sometimes conflict, in creative and innovative ways that make her unique. The more obvious of these influences include the European cabaret, the catwalk of the haute couture French fashion house, and Jamaican and African diasporic musical and performance traditions – a unique and potent admixture.

"Nightclubbing"

Jones was born in Spanish Town, Jamaica, into a religious family – her father was a minister in the Pentecostal church and her uncle the bishop of Jamaica. Jones attributes her rebellious streak to the restrictions imposed upon her by her family: "When you are brought up in church and taught as a woman just to have a family and stay at home until the man comes and takes you away . . . I rebelled against that!" she states in an interview.[11] Elsewhere she states, "I was dressed in clothing that covered me completely", referring to the codes of dress observed by the Jamaican Christian middle class in the 1950s and 1960s, the period when Jones was growing up.[12] Of the many and varied manifestations of Jones's rebellions, one of the most evident is her style of dress on and off stage, particularly the styling of some of the more infamous stage costumes from her early disco days that were remarkable for their scantiness.

Jones moved with her family to Syracuse, New York, when she was twelve. She studied theatre at Syracuse University, but dropped out after freshman year to pursue a career as a film actress. Her early efforts to break into films were unsuccessful, and in her twenties she embarked on a modelling career. Starting out in New York City, she found it hard to get work because of her dark skin and the "irregularity" of her features; as she explains, "when I started modeling I didn't really get many jobs – 'your nose doesn't match your eyes and your eyes don't match your lips – where the hell do you come from? What are you?'"[13] The American fashion industry, and the field of modelling in particular, was notoriously inhospitable to phenotypically black women. In the 1970s, the number of successful black models were few, and the few were light in skin colour – America's first black "supermodel" Naomi Sims, for example.[14] Jones left New York and followed the black Atlantic route to Paris, motivated to escape the constriction of opportunity resulting from American racism, like many Caribbean and African-American artists and entertainers before her. In Paris, the postcolonial fixation on the sable beauty of the *Venus Noire* and the celebration of her most popular twentieth-century incarnation, Josephine Baker, persisted – to Jones's advantage. Jones's beauty, her "unusual" facial features, dark skin and long, lean body, were received with appreciation in Paris, and she became a runway star.

In Paris, Jones adopted the severely cut Thierry Mugler suit, that, worn with high-heeled stilettos, was *de rigeur* among top models at the time and became a personal style signature. She also began writing songs and singing in small cabarets, intimate clubs that offered food, drink, music and dancing late into the night. In the mid-1970s, Jones gave up modelling for singing and returned to New York, already a celebrity of the world of fashion and, due to her unique, distinctive fashion sense and extrovert personality, an incipient fashion icon. She found a niche in downtown New York at Andy Warhol's Factory, and became a companion and muse for Warhol, whose patronage added ballast to her cultural capital. It was during this period that Jones erupted onto the downtown disco scene, as a singer performing in underground dance clubs and gay discos.

Jones discovered a productive synergy between the excesses and subversiveness of her early performances and the culture of the gay disco; her lack of inhibition and free expressions of sexuality resonated with the sexual politics and cultural values of the gay audience. In an interview Wresch Dawidjan asked Jones why she enjoyed performing for gay audiences, to which she replied: "There is no question about it: gays are more sensitive, more aware of form, more artistic, and much more open to accepting of something new and fresh."[15] The gay audience, visible in the 1970s for the first time, was itself something new and fresh and, moreover, receptive to transgressive, sexually charged performance.

In the 1970s, disco in New York was music, fashion and dance combined in an atmosphere of glamour and hedonistic excess. The flourishing of disco culture during this period coincided with the flourishing across the United States of gay communities that embraced disco culture with passion. Richard Dyer explains that, for the gay community, disco was more than entertainment; it was also, "a certain *sensibility*, manifest in music, clubs". That sensibility expressed itself in ways that subverted mainstream models of nightclub entertainments; the gay disco scene was erotically charged, the music and the space allowing intense bodily pleasure through dance. Dyer argues that, paradoxically, the gay disco was also romantic in its striving to create an uplifting alternative to what he terms "the banality of organized routine life".[16] In order to subvert the reality of the everyday, the interior of the disco club was necessarily materially excessive, "a riot of consumerism, dazzling in its technology ... lavishly gaudy", and, also, outrageously camp.[17] Dyer explains disco camp, as "a contrary use of what the dominant culture provides", which implies both creative *and* subversive forms of self-expression that, according to Dyer, are important in forming a gay identity.[18]

Music was the element that animated the erotic, romance and excess of disco. The driving rhythms of disco music fuelled the eroticism of disco dancing, and historically and typically, black music produced the most insistent, danceable rhythms. However, the songs of the popular black male artists who dominated the R&B scene in the early 1970s – Marvin Gaye and Teddy Prendergrass, for example – though suitably rhythmic and danceable, and often overtly sexual, were lyrically inappropriate for the gay disco, often celebrating black male prowess achieved by the sexual exploitation and objectification of dominance of women.[19] Theirs was a patriarchal sexual politics that neither reflected the libratory politics of the disco dance floor nor resonated with notions of sexual agency and freedom that informed queer culture at the time. The black female disco vocalists such as Donna Summer and Candy Staton and even Diana Ross, were much more in keeping with the ethos of the gay disco, which granted them diva status. As Judy Kutulas explains, for gay men the attractions of the disco included the performances of such divas. Disco music is dance music, and dance music is about sex. The divas, rising to prominence on a wave of feminist *and* queer consciousness, symbolized sexual agency and freedom, projecting images that resonated with ideals of sexual liberation and pride valued in gay communities.[20] Thus the phenomenal success of Donna Summer's now classic "Love to Love You", an eighteen-minute anthem to the pleasures of love and dancing, announces the triumphal transformation of a black woman from object into desiring sexual subject.

Enter Jones, whose disco set piece in which she is a roaring, caged tiger-woman, prowling on all fours, sardonically enacts an animal and predatory female desire emblematic of her performance style during this period. Jones was a radically *different* type of diva. Despite their lyrical claims to sexual liberation, the R&B divas were products of their record companies, groomed and schooled in correct public behaviour. Female artists signed to the Motown record label, for example, were required to attend charm school, where they would learn decorum and correct deportment, so they would not offend mainstream audiences with inappropriate dress or conduct.[21] In the 1970s and early 1980s, the only acceptable hairstyle for a black woman in the public eye was one achieved with straightened hair, wig, or flowing hair extensions. The required dress for a diva was a spandex tube top or sheath, as evidenced by Diana Ross and Donna Summers in photographs from that period. Jones's cropped hair and costumes, whether scanty or extravagant, boldly asserted her resistance to these norms and her freedom of aesthetic choice.

Jones's tiger-woman piece courted controversy as it reproduced, for a mainly white audience, the kind of sexual bestiality stereotypically associated with black people. The piece culminated with a confrontation between Jones and a live tiger, from which Jones emerged the victor – the tiger slinked away, leaving Jones in her cage, chewing a slab of meat. The piece offered a powerful spectacle: the fearless expression of predatory sexual desire – the tiger-woman is caged for the protection of the audience as well as for tigers. However, while Jones engaged deeply entrenched stereotypes with this enactment, she risked the probability that segments of her audience would have seen only exotica and missed the irony in her performance. Yet, transgressive performance and the attendant risks are intrinsic to the tradition of black performance in the United States, as Coco Fusco observes: "the spectre of the popular and the stereotype of the exotic entertainer loom large as part of an historical legacy that shapes the reception to 'culturally diverse' work in the US and Europe . . . the issue of how artists of colour relate to popular culture and to racial stereotypes has been central since the Harlem Renaissance".[22] Fusco implies questions about the commodification of racial stereotypes and their exploitation by black performers, but such questions are complicated by other, related questions about the freedom of black artists to engage images that, historically, have contributed to their oppression, and about the undeniable cultural value of ironic deconstruction of such images.

Rebecca Wanzo has drawn attention to the life stories of black female entertainers who "walked a fine line . . . between depicting stereotype and suggesting complex personhood", and who "remind us of how difficult it is for black subjects to escape the histories which inform their public selves".[23] Wanzo alludes to the limited choice of roles permitted black female performers and the difficulty they face finding complex roles that represent their lived experience – a circumscription that makes the likelihood of avoiding reiterating racist stereotypes unavoidable. Wanzo's comments bear a trace of W.E.B. Du Bois's notion of the entrapment of black subjectivity by the racist projections of a white world, represented in the metaphor of the veil. The veil divides and conceals the inner world of black people from the hostile reality created by racist projections and stereotypes. "Double consciousness", the mode of seeing produced by existence behind the veil, is explained by Du Bois as "this sense of always looking at oneself through the eyes of others, of measuring one's worth by the tape of a world that looks on in amused contempt and pity".[24]

Following Du Bois and Wanzo, I propose that the ironic and hyperbolic character of Jones's tiger-woman persona in this phase reveal the operations of double consciousness; Jones, fully aware of the stereotype of the sensual, bestial black woman, exaggerates it and takes control of it. Instead of being controlled, she projects it back to the fetishizing gaze of her delighted audience in a transfer of ownership that empowers her. This dynamic – of inhabiting a stereotype or projection in order to explode it – was, for a time, one of the signature elements of her performance.

Not every aspect of Jones's disco performances was profound, however, as commercial imperatives also influenced her artistic choices. One of the subtle ironies of Jones's disco phase is the contradiction between her stage performances and the lyrics of her most popular songs in this period, which were neither transgressive nor sexually suggestive. On the contrary, the lyrics of "I Need a Man", her first major disco hit, express a yearning for conventional romance: "Getting tired of lookin' / Wastin' all my cookin' / Endin' in a dreadful row . . . I need a man like you to make my dreams come true."[25] The lyrics respond to one of the contradictions inherent in disco culture: rebellion against constraints to fulfilment of sexual desires coexistent with the quest for romance. The song speaks to the dreams of straight women and gay men who imagine that the erotic encounters of the dance floor might lead to love. The selection of this song for the 1977 album *Portfolio*, and for release as a single, is only one example of Jones's characteristic awareness of, and responsiveness to, the desires of her audience, and the success of the single confirms her perspicacity.

Jones's disco performance style reveals the influence on her art of cabaret; even her more outrageous disco performances followed the conventions that define cabaret. Shane Vogel reminds us that "*cabaret*, like *theater*, refers to both a kind of performance and the room or building where such a performance takes place".[26] Cabaret performances emphasize the architecture of staging, whether the catwalk, or the cage or the moving staircase, all of which Jones deployed in her performances. Cabaret artists "esche[w] a singular narrative, offering a collage of forms", even in a popular cabaret presentation, such as "the one man/woman show".[27] Forced to compete for her audience against the attractions of drink, food, flirtation and dancing, the successful cabaret artist would develop distinctive gestures or behaviours, and change costumes and personae to attract and hold the attention of his or her audience. The video work *A One Man Show* displays the range of personae in Jones's repertoire and the skill with which she compels audience attention with her continually evolving play with image. She dances on set in a gorilla suit, beating on a drum and swaying her hips, or poses, caged and on all fours; she moves in strides assertively across a set invoking a construction site to perform the song "Demolition Man" and she strikes a tragic pose on a staircase, with an accordion as a prop, to perform her somber version of "La Vie en Rose".

Photographs of a performance staged at the Paradise Garage in 1985 show Jones's body covered in a design painted by artist Keith Haring and inspired by the body paint of Maasai warriors. The addition of a coiled metal breastplate and a towering headdress completed a costume straight out of a carnival parade.[28] Later in the same performance, Jones danced in a short skirt made of yellow neon spikes strung together, a postmodern version of Josephine Baker's iconic little grass skirt, that referenced Baker's own subversion of primitivist discourses on black women's bodies and sexuality. Miriam Kershaw's claim that "Jones' costuming and tactics . . . refer to those exploited by Josephine Baker",[29] is undeniable; Jones's satirical invocation of Baker indicates her awareness of her debt to Baker, who was undoubtedly a predecessor and a model for Jones's cabaret aesthetic.

However, Jones's aesthetic also draws on Jamaican traditions of Jonkonnu, the inherently subversive, vividly costumed musical street masquerade practice. Shaped by the aesthetic sensibilities and ritual practices of Africans brought as slaves to Jamaica, the costumes and dances of Jonkunnu characters satirize the dress and social mores of white colonizers. Growing up in Jamaica, Jones would have witnessed the parade of masked and costumed revellers dancing in the streets each Christmas and New Year, and may even have yearned to join them. Her varied costumes, and her use of masks on and off stage, suggest that Jones was inspired by African diasporic performance traditions to which she had direct access.[30] In this she differed from Baker, for, as Miriam Kershaw notes, "Baker's exaggerated performances in banana and tusk skirts have little to do with Africa's diverse cultures and everything to do with the exotic Other in the imagination and art of 1920s Paris."[31]

The musical style of the three albums recorded by Jones in her disco phase, under the direction of legendary disco producer Tom Multon, and released by Island Records, are most accurately described as cabaret-inflected disco. *Portfolio* was the most successful of the three, reaching 109 on the *Billboard* charts and 52 on the black album charts, with the single from the album, "I Need a Man", topping the US dance charts. Side one of the album is a campy, disco-beat medley of hit songs from Broadway musicals, and side two includes Jones's interpretation of "La Vie en Rose", signature song of French *chanteuse*

Edith Piaf and a cabaret classic. The side also includes "I Need a Man" and two other original dance tracks. If *Portfolio* established Jones as a recording artist, *Fame*, released in 1978, consolidated her success, shooting to number ten on the US dance charts. *Fame* followed the same format as *Portfolio*, with a continuous-play disco medley on side one, and a classic French *chanson*, "Autumn Leaves", leading on side two. The winning formula did not hold for 1979's *Muse*, however. The anti-disco backlash set in in 1979, and by the dawn of the 1980s, disco mania was over.

"Demolition Man"?

Jones's metamorphosis from disco diva into an elegantly suited, polished, performer and recording artist, seems to have progressed seamlessly, in step with the rise of the New Wave in US popular music and the increasing popularity of reggae. Jones found a new musical direction with the support of Chris Blackwell, the Jamaica-based founder of Island Records, and in collaboration with the French photographer Jean-Paul Goude, whom Jones eventually married. In the late 1970s, Blackwell developed a state-of-the-art recording studio at Compass Point in the Bahamas and gathered, from across the African diaspora, a group of the world's best session musicians to form the Compass Point All-Stars.[32] Jones was the first singer to work with the group, to record her albums *Warm Leatherette* (1980), *Nightclubbing* (1981) and *Living My Life* (1982). The All-Stars were the architects of her new sound that was austere, rhythm-heavy and reggae-inflected.

In his notes on these three recordings, Brian Chinn writes, "Jones made herself the perfect instrument of the best artistic elements . . . the song selection put Grace squarely in the company of the best rock writers." Jones herself was more modest in her comments: "good songs, interpreted well – nothing trendy; classics, whatever that might be. Songs that last."[33] Of the three Compass Point recordings, *Nightclubbing* and *Living My Life* were the more commercially successful; the single "Pull up to the Bumper" from *Nightclubbing* was Jones's most commercially successful single in the United States, reaching the top five on the R&B chart. "Private Life", also from *Nightclubbing*, reached the top ten in the United Kingdom. In 1981, *Nightclubbing* was named album of the year by Britain's premier music journal, the *New Musical Express*.[34] The following year *Living My Life* reached number fifteen in the UK album charts.

In this new phase Jones presented a new face to the world, typified by the now iconic sculptural suited images disseminated via music videos made in collaboration with French photographer Jean-Paul Goude. Goude has been credited with designing Grace's signature look, the close fitting, severely tailored clothing, tops sometimes open to the waist, revealing Jones's spare midriff, high-heeled stilettos and the occasional extravagant hat. But Jones had evolved her own personal style while a fashion model and had adopted the Thierry Mugler suit even before her association with Goude. Critics have described Jones's signature style – the look foregrounded in the video artwork *A One Man Show* – as androgynous, or a combination of feminine and masculine, based on her cropped hair, the severe cut of her suits, her spare, hard body, strong make-up and stiletto heels. Undoubtedly Jones plays with such perceptions, which are provocatively reinforced by lyrics from songs such as on "Demolition Man", in which she sings "I'm a walking disaster / I'm a demolition man"; and from "Walking in the Rain", where she sings of "feeling like a woman / looking like a man".

Carolyn Anderson asserts that Jones "eludes and confuses all definitions of male/female, past/future, real simulated and familiar/foreign . . . sometimes even escapes categorization as rational or insane, human or animal".[35] Here Anderson falls into the trap of an essentialist binarism that refuses to contemplate the possibility of paradoxical wholes: the possibility that Jones might represent female *and* male personas or aspects of herself in performance. But even binary thinking cannot explain Anderson's questioning of Jones's sanity and humanity. Anderson's speculation finds its apotheosis in the following statement: "Categorically other . . . Jones is adored by those who masquerade as the opposite sex because she even masquerades as her own sex."[36] Of the many possible ways of interpreting this comment, the most obvious refers to some of Jones's occasionally excessive feminine fashion choices, such as the extravagant hats she sometimes wore on stage and for public appearances. If so, Anderson has missed Jones's studied critique of prevailing constructions of gender; for Jones's play with so-called masculine and feminine dress – like those who "adore" her and "masquerade as the opposite sex" – interrogates the conventional association of gender with particular styles.

In Western cultures, long, lean female bodies topped by cropped hair are typically described as androgynous, which is not the case in African and African diasporic contexts, in which Jones's body type is not uncommon, and many women elect to wear their hair cropped. Anderson's categorization of Jones is vague, because the term "androgynous" has a wide range of meanings, referring to a mixing of characteristics generally accepted as masculine or feminine that can be seen as physiological, psychological or behavioural. In addition, the term may be used to refer to one whose person and/or psychology combine masculine and feminine traits in equal measure.[37] But it may also refer more perjoratively to one who is neither wholly man nor woman whose sex is indeterminate.

Miriam Kershaw is more categorical in attributing masculine qualities to Jones: she describes Jones's hairstyle as a "crew cut" that "makes reference to male-dominated military discipline . . . her trim gray suit offsets a bare chest of hard, flat muscle".[38] Clearly to Kershaw's gaze, Jones's body is not merely or vaguely androgynous, it is macho. The image to which Kershaw responds is, of course, that of Jones in the wasp-waisted suit and high heels that is projected repeatedly throughout *A One Man Show*. Whether the severe cut of the suit is inherently masculine is a moot point, for the exaggerated, padded shoulders anticipate the power suit, symbol of female empowerment, that, like the pant suit for women, became fashionable in the 1980s. Perhaps it is the severity of the suit that is, if not actually masculine, somewhat "unfeminine", especially as it clads a body devoid of "feminine" fat.

Kershaw's comment on Jones's hairstyle serves as a reminder that black women's hair – that is, the texture and styling of it – is a discursively overburdened feature of black women's already discursively burdened bodies. While Wendy Cooper argues that this is true for everyone, irrespective of race or gender,[39] Willie Morrow goes further, suggesting that for black people, hair texture, even more than skin colour, functions as a symbol of racial inferiority. Morrow argues that the black skin of enslaved Africans was much less repugnant to their white masters than their tightly curled, "kinky" hair, which became the justification for their subordination by and to their white masters. According to Morrow, "kinky" hair became a badge of racial inferiority recognizable by black and white people alike.[40]

For black women the nuances of hair politics are so charged as to merit further examination of the semiotics of the unprocessed, cropped hair of Jones.[41] Ingrid Banks explains, black women's hair worn in its natural state becomes an abnormality in a culture that valorizes the features and hair of white women while deprecating those of black women:

> Although "natural" relates to ideas about purity as well as being an act or state that is "normal", it takes on a different meaning when it is cast against straight and straightened hair. The altered nature of relaxed or permed hair is seen as "natural" whereas natural or unaltered hair is defined as "unnatural" . . . Nappy hair is not celebrated in a society that privileges straight (blonde) hair.[42]

As a signifier of social status, the natural hair of black women is charged with notions of racial and gender abnormality and by extension, inferiority, for as Banks explains, normal in hair terms, is straight, and preferably blonde.

Following Kershaw, then, it would seem that Jones's cropped hair "unwomans" her, rendering her masculine, as the description "crew cut" infers; and for Kershaw, the "crew cut" invokes a militaristic, disciplined masculinity, an impression reinforced by Jones's flat chest and muscular stomach. Such a reading of Jones's hair (and body) raises questions of racial and gender anxieties generated by difference interpreted as abnormality. By contrast, Jones's matter-of-fact comment on her hair style in an interview with Dawidjan is striking. "Why do you present yourself in such an unusual way? The shaven head, for instance?", he asks. Jones responds as follows: "I prefer it that way. I tried many different looks . . . Modeling gave me the opportunity to wear many different styles and I chose one I found more suited to my personality. It turns out that it is different from the ordinary."[43] Jones's experiments with style enabled her to find a look she could claim for herself: one that is not styled on her body by others. Jones acknowledges that her choice of hairstyle is not "normal", but lays claim to its non-conformity – its difference – simultaneously refusing Eurocentric aesthetic norms and affirming her own aesthetic preference.[44]

The remarks of Anderson and Kershaw invoke the very discourses that Jones's physicality and appearance subvert: colonial discourses that represent black female bodies as other, and even deviant and unnatural. Furthermore, they suggest an anxiety rooted in negative, historically determined, attitudes towards the black female body. As Janelle Hobson notes, "history – a history of enslavement, colonial conquest and ethnographic exhibition – variously labeled the black female body 'grotesque,' 'strange,' 'unfeminine' ".[45] Jennifer Morgan explains that from their earliest encounters with Africans, Europeans viewed African women's bodies as "abnormal", and thus, "evidence of a cultural inferiority that ultimately became encoded as racial difference".[46] Edward Long, an English planter settled in Jamaica, presents a striking example of such racist thinking. Writing in 1774 in his *History of Jamaica*, Long compares the enslaved African women working on Jamaican plantations to baboons.[47]

These early encounters and designations founded racist stereotypes of black women as less than or other than womanly, *different* from the norm for womanly physiology and comportment, which was always the white European woman, and therefore deficient. It is a matter of note that slavery in the West Indies influenced the development of gender roles in the region; the work of historian Sidney Mintz demonstrates that similarities in the treatment and use of male and female slaves produced in some areas an effect that he describes as "sexual equality still quite unheard of in Western societies".[48] This putative equality between the male and female slaves should not be seen as "empowering". For enslaved females it was based on the belief held by planters in some areas that, where health and strength and the capacity for hard labour mattered more than gender and reproductivity, it was neither impossible nor wrong to overwork a slave of either sex.[49] Nevertheless, recent studies have shown that the legacy of equality-in-labour on the West Indian plantation has been a considerable degree of female economic independence and resourcefulness in parts of the Caribbean, Jamaica in particular.[50]

To a casual viewer, Jones's stance on the video of the song "Demolition Man", combined with a set that invokes a demolition site and the seemingly male subjectivity that informs the lyrics, is an unsettling performance of gender-switching. I suggest an alternative view. The intensity of Jones's articulation and the power of her performance in this scene, which is one of the strongest in *A One Man Show*, expresses a conviction that she is *both* woman *and* a demolition man; the demolition man is a metaphor for her own strength and power, strength that society deems unacceptable in a woman. She sings:

> I'm a walking nightmare, an arsenal of doom
> I'll kill conversation as I walk into the room I'm a three line whip I'm the sort of thing they ban
> I'm a walking disaster
> I'm a demolition man.

The lyric reminds us of the discourse that designates black women as not-women by European standards of heteronormativity – black women are the "walking nightmare" of deficient femininity, and "the walking disaster" of failed gender attribution. The lyric calls attention to the fact that, because of their alleged deficiency, black women in general, and Jones specifically in this instance, are always already queer to the Eurocentric gaze – "the sort of thing they ban". Jones confronts and unsettles that gaze; she "demolishes" gender stereotypes by disrupting and problematizing gender categories, lyrically, performatively and personally. The words of Kalamu ya Salaam are particularly relevant to Jones's performance of "Demolition Man": "rather than a spectacle to be consumed, she was a knife that sliced the eye of every voyeur".[51]

"Living My Life"

Designed and directed by Jean-Paul Goude, the long-form video work *A One Man Show* showcases Jones performing a selection of the most popular songs from her repertoire, including "Warm Leatherette", "Pull Up to the Bumper", "Demolition Man", "Feel Up", "My Jamaican Guy", "Living My Life" and "La Vie en Rose". Filmed partly in studio in London and partly at live performances in the United States, the work is a vivid and compelling visual text documenting the defining performances of Jones's career. In his book *Jungle Fever*, Goude rather boastfully takes credit for the video's now iconic images of Jones, claiming that she surrendered completely to his direction.[52] However, elsewhere he acknowledges Jones's active participation: "she was no dope – Grace is an opportunist and she knew my vision was good for her career".[53]

Goude was insightful in his use of video to project Jones's image and songs to a wide audience. In the early 1980s, video was an emergent artistic medium, soon to become the medium of choice of commercial postmodernism. Video enabled artists outside of the mainstream affordable access to image production, manipulation and dissemination, and, combined with a computer, enabled the production of avant-garde, subversive or simply new aesthetic experiences. With Jones, a highly telegenic subject, Goude fully exploited the potential of the medium, in particular the possibilities for subversive aesthetic experimentation. *A One Man Show* is more than just a sequence of compelling images; the songs selected and Jones's vocal performance of them articulate an experience and sensibility that are both postcolonial and postmodern. The video represents this by means of artfully orchestrated images. Lyrically and musically, the songs invoke the span of Jones's broad and diverse experience: the rural Caribbean, the hyper-urban metropolis that is New York and the Parisian cabaret. The songs also illustrate the alienation produced by a peripatetic existence and perpetual displacement; they interrogate gender and sexual identities, exploring love, longing, betrayal, rebellion and existential struggle. The video itself made it possible to project Jones to a wider audience.

The "show" opens with sounds of cicadas and steel drums, sounds that instantly evoke the Caribbean, and an image of a black girl of about ten years old standing on the porch of small house. The girl holds the skirt of her dress high, exposing her naked pubis. This is Jones as she might have posed at that age had she grown up without familial and cultural restraints: precociously bold and sexual. A montage of still photographs shows Jones in her disco phase – Jones the tiger-woman, Jones dressed *à la* Baker, and Jones as a statue fixed in an improbable arabesque. In the prologue to the first song, "Warm Leatherette", Jones poses at the top of a flight of stairs clad in a gorilla suit, a grass skirt draped around her waist and lips painted grotesquely red. She leaps gorilla-style down a few steps before pausing to remove the gorilla head, standing defiantly to reveal her own face, fully made up, with brilliant red lips. It is a moment of defiant self-affirmation that also confronts the accumulation of negative stereotypes and negative images of black women that can threaten a black woman's self-esteem.

The lyrics and visuals of the song "Living My Life", the final sequence on *A One Man Show*, elaborate Jones's critique of racist stereotypes and provide further insight into the experience and politics that inform Jones's art. The sequence opens with a prologue of gradually intensifying melodramatic music, at the end of which Jones, dressed in an enormous crinoline and hat, wearing long white gloves, holds a gun to her head and fires. Smoke issues from the gun, but Jones does not die. Instead, half a dozen figures dressed identically to Jones spring from the hem of her skirt and twirl in a frantic ballet. To a fast, driving beat, Jones begins the song, her expression defiant, the lyric half-spoken in a solemn, near-monotone that only breaks when it rises to an angry shout:

> You cuss me for living
> You cuss me
> For living my life
> . . .
> I'm living my life
> As hard as I can
> Black as I am

> . . .
> You hate me
> You hate me for living
> You box me
> You box me for living
> For living my life
> You kill me
> You kill me for living
> . . .
> You brainwash me!
> . . .
> You can't stand me!

Close examination reveals that the dancing figures, which at first glance seem to be blackface ballerinas, have chimpanzee heads and human bodies – an obvious reference to the video's opening sequence and an allusion to the racist characterization of black female bodies as primitive and grotesque. The figures *pirouette* and *jetée*, suggesting the distorting imposition of European cultural forms and values on the non-European, while the hats, crinolines and gloves that they and Jones wear, refer ironically to the imposition of Victorian or European standards of dress, deportment and aesthetics. While the figures dance, Jones spins and flails in the prison of her crinoline, clutching her head to gesture rage and despair at the "brainwashing" that threatens her psychic integrity and even her life. The unspecified, all-inclusive "you" addressed in the lyric invokes every oppressor, every repressive stereotype or convention – parents who "cuss", partners who "box",[54] hateful stereotypes – or individuals, or institutions – that "kill" spiritually or mortally.

Jones's performance of the song "La Vie en Rose" also expresses rage, but the lyrics of the song suggest wrongs of a more intimate origin. Posed on a staircase, seemingly playing an accordion, Jones sings *against* Edith Piaf's ecstatic anthem to the joys of love, infusing it with a tragic irony that subverts the romantic euphoria of Piaf's classic. The bitter, clipped enunciation of the lyrics, the soaring, howling crescendos that punctuate the song, the single, hyperbolic teardrop that stains her face, the typically Caribbean hand-on-head gesture representing extreme duress – all dramatize the emotional pain of a woman for whom romantic love is a fantasy that can only bring grief. Lobato notes "the semiotic mismatch" between the "diva ululations" of Jones's voice, the flatness of her affect and the solitary tear; he finds the impact of the song "devastating".⁵⁵

Jones's frozen features in this song/sequence and in others – in "Warm Leatherette" and "Demoliton Man", for example – take on a mask-like quality representative of alienation. In these songs, Jones performs the culturally produced emotional and bodily repression of the multiply alienated postcolonial subject. Not only alienated from ancestral Africa and denied its gift of belonging, she is also displaced from her native Caribbean into a context in which she is both categorized and viewed as alien. In "La Vie en Rose", the mask slips momentarily, and the single tear that trails down Jones's cheek metonymically expresses the emotional trauma compressed beneath it.

"Not Sublime, but Strange . . ."⁵⁶

It is revealing that one of the few sequences on *A One Man Show* in which Jones's body is noticeably relaxed and in which she actually smiles and expresses warmth, is also one of two songs with lyrics that are partly or wholly in Jamaican Creole. The recurrent visual, musical and lyrical allusions to Jamaica and the Caribbean in *A One Man Show* have received little specific comment in critical work on Jones, which typically makes more general reference to the postcolonial or the African diaspora. For example, two important contributors to scholarship on Jones, Miriam Kershaw and Carolyn Anderson, situate Jones's performance art – as distinct from her music – in the performance traditions of African America and within the Afrocentric discourses of the African diaspora, without comment on the specifically Caribbean elements of Jones's performance. In my view, such an oversight produces a significantly incomplete reading.

Failure or refusal to acknowledge Jones's Caribbeanity facilitates the reading and fetishizing of her person and performance as "strange", readings that Jones, and Goude in his role as director of *A One Man Show*, encourage and exploit. It may seem paradoxical that a work that reveals so many defining aspects of Jones's subjectivity and politics (through her lyrics), should visually adopt an aesthetic of the strange. Goude's adherence to this aesthetic is most apparent in the creative deployment of novel computer-generated visual effects – the troupe of chimpanzee ballerinas in the "Living My Life" sequence and the army of Grace Jones replicas in "Demolition Man", for example. However, commercially and artistically, Goude's (and Jones's) embrace of this aesthetic is in keeping with the times. Herbert Grabes argues that the aesthetic of the strange emerged from postmodern desires for novelty and new aesthetic experiences. He states that "it is . . . a question of dealing with something which appears more or less strange in order to reach the type of 'pleasure' that results from an expanded perception and understanding".[57] According to Grabes, the possibility of creating something startling and new artistically depends, on one hand, on the technologies and media that enabled "the alternative production of ephemeral simulations" and, on the other, the presence or existence of the alien, alienating, other: "the creation of a new type of alterity by turning to and integrating the world-views and conceptions of the self of foreign cultures".[58] Thus the aesthetic of the strange makes visible the resurgence, in the postmodern cultural moment, of the Western impulse to manipulate and exploit the being of the formerly colonized other.

Grabes explains this resurgence by situating the aesthetics of the strange at a conceptual midpoint between the "sublime" and the "beautiful", raising questions as to whether the aesthetic of the strange represents a revision of the aesthetic of the sublime.[59] As Meg Armstrong explains, "the sublime is described not only through analogies of differences between the sexes (Burke and Kant), but also as a product of an aesthetic disposition inherent in sexual, national, and historical characteristics (Kant) and is sometimes provoked by images of racial difference (Burke and Kant)".[60] Following Burke and Kant, aesthetic discourse has located the sublime human "object" within a global schema of bodies whose difference from the European subject is evident in racial, gendered and cultural characteristics, and whose difference affirms the self-identity of the European subject, even while simultaneously provoking unacknowledged desires. Burke attributes sublimity to blackness and darkness, and beauty to light and femaleness, but in his schema, it is the black female, who is both dark and not properly female, who is sublime.[61]

I digress to make this somewhat reductive review of the originary discourse on the sublime in order to point to the double consciousness revealed by Jones's embodiment of "the strange" in *A One Man Show*. Jones's lyrical discourse reveals her acute awareness of the historical matrix of race, gender and desire, and her refusal to be crushed, or even subordinated within it. Simultaneously, the aesthetics of the video situate her within a synthetic and virtual universe where she can only be seen as other and strange, desirable to the white and/or Western audience as a *novel and pleasurable experience*. For, as Grabes explains, a significant and intrinsic element of the aesthetics of the strange is the awareness of the aesthetic power of difference, coupled with a desire for expanded awareness of difference through pleasure. He elaborates, "it is precisely its strangeness that causes an initial sense of alienation and only after this has been overcome allows for a particular kind of pleasure".[62]

Further evidence that Jones consciously and deliberately engaged this aesthetic can be found in her performance in the role of Strangé in the 1992 film *Boomerang*.[63] Jones's acting career merits its own article, but I refer to her performance in this particular film as it vividly represents Jones's self-aware, and, in this instance, self-parodic exploitation of the aesthetic of the strange. Her character in this film embodies it. Directed by Reginald Hudlin, the film stars Eddie Murphy as an advertising executive responsible for the re-launch of a range of cosmetics for black women, Lady Eloise Cosmetics. Jones plays a minor character, Strangé, a celebrity fashion model who is engaged to be the new face of Lady Eloise Cosmetics. Jones delivers an exuberantly comedic performance, dominating each of the few scenes in which she appears in updated recapitulations of some of her familiar personae. She arrives at a reception to launch the new advertising campaign in a helicopter. A wooden crate is lowered to the ground, exploding to reveal a chariot pulled by four muscle-bound white men, and a leather-clad, whip-waving dominatrix Strangé. When she descends from her chariot to address the gathering, Strangé speaks English with a marked French accent. She gesticulates fervently with her hands and frequently lapses into French, reminding her African-American employers of her difference; she may be from a francophone Caribbean or African country, but she is not African American.

In a subsequent scene Strangé enacts the uninhibited temptress who behaves outrageously in public. In an aggressive but unsuccessful effort to seduce Eddie Murphy's character over dinner at an exclusive restaurant, she lifts her skirt and spreads her legs, then hurls abuse at Murphy when he recoils in embarrassment. And in a hilariously bad television advertisement, she plays a primeval, beautiful yet grotesque swamp-woman who gives birth to a bottle of perfume. Strangé compels attention, but she is viewed by the African-American characters with whom she interacts as a wild black other, whose difference marks her a queer, outside the norms of African-American blackness and therefore objectifiable and eminently exploitable. By contrast, the film's female leads, played by Halle Berry, Robin Givens and, in cameo, a now tame Eartha Kitt, emerge as rather dull models of black female heterosexuality. All three are both intensely appealing to Murphy's character, a black, supposedly heterosexual, male, presumably capable of appealing to a mainstream audience. Strangé disrupts the fixed categories of African-American identity and sexuality and, in resisting assimilation, claims a freedom that is viscerally exhilarating: she steals the show.

This chapter has demonstrated, through an analysis of the music of Grace Jones, that no matter what persona she inhabits, no matter how steeped in racist narrative or stereotype, she has engaged in deconstruction, deploying irony and subversive hyperbole in her performance of her singular brand of music. From her beginnings as a singer, Jones has functioned with artistic double consciousness, simultaneously seeing herself reflected in the othering and fetishizing gaze of a largely non-black, non-Caribbean audience, while both resisting and reflecting back the objectification of that gaze. Jones challenges us to negotiate the obvious paradoxes in her performance and listen to her music, thereby engaging the complex subjectivity that informs both.

Notes

1. Grace Jones, http://www.gracejones.org.
2. Rob Tannenbaum, "The Devil Wears Zebra-Striped Catsuits", *Village Voice*, 5 August 2009.
3. Miriam Kershaw, "Postcolonialism and Androgyny: The Performance Art of Grace Jones", *Art Journal* 56, no. 4 (Winter 1997).
4. Carolyn G. Anderson, "En Route to Transnational Postmodernism: Grace Jones, Josephine Baker and the African Diaspora", *Social Science Information* 32, no. 3 (1993): 493.
5. Stan Godlovich, *Musical Performance: A Philosophical Study* (London: Routledge, 1998), 50.
6. Jeanette Bicknell, "Just a Song? Exploring the Aesthetics of Popular Song Performance", *Journal of Aesthetics and Art Criticism* 63, no. 3 (Summer 2005): 263.
7. Goodlovitch, *Musical Performance*, 143.
8. Ramon Lobato, "Amazing Grace: Decadence, Deviance, Disco", *Camera Obscura* 22, no. 2 65 (2007): 136.
9. Anderson, "En Route to Transnational Postmodernism", 508.

10. Nicholas Mizroeff, *An Introduction to Visual Culture* (London: Routledge, 1999), 162.
11. Wresch Dawidjan, "Grace Jones: Grace Jones Prays", *About.com*, accessed 5 November 2011, http://dancemusic.about.com/od/discoflashback/a/GraceJones.htm.
12. "Grace Jones Talks Fashion and Supermodels on *The Tonight Show Starring Johnny Carson* 1985", YouTube video, 2:31, posted by "johnnycarson", 19 August 2011, http://www.youtube.com/watch?v=jWHmvf2_tDQ.
13. Dawidjan, "Grace Jones".
14. Even *Essence* magazine, the fashion and beauty journal for black women, did not feature a dark-skinned woman on its cover until 1987, and that woman was a Jamaican model, Althea Laing.
15. Ibid.
16. Richard Dyer, *Only Entertainment* (London: Routledge, 2002), 151.
17. Ibid., 158.
18. Ibid., 151.
19. Judy Kutulas, "You Probably Think This Song Is About You: 1970s Women's Music from Carole King to the Disco Divas", in *Disco Divas: Women and Popular Culture in the 1970s*, ed. Sherrie Innes (Philadelphia: University of Pensylvania Press, 2003), 189.
20. Ibid.
21. Ibid.
22. Coco Fusco, "Performance and the Power of the Popular", in *Let's Get It On: The Politics of Black Performance*, ed. Catherine Ugwu (London: ICA, 1995), 159.
23. Rebecca Wanzo, "Beyond a 'Just' Syntax: Black Actresses, Hollywood and Complex Personhood", *Women and Performance: A Journal of Feminist Theory* 16, no. 1 (March 2006): 135–52.
24. W.E.B. Du Bois, *The Souls of Black Folk* (New York: Penguin Books, 1989), 5. Du Bois's formulations refer to "the American Negro", however, Paul Gilroy has argued for their relevance to all post-slavery societies in *The Black Atlantic: Modernity and Double Consciousness* (Cambridge, MA: Harvard University Press, 1993), 30.
25. Grace Jones, "I Need a Man", *Portfolio* (Island Records ILPS 9470, 1977).
26. Shane Vogel, *The Scene of Harlem Cabaret: Race, Sexuality, Performance* (Chicago: Chicago University Press, 2008), 61.
27. Ibid., 45.
28. Photograph, Keith Haring, untitled (body painting), 1984.
29. Kershaw, "Postcolonialism", 21.
30. Jones appeared on *The Tonight Show Starring Johnny Carson*, face covered in a hand-held mask (episode 16, November 1985).
31. Kershaw, "Postcolonialism", 21.
32. The band included "Sly" Dunbar on drums and Robbie Shakespeare on bass, who together had become Jamaica's pre-eminent rhythm team. Wally Badarou, from the

Ivory Coast by way of Paris, specialized in the synthesizer; Jamaican percussionist Uzziah "Sticky" Thompson, guitarist Mickey "Mao" Chung and the British guitarist Barry Reynolds completed the truly all-star group.

33. Chinn, *Grace Jones: Notes to the Compass Point Sessions*, liner notes, Island Records, 1998.
34. Ibid.
35. Anderson, "En Route to Transnational Postmodernism", 493.
36. Ibid., 508.
37. In late-twentieth-century feminist discourse, androgyny was debated as the potentially ideal human condition, one that would both subvert and overtly challenge patriarchy. See Kate Millet, *Sexual Politics* (New York: Doubleday, 1970); and Marilyn French, *Beyond Power* (New York: Ballantine, 1986).
38. Kershaw, "Postcolonialism", 24.
39. Wendy Cooper, *Hair: Sex, Society and Symbolism* (New York: Stein and Day, 1971).
40. Willie Morrow, *400 Years without a Comb* (San Diego: Black Publishers of San Diego, 1973), 15.
41. A case in point is the recent media frenzy over the African twists worn by Barack Obama's eleven-year-old daughter Malia while on holiday with her parents in Rome. This is evidence of the vitality of this particular manifestation of white supremacist norms. As noted in the *New York Times*, conservative bloggers "attacked her as unfit to represent America for stepping out unstraightened". A hairstyle that Malia and her mother, Michelle Obama, might have seen as just that, was perceived by Malia's critics as an insignia of inferiority inappropriate for a member of America's "first family" and thus, a representative of America. Whether a retention from the days of slavery or a legacy of the days of the Black Power Movement's politicization of hair, the decision to wear natural (meaning unprocessed) hair, or an African style, is commonly read as a political statement and/or an expression of black pride that contests Eurocentric norms.
42. Ingrid Banks, *Hair Matters: Beauty, Power and Black Women's Consciousness* (New York: New York University Press, 2000), 24.
43. Dawidjan, "Grace Jones".
44. It is worth noting that the style in question is an exaggeration of the "fade" cut worn by black women across the African diaspora since the 1980s.
45. Janelle Hobon, "The 'Batty' Politic: Towards an Aesthetic of the Black Female Body", *Hypatia* 18, no. 4 (Fall–Winter 2003): 87.
46. Jennifer L. Morgan, " 'Some Could Suckle Over Their Shoulder': Male Travelers, Female Bodies, and the Gendering of Racial Ideology, 1500–1770", *William and Mary Quarterly* 54, no. 1 (1997): 167–92.
47. Edward Long, *The History of Jamaica* (London: T. Lownudes, 1774), 2:476.
48. Sidney Mintz, "Black Women, Economic Roles, and Cultural Traditions", in

Caribbean Freedom: Economy and Society from Emancipation to the Present, ed. H. Beckles (Princeton, NJ: Markus Wiener, 1994), 243.
49. See Beckles's comments on the writings of A.C. Carmichael in *Centering Women* (Kingston: Ian Randle, 1999), 176.
50. See Janet Momson, "Gender Roles in Caribbean Agricultural Labor", in *Caribbean Freedom*, 216–24; and Janet Momson, ed., *Women and Change in the Caribbean: A Pan-Caribbean Perspective* (Kingston: Ian Randle, 1993).
51. Lalamy ya Salaam, "Grace Jones: Slave to the Rhythm", *New Black Magazine*, 11 May 2007.
52. Jean-Paul Goude, *Jungle Fever* (New York: Xavier Moreau, 1981), 103.
53. Jean-Paul Goude, qtd. in "Snapshot", *Guardian*, 19 February 2006.
54. In Jamaican Creole, "to box" means to slap or strike.
55. Lobato, "Decadence, Deviance, Disco", 134–38.
56. Herbert Grabes, *Making Strange: Beauty, Sublimity and the (Post)Modern "Third Aesthetic"* (Amsterdam: Rodopi, 2008).
57. Ibid., 117.
58. Ibid., 116–18.
59. Theorized in the eighteenth century by Burke and Kant, the aesthetic of the sublime emerged from the colonial encounter between Europe and Africa and Europe and Asia. I invoke the sublime here to refer to a heightened response of awe or fear produced by an object or phenomenon that is unfamiliar or unintelligible to the beholder.
60. Meg Armstrong, "The Effects of Blackness: Gender, Race and the Sublime in Aesthetic Theories of Burke and Kant", *Journal of Aesthetics and Art Criticism* 54, no. 3 (1996): 213.
61. Ibid., 215.
62. Grabes, *Making Strange*, 7.
63. *Boomerang*, dir. Reginald Hudlin (Paramount Home Entertainment, 2002, DVD).

Discography

Jones, Grace. 1977. *Fame* (1978). Spectrum Audio, B0059V5797, compact disc, 1993.
———. *Living My Life*. Island USA, B000001FU8, 1989, compact disc, 1982.
———. *Muse*. Island Records USA, LP, 1979.
———. *Nightclubbing* (1981). Universal/Island, B0059V5797, compact disc, 1989.
———. *Portfolio* (1977). Spectrum Audio, B000001FU7, compact disc, 2004.
———. *Slave to the Rhythm* (1985). Island Masters, B00000.1FT2. 2007, compact disc.
———. *Warm Leatherette*. Spectrum Audio, B000001FU5, 2001, compact disc, 1980.

11.

"LADIES A YOUR TIME NOW!"
Erotic Politics, Lovers' Rock and Resistance in the UK

LISA AMANDA PALMER

Introduction

I felt I needed to be taken seriously as a 'conscious sister' in my teenage years, and so I developed a haughty snobbish disdain for all sorts of music that sounded remotely 'smoochy' or 'romantic', things I considered highly damaging to my 'conscious credentials'. However, most of my female friends and cousins disagreed with my antipathy towards love songs. A reggae blues dance was 'lame' if the right selection of lovers' rock music was not played. The dance was a complete disappointment if my cousin did not '*get a dance*' with the right boy, to the right lovers' rock tune, in her case, preferably Peter Hunnigale's 'Won't You be My Lady', or even better, 'Hopelessly in Love' by Carol Thompson. My cousin's dad had the most meticulous and extensive collection of lovers' rock vinyl LPs and 45s which were lovingly and routinely polished with a special alcoholic fluid and a velveteen cloth. The fluid, the cloth and the treasured collection were all completely out of bounds to us children. Any evidence of scratches or smudges would automatically be traced back to us with serious consequences. Rather than face the consequences, we decided not to 'farce' (interfere) with his treasured lovers' rock records, and left them well alone.

"OK people, this is lovers' rock..."

This paper is concerned with the politics of erotic love as expressed through the genre of lovers' rock music and its emergence inside a highly gendered, erotic and political reggae scene that developed within the social context of Britain during the 1970s and 1980s. Lovers' rock was an integral component of the reggae music landscape of that period and has remained so to this day. Nevertheless, within scholarly, critical and historical reflections on reggae cultures, lovers' rock's fleeting if not invisible presence, is often obscured by the predominance of the genre's more raucous reggae relatives, namely 'conscious' roots reggae and ragga 'slackness' (Cooper 2004; Henry 2006; Noble 2000; Stolzoff 2000). On the occasions when lovers' rock has been inscribed into the historical and cultural narrative of the reggae music scene in Britain, its romantic and erotic expressions are frequently seen as apolitical and antithetical to the 'conscious' political impulses of 'roots reggae' (Barrow and Dalton 2004; Hebdidge 1987; De Koningh and Griffiths 2003).

The binary positioning of lovers' rock's soulful melodies against the hardcore political 'toasting' and 'chat' of 'conscious roots', is theoretically and culturally organised along the lines of gender. Here, both lovers' rock and conscious roots reggae are generally allotted respectively to categories of femininity and masculinity. Lovers' rock is gendered as strictly black female territory, whereas the oppositional politics of conscious reggae is primarily assigned to the interests and concerns of black men. Although lovers' rock is by no means exclusively performed, consumed or enjoyed by black women, the genre has commonly been designated as some sort of female sanctuary both within the dancehall space and within reggae culture at large (Barrow and Dalton 2004; Hebdidge 1987).

Below, I will explore ways in which lovers' rock has been rendered and interpreted as a 'special' form of reggae for black women (Barrow and Dalton 2004; Hebdidge 1987). Whilst there is nothing fundamentally wrong with the popularity of lovers' rock amongst black women in the reggae dancehall scene, I am arguing that its designation as a 'special' female space is problematic. The differentiation between lovers' rock from the politics of 'conscious roots' and culture reinforces rigid categories of gendered participation within the dancehall space. This process of gendering also works to downgrade and marginalise discourses on erotic love in such a way that erotic and loving identities are perceived as being at best unimportant and at worst irrelevant to the radical political ambitions of 'conscious roots'. I wish to demonstrate that such divisions obscure the discursive interconnections of erotic love with radical politics and thus undermine the complexity of black erotic/political identities. I will challenge the gendering of lovers' rock as a predominantly feminised space, aiming to retrieve a complex and sometimes contradictory interpretation of the ways in which lovers' rock both affirms and disavows its discourse on love whilst interrogating how these contradictions work through the politics of gender.

Lovers' rock is also a distinctly transnational cultural project emerging from the creative, political and erotic impulses of Caribbean communities in Britain. The transnational spirit and cultural formation of lovers' rock has been highlighted elsewhere by Paul Gilroy (1993). I wish to support Gilroy's claim that lovers' rock has a distinctive transnational sensibility by further suggesting that Caribbean communities in Britain have used the erotic and political intersection of lovers' rock and conscious roots reggae to reconfigure the stereotypical, loveless and nihilistic representations of their identities found within popular discourses in the British press (Gilroy 2006). Through the intersection of the erotic and the political, Caribbean communities created complex discourses that asserted a love ethic as a way of expressing and validating the complexity of their existence within Britain's hostile metropolitan centres.

My discussion of lovers' rock has been greatly influenced by black feminist discourses on love and the erotic (Hill Collins 2005; hooks 1992; Lorde 2007), in particular, the writing of bell hooks who argues that love is a highly political activity (hooks 1992, 2000, 2001, 2004). In her book, *Black Looks: Race and Representation*, hooks writes 'Loving blackness as political resistance transforms our ways of looking and being, and thus creates the conditions necessary for us to move against the forces of domination and death and reclaim black life' (hooks 1992, p. 20). I would add that loving blackness also enables us to highlight and reinterpret cultural practices of love amongst distinct and different black communities that illuminate the ways diverse groups of black people have expressed love beyond the perceived limits, myths, and narratives mapped onto our existence. However, in the erotic arena of lovers' rock this love ethic is often complicated and sometimes compromised by gendered conceptualisations of love and rebellion that re-inscribe binary gendered discourses that discount love as a serious and valuable tool to the politics of black liberation (hooks 1992).

I seek to rehabilitate lovers' rock within critical discourses on dancehall by taking seriously its erotic political import into the reggae dancehall scene. I wish to counteract the critical and theoretical tendency to routinely undermine and thus devalue lovers' rock's significance within academic scholarship on the emergence of dancehall reggae cultures in Britain and the wider diaspora. This paper seeks to explore the genre's discursive role within the dancehall space as a whole. It is at this discursive point of lovers' rock's intersection with other reggae genres that its more radical possibilities can be revealed.

The Emergence of Lovers' Rock in Britain

The 'lovers' rock nomenclature was coined in Britain by music producer Dennis Bovell, his co-producer and guitarist John Kapiaye, alongside husband and wife music producers Dennis and Eve Harris. Bovell, Kapiaye, and the Harris team are credited as the original architects of the 'lovers' rock sound in Britain (Barrow and Dalton 2004; Garratt 1985; Hebdidge 1987). During the mid-1970s in the early stages of lovers' rock's development, music producers such as Bovell were in search of a distinctive 'Black British' reggae sound beyond merely imitating the songs being produced in Jamaica (Cumming 2006; Garratt 1985). During this period, as far as Caribbean audiences in cities such as London and Birmingham were concerned, the best and most popular reggae was still being recorded and imported from Jamaica to England (Hebdidge 1987).

Love songs have long been a staple feature of the Jamaican reggae music lexicon. Male singers such as Dennis Brown, Owen Gray, Alton Ellis, Ken Boothe, Sugar Minot, and Gregory Isaacs are considered as some of the most important lovers' rock reggae artists of their generation (Hebdidge 1987). However, despite the success and popularity of Jamaican balladeers both at home and throughout the Caribbean diaspora, lovers' rock as a recognisable term was only named in London during the mid-1970s through the emergence of the British based lovers' rock trio, Brown Sugar (Garratt 1985; Hebdidge 1987). Their song, 'I'm in love with a Dreadlocks', was the first track to be released under Bovell and Kapiaye's 'lovers rock' label (Garratt 1985). By this time, the lovers' rock sound had already been established by artists such as

Louisa Mark, Marie Pierre, and 15, 16 & 17 before the term emerged. As Bovell began placing the lovers' rock name on to more record labels, the name gradually caught on (Garratt 1985; Hebdidge 1987). Indeed, it was after the term emerged in the UK that the lovers' rock name became attached to romantic reggae singers throughout the Jamaican diaspora who sang about love.

Bovell had previously co-founded the British roots band Matumbi in 1971. He went on to produce Janet Kay's lovers' rock album, *Silly Games* (1979), as well as writing and producing the soundtrack to Franco Rossos's film *Babylon* (1980). Many young female musicians had entered the lovers' rock scene through auditions and talent competitions organised by Bovell and Kapiaye at various venues across south London (Hebdidge 1987). Lloyd Coxsone, a hugely influential and important figure within the development of sound system culture in the UK, was instrumental in the recording of Louisa Mark's 'Caught You in a Lie' (1975), a track considered to be the first definitive lovers' rock song (Garratt 1985). Bovell and Coxsone saw Mark as the 'natural choice' to record a cover of the Robert Parker original (Barrow and Dalton 2004). Mark introduced herself to Bovell at a blues dance where his sound system, Jah Sufferer HI FI was playing. According to Sheryl Garratt, her yearning vocal wherein she discovers that the girl her boyfriend has been seeing is not his cousin after all, was recorded in one take and became an instant hit (Garratt 1985). Mark's brilliantly produced version of 'Caught you in a Lie' still remains a classic lovers' rock recording, belying any dismissal of the track as a foray into 'teeny popping' drivel and dross. The popular face of lovers' rock in the UK was frequently characterised by young black teenage girls, like Mark, who were supposedly eager to cover African American soul songs on top of the deep and heavy baselines of roots reggae (Garratt 1985; Hebdidge 1987).

Outernational 'Blak'ness

Lovers' rock's popularity was established through the 'free' (pirate) radio stations and underground local blues party networks and venues across the UK during the 1970s and 1980s (Barrow and Dalton 2004). Despite the recent demise of vital reggae music venues in cities such as London and Birmingham, these local clubs had previously served as both porous and hidden locations for engaging with lovers' rock as well as other transatlantic musical styles and forms. In these intimate subaltern spaces, working-class Caribbean communities came together for leisure, celebrations, and entertainment. Sound system nights, engagement parties, weddings, christenings, and Rastafari gatherings all provided 'safe' spaces of sanctuary where black urban music was central to easing as well as expressing the tensions of urban inner city life. Lovers' rock musicians were carving out their own dynamic vernacular and rhetorical spaces within the British reggae music scene. Lovers' rock brought soul and reggae so close together that it became a fusion of the two styles of music (Hebdidge 1987). Indeed, young Caribbean musicians and audiences utilised other black diasporic musical dialects and sounds by blending and interweaving the heavy Jamaican reggae baseline with 'soft-soul' vocal harmonies emanating out from Chicago and Philadelphia, thus creating a unique diasporic lovers' rock style and aesthetic (Barrow and Dalton 2004).

This new genre had its own transnational sensibility. Lovers' rock signalled the emergence of an early *Blak* British transnational soundscape that would later give rise to UK soul acts such as Soul II Soul, whose leading vocalist Caron Wheeler, had previously emerged as one of the early forerunners of first generation lovers' rock artists (Barrow and Dalton 2004; Gilroy 1993). At the age of 15, Wheeler was one member of the trio Brown Sugar alongside fellow band mate and lovers' rock veteran Kofi. Brown Sugar were amongst that first group of young women who attended Bovell and Kapiaye's auditions in south London (Barrow and Dalton 2004; Hebdidge 1987). Brown Sugar achieved early success within the lovers' rock scene with tracks such as 'I'm In Love With A Dreadlocks' and 'Black Pride' which also signalled the arrival of 'conscious lovers', a politically inspired sub-genre of lovers' rock music.

Following her later success with the group Soul II Soul, Wheeler's 1990 debut solo album entitled *UK Blak*, would be instrumental in cultivating and articulating the idea that British-born Caribbean decedents had an 'outernational' understanding of their 'blak'ness' in Britain. In other words, blackness in Britain was intimately formed within the social confines of black urban settings as well as upon the outward trajectory of postcolonial and transnational forms of blackness dispersed through the cultural mesh of Caribbean, African, and North American transatlantic flows. The cultural and political significance of the term 'blak' (as opposed to black spelt with a 'c') was subsequently cross-referenced into the cultural and political theories of both Paul Gilroy's *The Black Atlantic* (1993) and William 'Lez' Henry's *What the Deejay Said* (2006). Blak is mobilised within these theoretical discourses to underscore a countercultural black consciousness and the influence of the black diaspora in shaping the cultural politics of black Britain. Gilroy locates the transnational logic of 'blak' and its meaning within the formation of musical subcultures that emerged from Britain's urban inner cities. These subcultures drew heavily from a range of 'raw materials' supplied by transnational currents from the Caribbean and black America (Gilroy 1993). Henry further provides an explicit historical context for the emergence of the term 'blak':

> The usage of 'blak' emerged in urban London during the late 1980's and when Caron Wheeler of 'Soul to Soul' fame released an album entitled 'UK Blak' for EMI records, the word became known in mainstream British society. By omitting the letter 'c', Wheeler was making a profound Africentric political statement that reflected a conscious move by certain members of the black community to distance themselves from the negative connotations of black as the colour of doom, oppression, bad luck etc. This meant that the term blak, which was created within the counter cultures of the Afrikan Diaspora, had much currency and signified an alternative way of thinking about the black presence in Britain. (Henry 2006, p. 27)

As Henry further argues, Caribbean communities in the UK have continuously looked to resources outside of Britain to facilitate its cultural and psychological survival (Henry 2006). Dancehall culture in Britain, and in particular the role of the dancehall deejay in providing a 'critique from the street' helped to create countercultural 'self-generated concepts' such as 'Blak' (Henry 2006). These self-generated social critiques were created from African centred outernational resources that allowed 'downpressed' Caribbean communities in Britain to counteract their racialised marginalisation and social exclusion. The dancehall deejay's critiques provided an energetic and politically engaged intellectual discourse that highlighted the day to day problems of surviving within a racist social environment (Henry 2006). Henry further argues that the cultural templates of dancehall from the 45 inch single, 'sound (cassette) tapes' with live recordings of sound system events, to the dancehall space itself, furnished alternative public arenas for working-class black youth in Britain (Henry 2006). These cultural templates enabled young people to link 'disparate elements' of black oppositional histories, making their identities 'outernational and whole' (Henry 2006). 'Outernational' notions of 'blakness' provided important cultural, psychic, political and emotional links back to the Caribbean. It was also an important critical resource for developing oppositional critiques of the British nation state. By espousing an 'outernational consciousness', black Caribbean youths born in Britain developed critical perceptions and intellectual frameworks that deliberately transcended the racialised geography of Britain (Henry 2006).

Although I support Henry's insightful arguments, I argue that he proceeds to overlook the cultural and political context of lovers' rock in the formation and intellectual conception of an 'outernational consciousness'. After all, it was Caron Wheeler, a black female artist and pioneer of lovers' rock who mobilised the term 'blak' to demarcate the very specific diasporic journey of black Britain's post–Second World War emergence and cultural formation. The cultural context of the lovers' rock scene was indeed critical to Wheeler's emergence as a politically 'conscious' lovers' rock artist, and too, as a soulful musician who successfully and brilliantly utilised a 'blak' diasporic political sensibility throughout her *UK Blak* (1990) album. While acknowledging and mobilising the political and intellectual significance of Wheeler's use of the term 'blak', Henry does not situate this critical moment within lovers' rock's transnational tradition nor within the genre's discursive contribution to the dancehall scene in which both the erotic and the political are interdependent paradigms that inform the cultural aspirations of dancehall aficionados.

By overlooking the cultural interdependence of political and erotic discourses that emerge within lovers' rock, critical interpretations of reggae dancehall cultures obscure the significance of complex discourses by black women that affirm the intersection of erotic and political identities. They further undermine the ways in which the mutuality of these identities is indeed relevant to the development of oppositional politics and social movements in Britain. Within dancehall culture, this oversight can be explained by the fact that the position of the male deejay reigns supreme (Henry 2006). Male singers, and to a lesser extent female singers, remain highly valued but in general terms occupy a less elevated status in contemporary dancehall culture (Cooper 2004). This is true both within Jamaica and the diaspora. The skills of deejaying and singing are deeply attached to notions of gender that demarcate 'chatting' and 'toasting' (a form of 'rap' that precedes hip hop) as a discursive space that privileges talk between males, whilst singing and harmonising within the dancehall becomes a designated space of communion first and foremost for women. These demarcations become particularly evident through the overt gendering of lovers' rock as a feminised reggae genre against the more covert gendering of roots reggae and deejaying as the domain of countercultural or oppositional black masculinity. Of course, both men and women can be deejays and singers. However, it is the gendering and social construction of these musical forms that is under scrutiny. This paper situates lovers' rock at the heart of the reggae music scene to demonstrate that such divisions are not always so clearly defined and are in fact more discursive than is often imagined.

A Feminised Sanctuary

Within the dancehall space, lovers' rock became gendered by male selectors and DJs as specifically 'female time' – *'Ladies a your time now!'* This rallying call could be heard during the blues party after a 'serious' conscious roots session had finished to be followed by the 'softer' intimate vibes of lovers' rock. For the most part, 'ladies' would reply with agreement to this clarion call to take centre stage. Black women in particular were presumed to be waiting in anticipation for a well needed break in tempo from the serious 'toasting' and 'chatting' performed by male deejays during a blues session. At this moment, the erotic interplay of black female and male bodies would engage in a 'slow wine', an open, erotic, and public display where couples dance together. However, rather than this moment being engineered exclusively for women, it was in reality eagerly anticipated by men and women alike. The 'slow wine', sometimes known as 'big people dance' due to its erotic nature, blurred rather than reinforced the gendered boundaries of the dancehall space. Amorous dance movements where bodies would rock, rub, slide, dip, and whine, not only disrupted the borders of gendered demarcations they also challenged wider public perceptions of black erotic identities. Open public displays of erotic intimacy between black bodies were uncommon outside of the dancehall in the UK. Whereas black male and female sexualities were often fetishised and objectified in wider dominant cultures, lovers' rock provided safe countercultural spaces for the erotic expression of black sexual subjectivity. In this view, 'lovers' rock music sits in tandem to roots reggae as opposed to in opposition to it in providing alternative countercultural representations of blackness. For the erotic as expressed in the genre of lovers' rock furnished notions of hot spaces, sensual sanctuary and intimate communion where black sexual desire was juxtaposed with the politically combustible space of the dancehall as a countercultural revolutionary location for critiquing black oppression in Britain.

In the making of black expressive cultures, lovers' rock affirmed the importance of the 'erotic as an essential source of power' (Lorde 2007) in the formation and transformation of loving countercultural identities. As Audre Lorde reminds us, the erotic is often confused with the pornographic, although they are 'two diametrically opposed uses of the sexual' (Lorde 2007, p. 55). Whilst the pornographic 'emphasizes sensation without feeling' the erotic provides opportunities to share and feel deeply any pursuit with another person (Lorde 2007, p. 56). Loving identities in lovers' rock were not solely concerned with the 'trials and tribulations' of interpersonal relationships although the trials of romantic love are without question the genre's dominant focus. Lovers' rock suggests that the 'personal' erotic domain also shares much emotional and political investment in the 'conscious' politics associated exclusively with roots reggae culture. Again, Lorde helps us to understand that the dichotomy between our psychic/emotional selves from the political is a false one that results in an incomplete understanding of the erotic (Lorde 2007, p. 56). I am arguing that within the social context of the dancehall setting the music of lovers' rock and conscious roots reggae create a discursively flexible space where erotic and political boundaries are at once established and at the same time agitated and dismantled to open up multiple ways of feeling.

Black Female Vocalists Within the Lovers' Rock Scene

Lovers' rock has a distinctive Black British male tradition where artists and crooners such as Vivian Jones, Winston Reedy, Victor Romeo Evans, Peter Spence, and Peter Hunnigale have enjoyed popular success in the UK reggae charts on a par if not more so than their female counterparts (Barrow and Dalton 2004). However, it is the voice of black females within the genre that I wish to focus on to explore notions of the erotic, of love and blackness. As I have suggested, lovers' rock was not exclusively performed, consumed or enjoyed by women even though the genre was commonly designated as a feminised sanctuary within the reggae dance hall culture. Whilst lovers' rock created an important erotic space, conversely it also succeeded in creating essentialised notions of women and love. Dick Hebdidge argues that 'lovers' rock is important because it gave British Black women a chance to make themselves heard in reggae music' (Hebdidge 1987, p. 131). This view is also reinforced within the dancehall space itself where the genre's preoccupation with love and romance is often deemed to be the primary and sole concern of women. Within the critical commentary that exists on lovers' rock, most critics have been quite right to stress the popularity of lovers' rock amongst many black female audiences (Barrow and Dalton 2004; Garratt 1985; Hebdidge 1987). In Dick Hebdidge's account of the lovers' rock scene he states,

> What Lovers' rock did was to give young women a voice inside reggae without forcing them to deliver sermons when they didn't want to. It didn't ask them to lay down the law for the 'righteous.' In some cases, in records like *Indestructible Women*, it implied that all laws were made by men anyway and that women didn't have to bow down to any manmade law unless they wanted to. Most importantly, Lovers' rock made it possible for women to sing about real things close to home – things that affected *them*. (Hebdidge 1987, p. 135, emphasis in the original)

But the literature on lovers' rock has not attempted to deconstruct the popularity of the genre amongst black women within the broader contextualisation and socialisation of love as 'women's work'. What I am suggesting is that gendered notions of love combined with historical patterns of sexism and patriarchy have positioned women to be the 'natural' providers of care, nurturance, compassion and service. bell hooks argues that it is common for women to see themselves as intrinsically knowing more about love than men. In her book, *Communion: The Female Search for Love*, she writes,

> Women are not inherently more interested in or more able to love than are men. From girlhood on, we learn to be more enchanted by love. Since the business of loving came to be identified as woman's work, females have risen to the occasion and claimed love as our topic . . . Our obsession with love is sanctioned and sustained by the culture we live in. (hooks 2003, p. 75)

In reggae dancehall cultures, lovers' rock is one such space where women learn to be enchanted by love and are encouraged to see love's work as their business. There are spaces for women to claim contradictory forms of female autonomy within lovers' rock, in spite of the fact that lovers' rock can be legitimately critiqued for positioning women into roles of patriarchal dependency (Hebdidge 1987, p. 131). Indeed, it is also necessary to recognise that autonomy is never clear cut. It is always negotiated within relationships of power. It can be consciously fought for and gained, while imagined or frequently lost. Thus I am scrutinising Hebdidge's claim that suggests that black female vocalists simply found their voice, agency and autonomy in lovers' rock music, enabling them to articulate those 'things that affected them', namely romantic love, within the broader oppositional culture of reggae (Hebdidge 1987, p. 135). With good intention, Hebdidge's assertion sets out to support young black women both as active participants in the cultural production of lovers' rock and as active critical agents giving voice to 'their' own reality. Whilst this observation seeks to underline black female autonomy, I believe it can also dangerously essentialise the black female experience because it suggests that what actually affected '*them*', black women (as opposed to black men), was a specifically gendered female preoccupation with everyday love and romance. Thus love and romance are positioned by Hebdidge as being antithetical to those 'sermons' and chants of 'righteousness', voiced by male contemporaries in the 'conscious roots' reggae tradition. Although Hebdidge acknowledges that some common yearning may exist between our 'yearning for a lover and deliverance from Babylon' (Hebdidge 1987, p. 134) the assertion rests on the false dichotomy between erotic desire and political aspiration. Quite often the so-called 'sermons' were part of the everyday social realities that impacted upon the experiences of black men and women. Within the UK reggae dance-hall scene, racialised forms of oppression became entangled with complex gender politics and class marginalisation which were also interwoven into our loving and erotic relationships. Films such as *Burning an Illusion* (1981) and *Babylon* (1980) represented the intersection of these structural and social factors that affected both black men and women in very specific ways. The soundtracks to both films utilise a mixture of conscious roots reggae and lovers' rock as the cultural back drop to Caribbean life in Thatcher's Britain during the early 1980s. Within *Illusion*, the erotic is an important space for suggesting that loving relationships between black men and women (romantic or otherwise) served as critical sources of affirmative and transgressive power that sustained marginalised communities. However, these relationships were also under frequent pressure from social factors such as unemployment, poverty, social marginalisation, domestic violence, and racism. Directed by Menelik Shabazz in 1981, *Illusion* demonstrated that black consciousness as a counter-cultural critique of racism and imperialism was as 'close to home' for many black women as it was for black men. Furthermore, these political factors were intimately connected and determined the realities of the trials and tribulations of erotic loving relationships amongst black working-class communities in Britain.

Many female lovers' rock artists began performing as teenagers during the early development of the lovers' rock scene (Barrow and Dalton 2004; Garratt 1985; Hebdidge 1987). One group by the name of '15, 16 and 17' were exactly 15, 16, and 17 when they recorded their track, 'Black Skin Boy'. It is commonly reported that Louisa Mark, was possibly as young as 13 when she recorded her cover version of 'Caught You in a Lie' (Garratt 1985). In an interview conducted by Sheryl Garratt for *The Face* magazine in 1985, lovers' rock veteran Janet Kay lamented, '. . . I'm sick of the term "Lovers' Rock." It's got so that every time a woman opens her mouth to sing, she's stuck with that label' (Garratt 1985). Leading lovers' rock vocalist Carroll Thompson elaborates on how as a young black woman growing up in England, the struggle to be taken seriously as a musician informed the direction her career would take as a lovers' rock artist. This was equally determined by her deep love and enjoyment of both reggae and soul music,

> I grew up hearing the Supremes, Stevie Wonder, The Jacksons . . . Then there was Minnie Riperton, Aretha, so many. But *Catch A Fire* came out when I was still at school, and it really got to me – Bob Marley and the I-Threes. I really started listening and becoming aware of my roots, my culture, where I'm coming from, and how I should be. That's still there – I love reggae music, and that is my first, natural kind of music . . . In Jamaica, it's always been roots and the men singing about their culture and Rasta . . . And because of that, women always had a low profile. At first it was the same in England, because you only had Louisa Mark, Janet Kay, 15, 16, & 17 and Brown Sugar who had any real success, and I don't think the producers really took women seriously. They thought, 'Oh, they'll just get pregnant and give up, or a man will give them a whole heap of trouble, and there's no point putting money into it.' So they didn't really concentrate on them and give them the credit that was due. Then after awhile it changed as they realised that women weren't stupid, that they *did* want to make a career out of singing. (Garratt 1985, pp. 69–70)

As Thompson's commentary highlights, female lovers' rock artists were engaged in an uphill struggle to be taken seriously to achieve any level of autonomy or agency within the music scene. Indeed, Thompson was emphatic about establishing the parameters of respect which determined how women were both perceived and treated as credible musicians. Having the will to sing was not enough. Thompson suggests that young black women had to employ a high level of self-determination to navigate sexist obstacles and prejudices that faced many black females within the reggae scene:

> It depends on your mentality and what you want to project – if you're the kind of woman who wants to go through all that shit, then you go through it. If you show them that this is your profession and tell them that if they want a woman to mess around with, then they should go to a club and find one, then they'll treat you with respect. And in this business you have to have respect if you're a woman, otherwise you won't get far. (Garratt 1985, p. 70)

Thompson became so frustrated with waiting for attitudes and prejudices to change, that she formed her own company C&B, where she wrote, sang and produced her own records (Garratt 1985). In an industry where young women often felt pigeonholed by male peers into being merely 'lovers' rock singers', female agency for young women in lovers' rock could not be so easily claimed by notions of 'giving voice'. It is important to take seriously how such agency was negotiated and compromised by age, a lack of female ownership of recording studios, the rarity of finding female musicians to form female bands and the fact that some male bands were reluctant to be seen in public playing love songs for girls (Garratt 1985).

Thompson's account of her experience as a lovers' rock artist also challenges the presumption that black women as both artists and as listeners had very little interest in black oppositional politics (Barrow and Dalton 2004; Hebdidge 1987). Black women were assumed to be generally disengaged cognitively, emotionally, and socially from the political discourses and aspirations that were troubling black men. Hence, black conscious music was presumed to offer very limited expressive opportunities for black women in Britain in comparison to African American soul music:

> And to most black British girls living in places like Tottenham and Handsworth, Africa didn't look much like home. For behind the success and popularity of Lovers' rock among the female audience there was another message. The message was that the soul of the big American cities, of Aretha Franklin and Diana Ross and new singers like Gwen Guthrie, was there to teach women about a different set of options. (Hebdidge 1987, p. 135)

As Thompson's discussion above suggests rather than being an alternative option to conscious roots music, African American soul music was one option amongst the many discursive transnational sound cultures that contributed to the syncretic noise of lovers' rock. I would also add that whilst Africa may or may not have looked much like home, Handsworth and Tottenham did not always *feel* much like home either, particularly as it was these locations that exploded with successive urban uprisings ('riots') during the 1970s and 1980s. These urban areas were centres of intensified racial tensions and social resistance in the UK where black women were very much a part of, and in specific cases, the impetus for community struggles against police harassment and brutality. Take for example the shooting of Dorothy Cherry Groce by police officers in Brixton that sparked the Brixton uprisings of 1985, and the death of Cynthia Jarrett who died a week later during a police raid of her north London home in Tottenham, an incident which became the main driver for the Broadwater Farm 'riots' (Gilroy 2006).

When lovers' rock is constructed as a sanctuary for 'female concerns', we underestimate the complex relationships that black women have formed with oppositional black movements alongside sexual politics and the politics of gender. It is not only possible, but necessary for black women to be thinking through and feeling our way around our multiple political and erotic positionalities concurrently without these identities necessarily being at odds or separated from each other. The feminisation of lovers' rock does not allow for the intersectionality and multidimensional engagement of black female experiences. It also fails to recognise the ways in which sexism can create the conditions that keep these feelings and experiences disconnected. Our intersecting experiences can pull together the complexities of location, sexuality, race, and gender alongside an engagement with love and decolonising politics that permits lovers' rock not to be simply antithetical to roots and culture but engaged in a much more dialogic and discursive relationship with notions of freedom and black liberation within the social contexts of black people in Britain and beyond.

Blocking the Vibes of Jah

As discussed above, the cultural emergence of lovers' rock took place in a social context where reggae music was characterised by the predominance of sound system/deejay culture. The scene was also highly populated by reggae bands and artists from the UK and the Caribbean including Aswad, Matumbi, Steel Pulse, The Wailers, Burning Spear, and Third World amongst many others (Barrow and Dalton 2004). Roots and culture became synonymous with blackness, or indeed, Africanness, as a political identity in reggae music.

Conscious roots music incorporated an African centred narrative of Rastafari repatriation back to Africa, resistance to and liberation from 'Babylon' oppression, whilst articulating racialised discourses that affirmed and validated black humanity (Campbell 1985). Indeed, within conscious roots music, love as a political category had taken a revolutionary stance. Love was conceptualised beyond the domestic sphere and used to service broader political concepts of freedom and emancipation. Love as a form of psychological political insurrection demanded decolonisation of our minds from the self-destructive and harmful remnants of black subjugation and brutalisation as a consequence of three centuries of plantation slavery and white colonial rule. In one obvious example of psychic decolonisation, Bob Marley charged us to, 'Emancipate yourself from mental slavery, none but ourselves can free our minds.'

However, black humanity and black redemption in reggae music was framed predominantly through male vocal cords. Black female participation was certainly evident in conscious reggae music. The I Threes from Bob Marley and The Wailers and the African American, Sandra 'Puma' Jones from Black Uhuru are just a few notable examples. Indeed, black female audiences could actively choose to occupy their own positions of solidarity within narratives of Rastafari livication and liberation, whilst seeking, feeling and believing in the libratory messages that arose from songs and verses of redemption. However, our loving roles also remained tied to the domestic sphere as the backbone that supported the 'worldly' work of Natty Dread in the quest for righteous redemption. Take for example, the Jamaican lovers' rock track by Horace Andy and Tappa Zukie's 'Natty Dread a Weh She Want', where Rasta love is depicted as a superior if not a more righteous form of loving. Andy and Zuki inform the female object of their desire that she needs love from a Natty Dread, above *all* other men, so *she* can keep him and care for him without the need to share him! Thus, the 'girl' is enlisted, for her own good, to love, serve, and facilitate the needs of a 'righteous Dread'. Far from an ethical or equitable form of righteous love, this patriarchal form of love is supplied abundantly from women to nurture and care for men without any acknowledgement of how righteous love leaves women short changed, without any reciprocated desire to fulfil or cater for our own need for love and the erotic.

Female or feminised loving could also be seen to be standing in the way of 'righteous' men. Carolyn Cooper argues in 'Virginity Revamped' that the lyrics of Bob Marley's love song 'Waiting in Vain' expresses an ambivalent representation of women and male sexual desire (Cooper 2000). Cooper suggests that from a male point of view, the transgressive woman in the song becomes synonymous with Babylon as whore, becoming an 'alluring entrapper, seducing the Rastaman from the path of righteousness' (Cooper 2000, p. 350). Similarly, in the UK, it is said that many male reggae bands frowned upon playing lovers' rock music and felt that any female presence on stage could actually be 'blocking the vibes coming from Jah' (Garratt 1985). Lovers' rock was not only characterised as the softer, sensitive side of reggae it was also seen as an obstacle on the path to righteousness. Lovers' rock was disavowed as a musical interlude which allowed women to escape into the frivolity and utopian fantasies of romantic love. As these critics write,

> For teenage black girls, whose dreams of escape were more likely to involve marriage to a caring man than repatriation to Africa, lovers' rock 45s presented a welcome alternative to the diet of militant roots being presented by many UK sound systems. (Barrow and Dalton 2004, p. 396)

The separation of lovers' rock from the labour of radical 'conscious roots and culture' follows a pattern of sexist thinking that engenders what counts as 'serious' and 'trivial' to the transformative political concerns of black people. This creates a false and gendered dichotomy between erotic love and rebel politics which in turn become gendered as female and male respectively. As Lorde suggests, this pattern of thinking falsely separates the spiritual (psychic and emotional) from the political (Lorde 2007, p. 56). In a further example of this 'ism and schism' between rebel politics and erotic love, 'Poko' Walford Tyson, lead vocalist of the 1970s roots reggae band Misty in Roots from Southall, puts it like this, '[We] no longer wanted to sing about love and women. We wanted to do progressive protest music' (Simpson 2007). For Poko 'progressive' music was defined by the expulsion of both women and love from their repertoire of radical political songs. Indeed, for Poko, the frontline of serious struggle was shared not with women, but with white punk bands of the 1970s and 1980s at gigs such as 'Rock Against Racism'. The guitarist, Peter Harris, described the bond formed between roots reggae bands and punk bands as 'very simple'. He explains, 'The punks were the same ... They were seen as dregs of society. We were all anti-establishment, so there was a natural synergy between us' (Simpson 2007). Harris's comments suggest that much more rebellious camaraderie and bonding appeared along the lines of a 'natural' masculinity between black and white male dissidents than across the lines of gender between black males and black females. For 'Poko' and Harris, love and women were one and the same thing, monolithic obstacles that 'blocked' or 'got in the way' of serious rebel politics and spiritual matters.

Conclusion

Lovers' rock stands as a forerunner for a distinctly black erotic music tradition in Britain where sexual politics and public politics converge upon the discursive acoustic environment of the blues party and dancehall. Lovers' rock emerged against the back drop of successive urban uprisings up to and during Margaret Thatcher's reign as Prime Minister of Britain. Deep seated feelings of injustice, disaffection, and social alienation were not uncommon to young black people in Britain during this period (Gilroy 2006). Black communities in Britain on a social level were facing a crisis of deepening levels of marginalisation born out of institutional forms of racism. Irruptions of anger and rebellion against police authorities were not rooted in mindless violence but within a malaise of rage against repeated violations against black humanity (Gilroy 2006). The rage which permeated the inner city streets of Handsworth, Brixton, Toxteth, and Chapeltown, repeatedly during the 1970s and 1980s, was triggered by a cauldron of social factors including high unemployment, police brutality, and harassment alongside racialised social alienation (Gilroy 2006). I am arguing that this period in British history was filled with deep and abiding levels of social neglect, lovelessness, and carelessness ingrained within a vile disregard for black life amongst the British press and wider society. The event that seemed to epitomise sentiments of lovelessness happened in 1981 where The New Cross Massacre killed 13 young black teenagers while they were out attending a house party in south London. The fire is believed to have been racially motivated and remains a tragic yet powerful reminder of the British media's attitude and public disregard for black life which was commonplace during that period (Gilroy 2006). As Gilroy observes,

> The 'black party' had become such an entrenched sign of disorder and criminality, of a hedonistic and vicious black culture which was not recognisably British, that it had become fundamentally incompatible with the representation of black life and experience in any other form. (Gilroy 2006, p. 130)

Critically, within this social context of anti-black sentiment, lovers' rock amplified and affirmed that blackness, through a complex and contradictory gendering process, was nonetheless, worthy of being loved with all of love's imperfections. Lovers' rock articulated a discursive narrative that said black males and females were deserving of a space to express an erotic interlocking politics of desire, joy, pleasure, love, and justice. bell hooks argues that, 'Erotic pleasure requires of us engagement with the realm of the senses, a willingness to pause in our daily life transactions and enjoy the world around' (hooks 1993, p. 116). The public display of the erotic, in the form of song lyrics as well as by the intimate 'slow wine' dance to lovers' rock music, can be interpreted as an open expression and validation of black male and female sexualities and humanity through the public display of erotic pleasure. Indeed, it could be argued that love expressed through lovers' rock was, in of itself, an act of radicalism and rebellion. As Patricia Hill Collins (2005) notes, oppression works by not only forcing people to submit, it also works by rendering its victims unlovable: 'In this context, resistance consists of loving the unlovable and affirming their humanity. Loving black people (as distinguished from dating and/or having sex with Black people) in a society that is so dependent on hating Blackness constitutes a highly rebellious act' (Hill Collins 2005, p. 250). Erotic desire expressed through lovers' rock formed part of a wider discourse on rebellion and revolution that helped to revitalise black life in Britain.

Lovers' rock became a highly syncretic political and erotic concern in the vernacular traditions and transnational networks of Caribbean communities as both producers and audiences of the genre. I have attempted to challenge the way lovers' rock is frequently disavowed and overlooked both within reggae music culture and within scholarly and journalistic accounts that exist on lovers' rock. As suggested above lovers' rock and conscious roots are much more dialogic and discursive than is frequently imagined. Lovers' rock has since its inception remained an integral and consistent component of 'black expressive cultures' where a preoccupation with erotic concerns has long existed in tandem with pragmatic and utopian notions of black liberation (Gilroy 2006). As Gilroy (2006) has suggested both reggae and soul place issues of sexuality, eroticism, and gender conflict as prominent thematic concerns alongside discourses that were previously aligned with notions of freedom. Carolyn Cooper also asks us to reconsider the erotic in the oversimplification of reggae categories specifically in relation to reggae 'culture' and ragga 'slackness':

But even that politically conscious reggae tradition is much more textured than is often acknowledged. The erotic was contained in the protest and often disrupted the simple logic of ascetic cultural warfare. This seductive tension between the erotic and the political continues to energize the dancehall, rub-a-dub style. Acknowledgement of this carnal element in 'conscious reggae' makes it possible to hear the continuities in the work of the contemporary 'slackness' DJs and that of their forebears. (Cooper 2004, p. 76)

A closer 'textured' reading of lovers' rock that takes into account the politics of black consciousness, love and sexuality reveals the tensions between the erotic and political energies that Cooper discusses. I am arguing that the marginalisation of lovers' rock as an erotic soundscape, is due to the following factors: the feminisation of erotic love, the masculinisation of black public politics, and the false separation of erotic discourses about love from the radical politics of liberation found in roots reggae. The gendered fissures of blackness fashioned around sexuality, gender conflict, and the erotic exist in a much more complex and ambiguous relationship to black liberation and resistance struggles than is often imagined. Such complexities do not furnish uncomplicated readings of lovers' rock as a genre that simply expresses 'female' concerns for female audiences. The intertwined forces of erotic politics reconfigure the dancehall not only as a countercultural revolutionary space but rather one that exists at once as discursive location to engage the multiple energies of rebellion, joy, pleasure, and love.

Acknowledgement

This essay was originally published by Lisa Amanda Palmer as " 'LADIES A YOUR TIME NOW!' Erotic Politics, Lovers' Rock and Resistance in the UK" in *African and Black Diaspora: An International Journal* 4, no. 2 (2011): 177–92. Reprinted unaltered by permission from Taylor and Francis.

References

Babylon, 1980. Film. Directed by Franco Rosso, UK.
Barrow, S. and Dalton, P., 2004. *The rough guide to reggae*. London: Rough Guides.

Burning an Illusion, 1981. Film. Directed by Menelik Shabazz, UK.

Campbell, H., 1985. *Rasta and resistance: from Marcus Garvey to Walter Rodney*. London: Hansib.

Cooper, C., 2000. Virginity revamped. *In: Black British culture & society – a text reader*. London: Routledge.

Cooper, C. 2004. *Sound clash: Jamaican dancehall culture at large*. New York. Palgrave Macmillan.

Cumming, T., 2006. Dennis Bovell: the dub master. *The Independent* [online]. Available from http://www.independent.co.uk/arts-entertainment/music/features/dennisBovell-the-dub-master-472069.html [Accessed 31 January 2010].

De Koningh, M. and Griffiths, M., 2003. *Tighten up! The history of reggae in the UK*. London: Sanctuary Press.

Garratt, S., 1985. Lovers rock. *The Face*, March (59), pp. 66–71.

Gilroy, P., 1993. *The black Atlantic: modernity and double consciousness*. Cambridge, MA: Harvard University Press.

Gilroy, P., 2006. *Ain't no black in the Union Jack*. London: Routledge.

Hebdidge, D., 1987. *Cut 'n' mix: culture, identity and Caribbean music*. London and New York: Routledge.

Henry, W.L., 2006. *What the DJ said: a critique from the street*. London. Nu Beyond Ltd.

Hill Collins, P., 2005. *Black sexual politics: African Americans, gender, and the new racism*. New York: Routledge.

hooks, B., 1992. *Black looks: race and representation*. Boston, MA: South End Press.

hooks, B., 2000. *All about love: new visions*. London: The Women's Press.

hooks, B., 2001. *Salvation: black people and love*. New York: Perennial.

hooks, B., 2004. *The Will to Change: Men, Mascutinity, and Love*. New York: Washington Square Press.

Lorde, A., 2007. *Sister outsider: essays and speeches by Audre Lorde*. Berkeley, CA: Crossing Press.

Noble, D., 2000. Ragga music: dis/respecting black women and dis/reputable sexualities. *In*: B. Hesse, ed. *Un/settled multiculturalisms: diasporas, entanglements, transruptions*. London: Zed Books.

Simpson, D., 2007. Roots manoeuvre: Dave Simpson on what happened when reggae and punk went head to head in the UK. *The Guardian* [online], 17 June. Available at http://www.guardian.co.uk/music/2007/jul/20/urban.popandrock [Accessed 13 March 2010].

Stolzoff, N.C., 2000. *Wake the town and tell the people: dancehall culture in Jamaica*. Durham, NC and London: Duke University Press.

Wheeler, C., 1990. *UK blak* [CD]. UK: RCA.

12.

From Third Wave to Third World
Lauryn Hill, Educated and Unplugged

| CHERYL STERLING

LIKE EVERY OTHER PERSON who enjoys popular black music, I love the music of Lauryn Hill. Her album released in 1998, *The Miseducation of Lauryn Hill*,[1] won five Grammy awards and stands as the apex of the power of the spoken word, the songs of all songs, which generate electromagnetically charged, transformational dynamics in a universe filled with fissures and divides, and accessed through the relentlessness of our everyday reductionisms. This evocative title resonates with Michael Campus's coming of age film, *The Miseducation of Sonny Carson* and the seminal work of Carter G. Woodson, *The Miseducation of the Negro*.[2] Also, by including the poet and social activist, Ras Baraka, as the teacher on the album, it further gives greater transparency to its politicized edge. Her talent has sonic resonances; it transcends geopolitical boundaries, tropic desires, localizations and ghettoizations, suggesting a multivocality that only belongs to the greatest artists, and she knows it.

Hill's music belies simplistic categorization as soul, pop, reggae or hip-hop, for it is a fusion of all these genres. This fusion, however, generates a mythos, a personae that everyone wants to claim as their very own. Within her amazing career span, her public identity has shifted from Haitian to Jamaican, reflecting a Caribbeanity that flows effortlessly through her music, but few speak of the young, gifted, black girl from Jersey. Yet, do any Web search for her acclaimed title of "mother of hip-hop invention"[3] and it leads to Lauryn Hill. This chapter attempts to explore the shifting morphology of Hill as reflected in her music. Everyone can attest to the highs of *Miseducation* and the lows of her next album, *MTV Unplugged No. 2.0*.[4] Conjoined, however, these works stand as a subjective chronicle of a young, black woman seeking her own self-actualization and finding it through an interrogation of the spiritual and political. Thus, I read Lauryn Hill's music under the rubric of two distinct but intersecting theoretical paradigms: as a voice of the third wave of feminism and as exemplar of the processes of re-diasporization due to the ease in which she incorporates Caribbean aesthetics in her work and life.

She is a chronicler of our time and our quest for everyday inventions of self, and, ultimately, she manifests what I consider quintessential diva-tude. In her song "Superstar", from *Miseducation*, she rhetorically challenges the egoism that comes with fame and stardom, yet she engages in the game of braggadocio in representing the capacity of her expressivity to transcend momentary celebrity: "Unprecedented and still respected when it vintage / I'm serious I'm taking over areas in Aquarius / Running red lights with my 10,000 chariots." Linking her vocal reverberations to divine essence by evoking the "ten thousand chariots", which, in Psalm 68, symbolize the power of God, Hill knows she is transcending matter to access cosmic energy, and she is not afraid to express it.[5]

These days, she prefers to be called Ms Hill. Her struggles to assert herself as an actualized individual, artist, woman, mother, and a product of a history laden with strife, struggle, negation, oppression and dehumanization is understandable for all women of colour, and thus, she speaks to us in a way that validates not just who we are, but who we long to be. *Sin fronteras*, Hill's music is an expression of her becoming; her expressivity, performativity and politicization suggest a natural fluidity that crosses diasporic spaces.

Hill began her career as L-Boogie with the Fugees. Before the Fugees became the Fugees, there was Pras (Prakazrel Michel) and Lauryn who were high school mates. Vibing on their synergy as a production team, they began making music together. Wyclef, who was a friend of Pras, joined in the production team, replacing some other, unnamed, young women. Yet it wasn't until their second album, *The Score*, that their identity was fully fused and the bridge, the hook, from "Fu-gee-la", "Oooh la la la, it's the way that we rock when we're doing our thang / Oooh la la la, it's the natural la that the Refugees bring / Oooh la la la la la la lalala la laaah, sweeeeet thing",[6] became the marker of identity for the group. The Fugees, taking their name from "refugees", became the voice of a new Haitian Revolution, since Haitian in New York, and I daresay in the rest of the United States, was synonymous with hemophilia, AIDS and boat people. No longer was it a Haiti that existed in isolation; the music generated a resurgence of pride and became a vehicle to fuse pan-diasporic consciousness.

In the song, "Ready or Not", Pras centres this pan-diasporic identity in a discursive challenge to a system that denigrates Haitians, Jamaicans and African Americans. In the verse, "Ready or not, refugees takin' over", he inverts the power dynamic and the social landscape. Linking the mythic insurgency suggested by the identity of the buffalo soldier, to the capricious, unpredictable status as a refugee, he raps, "I refugee from Guantanamo Bay / Dance around the border like I'm Cassius Clay."[7] The video stands as a tropic revision, with the members of the group combating land and aerial troops while running for their lives. Their ultimate invincibility recodes the image of complete outsiderness conflated with the refugee identity because the visuality, in tandem with the lyrical import, allows for an examination of the systemic, political strategies directed against black peoples.

The message of the Fugees and their politicized stylization caused universal rejoicing (at least in Brooklyn) and a sense of validation among black people, who are internationally aware, that yes, "Good things do come out of Haiti." Yes! The Revolution! Yes! The first black nation in the West! And, Yes! Barbancourt rum! Yet the music was hip-hop; it was soul and R&B; it was dancehall. The music had a definite Jamaican flava and pure reggae beats. It fused idioms, taking commonalities to a creative height that became the standard for all such music to come. The Fugees were hip-hop innovators, re-creating the medium to intermix musical genres, add in live instrumentation, and feature a female MC that could not only drop rhymes, but also make you cry when she sang.

For Hill, the refugee identity fused with a naturalized feminism. She transcended the image of the "fly-girl" and the conscious female rapper to generate a unique space for female subjectivity in hip-hop.[8] "Ready or Not" becomes exemplar of her attitudinal engagement and rhetorical capacity when she renders a cognitive segue between the insurgency of feminist positionality and its objection to masculine posturing, rapping "So why you imitatin' Al Capone, I be Nina Simone and defecating on the microphone." Not only is Hill asserting her voice as a an emcee, but articulating a point of resistance that incorporates a vivid herstory from which she ascends. Her palimpsestic relationship with these activist foremothers helps launch her into the mode of quintessential *divatude*.

Craig Werner likens the way Hill communes with her forbearers to Yoruba musicmaking traditions where the younger generate incorporates works of the elders to create something new, or at times just inflect the old with a new creative element to allow both the ancestral and the present to co-exist in harmony.[9] With her acapella rendition of "Killing Me Softly", on *The Score*, Hill not only gave homage to Roberta Flack, who sang the original version, she reinserted her into lives of the hip-hop generation. And, like a cosmic flash, all who heard the Fugees version knew that Hill was the voice of the age and the period. It was only a matter of time before we would hear her solo debut, and we waited. The Fugees were live and rocking and, whether Haitian or Jamaican, their Caribbeanity combined so seamlessly with an African Americanness that allowed these multiple forms of blackness to at least musically overcome their fractured, conflicted and striated identities. Hill does indeed give us hope for a more unified future, when she sings, "Everything is everything / After winter must come spring / Change, it comes eventually."[10]

The Fugees created three original albums together and one remix of their greatest hits. However, they never finished their last venture, which would have celebrated their reunion. Through them, the genre of hip-hop bohemia emerged from its tired tag of socially conscious rap. Within this bohemian sensibility, we find ourselves in the middle of a re-diasporization: migration waves in and out of the Caribbean, Latin America, the US South, the urban North, Canada and Europe. It includes children who may have been born in these Northern metropolitan centres, for whom such movement is just a plane ride enabled by the sanctioned passport they carry, who easily transit from one urban environment to another, from one metropole to another, and who go "back-to-Africa" on vacation for at least two weeks. This re-diaporization to which I refer has resonance in Paul Gilroy's earliest concepts of diaspora as delineated in *There Ain't No Black in the Union Jack*.[11] Gilroy's diaspora, as a new form of migration from the Caribbean to the metropole, is a willing one, or as willing as the economic and political conditions of the home island allow, for these settlers are impelled to undertake these journeys because of lack of economic opportunities at home. The question of economic success becomes crucial to understanding Gilroy's diasporic subjects, who, living in a racist England, become automatic third-class citizens, denied both the longed for economic opportunity and possibility of integration in the national framework. The way in which I refer to re-diaspora is structured from Gilroy's concept, but I speak mainly of the children of the first waves of migration, who are simultaneously comfortable and uncomfortable with their Caribbeanness, their Americanness, their Canadianness, their Europeanness, but, who, moreover, can transform that "ness" through language, dress, political positioning, social interaction and economic status to become a different type of hybrid that can move across all diasporic spaces.

This re-diaspora simultaneously challenges and affirms Kwame Appiah's cosmopolitanism. Appiah defines his notion of cosmopolitanism as "the idea that we have obligations to others, obligations that stretch beyond those to whom we are neither related by ties of kith or kind, or even the more formal ties of a shared citizenship" and "that we take seriously the value not just of human life but of particular human lives".[12] Being "a citizen of the world" is his ideal, and it signifies both "universal concern and respect for legitimate difference".[13] By inference, it suggests a sophisticated, urbane, learned individual with a love of the arts and literature, who travels and enjoys travelling, cherishes and holds a network of social contacts across an international scope and, by extension, is comfortable everywhere and with anyone. While true, in this incarnation, it is a mythic construct, the subject of our re-diaspora often embodies the virtues of the cosmopolitan ideal. However, while Appiah never interrogates the subjectivity of persons in the Afro-Atlantic world, our re-diaspora is predicated on an intimate interaction within it. It may be seen as a movement from one black defined space to another, from Salvador da Bahia to Brixton, with a stop in Senegal. Yet, it does not preclude intimacy or knowledge of "white" defined cultural or social spaces or white peoples, but suggests genuine comfortability within these relationships, derived from the security of privileging one's own defined cultural identity, saturating oneself in it, and other Afro-diasporic forms of expressivity.

It must be noted this form of re-diasporization does not generate the "imagined community" suggested by Benedict Anderson.[14] Within Anderson's concept, the ties that bind members of an imagined community, even those that are personally or geographically separated, are its shared text of language and ideas. The community is imagined because members may never meet or have any level of concourse, yet they have an image of communion that results from access to connective texts, largely through the print medium. If we take this value into our current mediatized world, then global access to CDs, music videos, DVDs, television and satellite radio allows this imagined communion to flourish. While the re-diaspora has its shared texts, it is predicated on actual movement and social interaction, as well as building and sustaining a global affinitive network that may be based on nothing but the personal. It signifies generating connective strands, finding intellectual and psychic sustenance within these transcultural spheres with other black peoples, who are undertaking similar pan-African journeys. It is a network built on what Ralph Ellison refers to as an "identity of passions",[15] which in concourse can easily transit between understandings of what constitutes reggae from Birmingham, kompa from Haiti and kwaito from South Africa. In a more axiological form, it is not defined by or limited to race or class discourse, rather it forms an interlocutory web of political and cultural interactions that interpolates imperial and colonial orders, mediates capitalist commodification, and finds sustenance in multiple forms of aesthetic and artistic expressivity.

It is in the midst of this translocative fluidity that I find Hill. Centring her in this process of re-diasporization, Hill's music attests to the ways in which her quest for individuality and happiness transcends spatial constructs, as it is predicated on multiple chains of association that create this new type of identity for a young, gifted, black woman. Her concerns are about the world and the force of the spiritual within it, filtered through an experiential, empathetic affinity with the personal and the globally institutionalized struggles of black peoples. The field of identification radiates from the global to the local, but rather than suggesting a form of limitedness, it emphasizes instead our connectedness in the visceral real space where "Hip-Hop meets scripture".[16]

Hill is an African American, born in South Orange, New Jersey, possessing a Caribbeanness that is casual and natural. However, it is her rendition of "Turn the Lights Down Low" on the album *Bob Marley: Chant Down Babylon*,[17] which sealed that identification. While the song gives valence to the spirit of ancestral evocation that Craig Werner sees in Hill's music, the album's premise is to introduce the music of Marley to the new hip-hop generation. In debates with other scholars and lovers of her music, she has been claimed by multivalent Caribbean identities. We long for her to be Caribbean so much that what might be called her "Marleyfication"[18] becomes symbolic of a rightful ascendance to the throne of a musical dynasty. Hill, growing up in the midst of a musically oriented family, was weaned on soul and R&B music.[19]

As with so many young people growing up in the 1980s United States, hip-hop was the medium for expressivity, and, as she has said, she has an enduring love for Bob Marley's music.[20] Her music returns hip-hop to its pan-diasporic incarnation, as a fusion arising from the use of Jamaican sound systems in tandem with a rap overlay. Hence, her body of work nullifies what Tricia Rose characterizes as hip-hop's attachment to localities, the emcees grounding themselves in their community to articulate from that specific paradigm.[21]

Her journey and musicality transcend concepts of physical, geo-political borders to generate a new chord in the global sonic flow. We can attest, from her album *MTV Unplugged*, that the journey, for her, has less to do with physical space and everything to do with the spiritual. This spiritual quest has caused many to think that she is erratic and unhinged. I take her words to explain her behaviour, as she says: "The view is that I'm unstable, which is reality. But what I realize I've become is a mad scientist who does the test on themselves first."[22]

Dave Chappelle's secret block party in 2005 was the site for the reunion of the Fugees. We may never know what really impelled them to split apart, but in that intervening moment we saw an unparalleled Hill, in transcendent glory and in full abjection. When she returned as Ms Hill, she did not stay long and the Fugees reunion died before it was touched again by cosmic energy. She tells us that her absence from the public eye allowed her to find a safe space, to find that inner self, the fortitude needed to face the challenges of being a black woman, a brilliant woman even in spaces of negation:

> For two to three years I was away from all social interaction. There was no music. There was no television. It was a very introspective and complicated time because I had to really confront my fears and master every demonic thought about inferiority, about insecurity or the fear of being Black, young and gifted in this Western culture. It took a considerable amount of courage, faith and risk to gain the confidence to be myself. I had to deal with folks who weren't happy about that. I was a young woman with an evolved mind who was not afraid of her beauty or her sexuality. For some people that's uncomfortable. They didn't understand how female and strong work together. Or young and wise. Or Black and divine.[23]

Hill's focus is on internal transformation and personal fortification to combat her own private moments of self-doubt and social misperception. As a performer who helped define the hip-hop age, she is the *griotte* of the third wave of feminism. This third wave often refers to the current phase in the US women's movement, although Patricia Mohammed, professor of gender studies at the University of the West Indies, also locates Caribbean feminism in the third-wave movement.[24] From a US-based standpoint, the first wave speaks to the nineteenth-century woman and the suffrage and abolitionist movements; the second is the modern-day 1960s model, attached to the Civil Rights movement. The third wave is, in many ways, a deviation from and a rejection of mainstream feminism. Coined by Rebecca Walker in *To Be Real*, the third wave is defined by more of what it is *not* than what is:

> For many of us it seems that to be a feminist in the way that we have seen or understood feminism is to conform to an identity and way of living that doesn't allow individuality, complexity, or less than perfect personal histories. We fear that the identity will dictate and regulate our lives, instantaneously pitting us against someone, forcing us to choose inflexible and unchanging sides, female against male, black against white, oppressed against oppressor, good against bad.[25]

Kimberly Springer critiques this concept of the wave, as she suggests that it perpetuates the exclusion of women of colour from the history of women movements and feminist theorizing.[26] Yet it is Beverly Guy-Sheftall who articulates the position of the second waver in response to the third. Feminist principles, she points out, are cross-generational and still relevant. As such, they cannot be dismissed by third-waver positioning.[27] What is apparent is that the second wavers fear that feminism and the feminist movement may be deemed irrelevant, which is not a worry for the third wave. It must be understood that third wavers are not post-feminist; they do not dismiss feminism. However, they find the imposed categorizations, the definitional constructs of what it is to be a feminist, what it means to do feminism in one's work and live feminism in one's daily life, just as limiting as patriarchal discourse.

The third wave of feminism is the *feminism of the now*.[28] It is an acknowledgement of the struggles of the past for female inclusion; yet, it is less about conformity to feminist paradigms and more about the quest for individuality and personal creativity. The third waver thus defies categorizations, for she is in a state of constant becoming, living and envisioning life outside of socially imposed constructs. The concession has to be made that generational differences engender different social relations, attitudes and responses. The third wave is about the quest for freedom from all definitional categories, except those that are self-imposed; it is a quest for personal happiness from women who are already self-empowered. Third wavers give homage to the second wavers who brought them to the point of self-empowerment, but now they want to express that selfhood to the fullest capacity that they themselves allow.

Hill intrinsically epitomizes third-wave confidence in her positionality within the world. She may be the embodiment of what Joan Morgan calls "the daughters of feminist privilege", college-educated, middle-class black girls, who believe that their horizons are limitless, that they can achieve anything, even when faced with the dualism of operational codes like sexism and racism.[29] According to Lisa Jones, external burdens now include the glass ceiling and both mediatized and popularized images of beauty.[30] For third wavers, these issues are aspects of institutionalized social capital that can be subverted from within, in an inclusionary framework, rather than stormed as a Bastille of impenetrability. The point of contention is not one of recognition of differences, as foreground in the struggle faced by the second wavers, but one of reconciliation, of living "lives envisioning or experiencing identities beyond those inscribed on them by the surrounding culture".[31]

The confessional narrative becomes both praxis and theory for third wavers. The phrase "the personal is political" takes on inviolable status. Gina Dent lambastes this narrative, seeing it as "less about changing conditions than converting souls".[32] It is, however, celebrated by Lisa Jones, who relates that "Who we sleep with, how we dress, and the music we listen to define us politically in a more immediate way than who we vote for, what dogma we espouse . . ."[33] It is in Hill's confessional narratives that we see her transformational journey. How can we forget the first song in *The Miseducation of Lauryn Hill*, entitled "Lost Ones", where she allows us to glimpse some of the internal and external dynamics that led to the break-up of the Fugees. Warning us how the combination of wealth and fame leads to "miscommunication" and "complication", the song, at first, seems like another version, or maybe the original, of "Superstar". But it soon becomes apparent that it is a veiled reference to her relationship with Wyclef Jean, who she critiques on multiple levels: from his focus on fame to his preoccupation with women. When she raps "Now understand, L. Boogie's non-violent / But if a thing test me, run for mi gun",[34] it must be understood as more than the normative bombastic stance of the hip-hop artist, rather she is confronting a corrosive past and attesting to her capacity to overcome any struggle. According to Hill, confrontation brought her to freedom, and by giving such testimony, she becomes the "bulletproof diva", the woman who recognizes and has both a sense of agency and capacity to "raise herself up and the world".[35] Her impact is such that the hook to the song, its chorus, "You might win some but you just lost one", becomes the triumphant *coup de grâce* that so many women privately iterate when ending their relationships. The album's empowering messages and collective impact is best captured in Talib Kweli's homage to her entitled, "Ms. Hill". "What the album did for black girls' self-esteem was so important", he states, attesting to the power of her choric will in the world, "Ms. Hill got skills, that's a gift, it's real get ill / What you spit got the power to uplift a hill."[36]

Hill's ability as a messenger and artist flows from the sense that she is one with her audience. She is able to recover a sense of intimacy that transcends the impact of mega-million sales. This is apparent in "Doo Wop (That Thing)" when Hill is warning both sexes about their roles in dysfunctional relationships. By placing herself directly in the narrative, "Now Lauryn is only human / Don't think I haven't been through the same predicament",[37] she speaks from an experiential space, not one of judgment. Morgan, as a hip-hop feminist, calls for recognition of the music's transformative capacity: "I believe that hip-hop can help us win. We can start by recognizing that its illuminating, informative narration and its ability to articulate our collective pain is an invaluable tool for examining gender relations. The information we amass can help create a redemptive, healing space for black men and black women."[38] Hip-hop generates a shared code and impact that allows for what Gwendolyn Pough refers to as "public pedagogy".[39] This is the ability to politically educate and organize in the public sphere by using the energy and the creativity that flows between an emcee and her audience.

For Pough and Morgan, hip-hop must be a tool for feminist empowerment, and Hill galvanizes that energy to ask both women and men to examine themselves. Hill further enters into a crucial contentious point between second-wave and third-wave feminism, as third wavers call for feminism to also confront the ways in which women are complicit in their own oppression.[40] Through the song, Hill demands that women face and address their negative choices and develop a sense of responsibility to self. She enters into the critique of masculine misbehaviours by condemning a man who is "More concerned with his rims and his Timbs than his women / Him and his men come in the clubs like hooligans." Morgan views this as male-centred nihilism, or "straight-up depression *masquerading* as machismo".⁴¹ The ontic significance of Hill's message cannot be challenged. It affirms the ability of hip-hop narrative to be a mimetic form of representation, strategically informing and mobilizing action. Morgan, in also defining feminism as the effort to maintain black-on-black love, voices how Hill's struggle for radical subjectivity can also be seen as a quest for love.⁴² Hill says that "Love is my food. Truth is my oxygen" and, in "Doo Wop", she asks young women and men to undertake that journey to love rather than mutual objectification.⁴³

The confessional narrative also becomes the vehicle to illustrate how Hill's feminism conjoins with her use of the aesthetics and discourses of the re-diaspora. In a song like "To Zion", Hill exposes the conflict that surrounded her when fame and motherhood collided, giving us a depth of understanding of her reflection, deliberation and commitment to exercising her agency. When she plaintively sings, "I chose to use my heart", her message reverberates with all (proto) mothers; it is a visceral, real moment that cannot be defined because it exists beyond the verse and lives in the emotionality it conveys. Morgan calls for the recognition of "hip hop's ability to articulate the pain our *community* is in and then use that knowledge to create a redemptive, healing space".⁴⁴ With Hill, the redemptive quality of her music pivots on a purposeful interdiction of injurious choices and a celebratory manifesto of the good ones. However, it is also in the song "To Zion" that Hill profoundly engages in the "diaspora literacy" to which Vévé Clark gives voice: an understanding of the stories, tropes and allusions across different diasporic communities.⁴⁵ Such a hermeneutic sensibility is the ontological base for the communicants in the re-diaspora.

When Hill sings about "Zion", she simultaneously evokes the Zion of the Rastafari and the Zion in African-American folklore, with each predicated on the extrapolation of biblical mythos to their individuated circumstances. Zion is the biblical promised land and, to both groups, it became a symbolic evocation of Africa and an articulation of a desire for freedom from oppression alongside a desire for psychic wholeness, and acceptance of their humanity. While the song, "To Zion" is obviously about a mother's love for her child, it is in diachronic and dialogic engagement with these ancestral longings and political ideations. In Hill's live performance of the song with Carlos Santana at the forty-first Grammy awards, she elaborates her expression of Rastafari ideology. Even with its attestation of a "One Love" ideation, Rastafari demands an identification with Africa. In this performance, the background of the stage is at first ribbed with red, green and gold – colours that symbolize the blood of black people, the land of Africa and the riches it holds. It then morphs into a portraiture of an Ethiopian saint, recoding Ethiopia as a symbol of freedom and the land that gave birth to the Rastafari messiah Jah, Haile Selassie I, the former emperor of Ethiopia. Hill, dressed in white, the colour of purity, stands centre stage, and in-between her soulful rendition of the song, she periodically gives a little *skank* movement in response to the reggae beat in the music. As the background continues to shift from an image of the open savannah to row houses someplace in the United States, the visuality of the re-diaspora unfolds in tandem with its vocal and sonic reverberations.

Hill has not stated that she is Rastafari, but the visual tropes she employed in this performance of "To Zion" and the spiritual codes she renders in her music are so endemic to Rastafari beliefs that it is impossible not to see how Kwame Dawes's concept of "reggae aesthetics" functions in her music. Dawes postulates reggae aesthetic as part of an overarching Caribbean aesthetic. Reggae, according to Dawes, in its connection to Rastafarian ideology, "encourages dialogue between the temporal and the eternal, between politics, issues of current social interest, sexuality and spirituality".[46] Hill embodies the artistic image Dawes constructs of a prophetic figure, who stands outside of society and challenges its significations. The artist is in a position of uncomfortableness or outsider-ness because of the messages she has to give, but, ultimately, it is a dialectical relationship with the artist embodying the role as social activist in the community. It may in turn become a self-reflexive role through the engagement of the *world* through the *word*; the artist must delve internally to conjoin lyrical engagement with social commentary.[47] Hill's connection with Rastafari discourse emboldens that prophetic stance made most apparent in her album *MTV Unplugged*.

MTV Unplugged was the long awaited sequel to the mega tour de force of *Miseducation*. The only comparison that can be made to *Miseducation* is the continuation of the confessional, to the point that she has a crying outburst in the midst of "I Gotta Find Peace of Mind". Unplugged, as a musical term, signifies a live performance without acoustic or electronic accompaniment. With this album, "unplugged" takes on double signification as it attests to what critics have described as a breakdown,[48] but what I see as a process of enlightenment. The effects are natural, rather than constructed through electronic filters, allowing for the raspiness in Hill's voice to seep through, and for its receptors to immerse themselves in its unadorned sound because the only accompaniment is an acoustic guitar. Joking on the album that she "looks like a hip-hop folk singer",[49] Hill does indeed embody this awkward dualism. Dressed in a casual jean outfit with her head covered by a scarf and baseball cap, it is another visual testament to her naturalness of expression. In the first interlude on the album, she tells the audience the following:

> Every single one of these songs um is about me first. Me first. Um. It was like, you know, a period of time where I was just out, you know just, just gone from the public, and I came to terms with the fact that I had created this public persona, this public illusion, and it became; it held me hostage. Like I couldn't be a real person because you're too afraid of what your public will say. And, at that point, I had to do some dying and really accept the fact that look, this is who I am and I have to be who I am, and all of us have a right to be who we are. And whenever we submit our will, because our will is a gift, to someone else's opinion, a part of us dies.[50]

Hill repeatedly uses the phrase "this is reality" on the album, and for her it means taking control of her own image, voice, music, life, love, career and destiny.

In this work, Hill fully takes on the issues of the world and evolves a feminist sensibility that challenges systems of oppression and includes the need for love, family, motherhood and self-actualization. She claims what Morgan terms "the right to imperfections and vulnerabilities" in a way that subverts the "Strong Black Woman Syndrome", the myth of the black superwoman, the emasculating bitch whose forceful personality dominates all around her and always appears in control.[51] The "Strong Black Woman Syndrome" validates the socially sanctioned façade that places black women in this in-betweeness of obscure visibility, being simultaneously objectified because of the strength they are supposed to embody, and repressed because it denies them access to an articulatory capacity to express their emotional, psychic and physical traumas.[52] It differs from the "bulletproof diva" because the diva stance is a point of articulation that allows beauty and sexuality to be as equally important as voicing one's empowerment. Hill, however, states that she is shedding that model of divatude, her enslavement to the cult of beauty, and turning inwardly to develop her spiritual self and free her voice. In what seems to be her last public interview, Hill gives warning that the old public persona was just a front: "People need to understand that the Lauryn Hill they were exposed to in the beginning was all that was allowed in that arena at that time. There was much more strength, spirit and passion, desire, curiosity, ambition and opinion that was not allowed in a small space designed for consumer mass appeal and dictated by very limited standards."[53] Hill may have been the product of someone else's phantasmic vision, but in her purposeful subtraction from public life, Ms Hill emerges.

MTV Unplugged is the testament to that freedom, wherein Hill liberates her political voice and melds it with her spiritual beliefs. In a song like "I Find It Hard to Say",[54] Hill creates a nuanced invocation of the Amadou Diallo fiasco. She states that she wrote the song long ago, but did not perform it, because she was afraid that her call to "rebel" would be taken literally by the public. Diallo's story is well known and need not to be repeated here, but, in this death, he transforms from a sacrificial tragedy to a political tragedy. Hill laments, "I find it hard to say, that everything is alright / Don't look at me that way, like everything is alright / Cuz my own eyes can see, through all your false pretenses." Within this reflective analysis, she challenges the normalcy under which such brutal acts are viewed. Interweaving the past with the present, she gives voice to the often unchallenged, institutionalized devaluation of the lives of black folks: "You think our lives are cheap, and easy to be wasted / As history repeats, so foul you can taste it / His life so incomplete, and nothing can replace it." Diallo stands within a history of such brutality, ringed by slavery, colonialism and extirpation. The song chronicles a movement from alienation to representation for him, and countless others, insisting on the redemptive quality of truth. Its call to rebel is not a physical call to riotous action, but one that emphasizes the urgency, immediacy and nowness of spiritual and political acts to combat continued injustice.

In "Mystery of Iniquity",[55] Hill's ode against global exploitation, she creates a fragmentary collage of images that challenges institutionalized knowledge and practices. Using the courtroom as a metaphor for the evilness in the world or "Babylon benefactors", as she terms it, wherein "crooked lawyers", corrupt judges, and lying witnesses bear the "false indictments publicized". In this critical voice, she promotes consciousness about the conditions that constitute a system of judgment that revokes the power of God and, instead, promotes material corruption, legal extortion and "counterfeit wisdom". Appropriating biblical codes, she juxtaposes apocalyptic consequences with the healing energy of a posture of redemption: "It's time for rebirth / Burnin up the branch and the root / The empty pursuits of every tree bearing the wrong fruit / Turn AND BE HEALED." Her spirituality, which seems supremely grounded in Rastafari ideology, posits a lost origin or uncontaminated essence that can be regained from the acceptance of divine will and a rejection of materialistic values. Rastafari calls for a unifying understanding of the black experiences in the Western world; it sees the entrapment in the consumerism of Western society as a symbol of Babylon, the biblical site of evil. More so, it revisions the biblical text as both metaphor and actuality that addresses the historical and continued subjugation of black peoples. When she chants, "Renounce all your thoughts / Repent and let your mind be re-taught / You'll find what you sought . . . was based on the deception you bought", Hill is advocating the use of biblical knowledge as a source of truth and as a guide to greater awareness of the world and one's place in it. Hill tells her audience that the songs are ultimately about "the problem, the cause, and the solution" and that "true healing is from the inside out".[56]

Rastafari philosophy, in its mediation, is supposed to enlighten; the practitioner "reasons" (meaning to philosophically debate) to reach transcendental awareness of one's relation to the god-force, the world and the nature of the struggle to be both physically and psychologically free. From the outside, Rastafari philosophy appears to limit women, as they are required to comport themselves, dress and act in the world as exemplars of feminine virtue. It is often forgotten, however, that women also *choose* Rastafari as a way of life. Hill use of this discourse allows her social activism to flourish, embodying the prophetic role that Dawes attributes to reggae artists. It is most apparent in the song "Adam Lives in Theory"[57] that Hill fervently believes that she is offering illumination by sharing a new conceptual paradigm. The biblical Adam and Eve are reconceived through the traumatic lens of systemic delusions and personal failures. Adam now is self-centred and egotistical, more concerned with his appearance than his impact on the world. Eve is a confused, bi-sexual (pseudo) intellectual, who, in longing for love and acceptance, is tempted and exploited. Metaphors for humanity's fall from grace and the manifold problems of the modern world, they both are adulterous and diseased and cannot admit to their sins. Hill offers a simple solution: "Stop walking in pride . . . / Un-learn everything you know / . . . say goodbye, / To this decaying social system." Hill is calling for change in perceptions, for a new acceptance of God into one's life. In the context of the album, Hill exercises a form of performative agency that is consciously constructed to manifest power, but this is not solely the power of the self acting in the world, but the power of the self to choose the god-force. "He won't deny us", croons Hill and divine love brings wholeness to fractured lives.

Hill's spiritual quest has had the expected backlash that any fall from media grace carries. Ever present on various websites is a critique of her indictment of priests, at the Vatican in December 2003, who commit child abuse. Like Sinéad O'Connor's critique of the Catholic Church, the globalized, mediatized environ prefers to sensationalize her conduct rather than offer any understanding of the impetus behind the messages. Hill is accused of being erratic and imperious, such as in her insistence that she be addressed as Ms Hill. She is subtly accused of ruining the Fugees reunion.[58] Her cancellation of tours, lateness to shows and changing appearance are seen as manifestations of her instability. Her latest album, entitled *Ms. Hill*,[59] debuted in 2008, in the midst of controversy; it is unclear whether the songs were sanctioned for release by her or released by the record company without her permission.

Hence, the spectra of critique that surrounds her must be interpolated by an understanding of how the loss of the material capital that comes with her agency factors into media representation. Gloria Anzaldúa states the following: "We are 'written' all over, or should I say, carved and tattooed with the sharp needles of experience."[60] Before we judge Hill, we must also ask, what type of voice does a woman and an artist come to have as a result of her dislocation and self-reinvention in a hegemonic, consumer-based industry and society? Can our societies actually handle the fullness of a black woman's experience? And what does it signify to all levels of society for one of the most popular artists in the world to live a resistant ideology in her personal life and in the public sphere?

We know well that in the hegemonic paradigms under which we live, the black female voice remains authorized and sanctioned when it is in direct dialogic engagement with the black male voice. However, when it shifts into modes of social and societal critique, it is not given the same value as authentic, authoritative discursive engagement. If not given the same cachet in socially sanctioned critiques, what then happens to that black female voice when it speaks from what is presumed to be a site of radical alterity, such as Rastafari philosophy? Rastafari is a foregrounding narrative within the re-diaspora, for it is a pivotal concept in the lexicon of "diaspora literacy", fostering a connective dialogic engagement. It bridges the class divide seen in the intellectualism of diasporic subjectivity with lived praxis. Those who choose to live this ideation find that it promotes a freeing of the voice, and of the self, since one's identity is no longer tied to the material-rhetorical codifications that mark the everydayness of modern day life. Hill's fracturing mirrors her questioning of the interests that so many others had in her stardom. As well, her transformation comes from a social and psychic reinvention of her innermost truth. How can we possibly find fault with that? "Music is supposed to inspire",[61] sings Hill, and we can only hope that she *chooses* to inspire us again.

Notes

1. Lauryn Hill, *The Miseducation of Lauryn Hill* (Sony B00000ADG2, compact disc, 1998).
2. Craig Werner, *A Change Is Gonna Come: Music, Race and the Soul of America* (Ann Arbor: University of Michigan Press, 2006), 359.
3. See sites such as http://www.mtv.com/music/artist/hill_lauryn/artist.html.
4. Hill, *MTV Unplugged No. 2.0* (Sony B000065625, compact disc, 2002).
5. In this song, Hill is also affirming her affinity with Bob Marley's music. In his song "Midnight Ravers", he evokes the metaphor of "10,000 chariots" to signify salvation from the partying, raving lifestyle. Damian Marley also continues the tradition with a song entitled, "10,000 Chariots".
6. Fugees, "Fu-gee-la", *The Score* (Sony B000002B5L, compact disc, 1996).
7. Fugees, "Ready or Not", *The Score*.
8. Layli Phillips, Kerri Reddick-Morgan and Dionne P. Stephens, "Oppositional Consciousness within an Oppositional Realm: The Case of Feminism and Womanism in Rap and Hip Hop, 1976–2004", *Journal of African American History* 90, no. 3 (2005): 253–77. This article discusses feminist articulation in the music of women hip-hop artists and in relation to male rappers in the industry. Also see Cheryl L. Keyes, "Empowering Self, Making Choices, Creating Spaces: Black Female Identity via Rap Music Performance", *Journal of American Folklore* 113, no. 449 (Summer 2000): 255–69. In this article, Keyes categorizes female rappers into archetypal representational models such as "queen mother" and "fly girl".
9. Werner, *Change*, 357–58.
10. Ibid., 359–60. Werner attests to how the Hathaway-Flack duets influenced Hill's development as an artist and the title of Donny Hathaway's debut album *Everything*

Is Everything seems like an inspirational source for *Miseducation*. Hill not only uses its title for her song, but echoes other tracks in songs like "Superstar", "Every Ghetto, Every City" and "Nothing Even Matters".

11. Paul Gilroy, *"There Ain't No Black in the Union Jack": The Cultural Politics of Race and Nation* (Chicago: University of Chicago Press, 1991).
12. Kwame Appiah, *Cosmopolitanism: Ethics in a World of Strangers* (New York: W.W. Norton, 2006), xv.
13. Ibid.
14. Benedict Anderson, *Imagined Communities: Reflections on the Origins and Spread of Nationalism* (London: Verso, 1991).
15. Ralph Ellison, *Shadow and Act* (New York: Random House, 1964), 263.
16. Hill, "Everything Is Everything", *Miseducation*.
17. Stephen Marley, *Bob Marley: Chant Down Babylon* (Island B00003000M, compact disc, 1999).
18. I create the term "Marleyfication" to humorously refer to her partnership with Rohan Marley. It is unclear whether the two are legally married, but they are conjoined and have five children together.
19. Werner, *Change*, 357.
20. Claude Grunitzy, "The Prophet", *Trace Magazine* 57 (July 2005), 154–61.
21. Tricia Rose, *Rap Music and the Black Culture in Contemporary America* (Middleton, CT: Wesleyan University Press, 1993), 34.
22. Hill, *MTV Unplugged No. 2.0*.
23. Joan Morgan, "They Call Me Ms. Hill", *Essence* 36, no. 10 (January 2006).
24. It is important to note the issues facing Caribbean women in this wave are conceived of differently than African-American women. For instance, Caribbean women have the privilege of just being women in their societies, without a qualifying racially coded or ethnically coded prefix to delimit their identities. The central question that Patricia Mohammed asks is as follows: "What will feminism look like or what type of movement will they have, since the signifier 'woman' is now replaced by the signifier 'gender'?" See Mohammed, "The Future of Feminism in the Caribbean", *Feminist Review* no. 64 (Spring 2000): 116–19.
25. Rebecca Walker, "Being Real: An Introduction", in *To Be Real: Telling the Truth and Changing the Face of Feminism*, ed. Rebecca Walker (New York: Anchor Books, 1995), xxxiii.
26. Kimberly Springer, "Third Wave Black Feminism?", *Signs: Journal of Women in Culture and Society* 27, no. 41 (2002): 1059–61.
27. Beverly Guy-Sheftall, "Response from a 'Second Waver' to Kimberly Springer's 'Third Wave Black Feminism?' ", *Signs: Journal of Women in Culture and Society* 27, no. 4 (2002): 1091–94.
28. See Joan Morgan, *When Chickenheads Come Home to Roost: My Life as a Hip-Hop*

Feminist (New York: Simon and Schuster, 1999); and Lisa Jones, *Bulletproof Diva: The Tales of Race, Sex, and Hair* (New York: Doubleday, 1994).
29. Morgan, *Chickenheads*, 59.
30. Jones, *Bulletproof Diva*, 133–34.
31. Walker, "Being Real", xxxvii.
32. Gina Dent, "Missionary Position", in *To Be Real: Telling the Truth and Changing the Face of Feminism*, ed. Rebecca Walker (New York: Anchor Books, 1995), 75.
33. Jones, *Bulletproof Diva*, 215–16.
34. Hill, "Lost Ones", *Miseducation*.
35. Jones, *Bulletproof Diva*, 3.
36. Talib Kweli, "Ms. Hill", *Right About Now* (Koch Records B000BKCXQI, compact disc, 2006).
37. Hill, "Doo Wop (That Thing)", *Miseducation*.
38. Morgan, "Fly-Girls, Bitches, and Hoes: Notes of a Hip-Hop Feminist", *Social Text* 45 (1995): 157.
39. Gwendolyn Pough, "Do the Ladies Run This . . . ? Some Thoughts on Hip-Hop Feminism", in *Catching a Wave: Reclaiming Feminism for the Twenty-first Century*, ed. Rory Dicker and Allison Pipemeier (Boston: Northeastern University Press, 2003), 237.
40. Morgan, "Fly-Girls", 156.
41. Ibid., 153.
42. Ibid., 152.
43. Morgan, "They Call Me Ms. Hill".
44. Morgan, "Fly-Girls", 155.
45. Vévé Clark, "Developing Diaspora Literacy and Marasa Consciousness", in *Comparative American Identities*, ed. Hortense Spillers (New York: Routledge, 1991), 40–60.
46. Kwame Dawes, *Natural Mysticism: Towards a New Reggae Aesthetic in Caribbean Writing* (Leeds, UK: Peepal Tree, 1999), 129.
47. Ibid., 100–101.
48. For more information, see the following articles: David Bauder, "Hill 'Unplugged': Grammy Darling Makes a Baffling Return to Music Scene", *Associated Press*, 8 May 2002, 3D; Richard Harrington, " 'Unplugged': Lauryn Hill's Troubled Soul", *Washington Post*, 15 May 2002, C1; Nick Marino, "Lauryn Hill: 'Unplugged' and Unglued", *Florida Times Union*, 17 May 2002, WE-11.
49. Hill, "Interlude 3", *MTV Unplugged No. 2.0*.
50. Hill, "Interlude 1", *MTV Unplugged No. 2.0*.
51. Morgan, *Chickenheads*, 110.
52. See Sheila Radford-Hill, "Keepin' It Real: A Generational Commentary on Kimberly Springer's 'Third Wave Black Feminism?' ", *Signs: Journal of Women in Culture*

and *Society* 27, no. 4 (2002): 1083–89. Radford-Hill objects to Morgan's characterization of the "Strong Black Woman" and speaks to the desire on the part of second wavers to inoculate their daughters against racism and sexism by presenting an intact self.
53. Morgan, "Fly-Girls", 151–57.
54. Hill, "I Find It Hard to Say", *MTV Unplugged No. 2.0*.
55. Hill, "Mystery of Iniquity", *MTV Unplugged No. 2.0*.
56. Hill, "Interlude 5", *MTV Unplugged No. 2.0*.
57. An article that details the critiques facing Hill is Morgan, "They Call Me Ms. Hill", 154–61. Also see Claude Grunitzky, "The Prophet", *Trace* 57 (July 2005), http://www.trace212.com/new/edspage.htm.
58. Hill, "Adam Lives in Theory", *MTV Unplugged No. 2.0*.
59. Hill, *Ms. Hill* (101 DISTRIBUTION, B0014FC29C, compact disc, 2008).
60. Gloria Anzaldúa, *Making Face, Making Soul! Haciendo Caras: Creative and Critical Perspectives by Women of Color* (San Francisco: Aunt Lute Foundation Books, 1990), xv.
61. Hill, "Superstar", *Miseducation*.

Discography

Fugees. *The Score*. Sony, B000002B5L, compact disc, 1996.
Hathaway, Donny. *Everything Is Everything* (1970). Rhino/WEA, B0000033OT, 1995, compact disc.
Hill, Lauryn. *The Miseducation of Lauryn Hill*. Sony, B00000ADG2, compact disc, 1998.
———. *Ms. Hill*. 101 DISTRIBUTION, B0014FC29C, compact disc, 2008.
———. *MTV Unplugged 2.0*. Sony, B000065625, 2002, compact disc, 2002.
Kweli, Talib. "Ms. Hill". *Right About Now*. Koch Records, B000BKCXQI, compact disc, 2006.
Marley, Bob. 1973. "Midnight Ravers" (1973). *Catch a Fire*. Island, B00005KB9T, compact disc, 2001.
Marley, Damien. "10,000 Chariots". *Mr. Marley*. Universal Republic, B000WM71F8, compact disc, 2007.
Marley, Stephen. *Bob Marley: Chant Down Babylon*. Island, B0000300OM, compact disc, 1999.

13.

Whose Rihanna?
Diasporic Citizenship and the Economies of Crossing Over

| HEATHER D. RUSSELL

WHEN POP SUPERSTAR RIHANNA burst on the scene in 2005, with her hybrid reggae, hip-hop, R&B style, signalled by her highly successful hit, "Pon de Replay", audiences hurriedly Googled to find information about her origins: "Barbados? Yes, Barbados!" Conventionally known for its progressive civility, culture of cricket excellence, and internationally renowned writers like Paule Marshall, George Lamming, Kamau Brathwaite and Austin Clarke – that Barbados would be the site of national origin for one of the most internationally recognized and commercially successful major pop stars of the twenty-first century caught many by surprise. More curiously though, and decidedly more revelatory, have been the ensuing discourses surrounding Rihanna on configurations of citizenship, national pride, Victorian notions of female decency, the global tourist enterprise and global music marketplace, that her emergence and ascendancy have provoked. My chapter proposes to examine Rihanna's Caribbeanity in context of what Alexander Weheliye describes as an attendant "diasporic citizenship" that black popular cultural practice, translocationality, conflicting/contesting/reinforcing sites of national belonging and myriad realms of black expressivity often engender.

In the case of Rihanna, such dynamics dramatically resound within several discursive domains. Such discourses include a radically divergent public discourse in Barbados that on the one hand critiques her "sexualized", "morally questionable" and "scantily clad" representations in media, but on the other demands formal national recognition of her for having placed the nation "on the map" so to speak. In addition, Rihanna's self-conscious choice to feature the Barbadian flag, especially the Trident, in her cultural production, as well as her resistance to standardize her "accent" to conform to US expectations are noteworthy articulations of Barbadian national belonging. At the same time, however, the economic rewards attenuating "crossing over" signalled via the shifts in Rihanna's musical sound to coincide with changing US market dictates mean that there is a clear disjuncture between her musical/rhythmic and national soundings. For example, the variance between "Pon de Replay" (2005), her Caribbean vernacular-titled dancehall-influenced track, with the mainstream pop successes "Umbrella" and "Don't Stop the Music" (early 2007), and in comparison to her most recent seismic transformation towards a harder, edgier, pop-rock sound in "Disturbia" (later 2007) and "Russian Roulette" (2009), have assured Rihanna exponential commercial success. In addition, Rihanna is one of two female artists with the most number-one hits in the twenty-first century. There is then no question that the "Bimshire"[1] artist has unequivocally crossed over into the mainstream of popular culture through her musical production, if not in her public performance of national/cultural subjectivity. Thus, while Rihanna may be crossing, she is not passing.

The invocation of Rihanna as the "face of Barbados" produces, however, a veritable phantasmagoria of colonial history, nationalism, globalization and sexual politics. With her light complexion and greenish amber eyes, Rihanna is not phenotypically characteristic of the majority of Afro-Barbadians who constitute the principal racial group in the nation. Her acceptance in the global popular cultural marketplace as a sex symbol embodying crossover appeal therefore raises numerous, complex issues. The Barbadian public's imagination of itself is inevitably fraught with what Alice Walker calls "contrary instincts".[2] The nation-state invariably feels simultaneously *proud* and *protective* of their native daughter, yet from an economic standpoint the selfsame nation-state must concede the expediency of *marketing* their daughter as "Bajan" commodity at the same time fully aware that Rihanna's commercial viability rests upon enduring colonial legacies which idealize and reward brown skin.

Also, the challenge Rihanna poses to Victorian notions of female social propriety in the Barbados is ineffable. She is on the one hand a pop star, attiring herself and expressing herself within the popular cultural marketplace in ways that reify her commercial appeal, and (not to strip her of agency here) which perhaps conform to her own necessarily dynamic ideological choices about self-presentation. But, as the *first* Barbadian superstar, she implicitly carries the burden, the sheer weight of representing the entire nation (willingly or not); for it is especially true in the case of black people that, in the absence of multiple diverse public images, *the one* is always already construed as both representative and representation. The horrific events of 8 February 2009 add yet another appellative, another construction, another layer to this already highly charged and complicated discursive terrain surrounding Robyn Rihanna Fenty: domestic abuse survivor. In ensuing months, the public discourse framing the intersectionality of domestic violence, sexuality and representation, concerning Brown's abuse of her, would range from the progressive and enlightened to the obtuse and vile.

I attempt to tease out some of these dialectical configurations of nation, diaspora, gender, identity, sexuality and global economy into which Rihanna is interpolated. Weheliye argues that, for a diasporic citizen (such as Rihanna), "the problematic of belonging" concerns where "subjects locate their political and cultural affiliations" and these are "circumscribed by various political, economic and cultural constraints".[3] If this is the case, in the face of such competing, coeval, national and transnational intransigence, is there a modality in which such circumscribing imperatives can be mitigated against, or at least dexterously navigated? Can she be, or is she, truly free to "locate" her political and cultural affiliations where she chooses? In the end, if she simultaneously *belongs* to Barbados and to her global consumers, and is thus answerable to (at least) both constituencies, then whose Rihanna is she?

"Pretty Li'l Girl Rihanna"[4]

In the space of six short years, Rihanna has undeniably proven to be a iconic cultural tour de force. According to Wikipedia and the website Rihannanow .com, she has sold over thirty million albums, won three Grammys, four American Music Awards, numerous awards from Music Television (MTV), Black Entertainment Television (BET), Video Music Awards (VMA), and has received eighteen Billboard music awards. She is the only female artist of the past decade and youngest soloist to have eleven number one hits on the Billboard Hot 100. In addition, she has graced the covers of *Esquire* (named 2011 sexiest woman alive), *British Vogue, Italian Vogue, Glamour, Maxim* and numerous other major magazines. Her endorsements include Cover Girl,

Nike, Gucci, Totes (following her highly successful 2007 hit "Umbrella"), Secret Body Spray, and she has recently released her own fragrance, *Reb'l Fleur*. Furthermore, on 22 February 2008, one month after assuming his post as prime minister, David Thompson named Rihanna "honourary youth and cultural ambassador" of Barbados. I shall return to the transnational implications of Rihanna's cultural production and its global as well as economic dimensions, but for the moment, I want to explore the historical, ideological and political trajectory framing Rihanna's journey towards the bestowal of this national honour. As Weheliye relevantly reminds us, "being a diasporic citizen entails culturally and politically aligning oneself with communities beyond the borders of the nation-state in which one dwells, in addition to negotiating legal and cultural positionalities in relation to this very nation-state".[5]

The dialectical relationship between transnational and nationally inflected "cultural positionalities" (along with unmistakable gender implications) resound in the following poem which appeared in the Barbados *Daily Nation* newspaper honouring both Rihanna's Grammy award and her having been named youth and cultural ambassador of Barbados:

> Rihanna
> Pretty little Bajan island girl
> You have put Barbados on the map of the world
> Like of glimmer of sunshine
> You came with a song
> And had the world at your feet before too long
> Your sweetness and innocence go a long way
> To reach the hearts of those you endear
> Keep up the good work, pretty little island girl
> Keep on putting Barbados on top of the world.
> Keep up the good work and may you continue
> To be blessed.[6]

To many in Barbados, the honour bestowed by Prime Minister Thompson upon "the pretty little Bajan girl" was long overdue. In several editorials published in 2007, demands that the "Gem of Barbados" be given national recognition permeated the Barbados press:[7] "Rihanna is the 'biggest thing' (person) to come out of Barbados ever. Yet to date, not a word of acknowledgement at the national level. How can this be?"[8] While it is true that the Barbados Labour

Party had in fact launched an advertising campaign in 2006 to promote tourism, with Rihanna primarily featured and singing the melody for the ad, many in the public believed the government's move was an insufficient attempt at capitalizing on the ascendancy of the Bajan superstar. The ad featured Rihanna in an early incarnation, singing. She does not speak, and thus does not clearly, concretely and definitively situate herself squarely as *belonging* to Barbados and her history. The absence of such public proclamations of belonging was, in the opinion of many, bereft of vision and belied an ambiguous commitment to making Rihanna and her nation coterminous in the public's imagination.

On the eve of the 2007 MTV music awards, for example, one writer castigated the Barbados Labour Party government's inaction in publically recognizing Rihanna's achievements:

> Here, it is important to question whether the Ministry of Tourism continues to have strong links with this star, and if they do, what programmes are they hoping to put in place where her international recognition *can be used* to help develop and further penetrate markets to promote Barbados? Likewise, what developmental programmes has the Ministry of Culture established? . . . so far both agencies' silence on these matters has been deafening.[9]

At this time, much of the dominant pro-Rihanna public discourse that permeated the print media and radio call-in programmes was undecidedly yoked to an articulation of national pride on the one hand and an unmistakable and concomitant recognition of Rihanna as utilitarian commodity in the global marketplace on the other; for example, a newspaper column penned by the People's Empowerment Party: "Now, if the Ministry of Tourism and the Barbados Tourism had any vision, they would have already established a Rihanna tourism development project dedicated to *utilizing her* phenomenal international market penetration *to promote* Barbados as a tourism destination."[10] Implying that the Arthur government (Barbados Labour Party) lacked the "vision, intelligence [and] self-respect *to claim* [the] international musical sensation for Barbados", the People's Empowerment Party column claimed it would "step into the breach".[11]

There was in the end no need for alarm, as the Democratic Labour Party victory on 15 January 2008 inaugurated the stemming of "the breach" and Robyn Rihanna Fenty was finally given her "just desserts" as part of the youth manifesto of the Democratic Labour Party: " 'Where there has been exclusion there will be inclusion.' . . . Our Youth Manifesto as presented is a contract between the DLP and the young people of Barbados. It is against this background that the Prime Minister signalled the intention to honour our Grammy Award-winning superstar."[12] In addition to bestowing the aforementioned national honour, the Thompson government also gave Rihanna, "a piece of the rock", specifically a portion of land in Apes Hill. The question of claiming Rihanna was thus resolutely foreclosed: whose Rihanna? The newly elected Barbados government answered with a resounding, unequivocal: "Ours." It is clear that the Thompson government's rectification of what was, by their judgment, a monumental and glaring oversight by the prior administration's failure to bestow national public recognition on their daughter Rihanna was more than just political ploy, and yet, their capitalizing on the historic Grammy win alongside their newly acquired national mandate certainly added sweet succour to their political ascendancy.

It is important at this juncture to note that the artist herself has never equivocated on the subject of national belonging. Upon winning the Grammy in 2008, Rihanna's concluding remark in her acceptance speech, "Barbados, I love you, we got one", enunciated with unmistakable Bajan inflection was, of course, emblematic.[13] While it has been the case that artists from the Caribbean who win such international awards often retain their "mother tongues", and I am thinking here of Jamaican artists like Shaggy, Ziggy Marley, Sean Paul, Damian Marley and the like, these artists have won in the *Best Reggae Album* category. In the aforementioned instances, the artists' acceptance speeches are usually not telecast on the primetime airing of the award shows. When televised, however, their purposive West Indian inflections are also integral to the artists' promulgation of cultural "authenticity".[14] Oftentimes, though, Caribbean-born artists (from Harry Belafonte and Billy Ocean, to Heather Headley and now Nicki Minaj), who have been internationally recognized awardees, frequently don the American "twang" and linguistically pass for US-born Americans.[15] As the *Daily Nation* news commentator Mavis Beckles writes of the Rihanna Grammy moment: "Ya did not try to speak or act like other people who have gone there before; ya didn't act as though you were pretending; your Bajan accent came across the airwaves as clear as day . . . Thank you for holding the Barbados Flag high for the whole world to see it, without any prompting or help from any o' we bout here."[16]

The marginalization of Caribbeanity in the mainstream US music market is a point to which I shall return. Suffice it to say, although there has been a decided shift towards the mainstream in terms of the rhythmical and lyrical quality of her music, Rihanna's Bajan-speak remains consistent, evident even as recently as in the "controversial" interview conducted with Diane Sawyer for ABC's *20/20* in November 2009.[17]

Most notable in terms of this symbolic/semiotic articulation of Barbadian national belonging is the fact that Rihanna has featured the Barbados flag and the image of the trident emblazoned on its blue and gold bands, on several of her album covers and in many of her music videos. It is precisely this issue of "marketing" Barbados through her cultural products, however, that created a firestorm that began in June 2007 in the Barbados media. In an interview with *Entertainment Weekly*, the then nineteen-year-old musician responded to a question concerning her post-fame home excursions. Rihanna's response stirred the proverbial cou-cou pot:[18]

> **Rihanna:** A lot of them hate me, but a lot of them love me. I don't really let the ones that hate me stop me from doing what I wanna do. They always have something to say about what I'm wearing or what I'm not wearing, like in the "Umbrella" video. If I wear a swimsuit to the beach, it's a problem, they put it on the front of the newspaper and call in programmes. It really annoys me when people that I try to represent and I try to put them on the map as much as I can – you know, I didn't have to put Tridents in my videos.
>
> **Interviewer:** Put what in your videos?
>
> **Rihanna:** Trident, which is the symbol of the flag. I didn't have to talk about them. I didn't have to even mention that I'm from Barbados. But I do and people kind of take it for granted. They hate me. They talk s—— about me all the time. But I'm like, "Whatever. I'm still doing this cause I love to do it and you're not going to stop me."[19]

For the next few months, myriad and frequently ideologically incommensurate Bajan responses to the interview dominated the media. She was saint. She was sinner. She was the proverbial second coming, holding a distant second only to Barack Obama, to whom she was compared. She was the whore of Babylon, scantily clad, "gyrating" inappropriately and a terrible role model for young Barbadian girls to emulate.

This dichotomous configuration of Rihanna's identity imbricated within the conventional Madonna/whore paradigm has, of course, historical roots, particularly for black women. As Donna Aza Weir-Soley cogently points out, "from the time of the black woman's first appearance on the New World stage, her moral character was beleaguered by vituperative stereotypes steeped in pseudoscientific myth, virulent rumor, and salacious fallacy. As a consequence, black women were conflicted regarding the issue of sexuality. How could they not be?"[20] Such distortions of black women's sexuality, rooted in the racist discourse attending slavery and the commodification of black women's bodies, invariably drove their sexuality underground, especially in the aftermath of abolition, and particularly if they desired bourgeois respectability. Having been historically barred from and hence naturally desirous of assuming such status, many black women entered the twentieth century inadvertently and they also quite consciously reified conventional Victorian ideals regarding the dichotomy between sexuality and its expression, as well as Christianity.

These values invariably persist and perpetuate simplistic, overdetermined and rigid ideas about black female sexual expressivity. Although it can be argued that within the music entertainment industry there has historically been greater fluidity in terms of black women's sexual expression (and I am thinking here, for instance, of the early-twentieth-century blues singers, all the way through to contemporary R&B icons like Beyoncé and Janet Jackson), Rihanna bears the additional burden of singularly representing the entire Barbados nation on the international stage.[21] It is no coincidence, for example, that in the aforementioned celebratory poem, "Rihanna", she is necessarily constructed as a "sweet", "innocent" "girl", aesthetically and ostensibly stripped of sexual allure, sexuality and womanhood.

In one "pro-Rihanna" article, entitled "When Is Rihanna Going to Get Her Just Desserts?", as if anticipating the public's (and by implication the government's) moralistically steeped reticence at honouring Rihanna because of the perception of her sexual suggestiveness, the writer ends by asking: "What is going to happen if we produce a successful movie star who has to perform a bedroom scene similar to those in [soap operas]?"[22] In other words, the writer argues, Rihanna's questionable moral decency is at least manageable, since the Barbados public does not have to witness one of their native daughters simulating sex (the nude photos of Rihanna had not yet been leaked to the press). In her analysis of "the Rihanna debate", Alyson Holder, in the *Barbados Advocate*, reveals that "one of the strongest arguments I have heard so far [against honouring Rihanna] is that Barbados is a predominantly Christian society and therefore such 'behaviour' should not be condoned".[23]

As a consequence, many responses to the *Entertainment Weekly* interview castigated Rihanna for her "arrogant" articulation regarding having "put Barbados on the map", with a concomitant denouncement of her moral character. One of the most fascinating convergences of nationalism with Victorian and Christian idealism, however, is offered in a piece published in the *Daily Nation*, "Pray for Rihanna". In this editorial, Phillip Knight enjoins not only the Bajan public but all Caribbean Community (CARICOM) citizens to have a prayer for Rihanna *every six months* in all churches:

> This *young child* ... needs our prayers and 100 per cent Bajan support ... *her tiny body* is going through some mental and physical battering [referencing her work schedule] ... Do not envy her ... She is correct to return to Barbados every month or two ... We have to keep her in our prayers so her health, wisdom, understanding and compassion are endless, thanks to the blessings and mercy of God Almighty ... we must share her with the world. We must protect her from this same world. Yes, we must pray to God to protect her now and for all time.[24]

Here, the paternalistic infantilization of Rihanna is revelatory. She is a young, tiny-bodied child subjected to the potential evils of an immorally encroaching world. Safety and protection from such secular exploitation are to be found in the coterminously operative domains of the church and the nation-state, which must, according to Knight, necessarily operate in lockstep.

Responses to Knight's editorial were as ideologically problematic and as discursively revelatory as was his own. Beginning with a sardonic assessment of "this little country" which "possesses human resources out of all proportion to its size", Olutoye Walrond enjoins: "Where else would we find the extraordinary ideas of a Phillip Knight?" Continuing the idea of the proposed bi-annual CARICOM prayer for their Bajan daughter, Walrond offers her own spiritual recommendations:

> So let's all pray for Rihanna ... this poor "child" [who] has so much limited control over her own life, that she has to work like the proverbial "Kendal mule" ... Let us pray that one day she will regain this control [and cease] *the kinds of erotic gyrations* she indulges in on stage. And while we are praying *let us ask God to turn her into a true role model* for young girls, who may not want to walk around with three-quarters of their bodies exposed.[25]

No longer the eternal innocent, unequivocally not a "child", and certainly not a victim of the tyrannical entertainment industry, here Rihanna is the corrupter-incarnate, the despoiler of young girls bereft of decent role models, who properly covered, comport themselves with moral rectitude and Christian decency.

In a similar vein, Etta Best's piece "Who's Envying Rihanna" commences with the author's admission that she was "astounded by this man's [Knight's] foolishness about the people of Barbados envying Rihanna". Continuing, she rhetorically asks: "What is there to be jealous of . . . what is so important about a young woman holding a mike in her hand on a stage and gyrating? Is that the kind of role model you want our future generation to emulate? . . . What do you want Barbadians to do Mr. Knight – idolize Rihanna like an ancient deity?" Her concluding statement, the only declarative juxtaposed against a litany of interrogatives, recalls the moral admonitions of the previous Walrond response: "Accepting God as our mediator and being baptized is what we Barbadians should be very proud of, not Rihanna's accomplishments."[26]

Thus, in the months leading up to the bestowal of the 2008 Barbados national honour, Rihanna was caught up in a maelstrom of controversy regarding her suitability as national representative. Deified on the one hand, demonized on the other, in neither case was she liberated from the strictures of the society's ingrained Victorian codes governing female sexuality and the deeply entrenched discourse of Christian decency. To be publicly sanctioned in the public domain was to be necessarily stripped of all markers of womanliness – to be forever the "pretty li'l Bajan girl". To be acknowledged as possessing an autonomous sexuality was to be necessarily stripped of all legitimate claims to national recognition.

Good Girl, Gone Bad

In the midst of these dichotomous, dialectical national permutations, Rihanna's sound, her physical appearance, her demeanour, began to reflect a hardening, darkening, anarchic quality, so that by the close of 2007, Rihanna could no longer be legitimately claimed as the "pretty li'l Bajan girl".

Cutting her long tresses, and donning a sharper, shorter, edgier hairstyle, the aptness of Rihanna's 2007 album title *Good Girl, Gone Bad* was an unmistakable declaration of independence from the Bajan elders. In addition, the release of the single "Disturbia" in June 2008, with its bleak, dystopic, haunting sounds, its ominous images of speaking "faded pictures on the wall" and "disconnecting ... calls, the phone don't even ring", captured in dread terms a slow descent into madness, with the phrase "I'm going crazy" as its refrain. The "Disturbia" music video was equally haunting – a veritable meeting of Michael's Jackson's "Thriller" set to T.S. Eliot's "The Wasteland". The song, though not written by the singer herself, clearly symbolized the emergence of Rihanna as iconic pop star and unequivocally as hard-ass, bad-ass woman. Donning black leather, several tattoos (albeit carefully placed so as not to disrupt her "Cover Girl" appeal) and short black hair, it was clear that Rihanna was no longer concerned with national legitimization and approval. But what of her diasporic, transnational appeal? Are we to read Rihanna's aesthetic overhaul as a purely self-generated movement towards greater autonomy and freer self-expression?

It would be disingenuous to overlook the fact that, in terms of commercial and critical success, both of Rihanna's first two albums, *Music of the Sun* (2005) and *A Girl Like Me* (2006), were criticized for their "lightweight dancehall and R&B jams [which] lack [the]ear-bending boldness" of her critically acclaimed song "S.O.S.".[27] In truth, with the notable exceptions of "Pon de Replay" (2005) and "Break It Off" (2006), Rihanna's dancehall-inspired soft reggae and ballads had not enjoyed mass commercial support. Two factors seem relevant here in terms of global market dictates: one, reggae (dancehall in particular) has a shelf life of a few years each decade, in terms of penetrating the foreign pop market and the United States in particular. Rihanna's initial ascendancy coincided with the then huge successes of Sean Paul's *Dutty Rock* (2002) and *The Trinity* (2005), alongside his major collaborations which included Beyoncé and Keyshia Cole, and also with Damian Marley's *Welcome to Jamrock* (2005).[28] With these successes, dancehall crossed over into the mainstream in the early to mid part of the new millennium. By 2008, mainstream public interest in reggae was on the decline. In addition, loyal consumers of reggae and dancehall tend to expect lyricism coupled with an attendant sociopolitical consciousness critiquing and engaging issues such as racism, poverty, violence and government corruption, articulated in at least a few of the singles an artist releases. Or, conversely and concomitantly, both reggae and dancehall connoisseurs expect overt raw sexual lyricism delivered in authentic vernacular, be it Jamaican, Spanglish or even Kréyòl. Rihanna's songs heretofore have articulated no such broader sociopolitical implications, unflinching sexual expressivity, nor overt use of "nation languages".[29] Perhaps as her fame increases and greater artistic freedom is granted, we may very well witness such ideological shifts. Or perhaps her artistic as well as aesthetic interests will lead her in other directions. For the moment, however, Rihanna's clear flirtation with hard rock poses an interesting counterdiscursive narrative to both the encroachments of national and regional expectations as well as the pop music industry's facile dictates regarding her lyrical soundings.

In the aftermath of the 8 February 2009 incident in which Rihanna's then boyfriend Brown punched, bit and choked her, all of the previously discussed dialectics of citizenship, diaspora, identity, sexuality and global economy would coalesce. The national and international critique of her initial decision to return to him, coupled with the vitriolic accusations (mostly outside of Barbados) of her having provoked the abuse were at best disturbing, and, at worst, vicious. Rihanna's return home to Barbados for "safe haven" was both literally and symbolically significant in terms of the issues surrounding national belonging. At the same time, in Barbados, the internal discourse in the aftermath of the domestic violence incident concerned the fact that although Bajans never really approved of the union, her society remained unequivocal and unwavering (if a bit paternalistic) in terms of offering concern and support. Rihanna's subsequent public incarnation as Mohawk-wearing, semi-nude–posing, gun-tattoo–sporting pop icon, along with her highly anticipated and powerful public interview with Diane Sawyer for *20/20*, which coincided with the release of her fourth album, *Rated R*, altogether weave a fascinatingly polyphonous narrative around and within which our ideas concerning "whose" or perhaps who is Rihanna might be articulated.

When the news finally broke that Brown had physically violated Rihanna, the Web was inundated with the widest ranging responses imaginable. Many were outraged by Brown's brutality and deeply sympathetic towards and supportive of Rihanna. However, those who did not want to imagine their native son, the clean-cut poster boy of contemporary R&B, as violator, immediately began blaming the victim. In their Web posts, Rihanna's critics asserted everything from the idea that she had provoked Brown by hitting him first, she had been cheating on him with Jay-Z (long standing false-rumour) and she had given Brown a communicable disease: herpes. So pervasive were these rumours that when I began researching this chapter over two years ago and typed Rihanna's name into Google, tenth on the list of options was "Rihanna herpes", just below "Rihanna new song", and three listings after "Rihanna nasty pictures". Here we might do well to recall Weir-Soley's articulation of the "vituperative stereotypes steeped in pseudoscientific myth, virulent rumor, and salacious fallacy" that plagued New World African women in the eighteenth and nineteenth centuries. The degrading and dehumanizing responses to Rihanna's victimization are a sad commentary on and a reaffirmation of the myth of progress, particularly where racial/gendered notions surrounding black female subjectivity are concerned. As a consequence, Rihanna was unquestionably interpolated into the perniciously persistent nineteenth-century discourse of the black female exotic/erotic who is at once desirable and dangerous, sexually promiscuous and morally corruptive. After the horrific photographs of her ravaged face were revealed (by way of a leak) to the public, there were still numerous attempts to exonerate Brown, even in the face of visual, empirical proof of his guilt.

I was sadly reminded of the moment in Sherley Anne Williams's *Dessa Rose* (1984) when the protagonist, Dessa, a revolutionary, formerly enslaved, fugitive black woman, seeks to conceal her bodily scars, remnants of the whippings and brandings she has borne in enslavement, scars that are encapsulated in and by the "history writ about [her] privates".[30] Dessa has been beaten and branded, in between her thighs. When asked to provide ocular proof of her scars' existence, the white, pro-slavery witness views her wounds as evidence of a "history of misconduct", disobedience and insolence; the white female protagonist in the story, Rufel, "reads" the scars and fabricates a salacious story of sexual relations between Dessa and her slave master. Upon the affair's discovery, Dessa is, according to Rufel (at least initially), justifiably punished by his wife. Thus Williams's novel reminds us that in public discourse, the black female subject is always already simultaneously aggressive and promiscuous. Dessa, on the other hand, wants *only* to conceal this painful private history, perhaps because she knows too well that her scars will be – as they are indeed – misread.

The day after the attack, the *Daily Nation* ran a cover that announced: "She's OK!" and reported that Rihanna's grandmother had revealed that her granddaughter was "doing well". Subsequent reports from the family, clearly under Rihanna's instructions, were intended to diffuse public outrage and militate against public scrutiny: "Rihanna's injuries are not as bad as people have made them out to be. She was not bitten, she was not knocked out, her jaw was not broken."³¹ We know now, finally, from Rihanna's own lips that she was in fact bitten, nearly choked unconscious, punched and badly bruised. When asked in the Sawyer interview about how she felt after having had her criminal evidence leaked to the press, she said: "I feel embarrassed, humiliated, angry when I see the picture."³² At first blush, however, the viewer might imagine (as I did) that she was engaging in the kind of self-loathing and self-recrimination that textured her post-incident (brief) reconciliation with Brown, but upon further explanation, Rihanna clarified: "I fell in love with *that person* . . . it was ugly."

Although there was primarily a mixture of outrage, protectiveness and organization around domestic violence issues throughout Barbados, a few commentators initially, in the aftermath of the incident, could not help but engage in a kind of veiled, paternalistic, "I told you so." In the quite regular humorous column "The Lowdown: To Lou wif Love", in this case published a few weeks after the domestic violence incident, Richard Hoad writes,

> An' den dere is my girl Rihanna. I would like to tell her that for every lifestyle *there are predicted paths mostly leading to perdition*. As Matthew say, "wide is de gate an' broad de road dat leads to destruction". But small is de gate an' narrow de road that leads to life, an' few find it . . . For a pop star like Rihanna, de pattern is fame, fortune, naked in Playboy, abused, love-child for some poppet, drug rehab, downhill. But in each case, we can break dese cycles and stay clean. *Make de right choice, girl!* An doan let no man spoil yuh features.³³

In another piece, regular columnist Beckles comments on "this t'ing which the media all over the world say allegedly happen between our child Rihanna and dat American boy from up in the United States of America". Here Beckles clearly references, as other Bajan commentators did, the US media's continual use of the term "alleged" to describe Brown's crime, in the face of both legal and physical proof of his domestic abuse. Beckles continues by implicitly critiquing Rihanna's choice of an American suitor: "[Brown] did look totally out o' place [in Barbados] wid a piece o' tam pon he head and a T-shirt and talking 'bout he got a whole set o' bodyguards roun' he. Stuppppsssse, looka gimme a break do!"³⁴ In both instances, Rihanna is gently admonished for straying away from her truly authentic cultural values. In this dialectical configuration of diasporic citizenship, the discourse of tacit reclamation of their native daughter, if only for healing, nurturing purposes, is articulated. Brown is clearly cast as displaced outsider – the ugly American who is arrogant and condescending, incapable of integrating into or engaging with a "foreign" value system. In a similar vein, although overtly supported by millions of fans, compassionate contemporaries like Jay-Z, Beyoncé, Kanye West, Oprah Winfrey and many others, Rihanna still rested uneasily; she was not quite fully integrated into the discursive landscape of US national belonging.[35]

In this latter regard, I was viscerally affected by many of the unsupportive Web postings that followed Rihanna's deeply personal, vulnerable, heartwrenching and powerful *20/20* interview. Many of the posts queried Rihanna's credibility, labelling her a lying opportunist who "has run Chris Brown's career into the toilet", and articulating the belief that she had somehow provoked his violent attack, perhaps through physical means. But there was one post that was particularly emblematic of precisely the fraught dialectical relationship between diasporic and national sites of belonging: "All of her videos are disturbing to me. She has a theme of control in all of them . . . She doesn't smile. Those videos are too dark for me. *Those island women are something else, she may have messed around and put the roots on him as well.*"[36] Having exhausted all other avenues through which to disclaim Rihanna's quintessentially and fundamentally *American* narrative of success, abuse, resilience and transcendence, the writer recurs to the ethnocentric discourse of stereotype. In an ironic way, however, the writer is correct, "those island women are something else".

Whose Rihanna?

When, in a pivotal moment, interviewer Sawyer says to Rihanna, "but people have said, 'she seemed so strong' ", as if to imply that strong women do not suffer under domestic abuse, Rihanna interrupts her: "I am strong", she definitively affirms, "This happened to me." Refusing to be scripted into the predefined discourse of victimization, Rihanna articulated a clear refusal to have her life's meaning at twenty-one years old, reduced to one moment in time. Post-interview, the number of posts articulating disappointment that Rihanna did not break down and cry during the interview was striking. Here again, the master narrative imposes itself with expectations of tears and anguish, unable to encompass the quiet stoicism yet feisty resilience witnessed by viewers. A perspicacious (and perhaps honest) viewer would have acknowledged moments in which tears were forming but withheld, and would also have recognized that typically, anglophone Caribbean people just do not cry in public. To cry in public is cultural anathema in the anglophone Caribbean – it is just not done. Perhaps such cultural values can be attributed to the remaining "stiff upper-lip" cultural practices of British colonialism. In any case, what Rihanna's brutal honesty opened up, in particular regarding her reunion with Brown in the months following the incident, especially in Caribbean discourse, was, finally, an honest discussion around the frequency and complexities attending domestic violence. This is a discussion that had historically been foreclosed.

Between February and March, in the aftermath of reports that Rihanna had reunited with her boyfriend, numerous letters to the editor poured into the Barbados presses. An article in the *Daily Nation*, in which everyday Barbadians were polled for their responses to this reconciliation, was indeed revelatory: "She is a Bajan woman. Bajan women does get beat and go back to their men all the time."[37] In another piece, "Secrets Corner: Fleeing Not So Easy", Sanka Price posted and examined some of the public's responses to her question of the week, which was as follows: "Would you remain with a partner if he/she abused you, and if so, why?" Almost all of the respondents, the majority female, said that they would leave if they had the material resources to do so and no children with their spouse. Trapped in the economic realities of financial and parental dependency, for many Bajan women, "getting beat" and "going back" is their only viable option.

Other analysts attempted to place the Rihanna and Brown domestic violence incident in broader context. The regular *Daily Nation* columnist Tony Best revealed that the "central question of domestic violence and its pervasiveness" had "reached epidemic proportions", representing a critical component of global human rights abuses. Best went on to cite other Caribbean and Caribbean diaspora locales, St Vincent, Trinidad and Brooklyn, New York, where domestic violence abuses remain monumental social problems and pose imminent "public health" risks.[38] In a similar vein, the People's Empowerment Party column seized the opportunity to urge all Barbadians, "to use the heightened awareness created by the assault on Rihanna to launch a new and determined nationwide campaign against domestic violence".[39] Once again, invoked, appropriated, *utilized* as representative in Barbadian national discourse, Bajans interpolated Rihanna into the public discourse surrounding domestic violence, about which and for which she could serve as "poster child".[40] Most challenging in this regard, however, albeit the catalyst that forced domestic violence out of the proverbial closet and fuelled such spirited public debate and heightened awareness, was Rihanna's decision to "go back to she man".

In ensuing months, and after assurances that Rihanna had in fact left Brown, the furore of public activity and engaged organization around the global epidemic of domestic violence appeared to have died down in both Barbados and the Barbadian diaspora. Refusing to speak publicly about the case until after Brown's sentencing (25 August 2009), Rihanna finally broke her silence in her November interview. Although naysayers have criticized the interview as a mere publicity stunt designed to promote her album *Rated R* (2009), according to ABC News's records, the evening after Rihanna's interview aired, domestic abuse hotlines experienced a 59 per cent increase in calls, with the teen hotline witnessing a surge of 72 per cent.[41]

At this juncture, however, one was forced to wonder whether, having thrown off the historical, cultural and religious residuals which prescribe bourgeois respectability within her nation-state, and having liberated herself from the global economic industry dictates regarding commercially viable lightweight pop musicians, whose Rihanna would she be now? Would Rihanna now become "the face of domestic violence"? Would she now be *their* Rihanna? I think not. If, in 2006, the shift from "good girl" to "bad" was embodied by Rihanna's aesthetic transformations, her 2009 incarnation was even more powerfully symbolic and culturally resonant. If one has been so publicly abused, how does one refuse to be written into and scripted by such a hugely significant and politically charged moment as she experienced? How does one publicly, metaphorically and aesthetically inaugurate, and unequivocally signal, one's transformation from momentary victim to infinite survivor? To whom would or could Rihanna look to find a model? In whose footsteps could she or might she walk as defiantly Caribbean woman artist on the one hand, unfettered by the Victorian codifications of gender and sexuality, and crossover artist on the other, benefiting from having broken through the dominant culture's proscriptions and prescriptions of both Caribbeanity and urbane banality? Upon whose forbearing strength might she draw to help dramatize and affirm her Caribbean woman's power?

Iconic, iconoclastic, outlaw, powerful, erotic, androgynous and defiant, Grace Jones's self-conscious owning of her ‡*différance* in the global popular cultural marketplace has heretofore been unparalleled.[42] Playfully signifying on Western fears concerning Caribbean women's mystical powers, Jones (as Fulani's incisive analysis of her in this volume demonstrates) fully embodies Toni Morrison's idea of the New World African black woman as "uncontained and uncontainable".[43] Although Rihanna has herself playfully commented that she was invoking the *101 Dalmations*' villainous Cruella de Vil's "edgy, dark and hot"[44] style, it is unmistakable that Rihanna was purposively invoking and, I would add, despite her protestations to the contrary, paying homage to Jones. The August 2009 issue of *Italian Vogue*, featuring Rihanna on the cover, created quite a stir in fashion circles in this regard.

One fashion report was titled "Rihanna Pulls a Grace Jones for Italian Vogue".[45] On the Internet, numerous references to Rihanna's aesthetic channelling of her Caribbean forbear, replete with photographs comparing these two Caribbean female artists, were everywhere and abounding. Most notable, however, was Rihanna's album cover for *Rated R* (2009), the first album she released after her domestic abuse encounter: it features her signature "R" for "Rihanna", positioned so as to appear like the Barbadian trident and remarkably reminiscent of a famous picture of Jones holding a spear. In addition, the expressions on Rihanna's and Jones's faces are an almost identical admixture of raw power, Amazonian futurism and dark beauty.

It bears remarking as well, that all of the furore surrounding Rihanna's gun tattoo which she acquired upon her re-emergence, might well be examined in context of the numerous photographs of Grace Jones depicted expertly wielding a pistol. Self-possessed and self-generating, surely Jones remains a powerful, alluring icon and symbol of Caribbeanity, whose non-conformist deconstruction of traditional sex and gender roles, invocation of phallic power and hard, edgy sexuality explodes fully the dichtomony between victim and perpetrator into which Rihanna had been read in 2009.

Whose Rihanna? I am in no way suggesting here that Rihanna was merely mimetic, facilely replicating the already-done aesthetic self-representations of her Caribbean predecessor. The reality is that Rihanna has, in her early twenties, already achieved much greater commerical success and wider audience appeal than Jones has during a thirty-year career. But I would have to argue that if Rihanna were going to define herself alongside, or rather, read herself into a narrative of female Caribbeanity as survivor, warrior woman, bad-ass bitch, over and against a narrative of innocence despoiled, victimhood and weakness, an impressionable actor rather than agent – her invocation of Jones is brilliant.

Defying, as Rihanna must, the competing and contestatory co-optations of her personhood, perhaps what the "taint" of the 2009 domestic violence incident has freed her to do is to move towards fully claiming her Caribbean female erotic power. As another of our powerful Caribbean female forbears Audre Lorde reminds us, "the erotic is a measure between the beginnings of our sense of self and the chaos of our strongest feelings".[46] It seems to me that Rihanna's diasporic citizenship is located, therefore, somewhere in the intersections between sense and chaos wherein the erotic lies. According to Weheliye, "'diasporic citizenship' *refuses to sublate* the fraught and violent traffic between national and global assemblages; instead it *raucously* brings to the fore the tensions that require complex ways of mediating between contradictory forces as they are scripted and sounded through the bodies and psyches of Afro-diasporic subjects".[47] Such raucous bodily and psychic soundings reverberate in Lorde's admonition that "in order to be *utilized*, our erotic feelings must be recognized".[48]

In her fourth album, *Rated R*, Rihanna articulates precisely such a rupturous and raucous refusal to be improperly ultilized (be it globally, nationally or sociopolitically). This was captured quite potently in her single "Hard". Opening with a classic African diasporic sonic "call and response", Rihanna lyrically invites her pistol-wielding challengers, who are opening fire at the pedestal of her own making, to keep on shooting since "Rihanna range just won't let up". In her single, the Rihanna she presents is fearless, truth telling, tough, tearless, wide-ranging, dexterous and agent. The obvious trap that must now be avoided is to pigeonhole Rihanna once again, interpolating her into a discourse of anarchic individualism. In 2009, when I wrote an earlier version of this chapter, I asked, "Will there be further Rihanna incarnations?" My answer? "Of course, what fun will it be if there are not?" There have been several since then, and we should anticipate even more in the future. For the moment, however, it is I think safe to assert that while we may not ever conclusively be able to define who she is, we can affirm *whose* she is. Unequivocally, Rihanna is today her own complex, contradictory, fluid, Bajan, diasporan, Caribbean, modern female black self.

Notes

1. Bimshire is a familiar appellative for Barbados.
2. Alice Walker, *In Search of Our Mothers' Gardens* (New York: Harvest Books, 1984), 235.
3. Alexander Weheliye, *Phonographies: Grooves in Sonic Afro-Modernity* (Chapel Hill, NC: Duke University Press, 2005), 147.
4. The title of this section comes from an article by Mavis Beckles, "Good Tidings and Great Joy", *Barbados Nation News*, 22 December 2007.
5. Weheliye, *Phonographies*, 148.
6. Sylvia Barrow-Green, "Keep on Winning, Rihanna", *Barbados Nation News*, 21 February 2008.
7. Alaistair Haynes, "When Is Rihanna Going to Get Her Just Desserts?", *Barbados Nation News*, 20 November 2007.
8. Jerome Davis, "Let Us Recognize Rihanna's Success", *Daily Nation*, 6 November 2007.
9. "What Rihanna Means to Us", *Barbados Nation News*, 17 November 2007; emphasis added.
10. People's Empowerment Party, "She Is Our Rihanna", *Barbados Nation News*, 17 August 2007; emphasis added.
11. Ibid.; emphasis added.
12. "All Hail Rihanna", *Barbados Nation News*, 22 February 2008.
13. Full video can be seen online: http://www.dailymotion.com/video/x70cif_rihanna-2008-grammy-awards-acceptan_music.
14. These Caribbean artists primarily reside in their countries of origin, also contributing to their language retention.
15. "Twanging" is Caribbean vernacular used to refer to someone from the Caribbean who puts on a fake American accent to hide his or her national origins.
16. Mavis Beckles, "Well Done Rihanna", *Barbados Nation News*, 15 February 2008.
17. Full interview available online at *NY Magazine*, "Rihanna: The Full Diane Sawyer Interview", November 2009, http://nymag.com/daily/entertainment/2009/11/rihanna_the_full_dia ne_sawyer_interview.html.
18. Cou-cou is a part of the Barbadian national dish and is made of slowly turned cornmeal that is cooked in a pot.
19. Margeaux Watson, "Caribbean Queen", *Entertainment Weekly*, 21 June 2007.
20. Donna Aza Weir-Soley, *Eroticism, Spirituality and Resistance in Black Women's Writing* (Gainesville: University Press of Florida, 2009), 12.
21. Although Alison Hinds and Rupert "Rupee" Clarke have both enjoyed major national, regional and international acclaim, they have primarily done so in the area

of soca/calypso music and have not enjoyed the kind of broad crossover that is a hallmark of Rihanna's career.
22. Haynes, "When Is Rihanna".
23. "Our World of Entertainment: The Rihanna Debate", *Barbados Advocate*, 24 February 2008, 33.
24. Phillip Knight, "Pray for Rihanna", *Barbados Nation News*, 5 November 2007; emphasis added.
25. Olutoye Walrond, "Some Praying for Poor Rihanna", *Barbados Nation News*, 29 November 2007; emphasis added.
26. Etta Best, "Who's Envying Rihanna", *Daily Nation*, 16 November 2007.
27. Barry Walters, "Rihanna: Music of the Sun, Album Review", *Rolling Stone*, 8 September 2005.
28. Both Sean Paul and Damian Marley won Grammy awards in 2004 and 2006 respectively. Paul's *Dutty Rock* (2002) sold six million albums and *The Trinity* (2005), five million. Marley's *Welcome to Jamrock* (2006) went gold.
29. For a further definition and discussion of "nation language", see Kamau Brathwaite, "The History of the Voice", in *Roots* (Ann Arbor: University of Michigan Press, 1993), 259–304.
30. Sherley Anne Williams, *Dessa Rose* (New York: Berkeley Books, 1986), 14.
31. "Rihanna's Bruises Not So Bad", *Daily Nation*, 22 February 2009.
32. Diane Sawyer's interview with Rihanna aired on ABC's *20/20*, 6 November 2009.
33. Richard Hoad, "The Lowdown: To Lou Wif Love", *Barbados Nation News*, 27 February 2009; emphasis added.
34. Mavis Beckles, "No Fairy Tale World Rihanna", *Daily Nation*, 14 February 2009.
35. It is important to note that Rihanna performed at President Obama's inaugural ball, in aid of Feeding America.
36. "Fayewiggles" comment on the *20/20* interview with Rihanna posted at ABC.com, 16 November 2009; "bluegoose" comment on the *20/20* interview posted at ABC.com, 14 November 2009; emphasis added.
37. Carol-Ann Tudor, "Makeup After the Break-up?", *Barbados Nation News*, 6 March 2009.
38. Tony Best, "New York, New York: Rihanna, Brown and Domestic Violence", *Barbados Nation News*, 13 February 2009.
39. People's Empowerment Party, "Support Rihanna and Fight Against Domestic Violence", *Daily Nation*, 27 February 2009.
40. "Rihanna 'Poster Girl' for Domestic Violence Campaigners", *Daily Nation*, 7 March 2009.
41. Posted on ABC.com after interview aired.
42. I am using *différance* in the Derridean sense to refer to his notion of meaning encoded in language as always deferred but also trapped in terms of binaries/hierar-

chies which highlight difference and power. See Jacques Derrida, *Of Grammatology* (Baltimore: Johns Hopkins Press, 1998).

43. This is Toni Morrison's phrase in "Unspeakable Things Unspoken: The Afro-American Presence in American Literature", *Michigan Quarterly Review* 28, no. 1 (Winter 1989), to describe the protagonist from her novel *Sula* (New York: Plume, 1974) and the transgression of conventional gender codes.
44. Caustina, *PopCrunch*, "Rihanna: 'Cruella de Vil Is My Style Icon'", 24 November 2009, http://style.popcrunch.com/rihanna-cruella-de-vil-is-my-style-icon/.
45. *The Fab Life*, "Rihanna Pulls a Grace Jones for Italian Vogue", 28 August 2009, http://www.thefablife.com/2009-08-28/rihanna-pulls-a-grace-jones-for-italian-vogue/.
46. Audre Lorde, *Sister Outsider* (Trumansburg: Crossing Press, 1984), 54.
47. Weheliye, *Phonographies*, 150; emphasis added.
48. Lorde, *Sister Outsider*, 58.

Discography

Rihanna. *A Girl Like Me*. Def Jam, compact disc, 2006.
———. *Good Girl Gone Bad*. Def Jam, compact disc, 2007.
———. *Loud*. Def Jam, compact disc, 2010.
———. *Music of the Sun*. Def Jam, compact disc, 2005.
———. *Rated R*. Def Jam, compact disc, 2009.
———. *Talk that Talk*. Def Jam, compact disc, 2011.

14.

I and Ireland
Reggae and Rastafari in the Work of Sinéad O'Connor

| ADAM JOHN WATERMAN

THIS CHAPTER EXPLORES THE place of reggae in the work of Irish pop star Sinéad O'Connor. Far from being an aberration or a desperate attempt at pop cultural relevance, I argue that O'Connor's 2005 reggae album *Throw Down Your Arms* should be understood as part of a larger engagement with the Rastafari movement. Where artists like the Clash, the Police, Gwen Stefani and recent "Hasidic reggae superstar" Matisyahu have experimented with reggae as a genre – to radically different political and commercial ends – O'Connor's interest in reggae has emerged from a relationship to Rastafari that is as much intellectual and political as it is spiritual, aural or economic.[1] Although O'Connor remains engaged by Ireland as a site of cultural struggle, the Rastafari movement has provided her with the materials through which she might articulate a new vision for Irish cultural politics, one that seeks the renewal of their anti-colonial orientation through an explicit turn to the transnational. In O'Connor's music, the social and cultural specificity of Ireland is sublated, its distinctiveness preserved within the heterogeneous unity of anti-colonial struggles. Her use of reggae is, in this sense, but one manifestation of a commitment and a programme that is expressed formally, through spectacle, and in thought.

Music, the Making and Marketing of Ireland

When it was released in 2005, *Throw Down Your Arms* garnered largely positive reviews, yet many were puzzled by O'Connor's engagement with the genre. Since the release of her debut album, *The Lion and the Cobra*, in 1987, O'Connor's music had taken the form of an extended dialogue between traditional and modern aspects of Irish musical culture. As such, most critics treated O'Connor's reggae album as a novelty, an almost aberrant diversion from the body of her more serious solo and collaborative work.[2] Few, if any, considered the political context from which the record emerged; specifically, the social and cultural struggles around the "Irish economic miracle".

In order to appreciate the critique O'Connor levels at present formations of Irish nationalism, it is necessary to understand the social and cultural impact of this economic miracle. Since the late 1980s, republican Ireland has seen an unprecedented – and truly staggering – economic recovery, one largely built upon trade and tax liberalization. As capital has fled other high-tax regions of the European Union, it has found a welcoming home in Ireland. Despite centuries of vicious colonial expropriation, over twenty years, this wave of foreign investment has helped transform the island from one of the poorest to one of the richest nations in the Eurozone. One of the consequences of this turnaround has been the dramatic reversal of Irish emigration patterns. Although Ireland has been a net exporter of people since the mid-nineteenth century, over the course of the 1990s, the island became home to an increasingly heterogeneous community. Following this trend, immigration has become a political variable in Ireland, with right-wing attacks upon state-sponsored social welfare programmes often linked to questions of ethnicity, nationality and race.

Although O'Connor has never made this link explicit, it is difficult not to think of *Throw Down Your Arms* as a response to this moment in Irish cultural politics. Music has been one of the primary sites through which a sense of Irish nationality has been defined, both for itself and for its others; as such, it has been a significant site of struggle over the meaning of Irishness. O'Connor has been long engaged by such debates and, by and large, her work has been meant to confound the opposition between tradition and modernity that animates them. Equally at home performing with the Chieftans, the Pogues or U2 throughout her career, O'Connor has allowed the traditional and the modern to stand alongside one another, often in a heterogeneous, rather than synthetic, unity. This is itself symbolic of the fractures within the social and cultural landscape of greater Ireland.

Throw Down Your Arms further complicates this picture, adding to it an undeniably syncretic musical tradition with a nevertheless unmistakable point of cultural and political origin. In Ireland, to the extent that the campaign to pass a 2004 referendum on immigration and citizenship was built upon the media-driven hysteria surrounding African asylum seekers using *jus soli* as a backdoor into Irish citizenship, O'Connor's almost reverent engagement with reggae might be seen as an aggressive riposte to those who endorsed such a hermetically sealed conception of Irish national culture, particularly one that is organized around a specifically racial exclusion.[3] As she noted at the time of the album's release, "There are huge ties between Africa and Ireland going way back before Jamaica even existed as it is now. And we were colonized by the same people and by the same religion in a lot of ways. And we have the same . . . similarities in our music . . . there's a huge kind of longing, yearning, and calling in the music."[4]

Here, the putative blackness of reggae as a musical culture allows O'Connor to call into question the very notion of racial homogeneity that underpins present forms of Irish nationalism and, by extension, to evoke the ways in which the Irish economic miracle is built upon the articulation of Ireland within the political project of Euro-American whiteness.[5] To a certain extent, this critique merely reveals the already implicit racial politics of the debate over tradition and modernity in Irish music: the modern influences that have so scandalized traditionalists have generally come out of rock 'n' roll and R&B, both undeniably black musical idioms. At the same time, the relationship of reggae to Jamaica, Jamaica to Britain, and Britain to Ireland allows her to articulate the question of nationality within the context of imperialism and anti-colonial politics. It is not merely the racial exclusiveness of Irish nationalism to which O'Connor objects; it is the ways in which this racial exclusiveness works to undermine the expression of transnational cultural and political solidarities.

As an explicitly political musical form, reggae is perhaps the ideal vehicle for this critique, particularly insofar as reggae's status, within the postcolonial Jamaican state, is curiously analogous to that of "traditional" Irish music. Given the international success of reggae artists, Jamaica has used reggae to market the country as a tourist destination – a site of cultural consumption absent social or political conflict. Although the Rastafari movement has been brutally suppressed at different points throughout Jamaican history, to the extent that reggae has emerged as the international aural identity of Jamaica, the postcolonial state has attempted to incorporate many symbols of the Rastafari movement. Since the Rastafari community represents a challenge to the state's claim upon the nation, this symbolic incorporation has aimed at disrupting the oppositional potentiality of the movement.[6] O'Connor's work on *Throw Down Your Arms* thus confounds the cultural work of bourgeois nationalism operative in both Ireland and Jamaica, even as her reverential treatment of reggae classics suggests an appreciation for the differential histories of racialization that produce Ireland and Jamaica as culturally distinct zones of the Atlantic world.[7]

For O'Connor, Rastafari provides the cultural and the intellectual materials to elaborate this critique of the bourgeois nation, a critique that emerges – in the case of Ireland – as a critique of the Catholic Church and its role in the statist reproduction of the Irish national body. In O'Connor's estimation, one of the greatest accomplishments of the Rastafari movement is the effective separation of God from religion and thus, by extension, the separation of God from the state.[8] Whether or not this is an accurate characterization of a spiritual movement that venerates an Ethiopian monarch as God incarnate is, for the moment, irrelevant. For O'Connor, what is important about Rastafari is less the ultimate horizon of its prophetic vision than the prophetic form itself, along with the scholarly mode of textual interpretation and debate that orients the community. Here, the turn to Rastafari is, in itself, a critical practice, insofar as it allows O'Connor a relationship to scripture, interpretation and spirit that is foreclosed by the hierarchical structure of the Catholic Church.

In the Catholic Church, the clergy is the last word on textual interpretation, and the laity are meant to receive the word passively. The prophetic mode of Rastafari allows O'Connor to engage in the elaboration of the word, a position of relative power compared to that afforded her within the rigid hierarchy of the Catholic Church. In turn, Rastafari affords O'Connor the ability to see the space between Irish culture, the bourgeois nation, and the institutional state, thus giving her the perspective from which to re-imagine Irish cultural politics.

"There is no man or movement in modern Irish history that can be intelligently discussed apart from the Roman Catholic Church in Ireland", Emmet Larkin wrote in 1964. He continued, "That Church [has] for centuries been intimately bound up with nearly every phase of Irish life."[9] Although the movement for Irish Home Rule was marked by strongly secularist political tendencies, including avowedly atheistic socialisms, the role that religion played in the colonization of Ireland ensured that it would remain a critical variable in any movement for political and economic independence. As Nicholas Canny has pointed out, the sixteenth-century jurists who provided the legal cover for the colonization of Ireland routinely cited Irish non-compliance with doctrinal authority as grounds for the expropriation of land and resources.[10] Although nominally Catholic, the Irish were considered wild: pagans practicing under a thin veneer of Church pageantry. As such, Irish land and resources could be rendered subject to a colonizing power that would then tutor them in the particulars of proper religious devotion. This rationale would become the blueprint for English colonization efforts in the Americas, one made all the more powerful by virtue of the politics of the Reformation.

In Ireland, of course, the Reformation only exacerbated the sense of Irish religious distinctiveness vis-à-vis the colonizing English. The primitive accumulation of English colonization proceeded as a racializing project. Once the Church of England was officially established, persisting in the observance of Catholic rites became little less than a crime against the state. Although the observance of anti-Catholic laws, and the severity of punishments meted out against Catholic "heretics" varied from monarch to monarch, in response to larger patterns of social conflict between the aristocracy, emergent bourgeoisie and peasant classes, the persecution of Catholics worked to consolidate lines of class and racial difference that persisted well into the twentieth century. As Catherline Hezser has argued, during the high points of English-Irish social conflict, even Jewish religious difference was assimilated to the Protestant/Catholic counterpoint, while Irish Catholics were routinely described as "the blacks of Europe".[11] Until their repeal in the 1830s, laws prohibiting Catholic participation in British political life effectively prohibited Irish participation in Parliament.[12] Until the 1990s, Ireland was one of the poorest countries of western Europe, routinely cited as a Third World site in a First World milieu.[13] The poverty of Irish Catholics was so well and historically entrenched to have become a literary cliché.

Because of its role in the establishment and reproduction of socioeconomic relations in Ireland, religion was one of the most significant sites of cultural struggle over the distribution of political and economic power under British colonial rule. As Michael Carroll has pointed out, there is a not entirely coincidental relationship between the rise of Irish Catholic devotionalism and the agitation for Home Rule in the nineteenth century. The devotional movement for a more doctrinaire Catholicism was, at least in part, about embracing a more decorous mode of religious observance and social behaviour, one that could counter British charges of Irish impropriety.[14] While this ultimately conservative attempt at forestalling British constructions of Irish "noble savagery" was doomed to fail as a political tactic, it succeeded in producing an exceedingly "Romanized" mode of Irish Catholic religious observance, one that rejected a host of vernacular religious traditions that fell outside the scope of the catechism. Whatever hostility might have existed between the Catholic Church and the political leaders of the Home Rule movement, because of the implication of Catholic reform with the politics of Home Rule, contemporary Irish Catholicism is generally believed to be one of the most doctrinaire forms of Catholic observance.

O'Connor's critique of Catholicism emerges out of the lived experience of Irish Catholic fanaticism. In an interview with Hilton Als, O'Connor described the impact of the Church upon her early life. "I grew up in Ireland, a Catholic, which means I grew up in the church. The entire country was like a church. It was very closed . . . It was considered a sin to walk into the car park of a Protestant church."[15] Born in 1966, O'Connor's description of Catholic attitudes toward Protestants illustrates the lingering political charge of these identifications in later-twentieth-century Ireland, despite the much celebrated ecumenicalism that emerged following the Second Vatican Council of 1962 to 1965. Although Rome had backed away from its most strict and demanding obligations concerning Protestantism, during O'Connor's early life Irish Catholics retained an exacting sense of the sinfulness involved in associating with Protestants, one that crept into her emotional and spiritual life. Nevertheless, O'Connor's comments provide a helpful insight into the way in which she imagines the relationship between the Catholic Church and Irish politics. Describing Ireland itself as a sort of church, in the same interview with Als, O'Connor invokes the implication of one with the other, relating the structure of the state to the structure of the Catholic Church.

> Very early on . . . I knew the difference between God and religion. My father went to Mass. I would go with him and be very bored, but my ears would prick up when I heard something that rang true. I wouldn't take in everything, but there were phrases that rang true and also gave me a code for life. And one idea was turning the other cheek. I was getting the shit kicked out of me regularly at home . . . My

mother was the abuser. To help me cope with the violence at home, I separated the sin from the sinner. And that helped me in terms of relating to my mother. There was something wrong with her. And the thing that profoundly affected me was Jesus saying that he would come back as just another beggar on the street. And that really struck me: Jesus embodying every person. I love Rastafarian culture for that reason. The idea of "I" and "I". I never felt [f]ucked up by religion.

Here, O'Connor describes her embrace of Rastafari as a condition of her youthful experience of religion; this approach is further elaborated in 2007's *Theology*, which proceeds as a series of musical commentaries on biblical passages. O'Connor's relationship to reggae begins much earlier, however, finding its earliest expression on her 1995 album, *Universal Mother*. Featuring a catalogue of very quiet, down tempo originals, *Universal Mother* was taken, by many, as an appeal for forgiveness following O'Connor's well-known 1992 *Saturday Night Live* performance, during which she defaced a photograph of Pope John Paul II. This impression was underscored by O'Connor's decision to cover Nirvana's 1993 post-punk pop anthem "All Apologies" on the album. Those who took the song to be an all too literal apology for the *Saturday Night Live* affair missed the acerbic bite of Kurt Cobain's lyrics, particularly as it was amplified by O'Connor's delivery: "I wish I was like you: easily amused / Find my nest of salt: everything is my fault." Delivered in a plaintive whisper, O'Connor recast Cobain's Generation X ennui as a sly commentary on her shakedown by the American media. In her hands, "All Apologies" was less an act of contrition than a barely disguised critique of the American appetite for pop schlock.

Universal Mother opens with a track called "Germaine", a recitation of a long passage from feminist intellectual Germaine Greer, in which Greer spells out the role of the women's liberation movement in the emergence of a post-state, post-capitalist social order. Eschewing all forms of panoptic state governmentality as institutional manifestations of patriarchy, Greer suggests that society retains the capacity to regulate itself and to manage its affairs, despite the perverse appearance of hierarchical structures designed to expropriate these capacities.

> I do think that women could make politics irrelevant; by a kind of spontaneous cooperative action the like of which we have never seen; which is so far from people's ideas of state structure or viable social structure that it seems to them like total anar-

chy – when what it really is, is very subtle forms of interrelation that do not follow some hierarchical pattern which is fundamentally patriarchal. The opposite to patriarchy is not matriarchy but fraternity, yet I think it's women who are going to have to break this spiral of power and find the trick of cooperation.

Following "Germaine", *Universal Mother* proceeds with its most provocative track, "Fire on Babylon". In this song, O'Connor plays with the very public nature of her biography – particularly, the allegation that she had suffered terrible abuse, as a child, at the hands of her mother – in order to stage her critique of the church. "She took my father from my life; took my sister and brothers", O'Connor sings at the outset. Here, O'Connor's lyrics seem straightforwardly autobiographical, yet subsequent lines take on a deliberately ambiguous undertone. "She's taken everything I liked; she's taken every lover. And all along she gave me lies; just to make me think I loved her." As the song progresses, the referent of "she" becomes less and less personified, until "she" is no longer part of O'Connor's intimate, familial relations, but rather somebody else's mother, destroying somebody else's children. "Look what she did to her son", O'Connor intones, over and again.

As O'Connor reaches this point in the song, the identification of her mother with Holy Mother Church is laid bare. Christ's sacrifice becomes the ultimate act of child abuse, one that is attributed not to God, but to the theology upon which the church stakes its authority. In "Fire on Babylon", O'Connor's abusive mother becomes the instrument by which the church reproduces itself. As such, the *Universal Mother* of O'Connor's title takes on a monstrous resonance contrary to the culturally hegemonic conception of mother as caregiver, nurturer and protector. Here, the universality of O'Connor's *Universal Mother* is the universality of Catholicism. "She" becomes the church, and the church becomes Babylon.

In its resonance across cultural formations, the word "Babylon" becomes the nexus through which O'Connor's critique of the Catholic Church interfaces with her commitment to Rastafari. Babylon is, of course, a critical part of the Rastafari lexicon, an allusion to the ancient Babylonia that seeks to cast the imperial hegemon Anglo-American "West" as the inheritor to its legacy and its eventual fate: just as the Israelites were imprisoned in Babylon, so are people of African descent imprisoned in the "West". And just as impenetrable Babylon eventually fell to the Persians, so will the indefatigable "West" meet its eventual demise. This allusiveness is not unique to Rastafari, of course; it is built into the source material from which Rastafari draws, particularly the Book of Revelation, which cites the history of ancient Babylon to stage its critique of Rome and ground its eschatology. Crucially, during the Protestant Reformation, Babylon was also a common epithet for the Catholic Church, with the pope often described as the incarnation of the "Whore of Babylon". To some extent, the myriad articulations of Babylon within the rich and expansive tradition of Judeo-Christian eschatology serves as the model for O'Connor's more immediate and intimate allusion between the structure of her family and the structure of a religiously ordained society. Placing herself in service to this metaphor, O'Connor draws upon the weight of historical tradition that it carries while bending it to her immediate purposes.

O'Connor's engagement with Rastafari was not merely lyrical; it was also registered musically. Written by O'Connor and long-time collaborator John Reynolds, and produced by Bomb the Bass DJ Tim Simenon, "Fire on Babylon" marked a departure from the alternative rock aesthetic that had formed the core of O'Connor's work since her debut album *The Lion and the Cobra*. Although O'Connor had experimented with drum machines and other electronic instrumentation earlier in her career, most notably in the track "I Am Stretched on Your Grave", from *I Do Not Want What I Haven't Got*, by and large, such experiments remained well within the idiom of alt-rock. "Fire On Babylon", by contrast, drew upon elements of what would come to be called the "Bristol sound". Loosely associated with the commercial genre of trip-hop, the Bristol sound incorporated elements of ostensibly American hip-hop with acid jazz, reggae and dub. O'Connor's most important intervention with regard to this emergent genre was to underscore its origin within the cultural matrix of the black radical tradition. Despite Bristol's place within the history of the Black Atlantic, and in spite of the cultural provenance of its generic components, as it was commodified and marketed, trip-hop was largely feminized and deracinated as a counterpoint to the aggressively masculine and African-American market orientation of hip-hop. By referencing Babylon in its title, O'Connor distinguished her work from the emergent commercial culture of trip-hop, identifying, instead, with the larger diasporic cultural milieu out of which trip-hop's generic elements emerged.[16]

Layered over a set of heavy, programmed beats, much of the drama in "Fire" emerges from the jarring juxtaposition of the syncopated swing of its bass line to the mercilessly military precision of its melody. As rendered by O'Connor, the melody line in "Fire" proceeds in precise four-four time, one quarter note for each syllable of each word. Accordingly, the words of the first line, "She stole my father from my life", occupy eight notes over two measures, with the final note of "life" held over two more measures. This phrasing mimics that of a hymn, suggesting the overall religious orientation of O'Connor's work. By contrast, the bass line repeats the same irregular musical phrase, swinging on the off beat. The tension between these two lines provides the musical figure by which O'Connor signals her own vexed relationship between two conversant, but non-identical and irreducible, cultural traditions. This then becomes the figure for how each tradition is not identical with itself, the manner in which the resources that comprise each tradition are always potentially in excess of the manner of their articulation. This tension is the condition that allows for their potential conversation.

O'Connor's engagement with Rastafari finds perhaps its most explicitly political articulation in the penultimate track of *Universal Mother*, the revisionist history lesson "Famine". This song acts as sonic counterpart to the general movement within late-twentieth-century Irish historiography, in which revisionism implied a movement away from the nationalist historiographies that had served the anti-colonial agenda to an "empirical" historiography that sought to grapple with the complexities of Irish social and cultural formation. O'Connor's "Famine" was an attempt at dispelling one of the most pernicious narratives of self-fashioning in Ireland and its diaspora: namely, the narrative of potato blight and famine condensed in the tale of "Black '47". As Christine Kinealy has argued, the impact of the potato blight and subsequent famine of 1845 to 1852 was such that the "Great Famine" entered into Irish folklore as a social and cultural watershed.[17] According to some estimates, the famine cost Ireland nearly one-quarter of its population, with approximately one million dying as a consequence of malnutrition, and another one million emigrating to Britain or the United States. As such, Irish historiography continues to divide the history of the island into pre- and post-famine, and the famine continues to be heralded as the calamity that gave rise to intensified forms of Irish nationalist activity and a more devotional, "Romanized", Catholicism.[18]

O'Connor's "Famine" proceeds by way of a provocation. "Okay I want to talk about Ireland", O'Connor intones over the opening bass line. "Specifically, I want to talk about the 'famine': about the fact that there never really was one." After stating her thesis, O'Connor goes on to explain that her aim is not to question the truth-value of the famine narrative, but to radicalize it. "There was no 'famine'", she sings,

> See Irish people were only allowed to eat potatoes
> All of the other food
> Meat, fish, vegetables
> Were shipped out of the country under armed guard
> To England while the Irish people starved.

Connor's narrative of the famine, in other words, strives to replace a quasi-naturalized explanation of a proto-national crisis with an interpretation that locates its larger political and economic logic within the field of the British imperial state. The famine does not occur because of the potato blight, but instead as a condition of Britain's expropriation of Ireland's natural resources. The Irish starve not as a consequence of some inexorable divine logic, but because of the perfidy of British colonial policy. Having established this rendering of political and economic crisis, O'Connor goes on to expose the social and cultural consequences for Ireland:

> And then in the middle of all this
> They gave us money not to teach our children Irish
> And so we lost our history
> And this is what I think is still hurting me
> See we're like a child that's been battered
> Has to drive itself out of its head because it's frightened
> Still feels all the painful feelings
> But they lose contact with the memory
> And this leads to massive self-destruction
> Alcoholism, drug addiction
> All desperate attempts at running
> And in its worst form
> Becomes actual killing

Here, O'Connor uses her political and economic critique to transpose the social and cultural conditions of Ireland since the famine into the register of socio-historical processes, rendering stereotypes and tropes of Irish drunkenness and despair into latter-day manifestations of a quasi-genocidal course of primitive accumulation. The obsessive search for identity that purportedly marks modern Irish cultural production here emerges as an attempt at connecting a culturally memorialized and reproduced trauma to its proper historical coordinates. While "Famine" is an attempt at providing such an orientation, O'Connor goes on to acknowledge that such an articulation is not, in itself, enough, but that it needs to be augmented and realized through a cultural and political process.

> And if there ever is gonna be healing
> There has to be remembering
> And then grieving
> So that there then can be forgiving
> There has to be knowledge and understanding
> This process is hampered, however, by the very educational system that seeks to educate the Irish about their past.
> What finally broke us was not starvation
> But its use in the controlling of our education
> Schools go on about "Black '47"
> On and on about "the terrible famine"
> But what they don't say is in truth
> There never really was one

Moving from political economy and social relations, to cultural formations, and then to manifestations of social control, O'Connor's "Famine" replicates the structure and argument of Walter Rodney's *Groundings with My Brothers*. It does so by couching the history of Ireland within a narrative of political and economic underdevelopment in which the social and cultural characteristics of the Irish people are rendered as conditions common to those who have been conscripted to the project of British colonial modernity. Irish culture, in O'Connor's presentation, is less the marker of a unique and irreducible national heritage than the localized cultural manifestation of a transnational political economy built upon the exploitation of colonial resources. Yet, like Rodney, O'Connor's critique goes beyond the perfunctory declamation of imperialism to condemn the social relations that obtain within emergent postcolonial nation-states. By underlining the political economic relations that have contributed to the production of contemporary Ireland, "Famine" transforms O'Connor's critique of the Catholic Church into a critique of the postcolonial Irish (republican) state, and the ways in which it maintains its hegemony by exploiting and reproducing social divisions produced under conditions of British colonialism. Just as Rodney attacked the postcolonial Jamaican bourgeoisie for its ruthless suppression of the black working class, over the course of *Universal Mother*, O'Connor identifies the church as an adjunct to the Irish (republican) state and a barrier to the realization of human emancipation.

Embedded within O'Connor's critique of the nation is, then, a vision of anti-colonial transnationality. The elaboration of this vision, I argue, must be understood as a considered response to the triumphant narratives that have served to organize the globalization of capitalism in the post-Soviet era. This preoccupation with history and struggle emerges in what remains O'Connor's most iconic performance. During her 3 October 1992 appearance on the popular American television programme *Saturday Night Live*, O'Connor defaced a photograph of Pope John Paul II. The inattention to reggae and its influence on O'Connor is all the more striking after consideration that it was, in fact, a reggae track that provided the backdrop for this moment. O'Connor destroyed the picture after performing Bob Marley's 1976 classic, "War". Without backing vocals or instrumentation, staring into the camera, O'Connor delivered the Wailers' indictment of Babylon into the heart of the United States, raising the image of the pope at precisely the moment she hit the word "evil" in the song's final lyric. As she ripped through the photo, audience members and studio technicians could be heard on the audio track, gasping incredulously. After O'Connor enjoined her audience to "fight the real enemy", she blew out a ring of candles and exited the stage. For all its vitality only two years before, O'Connor's career in the United States was effectively ended by the ensuing controversy. American Catholics burned O'Connor's picture in effigy, while shocked music lovers gathered to destroy her CDs.

For all the controversy her performance generated, little was made of O'Connor's choice of vehicle until two weeks later, when she was booed off the stage at a Bob Dylan tribute concert held at Madison Square Garden. Even then, the question was whether or not a Marley tune was appropriate for a Dylan tribute.[19] This evasiveness came, in part, because of the incoherence, for American audiences, of O'Connor's protest. As Elizabeth Butler Cullingford has argued, O'Connor's performance on *Saturday Night Live* resonated with the cultural politics of religion in Ireland; for Americans, it read as little more than an unprovoked attack on a representative of religious orthodoxy.[20] Even fellow pop star and Catholic provocateur Madonna spoke out against

O'Connor's actions, despite having earned the ire of the Vatican herself for her playful appropriation of Catholic iconography during her infamous 1991 Blonde Ambition tour. Indeed, when Madonna appeared on *Saturday Night Live* weeks after O'Connor, she parodied her performance by asking the audience to "fight the real enemy" while holding up a picture of Joey Buttafuoco, the middle-aged Long Island native whose teenage mistress, Amy Fisher, had shot and wounded his wife.

In some sense, Madonna's send-up of O'Connor's performance reflected their difference of position relative to national and immigrant Catholic traditions. Where Madonna was the product of an Italian-American immigrant Catholic community, O'Connor was the child of an Irish national Catholic community. And where Catholicism in America has served to reconcile diverse national and ethnic groups within the political formation of American whiteness, Catholicism in Ireland has served as a vehicle in the struggle for independence. Catholicism in Ireland, in other words, has been a signifier of difference, where in the United States, it has served as a mechanism of homogenization and incorporation within the state. Catholicism in America has been a critical part of the construction of whiteness, while Catholicism in Ireland has been a critical piece of the resistance to English economic and cultural imperialism.[21]

Consequently, in the United States, O'Connor's *Saturday Night Live* performance was assimilated to the emergent discourse of the culture wars. Earlier that summer, in a speech before the Republican National Convention, traditionalist Catholic and Republican stalwart Pat Buchanan had lit this fuse, declaring that there was "a religious war going on in [this] country . . . as critical to the kind of nation we will one day be as was the Cold War itself".[22] Drawing connections between a range of popular and high cultural products, and condemning the liberal decadence of Hollywood, Buchanan claimed that left-wing extremists were attempting to undermine America by attacking its most cherished ideals and institutions through the medium of culture. From this perspective, there was little difference between O'Connor, Anita Hill and the feminists who forced the issue of sexual harassment on the national agenda during the Hill-Thomas confirmation hearings, the "welfare queens" of the right-wing imagination, and Murphy Brown, the fictional television character who crystallized the American debate over "family values" by having a child out of wedlock.

Inscribed within this set of media sensations, the political and cultural context of O'Connor's performance was evacuated. Made over as nothing more than a right-wing talking point, O'Connor's performance could be used in establishing the reality of the supposed left-wing attack on American values, thus substantiating the right-wing discourse of culture war. What this reading missed was the implication of O'Connor's performance within the history of the Rastafari movement, and the implication of that movement within the history of anti-colonialism, generally. Coming just after midnight on 4 October, O'Connor's appearance on *Saturday Night Live* came just two days shy of the twenty-ninth anniversary of Emperor Haile Selassie's 1963 speech to the United Nations. Five months earlier, in May 1963, Selassie had presided over the founding conference of the Organization of African Unity (OAU) in Addis Ababa, and in his speech to the United Nations, Selassie reiterated the resolutions of the OAU, calling upon its members to support de-colonization movements in Rhodesia, South Africa, Mozambique and Angola. "We Africans will fight, if necessary, and we know that we shall win, as we are confident in the victory of good over evil."[23]

Coming in October 1963, Selassie's UN speech marked the threshold between what we might think of as the "two 1960s". Often indicated, in the United States, by the assassination of John F. Kennedy in November 1963, and the "British Invasion" of 1964, the 1963 to 1964 period marks a more general transition, globally, between reformist strategies and revolutionary movements. This should not suggest some inexorable historical dynamic, but rather a response to the intensification of repressive violence throughout the colonized world, as well as an effect of emergent struggles for power within recently independent states. Within the history of Rastafari in Jamaica, perhaps the most significant, retroactive, index of this transition was the 1962 Jamaica Independence Act, by which the British Parliament granted Jamaica formal independence as a commonwealth realm of the Crown. Post-independence, Rastafari was just one of the working-class movements subject to repression by the bourgeoisie as it sought to consolidate its hold on the Jamaican state.[24] As the middle-class elite sought to expropriate the signifiers of the black liberation struggle while divesting them of their revolutionary contents, Rastas became symbolic of all that could not be incorporated within the postcolonial order, the radical remainder of an unfinished, living struggle.

Taken almost verbatim from Selassie's 1963 UN speech, the lyrics to "War" retroactively posited this as the moment of a transition within the broader field of anti-colonial, anti-capitalist struggle. O'Connor's decision to sing "War" on *Saturday Night Live* reflected a consciousness of this fact, a point underscored by the choice to release her reggae album, *Throw Down Your Arms*, on the same day, thirteen years later. Together, then, the 1976 composition of "War" and O'Connor's performance constitute an act of historiographic performativity, the sonic production of a temporal figure that seeks not to memorialize the past, but to articulate the present. Just as the Wailers' 1976 recording of "War" sought to assert some measure of Rastafari radicalism in the face of growing respectability and commercial power, O'Connor's cover disrupted the highly reified state discourse of temporal rupture that accompanied the end of the Cold War.

O'Connor had articulated similar themes well before her 1992 appearance on *Saturday Night Live*. In "Black Boys on Mopeds", the fifth track off her 1990 breakthrough album, *I Do Not Want What I Haven't Got*, O'Connor suggested that the "First World" euphoria in the face of "Second World" democratization movements was little more than the product of media hype and political manipulation. "Margaret Thatcher on TV / shocked by the deaths that took place in Beijing / It seems strange that she should be offended / The same orders are given by her." Identifying the universally decried tactics of the Chinese state with the equally repressive, yet largely uncontested, mechanisms of neo-liberal policing, O'Connor's lyrics undermined the self-serving discourse of difference that organized the ideological battles of the Cold War, pointing out the fundamental identity between First and Second World blocs.[25]

O'Connor's "War" came from a similar place of frustration, yet it ratcheted up the intensity. Where "Black Boys on Mopeds" pinned down the hypocrisy of Thatcherite discourse, "War" was delivered as a call to action, a subversion of the post–Cold War discourse on democracy and struggle. As Alain Badiou has argued, the "death of communism" narrative that emerged at the end of the Cold War mobilized a rhetoric of popular protest to suggest an epochal shift to what Fukuyama called "the end of history". For Badiou, the end of the Cold War was entirely a matter of negotiations between states; while many Soviet-style regimes might have been undermined by popular protests, the political potentiality of those protests was evacuated by their very inclusion within the representative order of the emergent post-Soviet states. Popular mandates were used, in other words, to evoke transformation, thus obscuring the underlying continuities between the pre– and post–Cold War periods.[26] Drawing upon the Wailers' reinscription of the 1962 to 1964 period as a new awakening in the struggle for social justice, O'Connor's cover sought to rearticulate the euphoric declarations of liberty and democracy in Europe as threshold moments in the emergence of new struggles for emancipation, struggles that would reactivate those subjects who had been conspicuously excluded from the liberal-democratic consensus of the emergent globalization. As she rendered it, "War" was a canny rejoinder to all who saw the end of the Cold War as a victory for capitalist democracy at its avatar, the United States. Less than six months after the Rodney King verdict had polarized the United States, O'Connor's interpretation of Marley's song channelled the rage that had swept through the streets of Los Angeles. In her rendition, "everywhere is war", was the politically necessary response to Fukuyama's "end of history".

Notes

1. Louis Kaplan, "Yahweh Rastafari! Matisyahu and the Aporias of Hasidic Reggae Superstardom", *CR: The New Centennial Review* 7, no. 1 (2007): 15–44.
2. Jon Pareles, "An Irish Singer Performs a Show of Classic Reggae", *New York Times*, 12 December 2005; and also "Sinead O'Connor Finds New Roots in Jamaica", National Public Radio online, 6 December 2005, http://www.npr.org/templates/story/story.php?storyid=5037072.
3. See Dianna J. Shandy, "Irish Babies, African Mothers: Rites of Passage and Rights of Citizenship in Post-Millennial Ireland", *Anthropological Quarterly* 81, no. 4 (2008): 803–31.
4. "Sinead O'Connor Finds New Roots".
5. Although it does not touch on the post-millennial moment, the iconic text on the relationship between Irish cultural politics, class conflict and white racial formation remains Noel Ignatiev, *How the Irish Became White* (London: Routledge, 1995).
6. Anthony Bogues, "Politics, Nation, and PostColony: Caribbean Inflections", *Small Axe* 11 (March 2002): 1–30; and also Charles Price, Donald Nonini, and Erich Fox Tree, "Grounded Utopian Movements: Subjects of Neglect", *Anthropological Quarterly* 81, no. 1 (Winter 2008): 127–59.
7. "Differential histories" refers back to Paul Gilroy's notion of the differential histories of racialization within the formation of the Atlantic world. For more, see Paul Gilroy, *Small Acts: Thoughts on the Politics of Black Cultures* (London: Serpent's Tail, 1993).

8. O'Connor makes this point in the liner notes to *Throw Down Your Arms*. The lesson of the songs that she sings, she tells us, is that God and religion are different things, and this is the message she hopes to share with her listeners.
9. Emmet Larkin, "Socialism and Catholicism in Ireland", *Church History* 33, no. 4 (December 1964): 462.
10. Nicholas P. Canny, "The Ideology of English Colonization: From Ireland to America", *William and Mary Quarterly* 30, no. 4 (October 1973): 575–98; and also Andrew Hadfield, "Spenser, Ireland, and Sixteenth-Century Political Theory", *Modern Language Review* 89, no. 1 (January 1994): 1–18.
11. Catherine Hezser, " 'Are You Protestant Jews or Roman Catholic Jews?': Literary Representations of Being Jewish in Ireland", *Modern Judaism* 25, no. 2 (May 2005): 159–88.
12. Ignatiev, *How the Irish*.
13. Reuven Brenner, "The Irish Economic Miracle: One Part Fiscal, One Part Openness", *National Review*, 27 September 2006, http://www.nationalreview.com/articles/218835/irish-economic-miracle-reuven-brenner.
14. Edward G. Lengel, *The Irish Through British Eyes: Perceptions of Ireland in the Famine Era* (London: Praeger, 2002).
15. Hilton Als, "Sinéad O'Connor: The Irish Firebrand Heats It Up All Over Again", *Interview*, August 2000.
16. O'Connor has repeated this intervention in her work with other, more identifiably trip hop artists. In particular, her featured appearance on Massive Attack's 2003 "Prayer for England", finds her praying to Jah for the forgiveness of England, presumably for England's historical role in re-constituting the metaphorical Babylon of the present. Massive Attack featuring Sinéad O'Connor, "Prayer for England", *100th Window* (Virgin 724358123913 V25967, compact disc, 2003).
17. Christine Kinealy, *This Great Calamity* (Dublin: Gill and Macmillan, 1994).
18. Michael P. Carroll, "Rethinking Popular Catholicism in Pre-Famine Ireland", *Journal for the Scientific Study of Religion* 34, no. 3 (September 1995): 354.
19. Jon Pareles, "Pop View: Why Sinéad O'Connor Hit a Nerve", *New York Times*, 1 November 1992.
20. Elizabeth Butler Cullingford, "Virgins and Mothers: Sinéad O'Connor, Neil Jordan, and *The Butcher Boy*", *Yale Journal of Criticism* 15, no. 1 (2002): 191–92.
21. Ignatiev, *How the Irish*.
22. Patrick Buchanan, "Address to the 1992 Republican National Convention", http://www.learner.org/courses/amerhistory/resource_archive/resou rce.php?unit Choice=21&ThemeNum=1&resourceType=2&resourceID=10155.
23. H.I.M. Haile Selassie, "Address to the United Nations", 6 October 1963, http://www.nazret.com/history/him_un.php.

24. Walter Rodney, *Groundings with My Brothers* (London: Bogle-L'Ouverture Press, 1986).
25. On the ideological struggles between First and Second Worlds during the Cold War, and on their fundamental identity, see Immanuel Wallerstein, *The Decline of American Power: The US in a Chaotic World* (New York and London: New Press, 2003), 13–27.
26. Alain Badiou, "Philosophy and the 'Death of Communism' ", in *Infinite Thought: Truth and the Return to Philosophy*, trans. Oliver Feltham and Justin Clemens (London: Continuum, 2005).

Discography

O'Connor, Sinéad. *I Do Not Want What I Haven't Got*. Ensign/Chrysalis, compact disc, 1990.
———. *The Lion and the Cobra*. Ensign/Chrysalis, compact disc, 1987.
———. *Throw Down Your Arms*. Chocolate and Vanilla, compact disc, 2005.
———. *Universal Mother*. Ensign/Chrysalis, compact disc, 1994.
Massive Attack ft. Sinéad O'Connor. "Prayer for England". *100th Window*. Virgin, 724358123913 V25967, compact disc, 2004.

Contributors

Ifeona Fulani is Faculty in the Liberal Studies Program, New York University. She is the author of numerous scholarly articles, the novel *Seasons of Dust* and the short-story collection *Ten Days in Jamaica*.

Frances R. Aparicio is Professor of Spanish and Portuguese and Director of the Latina and Latino Studies Program, Northwestern University. Her publications include *Listening to Salsa: Gender, Latin Popular Music and Puerto Rican Cultures* and the edited volumes *Musical Migrations, Tropicalizations* and *Hibridismos culturales*.

B. Christine Arce is Assistant Professor of Latin American Literature and Culture, Department of Modern Languages and Literatures, University of Miami.

Nadia Celis is Assistant Professor Spanish and Latin American Studies, Bowdoin College. She is co-editor, with Juan Pablo Rivera, of the anthology *Lección errante: Mayra Santos Febres y el Caribe contemporáneo*.

Lyndon K. Gill is Assistant Professor of African and African Diaspora Studies and Anthropogy, University of Texas at Austin.

Kathe Managan is Assistant Professor of Sociocultural Anthropology, Louisiana State University.

Frances Negrón-Muntaner is Director, Center for the Study of Ethnicity and Race, Columbia University. Her publications include *Puerto Rican Jam: Rethinking Colonialism and Nationalism, Boricua Pop: Puerto Ricans and the Latinization of American Culture*, and *Sovereign Acts* and her films include *AIDS in the Barrio* and *Brincando el charco: Portrait of a Puerto Rican*.

Lisa Amanda Palmer is an independent scholar and researcher from Birmingham, United Kingdom.

Heather D. Russell is Associate Professor of English, Florida International University. Her publications include *Legba's Crossing: Narratology in the African Atlantic*.

Andrea Elizabeth Shaw is Assistant Director, Division of Humanities, and Associate Professor of English, Nova Southeastern University. Her publications include *The Embodiment of Disobedience: Fat Black Women's Unruly Political Bodies*.

Cheryl Sterling is Faculty in the Liberal Studies Program, New York University. She is the author of numerous scholarly articles and her forthcoming book is *African Roots, Brazilian Rites: Cultural and National Identity in Brazil*.

Lisa Tomlinson is a doctoral candidate at York University, Canada, where she teaches literary and cultural studies of the Caribbean and African diaspora.

Adam John Waterman is Assistant Professor of American Studies, American University, Beirut.

Donna Aza Weir-Soley is Associate Professor of English, Florida International University. Her publications include *Eroticism, Spirituality and Resistance in Black Women's Writings*, the co-edited volume *Caribbean Erotic* (with Opal Palmer Adisa), and the anthology of poems *First Rain*.

Acknowledgements

THE EDITOR AND PUBLISHER WISH to thank New York University's Humanities Initiative for their support of this book. We also thank Taylor and Francis, Inc., and the University of Texas Press for their permission to reprint copyrighted material.

www.ingramcontent.com/pod-product-compliance
Lightning Source LLC
Chambersburg PA
CBHW021846300426
44115CB00005B/35